# No Pain, No Gain?

*Athletes, Parents and Coaches
Can Reshape American Sports Culture*

## Richard Taylor

MECHANIC STREET PRESS ❋ BETHEL MAINE

## Disclaimer

The information in this book is intended for educational purposes only and is not intended to replace the individualized guidance of a qualified coach. The publisher and author are not responsible for injuries or damages caused by following the exercises and programs in this book, some of which may not be appropriate for a particular athlete depending on current level of fitness. Each athlete is responsible for maintaining an ongoing consultation with a physician and knowledgeable coach and for listening carefully to his or her own body to prevent overtraining or injury.

*Cover photo of Vegard Ulvang:* Dennis Donahue
*Title page photo:* Olle Larson
*Back cover and author bio photos:* John McKeith

© 2002 Richard Taylor
All rights reserved. Printed in the United States of America by
        Mechanic Street Press
        P.O. Box 16
        Bethel, ME 04217

ISBN 0-9718865-0-4

## *Acknowledgements*

To acknowledge and give appropriate thanks to those many, many people who over the years have given me love of sport, the spirit to both inquire and master as part of its joy, to thrive on its broad experience, the support of colleagues and their intelligent provocation as well, would be both daunting and absolutely rich with memories. This book is an attempt to do sport, cross-country skiing and all those people some modest justice. Most distinctly I think of Gary Allen, who taught me to ski in the first place, and Al Merrill, who calmly but unrelentingly taught me to excel. Many and wonderfully varied others have coached me in all sorts of ways since. I am just as profoundly indebted to every athlete with whom I have ever worked. They have inspired me, challenged me fairly and shared with me a huge breadth of human emotion and an energy as durable and exciting as it has been graceful to witness. Even some athletes whom I have not known have given me their information, just from the way they moved, like a leaf blown along by the wind, an animal bounding across the landscape. In the world where knowledge is always collaborative they all have been the true and refining sources of this book, which I hope in return properly celebrates their efforts and their gifts.

I have also had many immediate practical supports in putting this book together, among them those who have given me permission to use their photographs. These include Dennis and Chris Donahue for their photo on the cover and in my chapter on technique, Fischer Skis, Herbert Klose, Editor of *Skilanglauf/Triathlon/Marathon-Magazin* (for the use of Arnd Hemmersbach's photos) and Olle Larson and Haldor Skaard (for photos from Haldor's book). I have enjoyed the time span these photos represent, for they suggest that humans with the understanding and gift for refined movement have always moved in ways which have changed little, the advances of technology notwithstanding. It is some comfort to know that human performance remains distinctly human, and that sport provides the stage on which that realization is constantly renewed. To the many researchers whose work seeks to better understand that performance, to grasp more completely what humans are and can be, I also owe a major debt. Among those who opened the door to the history of our sports and education culture with their loans of particular books I would like to thank local scholar-historians Stan Howe and Ken Bohr. My efforts were further decisively aided by the computer staff at Gould Academy, Randy Autry, Matt Murphy and Derek Dresser, for their patience and guidance through the thickets of cyberspace. They both lent a hand and held mine. Finally, as much the architect and contractor of this book as I am myself, Marion Lennihan has been the patient and exacting editor I needed in order to lend sequence, logic and clarity to my ten years' worth of reflections, investigations, theories, anecdotes and finally prescriptions for a more humane and successful experience for America's young athletes.

My most abundant gratitude and abiding love in this lengthy endeavor must remain for my wife, Sally. Without her enduring belief that I indeed had something to say and that it would do good to say it, this project would long ago have been stored in a dark corner of our barn loft. She too has been an exacting editor, above all as the staunch defender of readers' rights to clarity and sensible insight. She has kept her shoulder to the wheel with me, so patiently, and her stamina has been the equal and inspiration of my own.

I think finally about the deepest of all the human sources of this book. I dedicate it then to the memory of my father, who gave words the silence and time they need to gather their true meaning, and of my mother, who always painted until the bucket was empty.

Richard Taylor
Bethel, Maine
December, 2001

# Contents

Preface .................................................................................................. *i*

Introduction ....................................................................................... *iii*

## Part One
## An Overview for Parents and Coaches

1. A Letter to Parents ...................................................................... 3

   Some Basic Notions about Developing Young Athletes .............. 5

   Developmental Aspects of Teenage Sport ................................... 8

   Basic Principles of Exercise Physiology ..................................... 18

   Race Day ..................................................................................... 23

2. Coaches and Coaching ............................................................... 27

   How Coaches Communicate ....................................................... 46

   Myers-Briggs Types ..................................................................... 48

   Some Principles of Communication: Neurolinguistic Programming ............... 56

## Part Two
## Sport and Physical Culture
## In Our History and In Our Schools

3. Affirming the Flesh: How Tough Can We Be? How Can We Be Tough? .......... 73

4. "Charge the Hill!" The Origins of the American Attitude Toward Sport .......... 83

   The Post-Civil War Period as a Watershed ................................. 89

   The Pivotal Role of the Middle Class .......................................... 93

   Between the World's Fairs of 1893 and 1904 ............................. 97

   Stuck with Teddy ...................................................................... 101

   Education and Individual Achievement ..................................... 107

   The '20s and '30s: The Body Discovered and Contained ........... 115

   World War II to the Present ...................................................... 133

## Part Three
## Developing High Performance:
## Ingredients and Recipes

5. Putting Miles By: Training ........................................................ 145

   Ingredients in the Recipe .......................................................... 147

   First Elements of Training ........................................................ 167

6. Linking Base Training to Racing .............................................. 178

Strength and Endurance Training: How They Fit Together ............ 183

The Relationship Between Strength and Speed .................... 187

Speed/Tempo Training .................................................. 193

Terrain and Execution ................................................... 203

Peaking ........................................................................ 208

7. Racing: Farewell to "Charge the Hill!" .............................. 213

Preparing Yourself to Race on Race Day ........................... 216

Hills and Flats .............................................................. 218

Hill Tactics .................................................................. 221

Technique Factors ......................................................... 222

8. Technique .................................................................... 230

Basic Notions ............................................................... 230

Classic Technique (Traditional, Diagonal) ........................ 232

Learning Naturally ........................................................ 242

Poling ......................................................................... 251

9. Skating ....................................................................... 257

Poling ......................................................................... 262

The Kick/Push/Liftoff .................................................... 266

Some Ideas on Teaching ................................................ 273

# Part Four
## A Critique of Recent American Ski Science

10. The Limitations of Visual Perception in Understanding Ski Technique ........ 277

The Limitations of Perception, Visual and Technological ............ 281

Other Sources of Flawed Analysis ................................... 286

Pitfalls of Our Culture ................................................... 289

The Confusion of Work with Performance ......................... 291

Epilogue: Results of the 2002 Winter Olympics .................. 293

# Appendices

1. Speed Development Program .......................................... 294

2. Acceleration Training for Distance Runners ...................... 296

3. Examples of Enhanced Plyometric Exercise ...................... 297

Notes ............................................................................. 300

About the Author ............................................................. 316

# *Preface*

Sport in America presents one of the most troubling paradoxes of our time. After a century in which sports engaged an ever increasing proportion of our population, of all ages, we still have not seen the general rise to international standards of performance sports which our scientists and educators have promised, particularly in the endurance sports. Many nations with a tenth of our population routinely perform at higher levels than Americans have. That contradiction not only means fewer international medals, it suggest more importantly that too large a portion of our young athletes have been squandered on misguided notions and training behaviors. The waste of that potential points as well to a shameful abuse of each young person's right to develop optimally and enjoy the full human grace and excitement of which they are capable, not to mention the life-long health and mobility which ought logically to follow. Our sports culture is not only inexcusably ineffective, it has in fact shown little care for the very body it has sought to develop. That is just cause for deep concern.

The science of human physical performance has been widely available, but our application of it to our American athletes has been in too many respects misunderstood and misguided. In this book I search out the origins of these misguided notions and present modern training science through newly cleaned lenses. Cross-country skiing is the sport I write about as an example of how positive, scientifically sound and humane changes can be made. Like other sports, cross-country skiing in the U.S. exemplifies the ideal in clean, vigorous outdoor sport, the enthusiasm of thousands of every age. It also exemplifies a history of failure in international competition. It is a sport which remains caught in a net of cultural presumptions which have destined American athletes to frustration and unfulfilled promise.

At the turn of the last century American physical culture did have unusual promise. Broadly based gymnastics programs from primary school to university provided routine skill- and strength-building. The fundamentals of aerobic fitness were recognized as well, with greater clarity, oddly, than they are today. That promise was not to be realized, unfortunately. It was the era of Teddy Roosevelt, and no figure embodies the paradoxes of American sports culture more than he. He become the icon, and our woods and fields echo yet with his cry, "Charge the Hill!" at running and skiing events. His spirit looks on behind every locker room talk of competing on despite pain in order to win, for personal honor, for team, for community, for America.

We have indeed failed in endurance sport this century, and the pain has not brought us gain. Instead of learning from our poor international results, we have simply persisted with the American Way: if something is not working, just keep doing the same thing harder. Equally damaging has been the manner in which we have tolerated athletic failure by preferring to praise the spirit of human warmth and camaraderie, democratic inclusion of the downtrodden, with which that failure took place. At the same time we have ignored sports-political self-indulgence and excess at the expense of truly scientific commitment to our athletes.

This failure need not be tragic, however, if we can simply learn from it. So much is known virtually world-wide about training science and physiological development, but it will remain baffling and misapplied in the U.S. until we understand and overcome the historical cultural blocks to its acceptance which I discuss in Part Two.

Yes, this is a book about cross-country skiing, thorough and detailed, and it is dedicated equally to athletes, parents, and coaches. It is also written for the educational policy makers who decree the patterns of development to which every young American athlete must submit. More generally, therefore, it is just as much a book about American culture in the twentieth century and about how sports and physical education have been determined and limited by our culture. My motivation in undertaking this investigation has been to allow our young athletes to step out beyond the limits of past culture to their full potential in the century to come. That is their rightful heritage.

American sport can grow, and grow up, but first it must transform itself at its very roots, and they lie firmly embedded and deep beneath the surface of our cultural ground. Knowing what is there is worth the digging, for we have to know before we can change.

# *Introduction*

Like so many sports, cross-country skiing has blessed us generously with its pleasures over the years, and we have shown a love of the sport which is as unquestioning as it is irrational and heartwarming. And we have had no lack of talented athletes in our midst. As science informed us more about the necessary quantitative factors of performance, we also realized with great pride that there were a good number of American skiers with cardiovascular capabilities equal to those of the good Europeans and Scandinavians. Knowing what we know now, it is clear we trained at too high an intensity, all the time, and thus beat ourselves to death in training long before we ever reached the starting line. But we smiled the whole time. How we enjoyed it! What wonderful, life-long friends we have made; what magnificent experiences we have had! We have been good and decent people, of best intention, generosity, boundless good will.

When the exclamations have stilled, however, and in the shadow of that boundless enthusiasm, skiers and coaches alike have again and again asked themselves: "Why didn't we do better?" As we have offered each other advice, full of kindness and conviction, we have just as often silently faced our deep perplexity over a mystery, an ongoing riddle of mediocre ski performance which we admit in private we have not solved. With each new insight into updated training methods and types and systems, with every new commitment to sports science on every topic from sports physiology to biomechanics to waxing, at the end of each winter of racing we feel ourselves snapped back by some mysterious tether. Our hopes and native optimism seem to have been stepped off on an elastic cord which, when the stretch must be tested with results, rebounds into confusion and dismay. We attempt to fathom the silent spring. It is one many athletes experienced in their teens and twenties and have reflected upon since, especially when they have their own children. "Shouldn't I have been able to do better," they ask in their forties and fifties, "with better science and more informed coaching?"

Our athletes these days train more intelligently. We do not lack for science. But we still do not do very well, for we fail in the practice of what we know, or at least fail in the teenage years which are most critical. Is it too late for older skiers? We are not sure, but we see no results. Science should have helped by now. We must ask ourselves if there is not some astigmatic flaw in our vision and thought processes which produce the aberrant practice of the very same science we share with athletes and coaches from other nations.

The answer to that question, and to the question why our teenagers do not experience correct training in junior high and high school, and thus miss out on the fruits of their potential as mature athletes, must rest within some attitude peculiar to Americans which calibrates our mental compass incorrectly, so that though we follow the prescribed settings, we fail to arrive at our goal. These attitudes are not merely superficial mental sets, of a decade, generation, or region. We will find that they are among the most profound forces of our history, for they originate in deeply rooted cultural values which we have inherited, values which account not only for our particular successes as Americans but also, less often considered, our failures.

There have been a glorious exception or two, but in all, given the athletic talent and dedicated training, we have nevertheless indeed failed. There must be sources of that failure which we have not yet recognized. There seems to be something in American cultural values which both determines our deepest, and unconscious, attitudes and which leads our understanding astray, a hidden prescription which blurs our vision. To date, however, no serious attempt has been made to look beyond the sport itself or the limitations in the sports culture each of us has personally experienced.

In an attempt to address this omission, I have investigated the history of our attitudes toward sport, the cultural sources and effects of our particular notions of toughness. I discuss how those very notions have limited our perception and application of science and suggest compelling new reasons why we have been unsuccessful as a nation in international cross-country ski competition. The task of modernizing our attitudes and practices of sports culture needs to be taken seriously, and it is anything but simple. Our complex cultural values themselves must be tracked down in order to identify and remove that prescription which blurs our vision. We must finally let physiology speak its wisdom and free our younger people from the abuse they suffer under the banner of sport in our schools.

I would like to suggest this new starting point: our best scientific and humane purposes notwithstanding, we are not the free, unbiased thinkers we would like to

*Introduction*

*v*

believe we are. The cultural values which are the heritage of our parents and grand-parents operate like an unconscious but powerful set of lenses which not only pre-interpret what we learn but also limit, even distort it.[1] What we know is no more important, therefore, than our attitudes toward what we know. Those attitudes have a profound influence upon how we learn in the first place and upon how we then apply it to our sport through the years of development, training, and competition. Those attitudes comprise our training culture — how we actually move with what we know.

Beyond the truths of training and technique, therefore, it is our training culture which ultimately decides the success of our individual and collective efforts as athletes, coaches, parents, program administrators. I will present the science of the sport, but the training culture which forms the basis of my perspective is very different from the traditional American approach. As an athlete, coach, and teacher of every age and ability for thirty years or more I have watched that traditional approach fail. A different training culture is both necessary and possible. New vocabulary and metaphors, fresh ways of understanding can better illuminate and direct our young athletes, insure their higher levels of performance and our collective joy in that shared experience. After all, we need that too, joy. No culture or individual performer thrives long without it. Not only that; there is yet greater joy to be had, and more people easily included in it, if we but understand why change is needed and possible to bring about.

In Part Two, I go looking for the historical sources of our sports culture, and I find them most profoundly in the years from the Civil War through the period of Victorian America and World War I. I will then trace the changes which followed, the values which evolved from the 1920's and 1930's to the present. Surprisingly, we will see how our attitudes after WWII to a large extent eddy back around earlier notions and biases. Thus the critical importance of that period from the Civil War through the 1930's.

It is often overlooked that although the future is in front of us in terms of history, it is behind us in terms of culture, in the past. However distant from our questions about Olympic medals this exercise may seem, I urge our indulgence of a leap backwards as a means of relocating where a more inspired sports future may be. The watershed upstream in time needs another look before we can understand why the river we follow in the present acts the way it does. In any culture innovation and progress set a current vogue of ideas and values. Less seen but just as powerful are the older values which persevere to silently harness and direct the new. If new and old are by chance combined in a charismatic personality, the effect can be unusually long-lasting, both in inspiring and limiting future thought. That personality will turn out to be Theodore Roosevelt.

Americans made Teddy their model of man, deified him, and we are still stuck with him. He learned, exalted, and perpetuated the ethos of competition so central to American life and character, competition with self, rivals, wilderness, and nations. Whatever short-term gains that spirit brought to a young nation deeply in doubt of itself after the Civil War, competitiveness and the unquestioning faith in the value of adversarial competition have been disastrous for our performance in endurance sport.

One example which hints at how it can become disastrous can be found in recent studies comparing the effects of competition and collaboration in a wide variety of areas from education to business to social interaction which suggest that being and acting competitive do not lead necessarily to higher performance. In one study which will be of interest to cross-country skiers, children's attitudes and task approaches were measured. Norwegian children were markedly less competitive and more collaborative than American children.[2] That should suggest to us a thought-provoking paradox: Norwegians grow up in a less competitive culture than Americans but routinely perform at significantly higher levels in world cross-country ski competition. I will suggest that our unquestioning faith in competition has not only put us into contest with our fellow athletes, it has led us into an essentially adversarial relationship with both the body and terrain as well. When competition is confused with combat and conquest, the body, the athlete loses. As odd as it seems, sheer competitive drive itself has been one of the factors which have steered us astray in our approaches to sports and physiological development in our schools, to training, technique, speed, even race tactics.

As the most elementary beginning, two major conceptual hurdles must be challenged, if we are to begin to understand modern American sport at all. The first is the robust and classic notion that mind controls body. If the wisdom of physiology is to come into its own, that notion will have to be re-phrased: mind is body and body mind. Neither may dominate if we are to think clearly and without bias about physical performance. The second concept is the central Christian conviction, held with especially radical and humorless fervor in Calvinist America, that the body is rude and profane, the spirit alone transcendent. The notion still enjoys high authority, particularly in the secondary schools in charge of our adolescent youth, inherited reverently from our Victorian grandparents, who in their own time looked backed, as did Matthew Arnold, in quoting with approval Benjamin Franklin himself: "Eat and drink such an exact quantity as suits the constitution of the body, in reference to the services of the mind."[3] Arnold lends further gravity to that notion by tracing its ancestry even to Epictetus, who says of giving oneself up to things relating to the body, like eating, drinking and exercise: "All these things ought to be done merely by the way: the formation of spirit and character must be our real concern."[4] From our modern point of view, however, that mind — body dualism must finally and wisely be overcome: there can be no split into higher and lower organisms if we truly intend to see the body grow in its capacities and flower on its own best terms.

The modern expression of these notions began following the Civil War, and they will appear and reappear like different colored threads, combine, disappear, and re-combine as in a continuous braid. But they are strongly felt. They are the cultural harness which holds and directs us. And in it we are still held too tightly. Minor shifts of attitude to the short term contrary, old values turn out to be more powerful than new knowledge. New print has to pass through the old lenses. Particularly in those early days, before physiology was well understood, sport served the uses of morality, social adjustment and therapy, the purposes of industrial power through simple behavior management and control. It was fundamental to our concept of life, after all, that we must compete with the frailties of the flesh simply to survive. Thus the athlete was carved into the necessary social, religious, political posture of his day.

Even with part of our cultural bias understood (Chapter Four, "Charge the Hill!": The Origins of American Attitudes Toward Sport), there will remain yet another related bias which will turn out to be the notion that what we see provides adequate insight into what is actually happening, that observable behavior is all the reality we need in order to understand. Yet we know as well now that that is one of the very illusions which distort perception itself. Mere sight is not yet insight. In a chapter on "The Limitations of Visual Perception in Understanding Technique" I undertake a critique of American ski science and perception itself briefly in order to "clear our lenses" further. One is reminded of Sherlock Holmes remark to Watson: "You see, but you do not observe."

New culture and science combine in "A Letter To Parents," and "Coaches and Coaching" to address the chief sources of the athlete's supporting culture, exploring ways to understand training and development and the urge to racing performance. These chapters are basic handbooks to finding and guiding the powers in young athletes. They link insight with personal relationship, the instinct to help with the vast subtleties of effective communication. They recommend patience and lively, unbiased senses above all.

I urge the reader's attention to those chapters, for without thoroughly digesting them, it is doubtful that the chapters on training, technique and racing can be intelligently applied. It is my deepest conviction from my years so close to every aspect of this sport that we cannot renew our sport, or our notion of sport in general, without a change in our training culture which encompasses all ages and stages of athletic development.

In Chapter Three, "Affirming the Flesh: How Tough Can We Be? How Can We Be Tough?" I will discuss the broad ways in which in which the Christian split of spirit from body plays itself out in the use of sport in our educational system. It bears noting here, however, that other Christian countries (albeit less Calvinist than ours) have not failed so in their physical culture as we have. There must be some specifically American sources in our cultural experience of sport which have prescribed the particular lenses we wear.

Just as "Charge the Hill!" is the signal call of the last century, and Chapter Four of my book, so "Putting Miles By" might be the motto of a transformed training culture in the next, and Chapter Five. My manner of reflecting on every topic in cross-country skiing will reflect that culture, so I need to explain something of it at the very outset.

"Putting food by" is a phrase used in rural New England to describe processing the harvests of summer and fall for winter's sustenance and enjoyment. One lady said it this way:

> To "put by" is an early nineteenth century way of saying to "save something you don't have to use now, against the time when you'll need it." You still hear it today from old-time country people, and applied to food it is prudence and involvement and a return to the old simplicities. Putting food by is the antidote for running scared.[5]

I use that age-old process as a metaphor for the preparation of cross-country skiers, with twofold meaning. On the calendar of a given year it suggests that the purpose of training in the summer and fall is to turn the ground, fertilize, plant, weed, and cultivate, caring well for each need, and then be patient.

Across the years of a young skier's growth "putting miles by" also defines those teenage years as a time for gaining the physiological characteristics, according to wise process and recipe, which may be fully ready as the sustenance of his or her athletic maturity.

"Putting miles by" states the principle of preparing for winter by looking forward

*Introduction*

from May and June, rather than looking backward over one's shoulder in the winter time and suddenly remembering the rule: You race in February on what you accomplish in June, July and August. And by saying one puts miles by the counterstatement should be just as clear: If you use up those miles in summer and fall, your store room in winter will be spare and not provide for your hunger to ski fast when snow covers the ground.

Such wisdom is ancient. It represents the simple instinct for survival and well-being. In the hype of a "modern" industrialized society the conceit of progress has been to go those instincts one better, to speed up the pace of filling reservoirs and satisfying hunger, be it for food, wealth, power, or for athletes' speed. Most often the speed-up is draped in the banner of Resource Management, Productivity, Loyalty to Country, State or School. In the chaos of the last hundred years Americans longed for management and an abiding cause, the sacredness of individualism notwithstanding.

But the human body is not a machine, a factory, or the raw earth. It is a patient, conservative, evolutionary organism. It balances, manages and develops according to its own laws. Its independence in fact has gotten it into trouble forever, for it will not submit to the mind which confuses industrial whim or greed with science, or fear of the body's power with divine providence. It will bend, or break, but it will not submit. It abides in its own recipes, and if those are ignored or followed carelessly, it will either spoil early or not keep later. If the ground is thoroughly prepared, however, patiently and in its own season, and the plant as patiently nourished, then the harvest will be great and abiding, the winter a time of vigor and plenty.

"Putting Miles By" suggests there is a natural process through the seasons of the year and the seasons of any young athlete's development. The thicket of mind and culture can be cleared, both for new planting and for re-discovering fields of previous good advice. I try to lead us through some of those thickets.

In this book I will describe what science is saying, but also the records of experience. Those records are not only to be found in skiing but in constant cross-checks over the years with other sports like running, rowing, bike racing. Experience, each of us knows, is the narrow passage through which all of us humans receive and give back whatever approximation of wisdom we can. It is also the broader cultural landscape which is both the seedbed and compost of human insight, and it is where wisdom or ignorance is decided by the care and discipline of our thought processes. I regret their imperfection and concede their absolute necessity. For there and nowhere else will we be able to ultimately distinguish true knowledge from mere information or raw data. Information enters our minds; knowledge moves our feet.

There are those who will think that such study is unreasonably "heavy," or peripheral to the sport. Sport is for fun, after all, for "extracurricular" diversion, spontaneous and joyful. But if while having fun we unwittingly abuse the body, that is a contradiction which we should not tolerate in an intelligent society. There can be no morality, elevation of spirit, no store for winter in that.

I submit that the equation reads quite differently. Both fun and performance are in fact so severely limited by our biases about physical culture, we need to get beyond them if our athletes are going to experience the heightened level of joy they deserve. We only add to the fun when we accept the notion that real fun is a serious undertaking. The pleasures of the musician rise with his level of understanding and artistry. The shooter may like the bang and the smell of powder, but his joy is in hitting the mark. As the old shotgunner said, "It may be fun to be fooled, ... but it is better to know."[6] Despite elements of change, our culture, particularly our educational system, seems to have decided that sport serves our purposes just as well without understanding. That is a sin of omission at the very least, an apology for whimsical abuse at worst. That attitude has no logical connection with fun, only with laziness and fear. New insights must not only improve our knowledge, they must transform those old values, newly prescribe our cultural lenses, if we are to become able coaches, informed parents, if our athletes are to finally succeed.

Finally, it also does well to remember at the outset that the motive for understanding is not to enhance the performance or position of the coach. "The finger pointing at the moon is not the moon," runs the Zen saying. Our object as coaches and parents is not to make cross-country skiers with our understanding and energy. It is rather to see into the ways in which each athlete can discover his or her own resources, and through them the unusual vitality to be experienced in speed and endurance. In the meantime we may also remind ourselves that the object of our efforts is to render ourselves less needed, the athlete more wise and self-sustaining. The coach cannot run the race, after all, and the moon will shine no brighter for the finger pointing at it.

I want this book to add clarity to our knowledge about cross-country skiing. I also hope that it reveals how our cultural "glasses" are constructed. Has our vision been corrected or simply stabilized at its point of weakness? To what extent, we need to ask, is the correction a cultural prop, to what extent a means to true clarity. Do we tend to focus on a few select and simple targets, but lose the critical details in the rich and rational periphery? For whatever good or evil, these cultural glasses are the harness for eyes and mind, and hence the body as well. Without the presence of the historical and cultural chapters, the science and experience I gather afterwards to cross-country skiing, whatever its thoroughness, logic, simplicity, or insight, may well remain misinterpreted and thus misused.

In his story about a forest fire and smokejumpers, *Young Men and Fire,* Norman Maclean observes: "A lot of questions about the woods can't be answered by staying all the time in the woods, and it also works the other way — a lot of deep inner questions get no answer unless you go for a walk in the woods."[7]

Part Two of *No Pain, No Gain?* asks the questions about sport and skiing which cannot be answered by staying all the time in the woods. It searches out the origins of our sports culture, in some detail. It is only by means of discovering the real makeup and properties of our cultural lenses that we will no longer incorrectly apply the science we receive.

Part Three follows with the necessary walk in the woods, the renewed application of science, a look at skiing itself. As I discuss training, technique and racing, the new approach will be apparent immediately. My hope is that many readers will find it fascinating and useful. My singular goal throughout this book is to aid athletes, parents and coaches to thrive in a newly transformed, more universally successful and humane high performance culture.

## Part One

## An Overview
## for Parents and Coaches

# *1*

# *A Letter to Parents*

> I know of no more encouraging fact than the unquestionable ability of man to elevate his life by conscious endeavor.
>
> —Thoreau, *Walden*

I begin with a chapter to parents. Parents are the closest to their kids and closest to many of the sports their kids chose. Yet as their kids develop from youngsters to teens to college athletes and beyond, parents often feel on the defensive. Their kids soon seek information and affirmation elsewhere. The kids themselves become more differentiated and complex. Emotional and social issues overlay physical development, and coaches' personalities enter powerfully into the child's most dynamic years of growth. Parents may feel more and more separated from this relationship which they have cherished with both child and sport.

In the first instance this changing relationship is a result of the child's development itself. Whereas younger children (8 and 9) prefer adult feedback, by 10 to 14 already that preference declines in favor of peer comparison and the direction of the coach. The later adolescent years tend to individualize further, even with strong reliance on a coach. Multiple sources of competence evaluation are used, particularly internal criteria such as goal achievement, skill-improvement, ease in learning new skills and enjoyment of the activity.[1] Thus, as the child develops, the parents' role shifts from clear and simple major influence to something more complex, more collaborative, and much more subtle.

That may not always seem just to parents. After all, "it's my kid!" Still, we need to remember that the kid does develop as an adolescent by progressively separating from parents. As both parent and coach I remind myself, again and again, of the adage: each of us belongs to himself first. That holds for kids as well.

Parents themselves continue to develop in the midst of their child's growth, of course, so confusion and uncertainty remain familiar fare. One result is that they may tend to lose trust in their educated convictions and deeper intuitions about their kids. Then they may simply fret or attempt to re-assert their control as parents.

What is most welcome then is a forum of informing discussion which includes us all together. Then parents would indeed re-affirm what their inklings as former athletes and astute adults tell them: much is awry with our children's experiences in sport. We recognize too much which has not changed from our own experiences. I am a good example myself. I found out only in my 40's as a US Ski Team coach that my max VO$_2$ figure at age 21 was 82ml/kg/min. That means my cardiovascular capacity was close to international standards. That proved to me what I had known subjectively for years: harder-is-better type training produces only mediocre results. My guess is that many other parents and coaches are also motivated in no small part by a desire similar to my own: to provide young athletes with wiser training than we received, and that being more intelligent and asking persistent questions is the best way to do that. We start by simply saying what we have seen.

We have seen much new science following those 1960's, but still few hints of international success. Since then kids have worked hard at home and school and still have not yet developed as they might. We sense that, we worry about our kids, for we share their hopes and pleasures in sport. And we are justified in asking why American educators have not yet effectively responded to the advances of modern physical science and to a number of persistent but misguided notions of physical education.

We have seen, for example, how too frequent and too intense training and competition can be dangerously stressful for early teenagers, and even injurious over many years hence. Many a marvelous young athlete is wasted because of indiscriminate challenges to his or her obvious and fascinating talents. Fired up by the normal desires for recognition and proofs of self-worth, many young men and women, and many coaches, charge into sports with high motivation and competitive spirit but with too little real knowledge of the kinds of preparation required to achieve durable success.

On the other hand, while many obvious talents are used too hard, we see, too late, that others go undiscovered, for they have never received enough time and informed training to let their talents become visible. Aerobic and neuromotor developments require a basic prescription without which it will remain impossible to know what abilities lie within a young athlete. As with musicians, we do not expect ultimate artistry until the time for all intelligent and patient process has been given. Artist, athlete, journeyman and businessman alike have long known this: skill, toughening and refined performance cannot be hurried. Why then is it so hurried and dominated by competition in our schools?

We also live with our children's frantic school year pace. Is that good for them? We sense correctly that precious development time is lost in the fragmentation of three sports seasons every year. Prepped anew for speed and power, by a different coach, to win that season's championship, the young athlete too seldom receives the time needed for the crucial first step in the training preparation curve: basic aerobic endurance. No European or Scandinavian physical culture program would follow such a calendar, under which a youngster so often sparkles as a junior but then cannot reach higher levels in his years of maturity and greatest potential. To be sure, there is nothing more joyous than the exhilaration of a young winner. But there is also nothing more sad than to find him a frustrated twenty-year-old who, for reasons he cannot grasp, is unable to improve further. His education, his school, his sport have in fact unwittingly double-crossed him, given him pleasure in sport and hope, but not the means to realize its higher levels.

We are wise enough to know, of course, that a relative few rise to top performance. Yet staggering rates of attrition from sports, the distortion of social norms by some of our top athletes and coaches, and the lack of international results justify our misgivings about our sports culture. We have the right and responsibility to ask questions about it. It is, after all, the physical and social context in which our young athletes wish to thrive, and we have much at stake. What follows is an attempt to provide parents with a sound basis for asking those questions.

## *Some Basic Notions About Developing Young Athletes*

Parents and kids belong together. Nothing could be more necessary or logical. Their desires run together, different strands appearing at different times perhaps but braided tightly by physical interdependence and emotional bonds. Parental love is uncompromising in its urge to support a child's success and happiness in sport and it suffers also the anguish of the uncertainties, struggles, hopes, excitements and despairs of learning and developing through which any young athlete must go. This chapter provides the knowledge a parent needs in order to feel informed in his guidance and support. Where a parent will not always have the knowledge of a coach, he can at the very least be equipped to ask the critical questions. The child, after all, gets only one body, and it must be cherished and formed with as much delicacy and precision as possible. Young bodies may seem forgiving, but our observations tell us that the price for casual or partially informed training can be extremely high. And it is the kid who pays it, often life-long.

Parents may in fact even wonder at first if it is even healthy, or wise, for a young athlete to set very high goals and begin to focus and train toward those goals as a teenager. Should summer job time, for example, be sacrificed in part to training needs? Should other sports be low-keyed in order to maintain a year-round training plan? Isn't that approach a little extreme? Is the coach there for my youngster, or is my youngster there for the coach? Isn't this getting a little too serious, too single-minded, maybe even a little compulsive and out of control? Or isn't this too much time spent at play, frivolous young dreaming, wasting time better spent on truly "significant" tasks?

My answer is that any sign of serious inner inspiration to excel is to be welcomed and carefully fostered. (This is quite different from parents pushing their child to excel.) Certainly the young athlete will never know until he or she tries, and the willingness to try is heroic by itself. Each of us belongs to himself first, after all, and it is the child's right to make the attempt to excel. That will require at least three or four years, even longer, and regardless of the outcome, the life lessons gained in the process will be positive and profound.

I think of performance sport in the manner of other performing arts. We know how soon a young musician must chose an instrument. We admire the dedication and tenacity of his study and practice, the outright passion of his involvement. We are patient for the years required to achieve mastery. The young athlete is no different, except that the athlete is both instrument and player in one, and there is no more complex, sophisticated, or wonderful instrument. And quite apart from whether or not some ultimate level of mastery is achieved, the process of training towards it will bear deep and durable rewards in self-knowledge and expression, in an articulate sense of both personal humility and power. These rewards make the experience vastly more than mere diversion and games. The effort bespeaks a passion which can mark a person's life culture with a richness and humanity which is fundamental to education or career as well.

Such a commitment to training signifies as well an attraction to a deeper self-awareness; it demonstrates a courageous willingness to measure oneself in public contest. To do so requires both self-possession and maturity, the ability to look life straight in the eye. It hints at a new aspiration toward excellence, a willingness to strive, to fail at times and feel wounded in the process, to heal and try again. The urge, then the passion, for more refined and powerful movement not only brings higher performance; it hints at the core energy of the child's sense of authenticity as an individual, his or her sense of being singularly alive. That passion is a gift not to be set aside, for above all it signals that the child is casting off his need for protection and stepping toward adult freedom.

As psychologist Alice Miller has stated so clearly:

> The child has a primary need to be regarded and respected as the person he really is at a given time, and as the center — the central actor — in his own activity. In  an atmosphere of respect and tolerance for his feelings, the child, in this phase of separation, will be able to give up symbiosis with the mother [or father] and accomplish the steps toward individuation and autonomy.[2]

As the young athlete commits himself to the requirements of an informed training schedule, he moves into a realm of his own, leaving his parents "on the outside," in a state of unease, a sort of elastic tension with their distance from their child. These are some of the questions I have encountered from parents over the years:

- Given that the teenage athlete is often surrounded and affected by inappropriate pressure or messages from peers, coaches, and parents, how does one safely and effectively advocate for one's child?

- How does one identify and find good coaching?

- How does one make changes in the public school approach, with its short—term, seasonal focus, continuous pressure to compete and to win, with its thus fractured and often inconsistent or uninformed coaching?

- How does one equip the child to select the right, reasonable advice in the face of what is often a real chorus of bad advice?

- My son seems tired all the time. Is he training too hard, or is he simply going through a growth spurt?

- What can I do to calm my son down before the race? He is so irritable and brooding, or bossy, even impolite?

- My daughter never wants to talk to me after the race. What's the matter? All I want to do is be supportive.

◆ How can I, or my son or daughter, communicate questions and concerns to the coach?

Some of these questions clearly have to do with competition psychology, others with a knowledge of exercise physiology applied to the growing and changing teenage body. This section will give an introduction to developmental issues and to basic exercise physiology. An overview will be sufficient for most parents and can serve as a summary for coaches (who will enjoy the greater detail provided in the next chapter on coaching). This chapter ends with a section on competition psychology which will help parents understand their children's moods and behavior on race day.

# Developmental Aspects of Teenage Sport

Since teenagers' bodies are constantly changing, success in junior high and high school should not be seen as necessary predictors of success in college and beyond but rather as one of many steps along the way. In fact, if we drive children unrelentingly toward winning as juniors, we may even *inhibit* their success as a senior. Why? Because kids are different from adult athletes both psychologically and physically. Training methods for an adult athlete do not necessarily work for a youngster. Here are some reasons why.

Scientists from the former East Germany had learned by the 1970's that it is the actual state of biological development of a young athlete which determines the appropriate training loads. Writing in *Rowing,* Dr. Ernst Herberger notes:

> Particularly during puberty, high demands are put on the body; these vary greatly from one individual to another but are generally applicable. The blood volume increases by almost 50 per cent, and heart and lungs attain their final growth. This does not mean the training should be reduced. But it is important for the coach — supported by a good relationship of trust — to have a clear picture of his subject's state of health. Unexpected leaps forward in performance and stagnation form no real basis for judgment, but are caused by the normal, but individually varying, biological development.[3]

Herberger goes on:

> A further significant difference between a youth and an adult is the performance of the heart. Up to about the age of fifteen, the heart must work far

harder than in adulthood and can only achieve high performances with a higher beat frequency. The resting rate is about 80/min and reaches values in excess of 200 under load. The cardiac muscle strengthens itself gradually at first, and adapts itself to the load with a greater beat volume. Breathing frequency and depth of inhalation behave similarly. On these physiological grounds, the only justification for continuous performances at highest intensity up to the end of puberty is competition rowing.

In other words, one does not train kids with either steady schedules of competition or with competition levels of overall work intensity in training. Herberger concludes with the principle that loads of middle and low intensity are the best means of adapting to future high load requirements, and he adduces Shede's view that submaximum pressure load encourages growth, whereas excessive pressure load inhibits it.[4]

We enjoy the excitement of a young athlete's success, of course, but we need to be careful not to overestimate its significance. Boys and girls between the ages of 10 to 13 or 14 have the most advantageous ratio of cardiovascular capacity to body weight of their lives. With little muscle mass development yet, they tend to be "all engine." They may thus achieve really astounding results early. But then they will inevitably change both body shape, muscle mass, and chemistry in the next years. Their success will come to depend upon a different set of related capacities. To bank on early results too heavily is to set oneself up for later disappointments. Parents and coaches alike need to strike a balance of responses here, giving unwavering encouragement but avoiding excessive early praise or expectation. Too much praise runs the risk of both drowning the youngster's own responses or allowing him to imagine he has, in fact, "arrived".

Following the onset of puberty, teenage growth is asynchronous; that is, different parts of each child grow at different times and at differing rates. Kids display physiques which lead us to both despair and amusement, as well as hope. Often they look like a collection of spare parts. For the child the body is literally a mixed bag, and the momentary loss of coordination or "engine" can bring on a sudden downturn in results which can devastate his view of himself, his sense of power as a athlete. Reacting to the contradiction between an increase in size and muscle and poorer performances, many kids drop out of sport during this period of development, needlessly. They and their parents need to understand that such puzzling ups and downs are only the developmental deck being shuffled, and it will be shuffled many times more before the decisive hands are dealt.

I have observed this process many times with top European World Cup winners. The Finnish World Cup winner, Marjo Matikainen, went from being a skinny young girl to a teen grown rounder in the cheeks and full in the hips to a senior competitor in her early twenties who was more balanced in muscle structure and a little more trim overall. The same pattern characterized the development of Anfisa Retsova and Svetlana Nageikina of Russia. In 1984 Alexei Prokurorov was the gawky, ugly-duckling kid on the Russian team at the World Junior Championships. The best US skier, Joe Galanes beat him with an excellent 11th place. Prokurorov, however, was raced sparingly and brought patiently along with good low-intensity volumes and monitoring. He won a Gold Medal in 30 kilometers at the Calgary Olympics, while Galanes, one of our best, toughest, and most intelligent young skiers ever, had seen his speed development already falter and stop, a performance trajectory all to familiar to athletes mistrained in the American way.

If we become too excited about early results, therefore, and decide to "really train" a talented youngster with intense loads and lots of competition, we run a more fundamental physical risk. Competition pace is anaerobic and represents the extreme of physiological loading. In anaerobic metabolism the waste products of metabolism (lactic acid) accumulate faster than the athlete's capacity to remove them through oxygen intake. The athlete experiences this state when his breathing becomes rapid and his muscles begin to experience significant discomfort.

But up until the age of 18 or so an enzyme (phosphofructokinase) which is a major link in anaerobic energy supply system remains in distinctly sub-adult amounts. Thus, the younger athlete cannot adapt well yet to extended anaerobic (race pace) training or competition. As a result, overloading the youngster's body does not stimulate growth, it only causes shock.[5] The body does not regenerate and develop from pain; it simply repairs. Too many years of repairing will sacrifice those same essential years of cardiovascular development, the most significant of which are from 14 to 18. Pushing young athletes too hard and without informed plan has been a principle cause of both athlete defection from sport and, with isolated exception, dismal international results of our endurance athletes, cross-country skiers among them. Two Russian graphs display the optimal development years and the problems which arise when younger athletes are brought along too quickly.

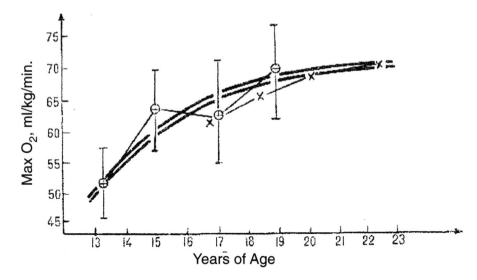

The increase in oxygen consumption (for the 16 – 18 year age group) was 4–5 ml/kg/min per year. The rate of increase then slows rapidly, despite an increase in the number of training sessions and the intensification of the training session.[6]

In other words, we must take advantage of the specific biological period which is optimal for aerobic development; that development cannot be made up for later.

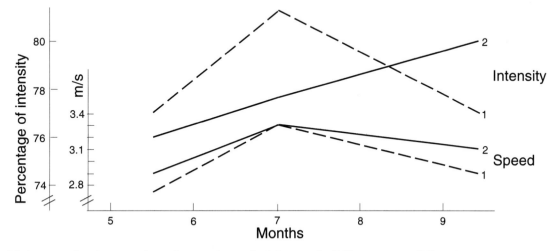

This graph shows the dynamics of skiers of different qualifications practicing together. Number 1 is skiers of the first degree, number 2 candidates for the masters degree. The % scale is intensity; m/s is speed in meters per second.[7] Notice the steep improvement of the younger skiers in the short term, and their subsequent demise because of trying to keep up with those with greater years and training background.

With these considerations in mind, the following chart reviews the training activities appropriate to the various ages.

| Age | (8) 10–12 | 12–14 | 15–16 | 17–18 |
|---|---|---|---|---|
| **Skills** | sports skills | speed of separate movements | speed of muscle contraction | |
| | | *(all complicated by puberty, then a new skill arrangement)* | | |
| **Speed** | | frequency/rate | power/length | |
| **Endurance** | aerobic | ————————————————————> | | anaerobic |

*Aerobic development is limited through primary school by peculiarities of circulation: heart is small, arterial vessel large relative to heart volume. It is hard therefore to increase the stimulus on blood pressure.*

*Anaerobic development is limited by youthful energy metabolism: creatine phosphate content and concentration of phosphofructokinase are lower than in adults. These two major factors in anaerobic glycogenolysis are not fully present until ages 17–18.*[8]

Furthermore, it is no surprise to any parent who has watched a youngster grow that the energy-fatigue pattern of youngsters is different from that of adults. Young people have higher pitches of energy and lower and often more extended periods of fatigue. Anybody who has witnessed a teenage boy in the midst of a growth spurt knows this. "Really training" a teenage athlete too often leads to an intensity level and day-to-day schedule which ignores the need for enough rest. An informed training schedule plans significant rest into each week and month as a safeguard, and sometimes young athletes will need more yet.

Yet sadly, when rest is needed, or requested, the younger athlete is too often thought to malinger, to be a wimp or ill-motivated. In fact, the vast majority of a youngster's training should be aerobic, where his efforts may be full but also fully ventilated with oxygen, and its progressions carefully planned, rather than constantly tested in competition.

The examples of early teenage athletes with great promise who have fizzled in a few years are legion in endurance sport. Young girls are particularly susceptible. Light, quick, and all heart-lung "engine," they are "naturals" for racing. They can run and ski like gazelles. Young and eager to please, they are only too willing to race for friends, school, parents, coaches, regardless of distance. In many cases I have seen, sport eats them alive. It so shocks their young chemistries and structures that they later cannot train for 4 or 5 weeks without becoming sick or injured. Essentially they have foundered and will not compete again. Polished and powered up, they dazzle us a few times around the track, but then "the wheels fall off". With everybody's best of intentions, they have been used up, or, more precisely, abused. That is a tragedy we cannot justify.

It is a fundamental principle that the goal of training is not exhaustion but adaptation to higher loads, speeds, distances. The body's response to exhaustion is repair; its response to adaptation is growth. Exhaustive levels of training for young athletes for boys are simply foolhardy excursions into superficial manliness, for girls celebrity stardom, or, as more often becomes the case, martyrdom. Exhaustion workouts prove nothing, make little real contribution to performance, and are really little more than a psychological quick fix, for both athlete and coach.

Overemphasized early success in young athletes also brings a risk not only of physical burnout and impaired development, it can cause a stunting of psychological growth as well. Success can be emotionally unbalancing in young athletes who lack the perspective to handle it. Ironically, kids who are big and strong early may be the most vulnerable. They may come to build their sense of self-worth too exclusively on their athletic prowess. Seeing sport as a vehicle for self-esteem, acceptance and admiration, they naively assume it is *the* vehicle. Yet I have seen many a fine athlete in his 20's suffer the frustrations of facing up to the need to recover his or her social and intellectual development, left on the back burner at age 14. Now, in order to become a whole, creative adult, as well as a truly accomplished athlete, he must finish his maturation.

The error made was a small but significant one. The young athlete mistook the part for the whole, took athletic promise for an assignment to herodom and its magical powers. Believing that to be a life-long given, as many teenagers do, he went to sleep, so to speak, on his white horse. He has been duped in fact by premature praise. Right from the beginning, on the other hand, it is our job to help him sustain the balanced perspective in which success is less important than skill, admiration less rewarding than learning, results less persuasive than the deepening intellectual and emotional experience.

Closely related to these concerns is another fundamental question: If a youngster wishes to become a good endurance athlete, when should he or she begin to specialize and for what reasons?

It is important to make a change in dominant sport type from sprint/field sports to endurance speed sports around age 14 to 15. It is important because if the body adapts to a preference for sprint type fuel sources, creatine phosphate breakdown and anaerobic glycogenolysis, the athlete's anaerobic threshold will remain too low to allow top distance results in his mature years. The following chart shows how anaerobic threshold stabilizes at lower levels, the shorter the distance of the event.

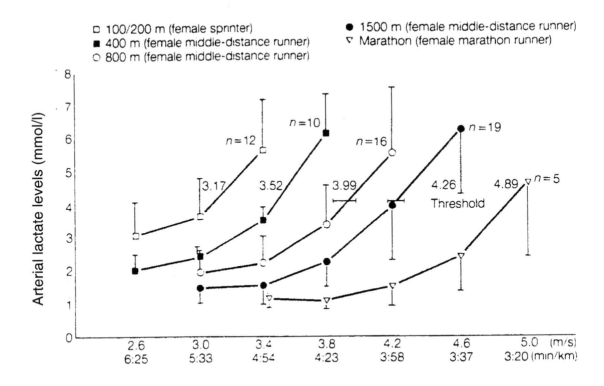

The anaerobic threshold of female sprinters, middle-distance runners (400, 800 and 1500m) and marathoners (from left to right).[9]

Field sports require even shorter distances than 100 meters. This was the situation with Joe Galanes, whom I have mentioned before. Even with an adjustment in his training, 2 to 3 years of predominantly very low level aerobic training (as recommended by the Finnish Team physiologist, Heikki Rusko), he could never reach international levels of speed endurance. As Rusko noted, Galanes used too much of his oxygen uptake at the anaerobic level. The problem was never that he, like many other American skiers, was not an extremely fit athlete; it was that his specific anaerobic threshold was too low. That is the result of both training at too high an intensity in the late teens. It is also just as profoundly the result of remaining too long in anaerobically fueled sports in the early teens. The specific endurance/efficiency work, which is central to longterm continuing development, was compromised. This is the case with most American field sport programs.

If youngsters do not adapt to and develop their aerobic energy mechanisms by their mid-teens, it is my belief and experience that they will be too far behind to catch up later, no matter how much endurance training they do. As Americans, we cherish our freedoms and find limitations basically unjust. Thus we strive to keep the options open for our young athletes. But unfortunately physiology dictates that they must make a choice in the early teenage years: give up sprint sports if they want to excel in an endurance sport. The body cannot wait; the years from age 14 – 18 are the critical ones for cardiovascular development. Making that choice is not a simple matter, for it may be the first life-directing decision a young person makes, one that requires sacrificing one joy for another. That touches the youngster with tragedy. We should therefore understand that supporting young athletes in making that choice can also help them mature as human beings. The overly kind and well-intentioned adult who compromises the budding athlete with indecision or a misdirected program will only doom him to unsuccessful struggles later as a mature sportsman.

A significant factor in American skiers' aerobic base deficit is thus to be found in the field sport types in the high school years. Whereas these types are excellent for skill building in the earlier years, Americans tend to continue with them into the years critical to aerobic development, and sacrifice that development accordingly. Atko Viru has documented the predominant mechanism of energy supply in various sports. In sports games characterized by phases of high activity and relief, the high activity phases in volleyball, for example, lasted 8 seconds, in basketball 28 seconds, and in ice hockey 36 seconds. Soccer was quite similar to basketball. These time periods of high activity all fall in the area where the breakdown of creatine phosphate and anaerobic glycogenolysis are the main sources of energy[10], as opposed to oxidative phosphorylation, the prime energy mechanism for endurance sport, as the following chart shows.

Jim Galanes (Joe's older brother and one of the most active minds and coaches in skiing) has further confirmed this phenomenon through regular lactate analysis of young training athletes.

My data to date confirms your statements concerning a reduction of lactate threshold [anaerobic threshold] in athletes who train too hard. More importantly, in athletes that have always trained too hard and/or have had little endurance training their lactate rises linearly to work load or heartrate. This shows they have little or no aerobic capacity and the organic acids that are destructive to aerobic development begin accumulating in their muscles at even the lowest levels of exercise. This was the case with a girl from Alaska whom you may remember. ... She was very successful as a junior but never developed a solid aerobic base, and her lactate profiles were similar to what I described above." (letter Aug. 21,1995)

The following chart lays out the various sources of energy.

### Bioenergetic Criteria for Working Capacity of Athletes

| | Oxidative Phosphorylation | Anaerobic Glycogenolysis | Phosphocreatine Mechanism |
|---|---|---|---|
| Intensity (power) | $VO_2$ max. critical power output level | Maximal rate of lactate production and excess $CO_2$ formation, highest power output in 'pure' anaerobic exercise (30–60s) | Maximal power output during 3–7 s, rate of phosphocreatine degradation |
| Capacity | Maximal amount of $O_2$ supply of exerrcising muscles, maximal exercising time on VO2max level | Maximal amount of lactate accumulation, total $O_2$ debt, the highest pH shift | Alactic $O_2$ debt, accumulation of free creatine, time of all-out exercise at the highest levels of power output |
| Efficiency | Velocity constant of initial 'tuning' of $VO_2$, coefficient of mechanical efficiency | Mechanical equivalent of lactate formation | Velocity constant of alactic $O_2$ debt payment |

From Volkov, N.I., *Tests and Criteria for Evaluation of Endurance in Sportsmen,* Central Inst. Phys. Cult., Moscow, 1989 (in Russian).[11]

Viru does make the important observation that even field sport athletes must develop good endurance in order to recover rapidly from the types of sprints they must repeat and in order to remain relatively lactate free. I would make the further point that field sport coaches could add a significant base endurance factor into their training sessions by planning for the sessions to be largely continuous rather than stop-and-go, particularly as youngsters reach the early teens. The result of base endurance training is also the enhanced capacity to maximize skill levels and alertness in the latter periods of games. I know of a lacrosse team which outscored its opponents 7 to 1 in the final quarters of its games and scored evenly in all four periods following such a program of continuous movement in its practices. Too few coaches include the endurance element within their practices. Among others who have learned to do so are the coaches of the Pittsburgh Steelers. The only alternative is to do 40 minutes to an hour of easy, continuous running before or after practice. Coaches simply have to plan the time into their practice day and use their imaginations to make it unusual and fun.

For example, if a young cross-country skier decides to keep playing soccer all through high school, without added aerobic endurance work, the impact on his skiing will not appear until it is too late to undo the damage. His ski development will flatten and end some time in the first two years of college, no matter how much talent he has, because he has not done the necessary amounts and types of training hours in his most critical years of development. Those deficits can never be fully recovered. "If a fool throws a stone in the water, even a hundred sages can't bring it back," goes an old saying.[12]

The need to decide and the initiation of more informed endurance training may not feel comfortable at first. Endurance work may not seem to provide the immediate results and personal validation that sprint type field sports offer. A coach, however, should be able to make it fun, a different sort of adventure.

Another important qualification needs to be made: the best training recipe for young athlete's primary sport will include not always training them to their strengths at every season of the year. A youngster who excels in cross-country skiing, for example, might well run cross-country in the fall, ski in the winter, and then want to do track in the spring. Everybody would wish to take advantage of this athlete's endurance capabilities.

Two factors suggest we should resist this inclination, regardless of the points to be gained for the team or the school. First, the youngster has already competed two seasons long in endurance events. Spring needs to be "down time". Secondly, in the long term this youngster will need more speed. Spring is the time to do it, by running 100's, 200's, and doing some jumps, rather than more endurance events. Speed often remains the endurance athlete's weakness. Spring provides the time to work on it, and running form. Both add variety to the year's sports and maintain the perspective on the youngster's overall development.

Thus when we support our young athletes in choosing their sports commitments, the real starting point must be physiology, be we parent, athlete, coach or administrator. I have written more comprehensively about training in Chapters 4, 5 and 6. What follows is a pocket version of the essential principles.

## Basic Principles of Exercise Physiology

**Distinguishing aerobic from anaerobic training.** This is the most critical distinction in all training development, for aerobic training is the ground in which all other types of training are seeded. Aerobic (with oxygen) training is low to medium intensity activity which is continuous for 30 minutes or more. It is the key to athletic stamina and efficiency and is 18 times more physiologically efficient than anaerobic (without oxygen) training. Aerobic pace can range from an easy, conversational extended run (special endurance level) to anaerobic threshold sessions which feel full and loose but are well below hard race pace or sprinting. Threshold runs feel like the swell of a wave which rises but does not break over, like a balloon that is full but not tight about to burst. Identifying both special endurance and threshold training zones, both objectively with a heartrate monitor and subjectively through feelings and images, is described in detail in Chapter 6. An easy method is based on determining the highest *sustainable* heartrate for a 12–15 minute, 8 lap run or rollerski on a track. This heartrate, minus 10–12, predicts anaerobic threshold (ANT) rather accurately. 20 to 30 below ANT gives the base or special endurance level (AT).

**Threshold speed, not maximum speed is optimal for developing speed (racing) endurance.** Aerobic training develops oxygen transport, which fuels speed endurance. And threshold training produces speed without shocking the still-developing system. Developing endurance toughness does not mean training to exhaustion — just the opposite. Think of a bellows: blasting hard makes brief white heat and blows the fire to ashes and out; relaxed, full and continuous air keeps the fire and heat both.

**Anaerobic training produces anaerobic endurance, not greater speed.** Speed is widely assumed to be the product of hard, anaerobic training. That is incorrect. Anaerobic training produces anaerobic endurance, or the ability to tolerate a given speed above anaerobic threshold. It does not produce the speed itself. Speed is a complex phenomenon dependent upon the whole spectrum of training activities, from endurance capacity building to skill speed or coordination work done fast but within threshold limits. Speed training is discussed in detail in Chapter 6.

**The effect of training is optimal at threshold pace** because slight improvement at threshold will result in the most lasting improvement in performance. An elevation of even 2 or 3 beats per minute (bpm) will result in significantly faster times. This change may seem small, but consider how a tiny difference plays out over a race distance. American skiers remain 1.0 to 1.5 seconds per 100 meters behind their European counterparts. In 10 kilometers that becomes 10–15 seconds per kilometer behind, or 1:40 to 2:30 out of winning time! Be patient with small gains; they will add up, and only if they are accomplished slowly, will they persist.

**By contrast, training consistently at hard race pace above anaerobic threshold (ANT) actually tends over time to nudge threshold downward,** reducing oxygen transport capacity and efficiency. When one of our best junior skiers was tested by Finnish physiologists, they observed that his unrelenting hard training had dropped his ANT to the point that it was too low for competitive performances. "Joe seems to have the greatest problems with his efficiency," noted Heikki Rusko. "He should train more at low intensity (heartrate of 130–145) and do exercises which improve recovery (walking, jogging at a heartrate of 100–130, stretching and calisthenics)."[13] After only three weeks of this training he was able once again to see his heartrate rise to a higher threshold and his performances improve. This advice needs to be more widely followed in all our juniors' training.

**Oxygen uptake levels drop slowly through the competition season.** This effect has been documented even among adult athletes. Oxygen uptake levels are at their highest at the end of the base and threshold periods (for adult skiers November, for juniors December). Most countries now allow a break in mid-season to restore some of that oxygen transport capacity, like giving an aquifer time to trickle full again. The drop in capacity will be the least among those athletes with the best developed aerobic base, and their recovery will be the most rapid.

I do not wish to imply that **hard training and competition** are bad in themselves; to the contrary. But they **must be in appropriate amounts (around 10% of the year's total training)** and timed for each youngster's stage of physical maturation and for the phase of the training years.

What conclusions can we draw from these basic principles? First, young athletes do not need a lot of hard training. In fact, **extended hard training is not only unnecessary, it is potentially detrimental to long-term physical development.** They thrive on a lot of fairly easy and medium continuous training. Recently European sports scientists and coaches have suggested a ration of 80% easy (AT) to 10–15% medium (ANT) and 5% hard (race pace). Competition is for fun, once a week, half that or less for youngsters up to age 12. Speed training is for skills, 15 to 20 seconds, not longer. All aerobic training, except for races. Competition is a learning experience. It is not training anymore than it is a measure of one's worth or character.

**Racing is not training.** The notion of "racing into shape" is a myth of times past. Competition takes money out of the bank; it is a check on one's resources. Training puts money back into the bank. What can fool us is that in the beginning any kind of training produces improvement. But without the base work in place from the four to six months previous, these early improvements will most often flatten in a few short weeks and prove illusory by the height of the season. Having used up his physiological "savings account" by the end of the season, the athlete is back to square one. Without net training gains beyond what that season required for itself, the young athlete begins each succeeding year at the same point of fitness, and makes little overall progress through his high school years. This can hold true for the athlete who does a single sport or who does three.

The concept that **training for a particular sport is a year-round recipe,** with various ingredients added at the proper times and in the proper amounts is known as **periodization.** The following graph gives us the year's recipe for skiers. The same general training plan applies to other sports by planning backwards from the specific competition season. For the winter competitor special endurance dominates summer, threshold work, and a few, well-spaced competitions, approached as time trials, are added in the fall, faster toward racing in winter. Skill speed work is sprinkled regularly throughout the year.

One activity provides the capacity for the next; the order cannot be jumbled or reversed. The smallest unit of training is 6 weeks, minimum, and 12 is better to give the body the time required for physiological response before new ingredients or intensity levels are added. (Physiological changes take 5–6 weeks to appear, 12 weeks to be significant. That is the reason physiological research is usually conducted over a period of 12 weeks. It simply takes that long for a performance change to be measurable.)

Thus the young athlete cannot wisely think to compete in each of the three school seasons without compromising long-term developmental goals in the sport in which he wishes to excel. There is simply no time for training if all the youngster does from September to June is compete. His recipe is all yeast and shortening but too little flour.

It is possible, however, for a young athlete to participate in three sports as long as he is not pushed to compete hard in all three and can keep his overall training plan going. Unusual knowledge and self-restraint is necessary for both coaches and athletes in this case, plus the enlightened collaboration among coaches of different seasons. A youngster who wants to focus on skiing, for example, could run cross-country in the fall, but limit competition and keep the training recipe for skiing. Allow time for supplemental roller ski work and hill work with poles. In the spring do track, but the track coach must recognize that this is necessary down-time for the skier's body and have him do 100's and 200's, and the jumps. The skier will also need a lot of rest, two or three days a week. It is also a good time to try a totally different, non-endurance type sport, not to mention catch up on studies.

But this subordination of two sports seasons to the child's primary sport season is seldom possible or understood. Peer and school pressures to win in every season intrude (even though I have proven that well-constructed aerobic training wins races,

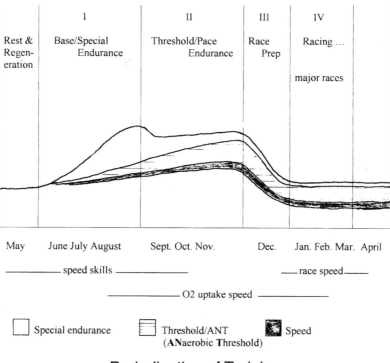

**Periodization of Training**

even championships). Most often ignorance of basic physiology is hidden by exhortations about the value of games and competition, with moralistic notions of overcoming ones limitations through pain, by reference to the socializing effects of team effort, the "higher good" achieved through sacrificing one's body to an ennobling experience or cause. If in all of this the real resource, the child's body, is misused, its potential for his or her own real future will have been foolishly, callously wasted. Such "soldiering," as I will call it in a later chapter, may save lives in war, but it kills young athletes on our trails and fields in school.

To return to parents' questions, the first response is this: your child's coach must be willing to discuss elementary sports physiology with you, a long-term plan, and the physiological basis for each of the types of training he assigns. In the next chapter on coaches and coaching I describe many of the skills you should seek in a coach.

**Who should coach?** Ideally the coach should have been a good athlete in the same sport. Generally speaking, however, currently competing athletes, particularly teenagers, are not appropriate. They are necessarily focused on their own competition and seldom have the interpersonal experience or emotional maturity needed for coaching. Certainly kids should not be allowed or asked to coach other kids. I would not even allow National Team athletes to coach each other. It does not work. Athletes make wonderfully inspirational models and companions for younger kids. That energy is best tapped in assisting another coach. Simply put, athletes are flowers, coaches are gardeners.

Nor do parents work well as coaches generally. Necessarily idealized by their kids, above all by the unconditional nature of their mutual love, there are too many other agendas between parents and kids to allow for patient and objective understanding of the child's physiological and emotional states in relationship to his or her athletic performance. It must also be said that in the teenage years the athlete will naturally begin to look beyond parents for critical information and want to become more responsible for his or her own progress. Understanding what is necessary for success both heightens the confidence and fun of sport and is the best insurance against needless risk. Sport is a wonderful, spontaneous diversion, but mindless whimsy is too often the forum for injury or less satisfying results. Nor despite the soothing effects of graceful exercise should sport become a sublimation of one's personal problems. Burying oneself in exercise has little to do with developing physical power, skill, and mobility. Training harder is rarely better. The thrill of the body in motion is not achieved through its abuse.

If there is any doubt about training or competing while injured, the answer is simple: stop. Never speculate what an injury might be, or hope it will go away, or think it a psychological weakness to be "toughed out". That is abuse. Stop, and consult with an MD who is practicing specifically in sports medicine as your first step to recovery. Physicians themselves without specific expertise in sports medicine cannot always be expected to give reliable advice. A young body is too magnificent and precious to be taken casually by anyone. You would not have a carpenter operate on a knee (nor a doctor build your house). Nor should moralizing about team values or school spirit be accepted as adequate substitute medicine.

Parents need to know that there are powerful, effective ways to support their special athlete from the sidelines, and the first place to start is by studying the principles of training and athletic development in this book. It will take a little time and require rereading. That is what any good coach or scientist does. That patience will demonstrate most persuasively to your child how profoundly you cherish him. Also, do not hesitate to ask your athlete the same questions you are trying to understand yourself. That can urge him to understand himself better and gain the true confidence of knowledge and command of himself. That is ultimately the kind of confidence any young man or woman will want on race day.

# *Race Day*

Finally, I would add some race-day hints about the behavior of young, even mature, athletes which can make it easier to understand and support a son or daughter. I will try to answer the bewilderment about peculiar behavior pre- and post-race.

First, you need to remember that competition requires the athlete to be alone and in a very compact, deep and exciting experience, a complex mix of long- and short-term preparation, confidence, anxiety, adrenaline, feelings of both daring and fascination, of both weakness and uncertainty. All of this may only belong to your son or daughter, alone. All of the feelings must be in his or her total possession. Your child must deal with them, convert them into excitement, calculation, strategy, presence of mind and body, power and speed.

Despite your love and anxieties for your child, your own deep wishes and most noble intentions, you cannot help on race day and should not intrude on the young athlete's necessarily private space. If you do, your child will unconsciously begin to take care of you. His energy and focus will be distracted from his race in order to satisfy your need to help. His focus diverted to you, your child's grasp of the specific task at hand will loosen; his ability to perform will diminish. Sensing this may elicit a belligerent, ungracious response from the athlete. Feelings may be confused, even hurt, on both sides. Nobody wishes this result, but it happens, again and again. I have even heard it described by Olympic Team athletes whose parents went to the Games to support them. It is perhaps the parent's most anguishing task to let a youngster own his performance, alone.

Parents should begin backing off several days before a major event. Feeling their bodies peaked, their "wiring is bare of insulation," young athletes may well become a more extreme version of what they normally are, more talkative, more brooding, more distracted, more feisty or emotionally brittle. Parents wish to make them feel good, be as normal as possible. Not knowing where to start, they ask the basic loving and courteous question, "How're you doing?" or "Did you have a good workout?"

Wrong questions! What under normal circumstances are so helpful and graceful may lead in an immediate pre-competition period to overdoses of self-evaluation: "How am I?" It is too late for that question; now it can only detract, and every athlete knows it. Inside there can be only one conviction: "I am excellently prepared, eager, ready." No questions. On the other hand, subjects which have nothing to do with skiing are wonderful — books, music, what is happening at home. I oriented late-arriving staff and guests to this notion with a World Junior Nordic Championship team I had in Norway for training in 1984, and the reduction in tension was palpable — as was the increase in quiet confidence and training execution. It also seemed as if we all had an overabundance of time to do what was needed. Nothing felt hurried. When that is the case, athletes grow more and more confident that they are prepared for the race.

More than anything else, parents, it is your mere presence which is most powerful, more so than any words you might say, more than any help you would most dearly wish to offer. I know the anguish of such separation and silence. Unfortunately, the coach cannot be of any help to you, to answer questions or provide information, for the coach, on race day, must be as totally fixed in his or her concentration as the athlete. He can be available only to athlete requests and the myriad compact requirements of the day. All the while, believe me, he too must also fight the urge to ask the same question, "How are you; how do you feel?"

Here is a good operating program for parents. Separate from your child 45 minutes before start time. An hour is better yet. The athlete's warmup must begin at that point, the last trip to the toilet accomplished, equipment set, number on. The warmup goes 20–10–5, 20 minutes easy, 10 at threshold, five at race pace (in some variation or other). This is completed as close as possible to actual start time, usually within a few minutes. Nobody should interrupt this warm-up, even a coach.

Enjoy all the skiers. Don't get too deeply involved in the competition, comparing your kid to others. Who happens to beat whom is really not very important, and measuring a youngster's performance in that way sets up external norms of comparison rather than more effective internal values of progressive mastery. Each is also so different a mix of things right now, and not one of them will be the same next year. A given day's results hardly approximate the complexity or mystery of it all. Each kid is giving 100% Their results need no interpretation. Accept, admire. I frequently ask my kids after the race, "How did you ski?" They often reply, "I don't know; I haven't seen the results yet." Neither have I, and purposely ask before they have seen the results. They need to feel each moment along the trail how they are going. Thinking in terms of results only distracts them from that task. I believe what they tell me and am satisfied. Any other, or contradictory, thoughts they may have later also come from them. They know, and must learn to know and trust their own feelings for speed and intelligence in racing.

And afterward? When he or she is ready, your young athlete will seek you out. Most athletes want to be alone for a while, to recover their composure, to reflect, warm down a half hour or more, until they have reflected upon the race and returned to themselves. Before they feel thus restored, they are still full with their effort. Inquiry or comment, great praise or expression of comfort, beyond the acceptance of a touch or pat on the shoulder feels like an intrusion. All kids are different, but everyone will seek out parents in a time appropriate to him- or herself. (Only in cases where an athlete's despair or pain extends solitary behavior beyond an hour should he be sought out, then most usually by the coach.) As for the coach, as joyful as good performances are to him, he must be just as thorough in seeking out his skiers who are not so happy with themselves. The coach is better again than parents, for often a young skier will feel the worse for thinking he has not done his parents hopes their due.

The separation before the race, the delay in contact after the race, are filled with certain despair, even anguish, at times a sense of rejection, by any parent. A righteous sense of injustice, even anger, may be felt. My child is fearful, and I should not comfort her? Why won't she let me? Can't I give my son some good advice?

The answer is no: The athlete must prepare and then recover alone, or with a companion. He or she wants to leave you for the separate world of the race, and to return to you on his or her own terms and under his or her own control. Less than friendly or courteous responses before or after the race should not worry you too much. They are born in the anxiety and emotion of performance and in no way alter the supreme importance a parent's simply being there has for a child.

How do you know what behavior your child athlete likes best? Ask him. Tell her you are not sure and do not want to intrude. You will get helpful answers, and that communication itself makes for empowering, loving moments for both parent and athlete. Your presence, however silent or distant, will always, mysteriously, impart strength to your child. You will beam strength with your smile, seen or unseen.

# 2

# *Coaches and Coaching*

When Disko thought of cod, he thought as a cod, and by some long-tested mixture of instinct and experience, moved the *We're Here* from berth to berth, always with the fish, as a blindfolded chess-player moves on the unseen board.

—Rudyard Kipling, *Captains Courageous* [1]

As young athletes develop beyond the initial skills and games of sport, as their joy begins to focus more seriously on improving capabilities and higher performance, a coach will take on significance almost equal to that of a parent in the athlete's life. Particularly in the teenage years the combination of dramatic physical and social growth (which includes greater independence from parents) along with the increasing complexities of training and competition make the coach's task many-faceted.

Training friends, for example, compete for the same team. One will make it, one will not. Both must be supported and encouraged to go on, for this is only this year. Another year can be different altogether. Then, once a team has been formed, its members must be turned from striving against each other to striving with each other. How is a coach to bring about that transformation? Another example: a coach wishes to inspire curiosity for more solid and sophisticated knowledge in the athlete, but how can he at the same time caution against pop-physiology, the latest training fad, the uses of the current hero's interview, or the 14 year-old's conviction that his key to success is in the weight room?

Human performance is a highly complex undertaking. It takes not weeks nor months but some years to marshal all of the variables of person and body into a plan and a shared mental set towards high performance. Above all, it takes human beings not as objects, marionettes to be directed mechanically, like machines or soldiers, by mail or by phone. Athletic development takes place not in dreams but primarily in a present, in the day-to-day execution of a training and learning plan, and thus depends upon the shared alertness and presence of athlete and coach. The coach's knowledge and sense for people are the raw resources; his own experience as an athlete is also critical. His presence alone makes something happen with the athlete.

The nuances of interpersonal relations are complicated enough, more so yet the shades and subtleties of language, at once powerful, imperfect, shifting, and above all highly personalized. Communication itself takes place unevenly, sometimes through many words, sometimes through a single word, perhaps the coach's, as often the athlete's. Often silence and waiting are best, sometimes a non-verbal signal most eloquent and precise. While there is much to accomplish, patience and a trust in detail are the two emotions most essential to success. While the coach is a powerful force with his many kinds of knowledge, success will come to the extent he can erase his own specific profile, turn the athlete into a true partner, enthusiastic and responsible. The coach has drive, but must "disappear."

How is the coach to do all that? Where are the sources of the coach's knowledge?

## The coach is an athlete

According to an old adage, the most reliable information comes up through the feet, in the lived experience. The urge to be a coach began as an athlete, and not in the intellect but in the sensations of movement. As with dancing, athletic motion, locomotion, and rhythm are deep sources of knowledge. (I say knowledge to distinguish it from mere information, data. Information becomes knowledge when it moves us physically and emotionally.) Knowledge captivates, impels, frees, seems magical. The urge to share that precious, mysterious knowledge turns athletes into coaches.

But being "fast in the pasture" is not the same thing as being an expert in the field. Being an athlete, however extensive one's experience, is only the most elementary beginnings of becoming a coach.  Since new coaches are often sought directly from the ranks of former athletes, not the least because these athletes are both attractive and inexpensive, there remains some confusion about the differences between the role of athlete and the role of coach. We serve each best by understanding the differences at the outset.

Particularly in an individual endurance sport the athlete must have combed through the myriad variables of life and selected out those which specifically help specifically him. He develops a highly refined, unrelenting singular focus upon the ways training and performance relate to himself. He may acquire this in the company of others, and that may be a group to which general information is directed. But he is a competitor, and he takes it as if it were only for him, a select type of body and psychological makeup, different from any other. His instincts are correct, on two counts. He is different, we all are from each other; and it is his reservoir which needs to be filled — that is only practical.

In the days, months, and years of filling, like the slowly rising water table trickles slowly but constantly into a dug well, he also struggles with every means of his understanding. Above all, language is constantly culled, selected, shrunk to minimal and powerful memory and effectiveness. Then he adds new words, better words, more ample, and discards earlier ones. Then he culls again. Ultimately his understanding and his language are as lean as his body, trimmed and muscled, and spare to the point of near silence. His single effort, along with his coach, is to transform the articulateness of language into the fluency of movement. That is the fundamental task of physical performance. The body "learns to speak" (and, as we will see, silence plays a large role).

The coach may have been an athlete, but he or she is now a fundamentally different person. The direction of forces is now outward, the focus is multiple, to the many sides of a number of athletes, each one different, to the most expansive dictionary and penetrating variety of expression in the language. Each athlete, he learns, will have something of his or her own personal vocabulary, and the coach will have to learn that personal code in order to effectively communicate. I will speak in a moment about both personality profiles and elements of communication in performance. Suffice it here to say simply that the coach must become outward-directed and athlete-motivated. The miseries and failures of athletes at the hands of self-directed coaches are thoroughly documented.

I want to further qualify this distinction between coach and athlete. I do not mean to suggest that the athlete is totally self-centered, or develops no social skills, to the contrary. Athletes train optimally in groups and function well, with experience and leadership, as teams. Yet they are still driven largely by a practical and efficient selfishness. That need not be seen as a mark of moral deficiency. Like a healthy plant striving to survive and dominate in its environment, the athlete takes all the sun and moisture it can for itself. Like the plant, the athlete "knows" something, up through its "feet" about how to flower most beautifully.

Nor is the coach totally altruistic. He is like the gardener. He loves the sight of growth, the green, but really seeks the flower. That splendor is his experience of beauty, of special life, a gift, a possibility. His hope is not without a note of greed, self-centeredness, for he wishes the thrill of final outcome. Any true coach will know, however, that he cannot possess that outcome, which is the measure of a common endeavor, a partnership. It is a shared joy, and one different for each, not to be confused by either, coach or athlete. It is a delicate, intricate undertaking.

The leap from one to the other is a sizeable one. The new coach's task is to look, ponder, and listen to everything. Be patient. You cannot become an expert by the day after your crossed your last finish line, even if you won the race. That is another of the perplexing, apparently ungrateful realities of life. Human endeavor is a ruthlessly collaborative thing. You will need to collaborate with the athletes with whom you work as well as forever with the athlete in yourself. And there are many other helpful, necessary, and equally fascinating sources.

## The coach is a student of physiology

Physiology is the "first base" of sport. It provides the basis for sound decision making for coaches, athletes, and parents alike. It is also the coach's most essential teaching tool, for an athlete builds a capacity to perform not only through physical growth but through motivation and confidence. In order to execute month after month of training, any athlete must believe in the physiological rationale underlying it. Simple obedience to a coach's convictions is never enough by itself, for at one time or another the athlete will find reason to be less convinced by the coach as a person. The coach can best convince the athlete, and thus strengthen that essential confidence, with clearly shared physiological principle. That is belief worth having. It adds cool patience to the passion to excel. Hurry, we know, is the athlete's enemy.

So coaches must simply wade in to the elements of biomechanics, aerobic and anaerobic metabolism, the peripheral and central systems, and on and on, deeper and deeper. I have provided a basis introduction to these subjects in the first chapter. Every coach needs several basic source books. As starters I recommend *The Olympic Book of Sports Medicine* and the journal, *Medicine and Science in Sports and Exercise.*

But it is not enough just to acquire knowledge; we must learn how to think. By that I mean it is important to test information put forth as science, to know how to challenge its assumptions, as well as one's own, to balance one's need to have the latest information with the intellectual skill to evaluate it. The coach thinks as a scholar, always checking the feedback from his feet. Above all, his zeal for the sport must not simply render him a believer. The power to accept as true knowledge the latest scientific results is full of barbs for both coach and athlete. I will offer some notes on recognizing the traps in scientific language a little later. For now I would only remark that the will to believe is usually attracted to doctrine or myth rather than to real knowledge.

That said, we know there is a risk as well in becoming too much the expert. Even if the athlete seems to thrive on volumes of information, he, like the coach, may start to confuse information with actual executed training. He is a flower being overwatered. Our best source of information then may be the athlete himself. We watch, listen, heed the feedback and adjust how best to proceed.

## The coach is a student of psychology

We all have our experience and our personal wisdom, and it is truly profound. Each of us, by himself, however, cannot encompass enough experience to be adequately prepared to deal positively with the infinite variety of personality types or psychological forces at work in training and competition, within the dynamics of individuals or teams. Some tools for understanding and communicating with different personality types are discussed later in this chapter.

## The coach is planner and administrator

In the first instance training is essentially time and stress management. Without a plan and systematic execution, the best talent and information in the world will surely be wasted. A plan is simply a budget for the body, taking optimal advantage of the time at hand, making that time predictable and recurring according to pattern, and thus reducing the stress of great and long effort. The cost per unit of effort drops; or, put another way, greater speed is produced for the same price. That is economy and efficiency. Chapter 5 gives a sample of a spread sheet training plan and how it works.

Given the myriad variables in any athlete's life in general, plus the variety of training types in the year's recipe, training must be planned at least a year at a time to ensure both accomplishment and pleasure in training. Some young athletes see a training plan for the first time and immediately say, "Oh! That's too complicated for me." If that is the initial response, a coach can begin with a smaller, three month piece of the whole, as long as he, at least, has the whole on paper and the athlete has a general idea how the plan is shaped.

It is the training plan which sets the stage for learning and growth, a sort of vintner's calendar. It is also the foundation of performance. Athletes or coaches who say they do better if they train by their gut or by how they feel are either lazy or deep down are afraid to really try to achieve something. Most athletes find a clear, extended plan both an immense time-saver and a great psychological relief. Training sessions can be reflected upon well in advance, the details set, so that the day-to-day execution can be accomplished well. The result will be what we all seek, "quality training". Without such an approach a coach and athlete are just toying with the athlete's body. That may be fun for the moment, in the sense of emotionally satisfying, but the gains will remain few. Over the long haul it will even be abusive.

I often find support and inspiration for my coaching activities by reading outside of skiing, physiology, or even sport. Books on management often have excellent insights into the processes of planning aimed at productivity, efficiency, in a word, performance. It is not happenstance either that a publication like the *Harvard Business Review* would become interested in a winning sports program and would interview Bill Walsh of the football San Francisco 49ers. Such reviews show that business management and coaching management of athletes have much to share. Walsh's ideas are clearly sensible and reflect a modern approach to sport:

> The role of the head coach begins with setting a standard of excellence. Successful coaches realize that winning teams are not run by single individuals who dominate the scene and reduce the rest of the group to marionettes. Winning teams are like open forums in which everybody participates in the decision-making process, coaches and players alike, until the decision is made.[2]

> You have got to be resolute in where you are heading and how you plan to get there. And even though you might fail … you never panic. A lot of people bring on failure by the way they react to pressure. … The more preparation you have prior to the conflict, the more you can do in a clinical situation, the better off you will be."[3]

Consistency and congruence must be able to inform each training session. Each session has a stated character, a physiological goal, a theme. Each day has its easily perceived "personality". And just as you prepare before a session, you finish after a session. The session does not simply cease. That is like a bag of marbles with the drawstrings left loose. It is time to ask the athletes what has been best for them today. They will tell you their most memorable points of focus. Select two for the athlete to remember and write down in his log. The coach keeps track of the others. He makes a point of telling the athlete to throw those others away. The athlete needs to travel light. Yet many will load up long lists; one young woman I worked with had 14 items she was currently working on. In that case her sheer fascination and desire to learn was ironically creating a block to her improvement. This case of too much information also can be controlled with a good, long-term plan, for it has all the details but is absolutely patient. It keeps space open in which both athlete and coach can move surely forward.

## The coach is a facilitator and collaborator

Such insights and words of advice are particularly helpful to coaches in light of the fact that we know that we all have certain limitations, certain strengths, weaknesses, and preferences. If we are dealing only with ourselves as athletes, these are somewhat routine to our development. If we are coaches, however, they can define our limitations in perceiving all the possible resources and ways of accessing our athletes. Such a limitation is neither productive, professionally acceptable, nor, for that matter, conscionable. It is, after all, someone else's body and spirit with which we are dealing, and that entails a major professional and personal responsibility.

It has been recognized generally that coaches, particularly those close to their athlete days but not limited to them, tend to coach to their own strengths.[4] This seems pretty natural, as is the coach's tendency to understand and relate to his sport in his own personal idiom.

A coach must quickly get beyond such a self-centered perspective. In his desire to help and his thirst for knowledge he naturally trusts his own words most. Yet he and his preferred vocabulary are in fact less important than the athlete and the athlete's language. Even if the athlete learns all the coach's words, and repeats them perfectly, that does not mean that a common reality has been shared, just as we know that mere imitation does not constitute learning.

The problems inherent in coach-centered coaching are both widespread and quite easy to overcome. We begin by recognizing two basic principles of coaching. The first is that the athlete belongs to him- or herself first. He or she will improve to the extent the coach can amplify that self-possession. So coach the person first, the sport second. The playing fields and trails are littered with the bodies of young athletes whose talent was recognized early, was "developed," with some success and, as became progressively more clear, considerable stress. The young person is treated as a mature athlete and soon thinks of himself as having a firm grip on the world at large. We admire him, for imitating adults is taken, mistakenly, for learning.

In fact, the youngster mimics the behavior, but his own body and psyche have somehow been left out of the equation.

The coach, of course, needs to take himself seriously and objectively and accept the fact that he finds himself in an athlete-to-coach continuum of personal and professional development. It also happens that people find themselves coaching and need to become athletes afterward. It is in fact both good comfort and challenge that athletes will always want the coach to be involved to some degree as athlete as well. That is simply a matter of remaining believable by doing what you are presuming to coach. It also demonstrates that the coach is using himself as the test animal for new ideas and not his athletes. It is fundamental to coaching, however, that the final height of an early athletic career, its end, marks the beginning of a coaching career, and not just in point of time but in understanding of the task. It is often a puzzling and bitter pill to swallow for willing, successful athletes to discover that their own experiences and convictions have only a limited, personal basis. Sharing those experiences demonstrates a generous and genuine desire to step out of themselves into the service of others, but it is really only exchanging their experiences for those of others, inviting others to match them, do as they have done. This may display a welcome generosity. It can also mask the need to be validated by the younger athletes. In this instance sharing is not taking place.

If both athletes and coaches could understand these notions, coaching itself might better be envisioned for what it is, the beginning of a fascinating exercise with the vast complexities of the body and the unending varieties of human being who have the odd spirit, who have the passion to find higher levels of physical performance in public competition with others and within their own vagrant, deepening and labrynthine interior worlds.

## The coach projects positive thoughts but is open and honest about the struggle to succeed and the hurts of failure

Given the complexity and charged emotional atmosphere of both training and competition, it only makes sense that a coach judge a training session, if he must at all, with distance, and above all confident enthusiasm. Let one lesson finish before speculating openly on the next. Any displeasure or doubt will have little positive influence. Save your concerns, then express them constructively in terms of the next days' or weeks' plan. It is one of the most difficult things a coach does — not showing his less positive emotions, at least not immediately. It is natural that he be worried at times, angry, frustrated, in despair, panicked. Those emotions are simply "not there," except perhaps a month later, expressed in the story telling. We all want our coaches to be full humans, and that fullness will be revered later. But too soon it will detract from the athlete's positive mental set towards a given performance. A training session, or following a race, is almost never the time.

This is not to say that a good coach must never get angry. To the contrary, we all know there are times when any athlete will behave in a way which cannot be corrected by calm rationality. To apply the softer touch of reason to every behavior can easily turn out not to be nurturing support for growth and progress at all but rather simple enabling of that behavior out of the lack of courage to state exactly what is useful behavior and what is not. No true athlete wants the coach to mince words, nor to be stripped of his true emotions. A coach who lives with his athletes as a full person will in fact implicitly dignify their full personhood in the process.

"Sometimes you just have to get ripped!" said my friend, Marty Hall; and he is right. And I can remember just twice when my former coach and mentor, Al Merrill, got really mad with me. One day I broke three skis, new ones just arrived. Full of enthusiasm, I attempted to glide over snow banks at trail crossings ... but three times? Another time he had arranged a penicilin shot with his personal doctor after I had been sick all winter. I did not show up for the appointment because I felt like I was finally feeling better. These are examples of bonehead behavior worthy of any coach's finest rage. They needed a lightning bolt to clean away the cobwebs in my head and clear the air in order to persuade me of the need to see my situation and responsibility to myself more clearly.

Once we think of it clearly, human high performance is so complex an undertaking in the first place, it is difficult, if not impossible, to keep every ingredient in a program in harmony and congruence, or each athlete in harmony with him- or herself and with the coach. Constant communication is necessary to keep the training and performance recipe moving forward. Now and then will come a time where some emotional heat fuses the coach's message together most succinctly and memorably.

What is critical, however, is that the coach expresses his rage with reference to the behavior which is the source of disharmony or ineffective training. No productive anger can be aimed at the whole person: that is malice, and that merely indulges the coach while it demeans the athlete. Good rage may better demonstrate the coach's passion and uncompromising commitment to that same athlete. It thus may build trust in the integrity and openness of the coach, his courage to confront an issue and reassert standards more worthy of the athlete when milder measures of communication have not worked.

Every now and then in technique work, when the myriad details become too many and confused, when progress is blocked and frustrated, we "clean it with speed." We go so fast the details are automatically combed out. A little high-quality, brief but articulate rage can have the same cleaning effect.

The knowledge of the coach as a full person himself and his knowledge of his athletes as full people becomes even more critically supportive in competition. The race is only a more compact version of training, so the preparation is even more careful, physically and psychologically as well. That means select training routines are followed. The workout from Friday of 20-10-5, with part of the 5 in the first kilometer, is repeated as the warmup for the race on Saturday. It means each competitor knows exactly when to start his warmup, I say 45 minutes before his start time, and thus the start itself is defused in its tension.

Calm must also be dispensed as well as the usual minimal information. In your behavior there is no hurry, no panic, even if there is. Racing mental sets, the cues which are the sensory anchors for the day, are reviewed. Each racer has his or her specific set. You position yourself on the course where you can help, and you retrieve each skier after the finish. Almost all would like to see you, soon, but most often only that, perhaps for just a sign or nod, not necessarily a word, and certainly not "How did you do?"

Just notice them, with your eyes, ears, sixth sense open. They will signal what they want of you.

You are tired out at the end of the race, but there is a very significant piece left. Sharing the joy of the successful is a wonderful reward for any coach. But you must tend to the less successful with even more sensitivity and support. Anybody who has witnessed Olympic Tryouts close up knows this. In the shadows among and beyond those who have made the team are a number who did "not quite" succeed. These are suffering dreadfully. They have just made a monstrous effort after long preparation and have sustained a devastating destruction of their hopes. Brave as they stand beside their friends, they are a shambles inside, and perhaps will remain so for some weeks. You need to reckon with that, and let them be how they are, dignify what are truly legitimate emotions and return them carefully to hope. They need a good lot of your time, if for no more than having you close and with them. They were as valiant, as good as the winners; the cards just shuffled wrong for them today.

It is only in the context of resilience and confidence that the compactness, duration, ups and downs of sport can be sustained, made fruitful and, after all is said and done, bring joy.

The source of this confidence is found only to a relatively small degree in the race result sheet. Race results, after all, are just that, results. Their source is elsewhere, in an assuredness of the causes. Americans seem forever to confuse causes and results, as I have suggested in my technique discussions and in my chapter on "The Limitation of Visual Perception in Understanding Technique." And we compete our youngsters unrelentingly in youth programs and in school, thinking apparently that results will somehow foster better results. But without adequate time given to the real causes of development through patient and proper training our young athletes have only short-term improvement, then mostly tension and fatigue. This fate has been documented world-wide; only we do not seem to understand.

Confidence and stamina and power are stored slowly in a huge reservoir in a systematic training plan, in the careful knowledge of the execution of the variety of training sessions, in the unpressured measuring of improving training capacities and speeds, in the feelings of improvement, greater mobility and quickness at any, sometimes surprising times, in the demonstrated convictions of the coach. Herein lies the recipe for excellent results.

Within that powerful framework there is ample room for the entire spectrum of human emotion, each perhaps more deeply tinted for the intensity of the desire and extent of effort contained in endurance sport. A coach must encourage and dignify all emotions, just as we accept all personality types. We know there is no particular athlete-type or athlete behavior.[5] As the body makes no mistakes, neither does the psyche. Familiarity with all the emotions forms the capacity to understand, select, control, to find strength in the widest spectrum of experience.

From the crash experience of a failed set of Olympic Trials, something I learned about in my first attempt in 1960, to the discouragement of an unimportant training race, the athlete must be allowed, supported in following his feelings down as well as up. We are so sad to see an unhappy fellow, we want them to be happy again as soon as possible. Suffering disturbs us, for ourselves every bit as much as for them. We equate pain with failure, and we do not want to be around that. (It isn't, of course, it is only loss, of a single competition.)

But the attempt to neutralize a powerful emotion, let alone change or suppress it, before it has run its full expression and course is really more self-serving than helpful. It is even brutal, callous, however well-intended. It is like stopping the athlete in mid-race; it blocks the sense of fullness, completion, and with it the true and necessary richness of the athletic experience, not to mention the dignity of the person. That experience will quite normally include both exaltation and despair. And there will be more pain in an emotion being blocked than one fully felt through. There is no particular toughness in suppressing feelings. That is no better than putting a kink in a hose. It is the whim and power of the one who wishes to manipulate the flow of energy, callously, at his whim and for his own comfort. Any compulsion to control or manipulate the flow of genuine feelings may even mask a rather cynical combination of disrespect for the child and demand for his achievement.[6]

Because any athlete must lose so many competitions before he wins, he actually has quite a highly developed sense for the basic tragedy of existence. He attracts this experience the more intensely for the presumption he makes to unusual human performance levels, for they are risky and public. To rob him of the circumstantial suffering may make us feel better, but it will also implicitly trivialize his experience. We must not regiment his emotions any more than we can regiment his physical development. If we do, we may achieve the appearance of calm and harmony in his obedience, of socially well-adjusted group behavior, but that achievement will likewise not lead to high performance. It will have "kinked the hose," too severely regulated the passion and triggers and flow of energy to excel. The simplest source of human performance lies in being totally alive, in finding aliveness at its outer limits.[7] For that the total human aquifer is needed and all spontaneous access to it is the prerequisite for any unusual human performance. As Alice Miller remarks, "Morality and performance of duty are artificial measures that become necessary when something essential is lacking."[8] What is lacking is a young person's sense of being an authentic self, somebody with full and spontaneous access to himself. Without that sense the motivation to excel cannot survive, for there is no personal strength without it. Obedience does not make the young athlete strong; it only makes him malleable. The coach rests assured, but the athlete has in fact been denied full access to himself. It also suggests an outside source as the better one, and thus implicitly trivializes him as an individual. Unfortunately, this remnant of 19th century pedagogy remains powerful in education circles even today.

Never, ever, is what a human being attempts trivial. It is complex, daring, mysterious, demanding, a frail but powerful undertaking. Whatever he feels has good reason. Let him be with it while he will or must. He will return to himself, and to you, strengthened, in his good time. Healing has its own pace, its own chemistry. In this athletes must be treated as no more and no less totally human than other humans.

It is for this reason that I have little faith in the various motivational programs we encounter. I do mental training, visualization, relaxation, some Yoga and Ki Aikido exercises, but I do no particular "psyching" or positive "self-talk." If an athlete has tapped the powerful intelligence of his body and his program, the process of development in its detail and spirit, then added mental manipulation or pump-up's can easily become distracting, make him more brittle in their facileness, and are dangerous in the romance of their goals. Positive, yes, but too often, with youngsters in particular, the mental program intensifies the desire and expectation to a point beyond which the preparation justifies. That again trivializes the process and makes performance seem to depend upon forces and influences more mystical. I have also seen several top athletes who have depended heavily upon them, not made an Olympic Team, including reasons other than fitness, and end up totally disequipped to deal with the loss. Of the non-winners of whom I have just spoken this last group are the most hopelessly and unjustifiably lost.

The strength of athletes is as complex and diverse as that of all other human beings. The key to athletic performance lies firmly in full access, constantly, to the total richness and spectrum of human experience and emotion. On that broad training ground, in that deep aquifer, the athlete prepares best for his sport. There is no contrivance, trick, or substitute which will heighten his performance any more reliably.

And in that enterprize coach and athlete must remain bound together in conviction and in generous partnership.

## The coach evaluates and applies scientific research

I would conclude this discussion of coaching with yet another re-affirmation of the reliability of feet, of the body in motion, in relation to knowledge and its language.

We tend to equate knowledge with science, for science, we assume, is objective and therefore trustworthy. For all the magnificence of its insights, however, science still has a few barbs coaches need to know about. Especially here in America, where individualism and enterprise tend to make science singular and competitive, a scientist has much at stake in being the authoritative voice. In that they mirror, and so often admire, athletes. We have already cautioned against the misequation of authority and power with knowledge, and we know that knowledge, untempered by broad culture and experience, often quickly presumes upon authority.

We need to think through the coach's relationship to science, moreso yet to the scientist. It is illuminating to start with Carl Roger's formulation that "Science ... rests on the assumption that behavior is caused— that a specified event is followed by a consequent event. Hence all is determined, nothing is free, choice is impossible."[9] It is quite easy to see how science and scientists are granted by us and thence readily assume the authoritative role of their particular work.

But Rogers goes on: "But we must recall that science itself, each specific scientific endeavor, ... each change in course in scientific research, each interpretation of the meaning of a scientific finding ... rests upon a personal subjective choice." Further yet, he stresses that, "each of these choices initiating or furthering the scientific venture, is a value choice. ... He interprets his findings in one way rather than the other because he believes the first way is closer to the truth, or more valid — in other words that it is closer to a criterion which he values."[10] Examples abound. I will mention one in another chapter: a team doctor/physiologist makes a sweeping pronouncement about how to train ... but has never seen, let alone experienced a modern year-long training plan. Our educational system is rife with the attitude that students must be directed from above, regimented in curriculum and sport. Coaches often turn with a curious quasi-patriotic fervor to the military command model.

We have begun to learn, on the other hand, that our students and athletes are not circus bears, nor bundles of chaos in need of total harness. We want to let them run because we see they do it better that way. And our discussion here has shown a very different, more creative, interesting, and productive role for coaches. Powerful in his own drive and personality, even his charisma, if you will, he nevertheless no longer plays the master or the general but rather the facilitator-collaborator. If he becomes a master, it will be master at that. In his experience up through the feet and his openness to the endless applicable resources he probably comes closer to being objective, to being a true scientist, than any scientist who insists upon or presumes to stand either alone, apart, or above.

Can we sharpen our eyes and ears to the clues of narrowness and subjectivity in the scientific research we all so eagerly consume? I think so. The answer lies in Roger's recognition that there are values implicit in much scientific research which are indeed subjective.

We tend not to see it, but we can learn how. We begin by learning to read more precisely. We read not only the results but how the experiments were run, who the trial subjects were and their characteristics. We compare with our own athletes and what we have known to date; we doubt, then give it a chance, and check again. We ask ourselves; we phone colleagues and inquire further. We find missing links, and while we need not hold them against the researcher, they may still effect the use of new information in our sport.

Above all, we develop a "nose" for qualifiers and the language of presumption, where doubt is deftly and almost silently admitted and where theory is extended to practice without previous trial by the researcher. This is qualifying vocabulary; the researcher shields himself legally with it as well as expresses honest professional care.

The sorts of phrases to remain alert to are these: "The evidence would suggest …" "It would follow that …" "Under most circumstances therefore …" "Theoretically it would seem …" Some qualifying words are "probably," "somewhat," "perhaps," "seems," "might," "may," "could."

The key element in each word or phrase is its statement of conditionality. The speaker is stepping back from fully identifying with the content of his own statement. He is being careful, not devious, mind you, but simply careful. He, like the rest of us, if he is good, knows that information can be intoxicating, heady stuff. Qualifiers are a way to stand more comfortably somewhere between yes and no.

Coaches need to be aware of this. It does not mean we reject the research out of hand; we simply recognize the distance at which we had best stand to balance our hunger for new and relevant information. If we leap in where the angels are fearing to tread themselves, we will routinely misequate the new to the best and the piece to the whole. For the scientist's qualifying vocabulary is usually no more apparent to the reader than the negative "don't" is to the athlete in motion. Immersed in the current of discovery, our senses pick up the content in its most bite size, handy bundles, like a fish a pretty fly, but we miss the barb, the qualifier. As coaches we will be too happily persuaded by the content if we do not read and mark every word and check the details of both the writing style and the research protocol itself, both in our intellect and our "feet." Do not accept the outcome until you have thoroughly checked the process. It is finally the coach who is uniquely equipped to provide the balance, for in him are mind and body most reliably and subtly joined. He works things through, so to speak, from head to toe.

A single example provides a case study. In 1977 an article by J.D. MacDougall appeared in the *Canadian Journal of Applied Sports Sciences.* Its title was "Anaerobic Threshold: Its Significance for the Endurance Athlete."[11] It is a key topic in endurance sport, and the author begins his conclusion in a sub-section on "Implications for Training" in which he says: "One can therefore hypothesize that any form of training which leads to an increase in the capacity of the muscle to oxidize pyruvate and fatty acids would be of benefit in elevating the athlete's anaerobic threshold." Fair enough to hypothesize at the beginning. He goes on, citing evidence, mostly from animal studies (his range is limited here) that duration of training has to date been thought the most important factor. He proceeds with an all too typical addition:

> In addition, however, it has recently be demonstrated that higher intensity 2-minute 'endurance-interval training of relatively short total duration will dramatically reduce lactic acid production at the same submaximal workload. In view of this and recent glycogen depletion studies which indicate that training intensity must be close to, or in excess of, $VO_2$ max in order to recruit the fast twitch fibers and thus provide a training stimulus for those fibers, it would seem that a higher intensity endurance-interval program might be more effective that the prolonged continuous sub-maximal type of program. Such a program would probably consist most effectively of 2-3 min work intervals at intensities equivalent to 90-100% $VO_2$ max, alternated with similar low-intensity rest intervals.[12]

We can hear the content, new, attractive, and the scientist's typically prescriptive extension of his personal conviction. And there is the catalogue of qualifiers. Still, it would be easy to walk away with the prescription, as many an athlete and coach has over the past fifteen years. Luckily, MacDougall provides the balancing approach in a major caveat.

> In some contrast to this recommendation, however, we have indirect evidence [i.e. from experience, not a part of a specific scientific experiment] highlighting the importance of long-duration sub-threshold training on the elevation of this threshold as well. Such evidence is furnished by comparison of the lactic acid responses of elite long-distance athletes whom we have tested (marathoners, 10,000m runners and cross-country skiers) with those of equally trained middle-distance athletes (in this case, 800, 1500m runners and oarsmen). Although we have found several exceptions, there is a definite trend for the long-distance athletes (who are more characterized by long-duration, sub-maximal training) to have higher anaerobic thresholds than the middle-distance athletes, who tend to rely more on the high-intensity endurance-interval type of program described above.[13]

Notice the total absence of qualifiers in the second section quoted. Experience not only balances his own prescription, it in fact contradicts it. He summarizes ultimately in favor of a mix of both kinds of training, but it his "new" information which still would have the most powerful attraction for the less suspicious ear. We also know that it is not only a question of either/or; it also a question of timing of the training types throughout the year's training curve. He seems unaware of this factor of periodization. No indication is given in the article as to the duration of the experiment, a critical factor in endurance training changes.

In another article on anaerobic threshold training which appears in Edmund Burke's *Towards an Understanding of Human Performance*, Ben Londeree provides an even more extreme example of a physiologist presuming to prescribe based on theory only:

> Now you might ask how you can best improve your A.T. We have not systematically compared various training programs as yet, so a conclusive answer is not available. However, we have produced increments in A.T. with an approach based on theoretically sound principles of specificity of training. Essentially this means that you must overload the specific physiological function in order to develop a training effect.[14]

"Essentially this means you must"? What kind of a combination of qualifier and command is that? One without the necessary support of measured comparison of training programs over a long period of time. His article should stop after the phrase, " so a conclusive answer is not available." He does not hesitate, on the other hand, to prescribe supra-threshold pace training, prolonged as much as possible and repeated often, again without consideration of the year-round recipe.

Finally, we have not seen the end of the speculation. Owen Anderson wrote in *Running Research* (Vol.9, No.1, 1993) in a similar vein as MacDougall and Londeree, 16 years later, though nowhere near as carefully as MacDougall. In "Planning Your Training for 1993: Should You 'Crash' Your Way To Better Times?"[15] he bases his prescription for supra-threshold training on an article written by a team of authors entitled "Endurance training amplifies the pulsatile release of growth hormone: effects of training intensity." Anderson, who otherwise has written quite carefully, advocates various "crash" portions of one's training in order to elevate anaerobic threshold. To his credit, he does bring in evidence for the dangers, including high cortisol and resting heartrate levels still present two weeks following the crash intensity approach. He overstates the degree of difference between the women runners in the study who ran at below threshold levels and those above: he describes the former approach as "far superior."

In the original article, the at-Lactate Threshold (@LT) runners improved in VO$_2$ max from 42.7 +/-6.2 to 47.4+/-8.0. The above threshold (>LT) group improved from 44.2+/-5.5 to 50.1+/-4.6. The spectrum of difference between the groups thus runs 39.4-55.4 for the @LT group, as opposed to 45.5-54.7 for the >LT group.[16] Whereas statistical analysis may indicate greater success in the >LT group, the variation within the groups, freely recognized by the researchers, renders Anderson's reading anything but conclusive or "far superior". Even with more compelling statistics, the caveat must remain that statistics seldom correlate directly with actual performance in the field. He does not say for whom his ideas are intended — young, mature, beginners, intermediates — or include any of the caveats contained in the article upon which he bases his "new" prescriptions. Finally, although Anderson speculates, rather wildly, about how to begin the training recipe and how to proceed with it in terms of paces/levels of effort, he concludes by saying:

> Although scientific research into the merits of various long-term training plans is still in its infancy [as with Londeree's article, not so in practice], it is possible to put together a fine overall training plan. Your best strategy is to use high-quality workouts which produce beneficial changes and to back away from hard training whenever you feel that you're not recovering properly between workouts. Systematically use races or test workouts to evaluate how you are doing. If your performances decline in spite of strenuous training, that's a good sign you are not getting enough recovery.[17]

This is a prescription for haphazard training at its most whimsical. Feelings follow the physiological processes which produce them; by the time you are feeling something, therefore, it is too late. It goes back to the time when we were all training by how we felt day-to-day and basically trained as hard as we could. Any coach with experience would recognize in this advice a plan for disappointment.

In fact, the merits of training plans had been rather well documented, not in laboratory quantification perhaps but in Olympic medals. Coaches and athletes knew, as is best exemplified by Arthur Lydiard's work which was validated point after point by sports scientists, among them the East Germans, through the late 60's and 70's. Training has come a long way in twenty years. Anderson wants to take us back to the 60's. He simply presumes to coach and cannot. The conceit of the scientist expert must not be thought to replace the feet of coach and athlete. Those feet are not mere clay.

At any rate, we need to track his source article. The first thing of importance is that the training group was comprised of untrained women between 18 and 40 years of age. That is a rather narrowly defined group. I would begin qualifying its conclusions based upon "untrained" and 18 to 40. In the first place these are definitely beginning adults, by statement and by their $VO_2$ max levels. They are also adults, which would limit the application of the research to youngsters through their early teens. One would have to go through the original article with a fine-toothed comb to gather all the data and consider its significance for general endurance sport training. It is an extremely complete and detailed study which admits of only limited generalization. Even the authors of this fastidious study state, "the long-term physiological implications of the adaptation in the pulsatile mode of GH release to endurance training cannot be determined from present data."[18]

In short, we have been down the supra-threshold road before, and our results have not improved. Yet physiologists keep on trying. Fine, I say, but we must be equipped to judge how good or bad their research and thought processes are, and be able to check the values and priorities their statements most clearly represent.

What do we do with the athlete whom we wish to understand? We put ourselves in his shoes to listen to what he is saying. We need to put ourselves into the scientist's shoes as well. Perhaps we can understand, or intuit, a small part of him at least. If science assumes human behavior, and thus physical performance, is caused, then it should be expected that the physiologist desires to cause improved performance. We do not mind if he wants that both for athletes and for himself, as long as his ego is not the primary one being served. We welcome his efforts, depend upon them. But we and the athletes should not suffer for his limitations.

For we know the leap from theory to practice is a huge one, at athlete expense foremost. So it must also be a leap of experience and documentation, not just a leap of faith. The leap is undertaken with the feet, again, not just the mind. The feet belong to the athletes and the coach. The scientist only rarely has the total array of equipment to be prescribing training. When he does, be interested, be a scholar, a student, an athlete, a coach, a physiologist, a full person - be as many people as you can be as you read, and read again, reflect, wait, ponder, check with other researchers and your colleagues, and then decide if everything, thought, feeling and feet tell you: "This information physically moves me over the ground better!" Then call it knowledge.

This is what is required of a coach. It is how he can best coach his athletes and get the most joy out of it in the process.

The most reliable information comes up through the feet.

—Local Maine sage

## *How coaches communicate*

What I should like is people to teach. I think I have patience. I teach the apprentices. You have to be understanding with these youngsters. Some are timid, some are pigheaded. I'm timid with the timid and pigheaded with the pigheaded. If you act the same as the person you are teaching he will be at ease with you and will learn better.

—Francis Lambert, old English blacksmith[19]

We have reflected here at some length upon the variety of sources of knowledge. Now we have the more complex and practical challenge: What are some of the ways to access those sources, both in athlete and in coach. What we are talking about is communication, no more or less than that.

It is important at the outset to remember the notion that one coaches the person first, the sport second, a being foremost and only after that his activity. If we coach the sport first, we may well produce a physical specimen who has learned to imitate adult behavior but who in fact remains, naturally, a very young person. It comes as a shock, usually in the late teens or early twenties, to discover this wonderful athlete is really still an early teenager emotionally and socially. One wonders why the final and upper levels of development remain elusive after so many years of promise. More often than not the reason is that the emotional and social development was unwittingly put on the back burner a few years back, in the euphoria over the athlete's special and very attractive gift for sport.

But particularly the intensified life of performance sport must remain a true life, and it takes a full person to achieve it. To be both fair and effective the coach must see this fullness both for its unavoidability and its necessity to human performance. Nobody truly excels with only part of himself, and rarely at that with the most obvious part.

It is obvious that I can give no comprehensive overview of communication. I will suggest a few ways, however, to make the step from athlete to coach, and to real coach-athlete partnership, to the quickening development and pleasure of both.

For some years now I have done small workshops with skiers with the Meyers-Briggs Type Indicator (MBTI). It is a self-reported personality measure done by the athletes which gives a basic but quite functional profile of their personalities. It gives words and description to the ways in which a person relates to the outside world, finds energy, learns most habitually, makes decisions for himself, and behaves with respect to all these activities. Starting from the notion that all personalities are strong, the profile is able to measure the strength of a person's preference (and thus behavior) in four areas:

(1) where one find his/her sources of personal energy;

(2) how one perceives and gathers information;

(3) on what basis he/she prefers to make decisions about that information;

(4) and how he/she relates to the outside world with respect to his/her preference for perceiving and deciding.

The following is a brief overview of the system.

## I. General Focus of Activity

| (E)xtravert | (I)ntrovert |
|---|---|
| E likes action and variety | I likes quiet and time to consider things |
| E likes to do mental work by talking to people | I likes to do mental work privately before talking |
| E acts quickly, sometimes without much reflection | I may be slow to try something without understanding it first |
| E like to see how other people do a job, and to see results | I likes to understand the idea of a job and to work alone or with just a few people |
| E wants to know what other people expect of him or her | I wants to set his or her own standards |

Although everyone turns outward to act and inward to reflect, E's turn mostly outward to the world of action, people and things, I's turn most often to the inner world of ideas and private things, just as each of us is either left-handed or right-handed,

## II. Ways of Gathering Information, Two Kinds of Perception

| (S)ensing | I(N)tuition |
|---|---|
| S pays most attention to experience as it is | N pays most attention to the meanings of facts and how they fit together |
| S like to use eyes and ears and other senses to find out what's happening | N likes to use imagination to come up with new ways to do things, new possibilities |
| S dislikes new problems unless there are standard ways to solve them | N likes solving new problems and dislikes doing the same thing over |
| S enjoys using skills already learned more than learning new ones | N likes using new skills more than practicing old ones |
| S is patient with details but impatient when the details get complicated | N is impatient with details but doesn't mind complicated situations |

S pays more attention to facts that come from personal experience. S can more easily see the details, while N can more easily see the "big picture." N pays more attention to the meaning behind the facts.

## III. Making Decisions With Information, Those Perceptions

### (T)hinking

### (F)eeling

T likes to decide things logically

F likes to decide things with personal feelings and human values, even if they aren't logical

T wants to be treated with justice and fair play

F likes praise, and likes to please people, even in unimportant things

T may neglect and hurt other people's feelings without knowing it

F is aware of other people's feelings

T gives more attention to ideas or things than to human relationships

F can predict how others will feel

T doesn't need harmony

F gets upset by argument and conflicts; values harmony

T makes decisions by examining data, staying impersonal and cool. T stands for thinking judgment. F makes decisions by paying attention to personal values and feelings. F stands for feeling judgment. You make T and F judgments every day, but you prefer one.

## IV. How We Deal With The Outside World

### (J)udging

### (P)erceiving

J likes to have a plan, to have things settled and decided ahead

P likes to stay flexible and avoid fixed plans

J tries to make things come out the way they "ought to be"

P deals easily with unplanned and unexpected happenings

J likes to finish one project before starting another

P likes to start many projects but may have trouble finishing them all

J usually has mind made up

P is usually looking for more new information

J may decide things too quickly

P may decide things too slowly

J wants to be right

P wants to miss nothing

J lives by standards and schedules that are not easily changed

P lives by making changes to deal with problems as they come along

J people show others their thinking or feeling judgment more than their sensing or intuitive perception. P people show their sensing or intuitive perception, information gathering side, more than judgment, decision-making in dealing with the world outside themselves.[20]

I have discussed the topic of "Personality and Performance" in the *PSIA Journal,*[21] so I will only give a few examples here to demonstrate how valuable a tool such a personality type indicator can be to a coach who must constantly strive to understand and thus communicate effectively with his athletes. Note that it is critical to this process that athlete accomplish two things before any coach is going to be able to hear them and respond to them with any significant insights and supports. The athlete must answer the questions on the reporting form spontaneously, from a relaxed, "feet up" point of view, and not as he thinks he ought to answer; and he must come away from the process with some fairly enriched perspective on him- or herself. It is also the athlete's responsibility, I am saying, to become an open source of himself to the coach.

I am not suggesting that the athlete should sacrifice his or her essential privacy. The coach is not a father confessor. Nor does MBTI purport or want to lay bare anybody's deeper and most wonderful mystery. The indicator is only the very beginning. In fact people with similar types invariably remark how different they are as well as how similar. The indicator is therefore more like the 4 bases; they define the basic field of play. The play itself is endlessly varied.

Above all this exercise is completely non-judgmental. All personalities are validated. Differences pop up for all to see clearly. Invariably people laugh at both themselves and others, and a genuine, affirmative electricity will begin to connect the group. It is simply great fun. More than anything else, however, I feel that as a coach I have formally given the athletes, as individuals and as a group, possession of themselves, lest they have any doubts about either my motives or their responsibilities in our partnership. They share my personality type indicator as well, of course, and there are invariably many smiles, many expressions of "Oh, that's just like you!" or "No wonder you always do that!"

## Extravert/Introvert

Two college teammates have become close friends over their four years and continue their loyalty at the National Team level. They travel and train together, depend upon each others energy and motivation. On occasion, however, there comes a problem which neither can explain to or about the other one. They get angry, have a tiff. It usually has something to do with race day. Whereas they are close friends, as the warmup and race time approaches the one's incessant chatter "bugs" the other. On the other hand, the stand-offishness of the second strikes the former as moody, suddenly unfriendly and thus fickle, too competitive, even a little manic.

The two shared three of the four Meyers-Briggs letters. Their friendship was not surprising therefore. But one was at the extreme of extroversion, the other just as extreme in introversion. In a psychologically compact situation like race day these traits become even more pronounced. So the one talked even more than usual, for extroverts talk to think. Every emotion spills into words, any words, whether they relate to anything real or not. This one becomes intrusively noisy.

The introvert dislikes verbal noise more than anything. He wants quiet and solitude, which leads to the second source of race day friction. The extrovert gets his energy from people, loves people, the more he finds, the more he is energized. Particularly on race day he wants to be energized. The introvert gets his energy from within himself, however, and beyond initial contact becomes quickly drained by people.

The conflict is now clear. The extravert naturally seeks out his friend to warmup and wax with before the race. He talks a lot and becomes all of himself. Right at this moment, however, the introvert finds that especially intrusive and inconsiderate. He wants to be left alone to his thoughts and task. Thus the tiff. And thus the instantaneous laughter from both when they understood their profiles. "Oh, my God," said the one (the introvert!), "This has been going on for five years!"

## Sensing/Intuition

How each of us acquires information determines in large part the manner in which we learn. A general example can show the difference in approach; then we can apply it to athletes. A group of budding automechanics is presented with an engine and a manual. Part of the group will invariably just start tinkering, then taking the engine apart to see how it works, and only then compare what they have found with the explanation and diagrams in the manual. They are the sensors.

The intuitives are panic stricken by the sight of their compatriots happily dismembering the engine. They prefer to understand it all first, everything in relation to everything else; then and only then are they ready to take hands and tools to the engine. Sensors do in order to understand; intuitives understand in order to do.

Think of teaching technique, or explaining the training of the day. The sensors want to just get going. They tend to be less fastidious about wax, where they are going, or the point of the day. In a word, they seem to be less interested in accomplishing anything in particular than they are in simply doing and enjoying. They sometimes give the impression they are undisciplined and not really serious about the sport. They are sometimes inattentive, even unruly, during pre-training explanations. They may even seem to disrespect the coach.

Don't be fooled; they just do their serious thing differently. Let them ski for a while; then pass along a new element or short(!) explanation of what you are after. The intuitives will more than engage you at the start of the workout anyway. They want everything in principle and design before they move anywhere. They usually get more credit for knowing what to do, but that does not mean they will necessarily do it better than the sensors.

The problem arises with any team of dealing with both types simultaneously. How do you avoid plain chaos. If you run with the sensors, the intuitives may never get their skis on, or wander around without any plan for the day. So you have to catch both in different ways. Have it written out, large and short, on a flip chart, ahead of time: workout and technique cues for the day. All get the message and can begin together. The intuitives can get their information before starting, the sensors out in the woods. The intuitives will be happy all workout long; the sensors will enjoy the added bits of information during the session. Where the intuitives may have needed a paragraph or two, the sensor will only want a word or two.

Any attempt to provide information to both types in the same way at the same time will only result in the agitation and wasting of quality training for one of them. Certainly a mustering of the troops for receipt of the coach's words for the day will be largely unproductive and serve only the coach's need to feel essential.

## Thinking/Feeling

Both thinking and feeling type decision makers have feelings. The point of the distinction between the two is the basis upon which each comes to a decision on using the information he has. Thinking types work from logic, cause and effect, reason; feeling types decide based on personal values, factors of fairness and harmony, how what they decide will effect others. Men dominate the first group, women the second, but there are many of both genders in each. This distinction needs to be understood because it most profoundly effects interpersonal relationshipsas well as team harmony.

One athlete will say: that is the task; it is most logical to accomplish it this certain way; its obvious (things are always obvious to thinking types). The feeling type asks: How can everybody get it done best together? Is it convenient at that time? Particularly for my favorite training partner? How can I take care of my other obligations to people, family and profession at the same time?

As with the intuitives, the thinking types are often given credit for being more task-oriented and organized, more objective and clear. That is an error. Feeling types are equally organized; they are simply more subjective in their approach and routinely need to clear a number of people-oriented issues before they proceed, even in the course of a given training session. The thinking types can seem utterly arrogant and impersonal, cold and brutal to be around. Feeling types may seem distracted and too "personal". Thinking types seem not to care about how others do, or if they perhaps are hurt by something done, said (or even worse, not said) by a friend or coach. It is easy to imagine, or remember, the many instances where such distinctions have distracted from team efforts, either in training camp or competition tours.

## Judging/Perceiving

In terms of overt, day-to-day behavior toward the outside world, this final difference is as influential as the thinking/feeling spectrum. The judging types love routine, structure, closure (no frayed edges, uncertainties), lists, training programs in detail (and typed, thank you, for they tend to be neat). They are disrupted by too constant questioning and tend to live by the statement. They like to take command of the situation and are often in leadership roles. They are deciders, outcome people.

Perceiving types like to stay open to the possibilities. They are process people. They are spontaneous and flexible, are always receptive to, and seek, further information. If they seem indecisive, it is because they value the question so highly. They are circumspect and irrepressible detail gatherers. They also make lists, but seldom follow them. They seem disorganized, invariably late, with too much luggage. They have too many pairs of skis and cannot decide which pair to use. The wax can always be improved upon. They are easier for coaches to coach and harder for coaches to organize.

The judging type is compelled to come to closure, to a conclusion which can be converted into action, and he will do so with whatever information he has at hand. Even if the information at hand is minimal, it will do. He has no problem coming to a conclusion, leaping, some of us might say. If he is in a leadership role, that conclusion is all important, above all for his particular peace of mind. Last minute wax changes tend to unnerve him. Checking further, asking more questions, drives him crazy, seems wishy-washy and aimless. It maddens him that the perceiver type notices a missing link in his data, even though the perceiver may have so much information, and gathers it so continuously that he never decides what it all might mean, or how to make it functional (this book is my attempt to overcome my own type). The judging type jumps the gun and finishes early, even when he has little interest in the process. The perceiving type arrives at the start the last second and seldom can tell you where he finished. One is rigidly "with it". The other is hard to figure out and seems to forever procrastinate.

I know an inventor of a computer designed to calculate hundreds of variables in any given genetics trial. His programmer and he were in constant conflict until they understood the difference between these types. The inventor kept thinking of a new variable; the programmer was driven to conclude the program. Scientists and coaches run similar risks of confusing conclusion with knowledge and too often in the National Team's history have run with the latest new information or current "expert" rather than truly researching each topic. Our leaders in both sport and medical research have too often needed to be expert more than they needed a truly comprehensive grasp of the phenomenon they were studying. Put more generously, once invested with a certain position of responsibility, they felt obligated to make some authoritative statement. Where authority either suggests or requires that decisions about parts of a program be made, decisiveness or the mere willingness to decide is too often confused with having adequate knowledge with which to decide. Power again becomes misequated with wisdom (I speak to this issue in Chapter 10, "The Limitations of Visual Perception.").

Science, of course, is generally expressed in terms of statements, however couched in qualifiers, and statements are convenient, short, and thus persuasive. They have the form and authoritative tone, but this alone can trick us into believing all the evidence is in. We perceivers may start feeling inadequate, like we are still learners, because we are not ready to draw a conclusion so quickly. Judging types might even find us slow on the uptake, and we might feel a little intimidated. But where all the world loves a decision, we ought to intelligently caution that our very hunger for answers makes us often too willing to believe any answer with the shape but perhaps not the substance of reliable knowledge. I would use my distinction and say we have information, but that is not yet knowledge.

Where coaches fall victim to "the latest," or whatever it is they know at the moment, so do athletes who are too strongly judging types. They tend to confuse the latest item of training or technique with the whole thing. This latest thing becomes of no use to them, in fact, and may actually retard their improvement because they allowed it to masquerade as the whole.

The most productive characteristic of this personality profiling, however, is that it both validates the way each person is, to himself and to others, others with whom he must train and against whom he must compete; and it suggests other beneficial ways of doing things. These other ways are not presented as weaknesses then but rather as other potential approaches to a task or situation. The point is that the collaboration of the varying types is the key to strengthening the whole enterprise through providing greater reliability and common power, not through choosing one approach and attempting to homogenize an individual athlete, program or group accordingly, but through finding in all the variety the richest possible sources of success for each athlete. It should also be clear at this point why the individual athlete cannot effectively coach solely from his or her own experience and why the coach who coaches to his own personal strengths will remain severely limited in his ability to educate and develop athletes.

In our reckoning with the variety and types of sources of the coach's information, we have been implying a truism all along: information will be effective only if it can be communicated. This goes along with my initial distinction between information and knowledge: knowledge is information which succeeds in moving us physically. We have an idea now of the sources and targets of knowledge, and we constantly reckon that every source is evolving and every target moving. Now we need to know something about how the knowledge is in fact moved from one person to the other. In this regard we know that conventional speech is only a beginning, for as I cautioned in the beginning, repeating the same words does not mean we have shared the same reality. How can we get closer to a "grammar" of effective communication with athletes?

When we think of the old blacksmith and his wisdom about his apprentices, we also think of the many wise communicators whom we have encountered in our own lives. These were the men and women who in some mysterious way were able to get a message to us, one way or the other, usually in something well short of a lengthy explanation or more than a few words. Even the few words seldom made up whole sentences. Often they mixed and matched some gesture, however broad or subtle. And then, of course, it was their tone and manner which was the truest document of their intent. We say of these people that they were easy to understand, clear, direct, engaging, perhaps a little colorful, oddly complicated in their simplicity and candor. Sometimes we even called them "characters," and even wonder how they did it. We sensed they liked us easily. Perhaps we sensed less well that our feeling of "rightness" with them was rooted in some odd way in their being willing to be like us.

I want to protect the mystery of anybody's special mix; yet I would like to adapt some of its energy to coaching. In the 1970's I encountered NLP — Neurolinguistic Programming — and was pleased with the depth and simplicity of its insights into human communication. Despite its highfaluting scientific name (as an approach to communication and interpersonal therapy it simply had combined the science of perception with linguistics — how people perceive reality with how they speak about it), I thought the title of the small book reassuring: *Frogs Into Princes.*.[22]

I met up with NLP long before MBTI, which I learned about in 1987 and became certified to use. MBTI has a history of 30 years or more, and I mention it in this discussion first because personality is more general. The modes and attitudes of language in communication are more specific and task-oriented. It that regard a cursory, by no means thorough, review of some principles of NLP is more immediately useful to a coach in his day-to-day interactions with athletes. If his personality is his basic cannon, some notions about communication are his artillery ordnance. Basic to all of these ideas is the notion that the athlete is as critical to the nature of communication as the coach. This may come as a wrench to the ego of the coach, but he will have to admit that hitting the target is more important that doing it "his way".

**Some Principles of Communication**

### 1. The meaning of a communication is the response you get.[23]

A communication is thus located between people, and its content is what actually was transmitted. That is the salient question in every case: what was really communicated finally? The relevant question is not: Did the athlete get what the coach wanted to say? We have already heard that shared words do not mean a shared reality.[24]

### 2. There are no mistakes in communication, only helpful or unhelpful outcomes. [25]

The coach's understanding is thus quite useless if it cannot be communicated and effect the desired improvement in the athlete. When the outcome is not the desired one, it it nobody's fault; the coach simply has not "listened" enough to his athlete, seen or felt how he or she "works".

There is a useful example in the introduction to *Frogs into Princes*. [26]

There is an old story of a boilermaker who was hired to fix a huge steamship boiler system that was not working well. After listening to the engineer's description of the problems and asking a few questions, he went to the boiler room. He looked at the maze of twisted pipes, listened to the thump of the boiler and the hiss of escaping steaming for a few minutes, and felt some pipes with his hands. Then he hummed softly to himself, reaching into his overalls and took out a small hammer, and tapped a bright red valve, once. Immediately the entire system began working perfectly, and the boilermaker went home. When the steamship owner received a bill for $1000 he complained that the boilermaker had only been in the engine room for fifteen minutes and requested an itemized bill. This is what the boilermaker sent him:

| For tapping with hammer | .50 |
| For knowing where to tap | $999.50 |
| Total | $1000.00 |

The point for coaches is to prepare themselves for a successful communication by being patient, by listening actively to the athlete's sounds, watching his motions, hearing what other sports and interests he has (music often provides useful vocabulary), then reflecting to himself. Humming to oneself is excellent.

Since technique is a response to speed and terrain, it is also important not to focus too severely on the athlete but rather to perceive more broadly the terrain of which the athlete's movement is a part. Or see the whole of his movement, not so much the individual parts. Even thought we love the microscope, zoom out instead of in. Put the skier "off center" in your vision, and let your peripheral vision pick up the essence of his movement. That is a critical principle in visual perception: "The periphery of your eye is physiologically built to detect movement far better than the foveal portion of your eye."[27]

That explains why if we center on one point or position in a movement, we will mistake its nature and timing. We will do what we think we have isolated as important, but we will invariably be late in everything. We will move as if we were perpetually just behind the crest of the wave instead of just in front of it. We also know this phenomenon as night vision. At night it is a way to sharpen the shape of shadows; in shooting it is looking past the target. Sometimes putting the athlete at a distance, into his landscape and speed can reduce the dizzying number of details one sees and heightens the one or two which are most decisive in determining the way the skier is moving.

Zoom yourself to him rather than him to you, and not just visually but kinesthetically, physically. Ski with him. fifteen minutes, a half hour or longer. Match his every move. Soon you will feel his manner of moving and better sense where to locate the operative valve or button. His kick may best be improved by doing something differently in the arms. The arc of his arm swing may "clean up" by moving only his shoulder, ever so slightly. When you sense what you wish to say, say it while moving with him. Asking a skier to stop for information can create an instant fiction, change of environment, in which the cue quickly loses its sharpness. How is a cue about movement to be used in the absence of movement?

Then use a word, a minimal cue to trigger the one improvement you wish. Not a long explanation — if your skier is good, or you old, you won't have the breath for more, which is good — just a word or two, the athlete's, your own, whatever small hammer taps the right valve. To whom the hammer belongs is irrelevant.

### 3. If you do not get the response you want, try something else.[28]

Don't be proud. Is it more important that you be understood your way, or that the content you are hoping to share be grasped in the form of improved response, improved movement? It is easy for a coach to be so convinced of what he wants and his understanding of it that he sticks stubbornly by his one approach. Athletes often do the same. As the authors of *Frogs into Princes* note, "That's the amazing thing about people: when they find something that doesn't work, they do it harder."[29]

It is better advice to stay with the same point of technique or training execution, just change the cue. Being patient is also being focussed, convinced about the simplest point of needed change. Too often, once we have given up on our single approach, if we are not seeing the desired improvement, we cut and run, switch both our point of attention and our vocabulary. The result is distraction and confusion in the athlete's mind and body. It takes a long time, weeks, more likely months, to change a movement pattern. You can be patient, but tough. Don't panic. You will get the response you want.

I do not mean to suggest that complete explanations are not important or helpful. They are essential. The athlete must understand with mind, body, and every one of his senses what he is doing. Only then will he be able to have the deep confidence to put it all on the back shelf, not think any more, and truly be able to race with a cleared out, spontaneous, alert passion for terrain and speed. Give him all the information and all the wisdom and conviction it brings … in order that he be able to do without it. He needs to travel light. I call this process learning by subtraction.

Theory and science, yes, but best communicated, not surprisingly, in the athlete's own environment, sitting around, with a blackboard, model, diagram, frequently one-to-one when the athlete asks. Then you can utilize the athlete's questions and responses as the source of the information. The athlete, without realizing it, will have begun taking responsibility for his own development. He is becoming the partner you wish. And then visuals are usually more effective than words. Or when you sense some bewilderment, you can say, "This is how this works, why it helps;" or "The biomechanics of how you feel are …" or "The physiological processes you are working with here are …."

**4. You can get answers insofar as you have the sensory apparatus to notice responses, both verbal/conscious responses and unconscious responses which are expressed in movement and behavior.**[30]

This notion may amount to the very foundation of learning, for coaches and athletes both, but most essentially for coaches.

> Your ability to perceive is something learned and you can learn to do it better. Most people act as if the senses are simply passive receptacles into which the world dumps vast amounts of information. There is a vast amount of information, so vast that you can only represent a tiny fraction of it. Learn to actively select in useful ways.[31]

As an athlete one has progressively selected the fractions of information he finds useful specifically to himself. As a coach you need to understand the selectivity and organizational habits of your senses themselves and make them open to the uses required by other athletes. Much of what I have been talking about in these recent pages, if not in the entire book, revolves around this requirement to open up, to be functionally selective for a variety of other individuals, not just for oneself, and let that be exemplary or learned enough. That can become the barb in one's own athletic success. Catch yourself when you hear yourself begin explaining something with "When I …" It is worth considering that "one of the most dangerous experiences human beings can have is success — especially if you have success early in your career — because you tend to become quite superstitious and repetitious."[32]

Coaches can thus in fact be handicapped by their athletic success as much as helped by it. As the authors of *Frogs into Princes* say (though they are not talking specifically about coaches),

> Most of the people I meet are handicapped in terms of their sensory ability. There is a tremendous amount of experience that goes right by them because they are operating out of something which to me is much more intense than just 'preconceived notions.' They are operating out of their own internal world and trying to find out what matches it.[33]

Asking athletes to match our worlds is the most limiting of ways to their best development and performance. The authors summarize:

> You need only three things to be an absolutely exquisite communicator. ... The first one is to know what outcome you want. The second is that you need flexibility in your behavior. You need to be able to generate lots and lots of different behaviors to find out what responses you get. The third is you need to have enough sensory experience to notice when you get the responses you want.[34]

Does this mean the coach should give up his athlete self? Not at all. I want to make this point especially after having said so emphatically that being an athlete is not enough preparation for being a coach. For all the feedback you receive from other sources — from athletes, study, from medical, physiological, and biomechanical research — you must test yourself. And the best test will remain in your feelings. That is what I mean when I say the most reliable information comes up through your feet.

We need also to further qualify the maxim which says coach the person first and the sport second. It is not some vaguely humanistic generality designed only to warn us of narrowing our focus on the special aspects of the sport alone. There is, it is clear, so much to learn both about athletes and from them that a coach's sheer fascination with people will become his greatest teacher. Coaching the person first simply recognizes in a very practical way the primary source of the coach's information, more so even than his own fascination and love for the sport itself. It is his utilization of the athlete as a principle resource in behalf of the athlete's own development that assures that that development will be sound and continuous.

The sense for planning and pacing and specificity which is the foundation for physical training is mirrored in the patience, pacing, and selectivity which forms the basis for communication. Another word we repeat resolutely about training is "rest." My former coach, Al Merrill, used to say rest was sixty percent of training. The equivalent in communication is silence. It is another critical factor, little mentioned, often even tacitly feared by coaches. We have as little conscious awareness of the uses of silence as we do of how to truly, "aggressively," rest.

A handbook of silences could be very useful. When we think of it, our event and its training take place in silence. Silence is like a perceptual blackboard which needs to be erased again and again back to silence, emptiness, in order that select information can be again set out, arranged, culled, highlighted, the waste erased again. Silence is also the nature of things not said, or not said yet, as powerful, we well know, as those things stated verbally. It can either indicate the absence of a thing to say, or negative information withheld, or provide the perfect backdrop for the richness and remarkable precision of non-verbal "vocabulary." We are, among other things, kinesthetic creatures, and our joy in cross-country skiing is forever renewed out of our sympathy with its movements. And how can we improve, for example, upon the speechlessness of dancing together? Is that not close to the best communication of all? Is that not why we were hooked by the sport in the first place?

But how a coach often suffers from silence. If words are not to be used, they seem to want to sit there, fidgeting like a small boy at an organ concert, and itch until the sufferer cannot but scratch. Most of all we coaches soon begin to feel guilty if we are quiet too long. If communication is so essential, should we not maintain it as obviously as possible? Is that not what we are paid to do; isn't it our profession? And who will know that if we don't speak up?

We forget, however, that talk, by itself is by no means necessarily informative, to the contrary, and even though the sound of his own words is soothing to the coach. They are, of course, the extraverts chief food and pleasure as well. Having said this, of course, it immediately strikes us as no surprise. We have noted already how much words require selection, sequencing, pacing, and these all use silence constructively. To make silence easier to accept I might say that a good coach will go quiet for the same reasons that a poet pauses at the particular point in his lines.

In fact communication begins before we speak as well as ending after we have gone still. We must set the before up and let the after be, give the message its time to sink in and "work." There is a loop traveled in the receipt of any effective message. Like the skills of the sport itself, we can learn to run the loop with greater speed and lower cost. The before takes place with release of tension and clearing. One way is what I call "going to zero." One simply stands in a slight slouch, in total comfort, bad posture, the "drug store slouch," perhaps with eyes closed or at least looking astray, and let all the tension in your joints "run out," run away from your fingers and toes like water from the holes in a bucket, until the joints feel empty.

The purpose of these few moments, usually less than a minute, is to release the athlete from the circumstantial stimuli of all sorts which surround him. It clears his blackboard of clutter, his internal "ear" of noise. Depending on the individual athlete, the coach may be able to put forth his message, cue, metaphor, at that point. He may also have to wait further, particularly in a competition situation where the tension is higher.

With one athlete I could see he needed to "get further away." High-strung by nature, he stood in the Start pen at the World Junior Championships, trumpets blaring, instructions to racers being delivered in three languages. We had worked out an added loop for him. Once he was clear, he disassociated from the present and focused on his grandmother's rocking chair at the end of the dock at their summer cottage, a place of sublime comfort. With thirty seconds to Start he came back to clear, received his two racing cues, anchors, mental set, and took off in control. During the race he could return to these anchoring cues again and again, from within himself or cued by the coach beside the trail, to maintain his focus, sense of control, and good technique.

A mental set is the particular sensory image/psychological perspective you use for each training session or race. It is your strategic mental recipe of the day. Mental sets are essential race support in particular. Racing without one is like sailing without a compass. Good focus is never the absence of thought or just the single, simplistic imperative to go as fast as you can, or to win. Each training session and race needs to be framed in advance. Lack of a clear and simple frame leaves the racer open to distractions and without any perceptual anchors to keep him on track, particularly at stressful points of the race.

There are no universal frames, or mental sets. Each guides the individual skier and an individual day. Even for the same skier the frame will change in varying situations, points of the season. Almost every skier, however, will work out one or two mental sets with a coach which are the most effective and then use them routinely. I have given one example above. Here is another.

It is late March, a week after Junior Nationals. The skier has done well at the Junior Nationals and is having trouble getting enthused for the New England High School Championships. She feels tired and says, "I am just not ready to race. I was done racing for the year last week. Its just too big to think about so soon after JO's."

My response was to change the frame. "Forget the *race*," I replied. "You won't race today. Just think about playing with speed over the snow between where you are and where the track disappears over the rise or around the bend in front of you. That is all. Once one section is by, do it again, and again. No racing, just speed ... and the technique thing we worked on again this week." She signaled with a simple nod from across the stadium after she finished that she had done the mental set. She did not know until 30 minutes later that she had won the race.

The scheme of the loop looks as follows.

*Clearing*
/
/
– empty our the joints
– tension slips away like
drops from a leaf, runs out
like water from holes in a bucket
– erase blackboard
– turn down noise from a radio
– conductor quiets orchestra
- tap-tap-tap
/
/
ZERO
/
– clean slate, empty of thought
– focus on nothing, "zero," or
disassociated image of comfort,
soft, quiet
/
/
ACTIVATE
/
– breath out into joints, let them
become large with emptiness, feel liquid
– float, move "under water"

/

/

*New Cue*

/

– word, image, movement response
(maximum 2, if more, repeat loop)

The factor of environment or context is often taken for granted, and ignored largely because it is nature and apparently passive. Yet particularly for a cross-country skier the landscape is alive and co-active. His personality as a whole is likewise a continuously co-active "landscape."

For these reasons the same cues will not work the same with all athletes. They need to help find the ones which will work best for them. They have to grow in confidence in their own loops. Even mid-course splits are not always equally effective. I have seen some use them well, others, thinking to be like some "better" skier, have their race mental set destroyed by an early split. They have decided in essence to ski someone else's race.

The point is that the athlete is never a blank piece of paper, his senses never passive, indiscriminant receptors for whatever information, jewels or garbage, comes along. He is totally dynamic, active, and, above all, contained in his own complete world of the moment. As coach you gain entry to that world by preparing him for your presence and thus your message. If it is in a race, it must be a message familiar to him. Even in training over a period of time the number of messages needs to be progressively more limited and specific. Their source will as often be the athlete himself, if you check the vocabulary and images he uses.

For the athlete who uses visual imagery, for example, clearing may happen best by "erasing the blackboard." If he is auditory, he does better by slowly "turning down the volume on the radio." If he is a kinesthetic type, he will clear best through tactile vocabulary, words of touch, warm, cool, smooth, liquid. Clearing brings him to a state of receptivity for your cue or image or metaphor for what he needs to do, given itself optimally in his same preferred type of vocabulary. Silence is just as powerful, providing space for some non-verbal sign or motion. Remembering introverts, and the high percentage of introverts in endurance sport, non-verbal signs may even be the better.

The need for the most minimal articulate vocabulary is all the more compelling when we take seriously the skier's most fundamental reality: movement. In that sense the point of all vocabulary is to become kinesthetic, to facilitate movement and the feeling for movement. Standing still while communicating about movement puts both athlete and coach at a severe disadvantage. So you look for ways to use movement itself as a means of clearing. Here are two examples.

The most obvious one is to communicate while training, moving with your skiers. It is easier to tell how much talk they can handle, given their level of effort at the moment. You also learn in this way to tell during races what their breathing levels and sounds indicate about their effort and thus where on a course they will be able to receive information at all, at the bottom of the hill namely, rather than on top.

Experience reminds me, however, that the top of hills is a coach's favorite spot. How many times I have seen coaches screaming at their skiers as they labor up the hill trying to please their coach. Finally I said to one coach, "Go back along the trail a ways, then ski back up through this hill. Let your feet tell you if your skier could do what you were asking of him." Exhortations like "Charge the hill!" are more apt to cause the skier to over-ski the bottom of the hill and leave him with nothing to continue with over the top, where the speed becomes cheaper and the competition suddenly disappears. American skiers have told this story so many times of racing in Europe, you would think we would have tried something else. No, we just try it harder.

If it is a race you also learn that you need to jog along beside your skier a number of paces, accustom him to your sudden presence in his complete world, before saying anything to him. Otherwise you will so startle him he will not hear you and may as likely be distracted, lose his concentration, and stumble.

As well and as minimally as we might communicate, there are times when a great deal of information has been given over a period of time. The athlete has been working on many things, tells you of them openly, asks other questions. You get the feeling of information overload. The variety and amount of information is creating distraction and fractured focus all by itself. From time to time to say "Today we are going to clear it with speed."

Think of learning to ride a bicycle. You could think all you wanted about how to do it; ultimately it took a certain basic velocity to put balance and mechanics together. Speed was both lubricant and glue. The same can be helpful, occasionally, on skis. A session specifically without words, or better, a series of hundred meter accelerations, or timed sprints (fast floats) with flying starts, has a way of "combing out the junk" and leaving the skier with the only two or three things, one is better, he really needs to be thinking about. He can give the other stuff back to the coach for safe keeping.

Learning is not measured by the amount of information we have in memory but by the actual movement in improving performance. In skiing, as in dance, movement is the form of knowledge.

The best language a coach can use is sensory, colorful, metaphorical, figurative, and simple. The notion that a picture is worth a thousand words applies particularly. There is time, and good time, for more complete analytical or conceptual discussion, but training sessions, moving, are not that time. In our need for professional identity we have at times believed instructors ought to use only scientific, technical-sounding vocabulary because it was supposed to be the most exact and clear. Figurative language was frowned upon. Once we truly understand communication, however, and practice it, we know that metaphor and figurative images are the more exact after all in terms of content received and transformed into performance.

You want to hit the target not shred it, and certainly not explain the bullet, why it does what it does. Only then will the message be received without the skier's concentration being overloaded or fractured. And if you and the athlete have prepared well, you may speak as softly as your non-verbal signals can be both minimal and absolutely articulate. Too great an emphasis, a loud voice, too flamboyant a motion only buries the content of the message in theatrics.

How often have we heard a coach beside the trail shout in a strident voice, "Relax!" That is an example of delivery burying content. In fact it reverses the meaning because it is incongruent. The sensory message is the one received, the lexical message lost. Especially while at great effort in racing, we respond to our immediate senses, not to the dictionary.

Do not repeat, unless the athlete specifically asks you to do so. Even if he does not respond immediately, give your cue the time to work. If the ground is well-prepared, the seed will root quickly, and, of course, it will not announce the fact. You will seldom see the change right away. Be patient, perhaps tomorrow or the day after. Maybe next week. But it will happen.

"When you have given a command and the dog begins to respond," says the old shepherd, "never add another command until he has completed the first one. And don't repeat the command. So long as he's doing what you have asked, don't say anything. Never shake his confidence in any way."[35]

I am not suggesting athletes are dogs, of course. Still, we are all creatures and respond from our instinctive animal selves, particularly racing through the woods. I do make the point again that the notions of communication need no real science to make them known, rather only men and women of experience and a generous and sensitive curiosity about others. The shepherd would quickly agree the coach must not repeat a message to a skier racing by. What happens? The message hits the skier in the back. It has been repeated, so he assumes he did not get it right the first time. Confused, he hesitates and looks around, his concentration broken, his rhythm blocked. The net effect of the message is that the skier stumbles. The repetition has actually changed the sensory message rather than intensified it!

Not repeating is another of the wise uses of silence. Another follows from this first one. Let the athlete close the loop. Once the coach has set out the message he "disappears." From that point the athlete's subjective feelings are the most reliable. (They have even proven to be accurate measures of lactate levels.) Feelings finish the communication, embedded now in the athlete's movements. The worst you can do is shout verbal approval, even if you do not repeat the command. That is distracting again and means only you have gotten what you wanted, which is not something which should concern the racer at this point — which is qualitatively different than the skier getting what he can use.

If the coach completes the loop, he in fact takes back the control, implying the athlete still is dependent upon him. At most a wink, sign, touch, thumb up leaves the athlete in control. Let the message go, once you have said it, quietly, once. You have what you should want, a faster, more efficient skier, owning his own performance.

I purposely talk about racing and training situations interchangeably. The communications in both should be as similar as possible. Race day should be as routine as training days. This goes a long way toward neutralizing any amount of extra tension and surprises which inevitably accompany a day of competition. There is great confidence for an athlete in knowing that nothing will happen this day which he had not done already. His preparation is routine, the words and gestures he receives all comfortably familiar.

That is a time when it may be more difficult for the coach to stick to the simple, familiar stuff, for the athlete is often in a state of heightened anxiety and excitement, and may well be speaking all kinds of unpredictable things. The coach must know when to let the barrage of emotion flow by him, noticed but left untouched. It is a time not to let the athletes supercharged vocabulary fool you into changing your routine, for that will only confirm to the athlete the worry or panic he is expressing. The coach may then seem unfeeling or rigid, but at the moment it may well be the particular power source the skier needs most.

So whereas the requisite flexibility and variety of vocabulary and behaviors is essential to the coach on the one hand, on the other consistency and congruence provide the requisite structural predictability which forms the very base of the athlete's physical capacities and resilient confidence. There is much, much place for the former; race day is time for the latter.

As with silence, no sooner have we mentioned consistency and congruence than we notice their many extensions. They are the basis for patience and preparation. Just as a coach helps his athlete clear before suggesting a new cue, so that same congruence is achieved by setting up each training environment with an expression of positive evaluation. "The right arm is finishing out behind nicely now;" "Holy smoke, that's wonderful!" This can create a relaxed, confident openness to a new element of improvement.

I also give cues sometimes by saying what I want is already happening. It is possible to short cut the clear-cueing-executing loop by simply making a statement about the execution. "You're toeing-down sooner now" emphasizes the activity of it, toeing, rather than the concept: toe-down. In fact a change may well take place without the skier even thinking about it. Since motion is what we are after, -ing words are good matches. In grammar -ing words are also present participles ("What are you thinking about?") So they give both motion and presence to the skier, immediacy to the communication. That is what performance is about — moving, now.

Setting up a positive atmosphere which is fundamentally complimentary to the skier suggests in the coach's words and behavior his abiding belief in his athlete's ability, both current and potential. In belief is where partnership thrives. There is no horse, no driver, no anvil, no hammer. There is collaboration and mutual effort, not just athlete obedience and a coach's judgment.

In belief and partnership with himself is where the athlete's execution of training and ultimate performance thrives. And whereas there will be the necessary and growth-inducing up's and down's, I do not like to see athletes get into a habit of evaluating themselves. In a way, what goes for the coach also applies to the athlete looking at himself. I have encountered forms with which the athlete may evaluate a race or even workouts. I have read training logs which contain extensive evaluations of relative success in execution, of feelings throughout training and the day, of general health and mood. At times such evaluation required 15–20 minutes a day.

That is too much. The athlete may become so sensitive, so aware of each moment, mood, and sensation that he in essence becomes two people: one doing and one watching. Such fastidiousness takes away from the alertness to what is ahead and points of moving better and faster, and can turn the athlete into a virtual hypochondriac. The sheer amount of self-analysis and judgment may begin to clog the senses and reduce the athlete's confidence is his plan and his basic spontaneous joy in skiing.

I believe in keeping a training log, but it should be kept spare. The real log is the year's training plan, written in May. The athlete need only check off workout types, minor changes or differences, a couple of each day's technique cues, a thought or two perhaps, a new image which may be helpful or simply one he just happened to like. In the latter case the image might just as well come from some other part of the day, from a totally different area of endeavor, from a book, from dance, physics, a new acquaintance, an expression overheard at the post office, or some unusual thought or occurrence of the day. In this way the athlete brings other worlds and their power into his training. Too much self-evaluation, on the other hand, leads only to narcissistic distraction.

There is really little use for judgment in development and performance, even where there come moments of objective evaluation. If we think of it, there never is anything really wrong. What we see as coaches may just not be the most efficient movement yet or the desired outcome response. But it is of no use to establish its incorrectness, except perhaps to validate the coach's higher position. It does well to remember the notion from NLP that it is not the athlete whom we may judge to be "resistant" to learning but the coach who has not yet discovered the behavior or vocabulary to elicit the response from the athlete which he wishes.

Bodies themselves do not make mistakes, unless they are encased in some alien harness. I always say the body "knows" already everything we hope it will learn. It is only the veneer of cultural attitudes which place an intellect in control of a body of doubtful moral inclination which gets in the body's way to performance.

Negative judgments and "don't's" are therefore of no productive use whatever in coaching. Even if I must be honest in the negative to a skier's question, "Am I doing it right now?" my answer will be "All but 5 percent."

We know also from communication theory that our senses to not respond to the negative particle, "no," or "do not ..." They respond only to the sensory content of a statement. "Don't twist so much in the hips" simply objectifies and thus reinforces the notion of twist, the very thing the athlete is trying to forget. I coached a top skier for some years who told me an all-too-typical story after a National Championship race. She said that going down a steep downhill she suddenly thought "I'm going great, but someone is going to fall here for sure." A split second later she was on the ground. And she was an excellent downhill skier! The negative "don'ts" in fact anchor the content of the statement and in doing so produce more often the very response we are trying to avoid. Congruence and negative statements are clearly mutually exclusive notions.

There will be times when you will hear negative statements from athletes, of course. But regard them in relation to their context, the heat of a frustrating moment perhaps, following a race. The comment will always be congruent with its context, the athlete's physical state, his psychological landscape. Be patient, listen, but don't take everything for the truth. Most often it is the raw emotion of great effort come up short, or even the athlete covering his tracks in advance of hearing the real results.

Think of it, however; it was raw emotion, the pleasures of pulsing effort and movement, that got this whole process going. In that it is utterly compact and deeply human. Small wonder then that at the end of race day one receives that fine raw emotion back. But now it has with it all of what one has learned through the years, months, days and races: one comes to know athletes gradually, some more easily than others. Some require closeness, others space. One will talk all the time. Another speaks barely at all. At best it takes time, more time yet for highly individual athletes, to understand and appreciate their differences, accept them, work with them, enjoy them. Be patient with it all, learn the details, link them together and to your particular athletes, listen and watch, give what you say time to sink in and make movements more efficient and graceful. If your athlete becomes truly successful with your direction, he will excel because you have brought him to final self-sufficiency, when you are no longer needed, your presence simply powerful and welcome.

> I am the teacher of athletes,
> He that by me spreads a wider
> Breast than my own proves the width of my own,
> He most honors my style who learns under it
> To destroy the teacher.
>
> —Walt Whitman[36]

# Part Two

# Sport and Physical Culture
# In Our History
# and In Our Schools

# 3

## *Affirming the Flesh: How Tough Can We Be? How Can We Be Tough?*

Our attitudes about sports in education exhibit numerous ironies and contradictions. Since vast energy and value is found in sports in our culture, not to mention a preferred source of self—image for our youth, it makes sense to try to unravel our thinking a little. Perhaps we can discover how powerful an experience and educational tool sports can become. Implicit in this discussion is also the question, of course, whether we want sports to really be anything of value at all, or believe it can be.

There is an ethic, widespread in secondary schools, that a young athlete ought to compete as hard as he can, to give his all, always, in every competition, in every training session, from beginning to the end of every season. That is said to be the essence of toughness and a moral imperative.

Any expressions of other mental sets — "run full but not hard," "threshold," "90%," "threshold the first half, race the second"— make the athlete then seem less than totally motivated to parent, coach, or school administrator, and seem to being giving excuses for a lower result than could have been expected or hoped for. This perception is often frustrating, even maddening, for coach, parent, or spectator.

To be sure, such expressions are confusing. What is competition for, if not for winning? It is fair to admit at the outset that winning is wonderful mainly for its simplicity and for the way it validates the moment, in retrospect rendering the struggle easy, euphoric.

But even in the driven world of professional football, successful coaches know better. Bill Walsh of the San Francisco 49ers and Stanford put it simply:

Winning does not necessarily mean being a victor in every game … It is a season and series of seasons in which a team wins more games than it loses and each team member plays up to his potential. If you are continually developing your skills and refining your approach, then winning will be the final result.[1]

Athletic performance is so much more than simple competition or the drive to excel. The notion of competition itself is more than each race; each race is but one element in a pattern of growth and improvement toward a true, "all-out" performance when the preparation has been carefully conceived and executed. Before that time being "tough" is unrealistic, even damaging, a hapless confusion of outcome and process.

One explanation for our confusion may be found in recent studies comparing the effects of competition and collaboration in education, business and social interaction. The results suggest that being and acting competitive do not necessarily lead to higher performance.[2] Our unquestioning faith in competition has put us into too-persistent contest with our fellow athletes, and it has led us into an essentially adversarial relationship with both the body and terrain. We squander our energies.

The old-time carpenter provides a wiser model of patient preparation and collaboration. A local plumber, now old himself, describes how the carpenter seemed forever to sharpen his ancient hand auger, while the plumber waited impatiently with his pipe. Then, without hurry but with sudden suddenness, the carpenter effortlessly spun a pipe hole through the beam with his augur so carefully honed. That is my idea of "tough." Great effort can produce speed, but patience in sharpening for a task well understood produces true performance. The carpenter is my idea of a competitor.

Or if the mower's scythe is dull, he does not simply double his "motivation" and flail harder at the hay, as I have done many a time as a youngster. No, he stops and sharpens further, then goes again. Let's say he learns not just to mow but to mow a stretch. That is his event.

Not all performances are equal. Some are work, others are recitals, refinings, some are trials of the many ingredients in a recipe for game, speed, or distance. Still others are championships. Only championships are championships. To treat all races as championships, under whatever guise — toughness, character building, school spirit — is unproductive, foolhardy, even damaging, like sailing off without the fittings checked and the guys set. Or like playing all your music loud and fast: it just wears out both player and instrument. The athlete is both player and instrument.

The damage has been documented. For decades, overloads of hard-as-you-can training and relentless competition schedules throughout the school year have produced exhaustion and overtraining rather than performance levels of which individuals might have been capable, had they had intelligent guidance. Overtraining has routinely produced conditions of blood acidosis (low pH factor), the symptoms of which are poor sleep, lost of appetite, and listlessness. The effects on both sport and studies for a young person should be obvious.

On the other hand, research has also shown that systematic aerobic training, which means oxygen-supplied and not breathless, is not only able to keep the body healthier for sport (because it combines more training with less frequent competition and fatigue) but also aids significantly in coping with stress. In terms of the spirit this means that routinely stimulating body and mind with ample but informed doses of training over a long period provide a peace and alertness which is much more productive and liberating to the spirit than scourging it haphazardly, season after new season, with "toughness" regimens and "hard work." Practical minded souls in the corporate world, in fact, found this out before even the physiologists and coaches came along and validated it. A treadmill in a basement room at Harvard Business School was the site of the first studies of the effects of physical and mental stress on the productivity of both line workers and management. That was 1927. The fitness boom in the 70's was again initiated by "bottom-line" business types, not by recreationists.

Why has such insight not taken better hold in our educational institutions, where it should have originated in the first place? It just does not make sense to be feverishly disciplined with strictly academic subjects and then calmly ignore developmental physiology in the conduct of our sports activities. I am puzzled by another paradox as well. The accepted maxim is: you should be "tough" each competition, but resorting to serious long-term preparation, calculating the tools of movement, learning sharpening and power is considered elitist, "Eastern Bloc," Prussian, too severe. Since national or international level athletes are terribly rare, people ask, why don't we just have sports "for fun," for diversion from work, from study, or from getting into trouble born of idleness. That would be appropriate for the majority, who, after all, realistically are without potential for top performances.

To answer is to remember carpenter and mower. Each prepared carefully, without hurry in his work, matching patience with the realities of time, task, and materials. He gives his body and its capacities time to grow and integrate into efficient motion. Only after each man did that could he discover whether he was carpenter or mower at all, was inspired to do either, was good at either.

To assume that being good is probably not possible only guarantees in advance that it will not happen. This may seem humane at first, and it is surely comfortable for some coaches and some kids, but it is an unconscionable limitation on young people, on their potential and on their rights.

Knowledge of true potential comes after training, not before. Each will thrive to higher personal performance with an informed plan, a plan which matches physiological development and fosters higher, more focused emotion. Simple excitement, diversion, fun can be cultured into a more articulate joy, at any level of ability, and into the heart of a more vital education.

Whence the disenchantment with systematic physical culture, whence the distrust?

One source could be the unnerving notion in our schools that a traditionally extra-curricular set of activities is gaining enough in its substance, science, and thus self-awareness and life-significance to claim strengthened stature within the general academic curriculum. It may begin to form a larger, more complex whole within the strictly academic values and will require re-balancing, like a new set of tires, with different weights placed at new points on the rim. We may have to re-think relative academic values with regard to physical culture and sport which we have long shared and which for many years have been, it seems safe to say, in well-fenced conservative pastures. Implicit in this process, once the mind-body dichotomy has been successfully blurred, will be the problem of the distribution of power among areas of education which have traditionally been perceived as curriculum (serious, academic, the mind) and those perceived as extra-curricular (play, recreation, the body).

The implications of blurring the distinction between mind and body have both ancient precedents and modern scientific examples. In the late 1960's even social and political philosophers got into the act. The Marxist Jürgen Habermaas argued that the capitalist elite looked to sport as a means of occupying and subduing the excess energies of the working class in order to distract it from a deepened political consciousness, to exhaust its acuity to social and economic injustice, to emasculate in advance its search for a distinct political identity. The imperative to "keep 'em off the streets" meant keep the workers dumb and unaware; in sports they could be kept amused and harmless.

Parents and school boards have used the same rationale with youngsters, and coaches have even gone them one better, using sport to "shape up" performance or behavior. If a youngster does not perform well or makes a mistake, he is punished by having to run laps or do pushups. We should know enough by now to recognize that sports are ill-used as mechanisms of negative reward or instruments of social therapy. Just as not training in the summer time is like suggesting to kids that they ought not to read during their vacations, so using one sport activity as punishment for another is like making a student do geometry problems because he did poorly on a French test.

In the context of schools, we can pursue our discussion by first asking students where the sources of their sense of self-image and personal power is best found. A majority will say sports, and then explain that sport is for the body, studying for the mind. Study is so hard and unrewarding; sport is invigorating and fun, even when you are tired. While many students will agree that an engaged mind will enhance most sports experience, they will still emphasize that physical activity gives them power, while mental activity yields some rare power but mostly headaches. In a practical sense the dichotomy between mind and body in American culture has dug these students' grave, for it has divided their perspective on human activity from within. It has, in fact, divided them from themselves … to the detriment of their intellectual engagement and their insight into the basic physical aspects of human life.

That is a large topic, and it deserves thorough reflection beyond the scope of this book. It is possible, however, to look for some of the sources of distrust in systematic physical culture.

One source is in itself cultural. Whereas for the ancient Greeks the *agon* of the athlete was ritual celebration of deity, right along with the "games" of theater, poetry, and dance, Christians were inspired by a more gentle spirit. In the new theology spirit and flesh divided. No longer was there interest and inspiration in the flesh, for it was the spirit alone which was eternal. No longer was there trust in the flesh, for its expressions and pleasures were the accomplices of temptation and evil. Sixty years after the Council of Nicea, at which the doctrine of the Trinity became the *de facto* imperial Roman religion, Theodosius II, quite logically, banned the Olympic Games at Elis in 394 AD.

The Dutch historian Johan Huizinga has chronicled the role and evolution of play in human culture in his seminal work, *Homo Ludens* (Man Playing) (1950). Looking back from the 19th century, which he observes "had lost many of the play-elements so characteristic of former ages," he reviews more recent history up to that point in an instructive way. He suggest that the "one-sidedness of medieval sporting life was due in large measure to the influence of the Church. The Christian ideal left little room for the organized practice of sport and the cultivation of bodily exercise, except insofar as the latter contributed to gentle education. Similarly, the Renaissance affords fairly numerous examples of body-training cultivated for the sake of perfection, but only on the part of individuals, never groups or classes. If anything, the emphasis laid by the Humanists on learning and erudition tended to perpetuate the old under-estimation of the body, likewise the moral zeal and severe intellectuality of the Reformation and the Counter-Reformation. The recognition of games and bodily exercises as important cultural values was withheld right up to the end of the 18th century."[2]

In America since that time our particular Puritan heritage has remained alive and well, conspiring to elevate that Christian distrust of the flesh to the need for its unconditional mortification. And among our fathers and grandfathers the Depression only abetted this notion, for people were seldom able to work doing something they wanted to do. Survival instinct dictated that the flesh be disciplined, that natural talent, want, or reasonable preference be stilled. Since that time it has been a difficult task to define work as something other than "something I do not really enjoy" or "effort which pains."

In American sports pain is almost universally used as the measure of upright, adequate effort, as the key to success. To subordinate, subdue the flesh, beat it into shape is part of the work ethic. But that moralistic beating to exhaustion in fact only cripples the body; it does not condition or expand its performance. It is a horrible paradox that our methods of sport trivialize the body. But that is little recognized. To the contrary, the outright subjugation of the body is itself experienced as success.

Many professionals in human development and culture have observed this phenomenon, among them Rollo May:

> As a result of several centuries of suppressing the body into an inanimate machine, subordinated to the purposes of modern industrialism, people are proud of paying no attention to the body. They treat it as an object for manipulation, as though it were a truck to be driven till it runs out of gas.[3]

This view grew particularly, even perversely strong in the Victorian era in which I have sought out the origins of our values surrounding sport. Kenneth Murphy has traced its evolution by noting that

> Victorian Americans in particular shared a view of machines in the promise of technology: unlimited domain over earth and humanity. If earlier times found that view contained many an element of brutality, the late 19th century

middle class was less qualified in its faith: the machine is good — strong, stupid and obedient.[4]

Bill Moyers brings to the present the same deep struggle of values with respect to health and medicine as I do in physical culture and sport.

> Well, to us in the West, the body is a machine: If something goes wrong, you find the part that's awry and replace it. That's a useful metaphor, but their [Eastern doctors'] metaphor is that the body is a garden... The physician then becomes a gardener, not a mechanic."[5]

My title for Chapter Five, "Putting Miles By" is derived from the gardening activity of putting food by and is just as seriously intended as a new way to understand training development and performance.

In his study of physical expression in dance and ritual, Jamake Highwater has portrayed the same struggle of values in our culture from which we still suffer in practice of sport. "It is difficult, after centuries of belief in the mortification of the flesh (and the celebration of the disembodied soul), for most Westerners to grasp the possibility of a 'spiritual body' in which spirit and flesh are united, in which feeling and thought are unified."[6] In particular, "Twentieth-century people are products of their gradual withdrawal from an awareness of nature and their place in it. They believe that nature serves them and that divine intention makes them the dominant being of the world."[7]

It should be no surprise that in sport as well we remain essentially in combat with the natural landscape, our rivals, and ourselves. It is still the word according to Teddy Roosevelt. But for human performance that combat is most assuredly destructive. We batter the landscape on foot and skis, righteously lashing our bodies. We feel securely validated in the pain endured. In fact we remain isolated from the very sources of power we seek and need most dearly.

Modern dancers are among the few who have evolved beyond that sad point: "they do not simply perform the movements of the choreographer," observes Highwater, "they become them."[8] But that is a state of mind and body, a culture yet barely conceivable to most people; it would be an affirmation of the flesh too primal, too frightening: that the flesh itself co-possess our spirits and behavior. We not only deny the flesh; we go a yet step further by trivializing it in our way of sport. So evangelical are we in our cultural ego, it is in fact our dread of the basic tragedy of existence, the necessary fading and passing of the flesh, which drives us to win at every turn, to prove our worth, our righteousness, our right to life's promise, each of our "moments" made eternal. But hurry in sport is impotent; it may be good for business, but it kills bodies. In the late 1920's business research began to discover it was not even good for business. Europeans are "old" enough culturally to know no such hurry, and wind up being more productive and going faster at lower intensities.

An ironic by-product of such trivialization of the body in sport, industry, and religion has been the relative failure of our increased efforts in recent years to get young people to take their own bodies seriously in sexual relationships or with the use of tobacco and drugs. The potential for tragedy in careless sexual activity will not be readily accepted by those whose bodies are routinely battered in sports on the notion that some false moral battle is taking place, either against the next town or the young athlete against something in himself. To subdue the flesh is to indeed control it, but also to render it unimportant, expendable. Thus we usher in the very misuse of the body which we profess, when it comes to sex, to protect. This overpowering and dangerous contradiction in our attitudes as educators carries an implied but eloquent message to kids, and it documents how untrustworthy we will remain so long as we still are burdened with our outdated Calvinist values.

Despite growing knowledge of the relationship between health, fitness and productivity of all kinds, sports have largely remained firmly, and safely in the area of diversion and relief from real life, rather than providing information, expression, or insight into it. Huizinga observed further how

> Modern social life is being dominated to an ever increasing extent by a quality that has something in common with play and yields the illusion of a strongly developed play-factor. This quality I have ventured to call by the name of Puerilism, as being the most appropriate appellation for that blend of adolescence and barbarity which has been rampant all over the world for the last two or three decades.[9]

For three generations in American schools, sport has been understood as an exercise in letting out our young people's fleshly demons in a harmless setting. But do we cheer for the elevating performance of the physical self or for the knowledge the demons have been quieted for another day?

The renewal of the concept of lifetime sport is but one example of how much better we know now; nevertheless, the concept that sport is only of passing and metaphorical value to real life is not dying easily. Our more persistent sports ethos runs roughly: to subdue the flesh is noble and Christian, frees the spirit for higher goals. Go hard in all things, "be tough." These are the messages of mind over matter, of intellect over senses, of psyche over sensation and sensibility. The flesh conquered, the win is achieved. We exult ... and are not a little relieved.

If we are to train or cultivate the flesh systematically, however, stimulate it to growth and self-awareness, give it dignity, that is somehow disturbing. It seems pagan, out of harness, oddly adulterous, or at the very least not worthy of true spirit.

When the systematic approach is undertaken, however incidental its physiological soundness, the accusation is soon heard that this is too Prussian, rigid, elitist, even distinctly undemocratic. The facts show just the opposite. Systematic physiological stimulation/development is inclusive of more levels of natural athletic ability because the premise to simply perform, "be tough," to win is tempered by the understanding of natural physiological stages, by the resultant patience, adequate skill development, and psychological/sensory sophistication. Though competition is included as one of the elements in development, the wholesale commandment to simply "be tough," to compete often and to win is justly exposed as simplistic, even crude.

Development should be defined as progressive freedom and refinement of movement. It should be a balanced discovery of self within the natural constraints of our exterior and interior worlds. Those realities are in fact the harness within which every human being develops. To stimulate growth systematically does not remove the harness, it rather defines it accurately. In doing so the harness can become the vehicle of wisdom rather than suspicion, allowing the creature within greater mobility, speed, articulateness, humility, indeed even more expansive experiences of spirit. In that adventure grace and gracefulness join, cultural elevation and efficiency of movement become mutual sources of power.

This notion is no different from providing all people the best applicable medicine for their basic limitations. Lack of an appropriate and available prescription leaves people where they are, imprisoned in the status quo, and this is both unfair to the patient and lazy on the part of the doctor, both in philosophy and execution.

Unease with a deepened notion of physical culture may go along not only with issues of balances of power within our schools' curricula but with issues of our senses of personal power as well. The freedom and inhibitions in our own personal experience, be we coach or parent, should inspire and inform, but never coerce or limit the athletes with whom we work. The thoughts might run as follows:

(1) If I go as hard as I can, every moment, I will feel good in the trying, and I will win with my individual talent.

(2) If I do not win, I can say this is what I have given; the effort was noble. I am a creature of spirit, after all. Besides, I couldn't really prepare. Other things were more important. The effort was the point, not the win.

(3) But had I trained well, and then lost, I would have to face a different conclusion: I made a noble effort but could still not equal or better my peers. My "noble" was not of ultimate value in the realities of human performance. My self-image is a bit smaller, and I don't like that. Humility is one thing, but my self-image is pretty precious to me. I'm not sure the two can live in me in comfort.

We must face the notion that there are all levels and kinds of "noble." Once again, accepting this fact is to also admit that personal power is a modest, fleeting, and very relative thing. The implications of this realization on one's power/position status (or one's view of it) in relationships, family, profession, or team are profound, to say the least … but not dangerous, so long as one's ego derives from one's humanity and not simply from power itself or professional position.

And lest our definitions of humanity run about erratically afield in the loose harness of this or that glib philosophical or educational concept, it is high time that the understanding of the body, how it moves and works and grows, when, how and under what optimal circumstances, is deepened and put into serious practice. To do any less is to discount, even trivialize, what we seek most to advance and to understand. The imperative to understand the body on its own terms is not to be taken lightly. As Norman Cousins so clearly put it, "Knowing more about the gift of life is not merely a way of satisfying random curiosity. In the end, it is what education is all about."[10] Year after year when I ask my ninth grade students where they feel a sense of power, personal clarity, where they feel plain good in and about themselves, in a word where they feel gifted, ninety percent say sports. Like a dowsing rod, their words point to a source of gift too powerful to be ignored or wasted.

And not for a minute can this requisite knowledge of the body and its spirit be provided by book and intellect alone. It must logically grow each day, routinely and naturally, as a garden from a ground, through the actual experience and practice of informed physical culture in our wooded trails and rolling hills, in our gyms and on our playing fields.

Not a small part of that knowledge must be of the historical origins of the particular American attitude towards sport. If we are to reform our sports culture intelligently, we must first understand what it has been in our culture which we need to reform. That will require a little patience in the following chapter, but it will render the remainder of the book the more informing and persuasive.

# 4

# *"Charge the Hill!"*
# *The Origins of the*
# *American Attitude Toward Sport*

Two basic factors have determined our attitudes toward sport and physical culture in America. These two fundamental cultural values have proven unusually resistant to change and thus have become the background against which individual changes have had to assert themselves. They are also two of our abiding sources of failure in endurance sport.

The first factor is that the body is not valued on its own terms for its potential to grow, to expand its capacities, to strive and enjoy higher levels of physical performance. The body exists rather to serve other areas of social concern and belief, not the least of which is the practical and moral imperative of productive work.

The second factor lies in a paradox of our democracy: despite the equality implied in the original notion of democracy, Americans soon came to be dominated by hierarchical notions of society and power and by the class system the industrial revolution and market competition made possible. The two factors are linked in a complex manner which is essential to discuss if we are ever to reveal the subtle and often hidden forces which have formed America's particular sports culture.

The distrust of the body as our weaker, less trustworthy part, of course, had its origin in Judaeo-Christian myth about the origin of evil and the Garden of Eden. Our particular Puritan heritage deepened even further our root fear of the flesh and its profanity. The body is rude and passing; only the spirit is worthy and eternal. The necessity for its subjugation (if not mortification) placed its value strictly in its capacity to serve other "higher" social concerns and beliefs. Applied to community life, that meant liberty was synonymous with both prescribed order and the ideal to improve the time in which one lived. Applied to raw nature, of which the body was considered a part, improvement meant domination and control. The imperative to control the flesh thence fit neatly into the ethos of selfless work and industrial productivity. Religious conviction merged with social and industrial creeds in the notion of manifest destiny: "The destiny of man is to possess the whole earth; the destiny of the earth is to be subject to man. There can be no full conquest of the earth, and no satisfaction to humanity, if large portions of the earth remain beyond his highest control."[1]

In this notion of destiny there lies the peculiarly American conceit about the human body. I have already cited Rollo May's remark that "as a result of several centuries of suppressing the body into an inanimate machine, subordinated to the purposes of modern industrialism, people are proud of paying no attention to the body."[2] That strange pride rises to sad and misguided bravado when cloaked as virtue: in the "no pain, no gain" credo of modern sport, man is presumed to be spiritually elevated by the hurt endured in the process of dominating his physical self.

Such axiomatic domination of the flesh, practiced with particularly humorless fervor in Calvinist America, is physiologically unsound, psychologically limiting, and intellectually simply untenable. The notion is so ingrained and so appealing to Americans, however, that it remains difficult for physiologists, athletes and coaches alike to approach sport in any other way. For years we have pursued pain as the measure of effective training, and we have done so almost as fervently as we have fled pain in every other aspect of our lives. One must wonder if our trust in punishing the flesh in sport has not been oddly abetted by pain's reliable connection with feeling, some vestige of real life we seek for ourselves in an anaesthetic technological world. There have been signs of growing beyond this level in our approach to sport in the last fifteen years — more in clubs, where year-round development in a particular sport is practiced, than in our schools, where seasonal sport fragments physical development and where moral and character ideals range dominant in its place. Yet the heroism of wounding ourselves in "battle" has remained a more prominent basis for pride than truly high competitive performance.

The inherent inconsistency in that view has never shaken our faith in the Divine Promise of America nor advised us of any incongruence in our adversary relationship with nature. The contradiction of believing in the promise of nature on the one hand and battling nature on the other is played and replayed in sports, where frequent public competition serves as an exercise in both moral cleansing and the demonstration of control. Conquest documents success and moral superiority.

How well such ideals fit the needs of an industrial society is quite clear, and it is not surprising that religion and industry have reigned over American culture with hands barely distinguishable from one another. Their domination has held the body mute and in bondage to a "higher" but alien world. Even where modern ecology has come to understand man and nature as partners, whether man likes it or not, an ecology of the human body has barely begun to surface in the awareness of educators or in the consciousness of our society as a whole. The imperatives and insights suggested by advancing knowledge in human physiology have barely been noticed and little heeded. Serious, informed sport has therefore had to wage an almost guerilla war against the trivialization and unwitting abuse of the body in the service of the "higher" purposes of our culture.

The body placed in harness exemplifies the control of the lower being by the "higher" self — the mind or spirit — for the domination of nature and the well-being of the community and nation: the first factor. The second factor: in like manner, the masses, all those men created equal, were harnessed into classes according to strength, skill, and productivity. Democracy became elitist: the wealthy became successful and thus were deemed gifted, the wisest and most capable of governing (controlling) the rude masses. It also became paternalistic: the masses, like children, were seen as needing guidance from the benign fatherly elite. Yet the elite remained steadfastly convinced of its democratic values, even though class divisions were tacitly justified, if not deepened. The moral imperatives of the social code mirrored beliefs in a natural hierarchy, more oligarchic or plutocratic than democratic. The belief in the inherent wisdom of social stratification rationalized binding the developments in sports, fitness, and education in general, to ideas of social adjustment — team building, sacrifice of self for nation and community, civic character — rather than to truly scientific enthusiasm for the body or inspiration from its physical nature. The middle class plays the decisive role in this arrangement because of its particular concern with position of social and economic power. This overriding concern with power and position ultimately elicits perhaps the most damaging misconception of all: the authority of power misunderstood as the authority of true knowledge. Power is construed as knowledge, not the other way around. And administrative bureaucracy misconceives its power as informed and scientific.

One of the most powerful influences in this phenomenon (we might call it even role-reversal) was the principle of democratic inclusiveness itself, which suggested the equal right, even duty, of every man to participate and yet discouraged unusual, separate individual efforts. By contrast, Europeans have never suffered from fears of selectivity. Perhaps Europeans' long history of monarchy, of class structure, of war and post-war reconstructions, has inured them to both the whim and possibility of selectivity, a personal destiny. Paradoxically, Europeans have also enjoyed a rather broad, one might even say democratic, tradition of fitness and gymnastics education based upon sound physiological principles for a hundred and fifty years or more. With many centuries of history behind them, they have labored under no democratic illusions of kind-hearted inclusiveness in life which might make them uneasy or suspicious of the unusual, select potential of singular individuals. The singular, selective nature of human destiny has in fact been part of European heritage since the Greeks, whether on the battlefield or in Olympic Games.

In America, on the other hand, the need for stability in our chaotic, diverse American society after the Civil War made us prize conformity and justified centralized dicta about the nature of organization and team (witness the large number of retired military people in sports governing bodies today). In the same breath, however, elitist gut response adores the maverick, colorful heroes who buck the constraints of rules and regimentation. As examples one thinks of Alpine Gold Medalist Bill Johnson, Nordic Silver Medalist Bill Koch and, perhaps better known, the US Hockey Teams of 1960 and 1980 whose youthful, spontaneous dash, all innocence and purity, untrammeled and unharnessed, was forever contrasted with the methodical, automaton-like regimentation of the Russians. Implicit in this adoration, however, is the idea that winning the status of hero, in its very selectivity and magical appearance, and in its extended privileges, dare not be available to all. Heroes thence confirm the divine right of administrative powers to elect, to mete out the gifts. Bill Koch wins a silver medal in 1976, and the US Nordic Program "has arrived". (Achilles wins, so the Greeks were right.) Now everything and anything its leaders say is correct, and the power to gift others remains with the already powerful. Subjectivity and "discretion" in the organization of training and team selection are the domain of leadership only.

As far afield as these theories may seem, they have been ultimately illuminating to me in my loving and sometimes despairing thirty-year search for answers to the American malaise in competitive cross-country skiing.

How did this contradictory set of notions come to inhibit the promise of sport in America? I begin with a period which many view as the decisive source for contemporary social values, among them our attitudes about sport and physical culture. That period runs from the Civil War to the end of World War I. It overlaps closely

*Charge the Hill!* 87

with Teddy Roosevelt's lifetime (1858-1919) and ends with his elevation as the icon of American manhood, the sports hero and model of American character in general. The evolution of views about physical culture is illustrated by comparing its presentation at the 1893 World's Fair in Chicago and the 1904 World's Fair in St. Louis, the year Roosevelt was elected to the Presidency. Ideas do not change suddenly, of course, even within a span of ten years. Yet there are junctures of history where a new attitude gathers enough dominance to be articulated more powerfully and thus clarify a broad change of cultural direction. In like manner changing ideas in education during that period can be documented by comparison of two National Education Association Commission reports, one also from 1893, the next from 1911.

The bridge from the Civil War to the present is embodied in the domineering figure, real and legendary, of Theodore Roosevelt. Perhaps more than anybody else he is the American our fathers, and particularly grandfathers, adored and whom we have inherited, like it or not. His status as cultural icon is easy to understand, for above all he recovered the notion of manifest destiny for Americans, and not just nationally but globally as well. Enshrined as "Teddy," both man and bear, he embodied the youth, fantasy and eternity of the American vision he personified. He lived the evolution of ideas about physical culture between two world fairs, and he then galvanized contemporary thinking on physical fitness and transformed it into the image of social and political robustness which still dominates, particularly in our schools. That view blinds us still when it comes to the informed physiological development of modern young athletes. No figure in our history has so powerfully cast our vision of modern American manhood and womanhood and their relationships to the physical self.

Teddy also represents the evolution of American sport away from the health-through-gymnastics movement, described at the 1904 World's Fair, towards competition and games skills. That bias has never been seriously countered since. Winning neatly separates the more powerful from the weak, heroes from spectators, rulers from subjects, participants from non-participants. Thus is society stratified and "stabilized," each ranked according to his allotted, or presumed physical ability. Curiously, it was the business world, oft pilloried as the arch exploiter of the working masses, which in the 1920's began to discover the connection between wealth and health through physical fitness. Our modern fitness boom began on a treadmill in the basement of the Harvard Business School in 1927.

In the 20's and early 30's it did seem that the body in harness might be set free, that a simple, accessible physical culture might indeed serve wealth and health alike.

There was a flurry of liberating new attitudes about self-development and individual expressiveness, both physically and emotionally. The Depression, however, quickly reestablished the necessities and virtues of castigating the flesh, a value thence hoisted next to the flag itself by the glorious nobility of painful sacrifice in World War II. Ultimately Americans have reaffirmed the old ways of 1911. Our bodies remain in harness, if not a subtle straitjacket of earlier notions.

Those ideas and behaviors document the implicit governing culture of the people who live in their time. That culture tends to be most clearly institutionalized in our schools, so I also pay particular attention to public education. It was in the public schools of America that conservative notions of sport became and remained most firmly embedded, and still are. Only when we have understood our American sports culture in its uniqueness, will we perceive with any clarity the urgency for change and the means of bringing it about. In the meantime our young athletes wait, or travel in harness in a direction which will fail them.

Understanding the origins of our American sports culture thus becomes the first step in changing that direction in the new century.

## *The Post-Civil War Period as a Watershed of American Attitudes Toward Sport*

What were the visions of play and physical fitness our grandfathers, including Teddy Roosevelt, encountered after the Civil War?

In Eastman Johnson's 1871 painting *The Old Stagecoach* a group of children plays in the wreck of an old coach. The art historian Jean Baxter describes the context and perspectives of the painting.[3] She notes how the children gather enthusiastically around the skeletal old coach, a broken remnant of the past. They look forward, as if to the future, pulling together in harness, in the luminous air of hope.

Reconstruction itself is the first post Civil War theme. New and youthful bodies will restore the fallen body politic. The children embody purity, hope, rebirth and promise — a second theme. Their play is purposeful, a team effort, a third theme. They play at working together in harness, hitched to the past, pulling to the future, a renewed promise in America.

The harness brings discipline, a powerful fourth theme, and unites their efforts. Play must not be allowed to exemplify random activity or chaos, for that might renew doubts about the American spirit of union and nation so rent in two by the Civil War. Order and stability build the foundation of hope. The uses of physical activity are founded on control. Despite their play, the children are learning about harness. The flesh remains essentially animal and rude, a part of raw nature, to be subjugated by intellect and spirit.

The themes Baxter takes from this 1871 painting give a beginning picture of the social values of the last quarter of the nineteenth century. Each of these themes was to recur, in one form or another, to powerfully influence Americans' attitudes about play, team spirit, discipline and physical prowess for decades to come. Even with the development of physiology, the body was still seen as an aggregate of mechanically arranged parts rather than an organism with its own informing "mind."[4] We have always been most comfortable with the horse or engine as a metaphor for the body, something we could get onto or harness, and spur or drive headlong.

Whereas the first three themes of post Civil War America clearly run through all of our sports history, there is a fourth which is more complex. It is mourning for lost tradition, a sort of heightened emotion of nostalgia. The stagecoach is dead, but it can become the locus of reminiscence in play, a fantasy world where the lost past and a visionary future are experienced in the imagination. At the same time, play is able to divert our attention from the harsh reality of the present. Certainly Americans experienced the depths of national mourning in the Civil War, and we have long since understood the necessary and positive emotional powers of grieving over human losses, however great or modest.

But I would suggest that as sports enthusiasts and fans we have also nurtured a more trivial version of mourning as a sort of defense mechanism to balance our frantic need to win, for we know at the same time that winning will be painfully rare. Mourning can bridge the promise of perfection and the fear of the body's physiological potential, the peculiarly American distrust of the flesh out of harness. There is an odd relief, almost sensual itself, when the flesh does not triumph. We can celebrate defeat in grieving together for our athletes and teams, and that is somewhat more comforting and simple than celebrating extraordinary feats of the flesh in victory, which seem somehow out of control, however wonderful. Commiserating can put off the implications of poor performance, and delay resolute examination of the necessary remedial measures. It may even excuse mediocrity over time because fans, volunteer groups, and association members of long standing, even sports administrators in schools and governing bodies thrive more by participating in the lore of a sport than in the actual score. That is understandable, necessary, and welcome. It is part of a lifelong involvement with the pleasures of sport.

But in sports administrations this form of indirect participation can become insidious when it shifts the focus of attention away from objective scientific evaluation and execution of the sport to notions of sports government, administration, logistics, and the usual peripheral folklore, myth and legend past and present. When those concerns preempt physiological goals, the body again loses. Tradition can become more important than performance itself. The personal satisfactions of sports politicos and even volunteers with the most noble of motives in being co-actors in that tradition can become justification for not improving training science in any fundamental way and for accepting loss, filled with either righteous indignation or sadness, or philosophical resignation over the inevitability of human frailty.

Americans strive, we must strive, it is the moral imperative; but we must never loosen control, whether it be administrators over their charges, teachers over their students, priests over their parishes or athletes over their bodies. The value of harness remains unquestioned, particularly in our educational system. Nor may we be patient in our efforts, for we must daily affirm anew the culture of striving to win, of displaying the virtue of work and control. It is not by chance that "hustle" is a by-word of both business and sport. We enshrine winners. To others who struggle we show our "understanding" as we mourn for the great, if unsuccessful, effort. We even admire the body in its loss, as if, despite the heroic attempt, it was not capable or worthy of more — and we knew that all along, for it is but flesh.

In "understanding" such loss, however, we implicitly trivialize the body and sell too many of our young athletes short. We sustain our optimism through defining failure euphemistically in terms of socially redeeming values - the morally elevating noble effort. Meanwhile we have seldom dared to be truly committed to the higher physical and intellectual requirements of high physical performance. Americans seem more able than Europeans, Russians and Scandinavians to accept great effort together with low yield. There is an odd affirmation of the standards of the masses in the failure of its few who dare excel. It seems enough, for it is safer, to demand total wins from a few heroes, enough namely to symbolically validate patriotic ideals in which success remains both blessed and God-given. Mourning the failure of the remaining non-heroes combines sympathy with the superiority of the survivors, a perfect combination for sports administrators. They are left both in control and relieved of any direct responsibility for performance. The administrator may still preach the high ideals while feeling absolved of undertaking positive measures to see them more widely attained. The usual justification is "We just don't get the good athletes."

Donald J. Mrozek traces many of these same ideas in his excellent essay, "Sport in American Life, From National Health to Personal Fulfillment, 1890-1940." In particular, he links our themes directly to corporate values and to broader adult cultural values.

The rise of corporate thinking in the nineteenth century and the growth of scientific management affected sport as much as they did industrial life, and since then the emphasis on order and discipline within the hierarchical society became one of the dominant themes in the history of play, sport, and physical culture. Subordinating the drives of the individual to the needs of the group became intense, as many historians have observed. Almost as a logical corollary, turn-of-the-century Americans showed a deep purposefulness in their sport, justifying their own participation in games and athletic events by the social benefits they supposedly gained from their efforts.[5]

The emergence of sport to prominence in America after the Civil War depended largely on a tide of justifications offered by the protectors of old-fashioned respectability, disciplined individualism, self-sacrifice and dedication to common cause, and a code of 'real manliness' and 'true womanhood.' The professed interest in using sport to mold personal character reflected the bias of the genteel middle class that personal character was the basis of public morality and social stability.[6]

Mrozek also notes how the physical assertiveness of organized sport following the Civil War was seen as a means of ingraining principles of ethical conduct. Spectator sport, on the other hand, was frowned upon because the entertainment factor detracted from the emphasis on moral training.[7] Dudley Sargent, Harvard University's first professor of physical education in the 1890's, and one of Teddy Roosevelt's professors there, typified this view. He encouraged competition but then became disappointed in his later years that it had led to an overemphasis on winning, spectator events and their attendant collegiate fanfare.[8]

It was the job of physical educators like Sargent to restrain their charges' energies and direct them to socially and educationally positive purposes. The durable Calvinist ethic of work and social utility therefore applied directly to sports. More recent development in the "sciences of the body" such as nutrition and physiology were quickly enlisted in the service of re-constructing the raw, animal body in the interests of social health. Wherever we look, purpose and work are the key words.[9]

Even the playing fields themselves were to serve social purpose. Larry Owens describes the 19th century playing field as

a "republic" intended to stress character and discipline just as strongly as the lecture hall and recitation room. Its government promoted deference to one's superiors, respect for legitimate rules, and obedience to properly constituted authority. But this athletic republic also exhibited important differences. The ethos of team play demanded aggressive participation in contrast to the receptive piety of the lecture hall. Competitive games, and the training required by them, offered new models of deference based on the demonstrated mastery of technique. Not least, team sports showed it was possible to reconcile the aggressive individualism that so worried many Americans with the cooperation and respect for authority demanded by the social order.[10]

This fear of aggressively expressed emotion has had an abiding history in the U.S. Mrozek reminds us that Van Wyck Brooks had "blamed the Puritan tradition for diverting all American energy into utilitarian pursuits, both expressing and reinforcing a fear of pleasure."[11] Social utility thus dictated that mere personal fascination with excellence or personal physical performance could in no way legitimize participation in sport.[12]

By the end of Reconstruction almost all the elements of twentieth century mainstream sports culture were firmly planted in the American consciousness:

- ♦ social harmony, adjustment
- ♦ moral vision, cleansing through work
- ♦ harness, control, directedness, team
- ♦ deference to authority more than individual mastery and performance
- ♦ simultaneous admiration and fear of elite physical performance.

## The Pivotal Role of the Middle Class

No group drove the engine of social mores more than an ever self-aware and righteous middle class, and for the traditional middle class sport was pursued no more for its own sake than was work itself. Play was to imitate purposeful work.[13] By the beginning of the twentieth century a new middle class, however, had moved beyond subordinating human effort, work or play, to standards of public morality.

The new middle class ... accepted order as a kind of value in itself. And to the extent that victory was viewed as proof of effective organization, this attitude contributed to the 'win at all costs' attitude which split the practice of sport from its former social purposes.[14]

Order based on the rules of economy and competition thus took on a practical and distinctly secular morality of its own. The ethic of the social order, pure and simple, was productivity and material success. With winning the new test of character, sport became both a measure of that success and a demonstration of one's right to pleasure.

The paradoxes and incongruities which characterized middle class values around the turn of the 19th century remain powerful in our own day, particularly in education. For a class of society marked by its middleness, few people ever ask what that middle realm looks like. Seeing the middle as the fulcrum of social values, however, provides a number of enlightening insights.

It was the middle class' curious set of allegiances, its paradoxical combination of assertiveness and dependency, aggressiveness and fear of the flesh, which has decisively influenced our attitudes toward sport and physical culture. Above all, the notion of class itself provides both opportunity and powerful constraints. What is good for the group, ironically, becomes dangerous for the individual. Thus for men and women of the Victorian period, as Kenneth Murphy has remarked, aggression had to be policed as vigorously as sexuality, but it was seen as natural, even obligatory in business or politics. The popular notion of Social Darwinism as survival of the fittest suited the middle class perfectly, for it not only justified aggressive self-assertion as a privilege of business, it rewarded successful self-assertion with wealth. At the same time it confirmed the logic of warding off that same assertiveness as an acute danger when it appeared either in the individual's sexual or general social behavior, or in the competing and always potentially chaotic lower class masses.[15] It is clear in this regard how the middle class aped the attitudes of the aristocracy, and it explains why in casting himself as a middle class man come down from his privileged origins Teddy Roosevelt would become the American hero.[16]

The middle class was also especially driven by the idea of upward mobility as a sort of domestic and economic manifest destiny. Everything is perfectible; the promise of America is buttressed by the spirit of improvability both of one's station as well as one's body. Like the automobile, the body was to be sleek, maneuverable, and powerful. Appearance is the mark of prowess, and that is valued both as a measure of advancement as well as the ultimate vehicle upward it provides one in getting along in the group just as along the road, particularly in business.

Elements of class allegiance also fueled the middle class' fundamental drive to establish its difference from the lower working classes, a difference defined by one's freedom from the constraints of that lower level of life. At the same time as flight from the life of hand labor (farming, labor, the trades) was important, so were two sorts of fears: the fear of the uncultivated, unordered masses at one end of the social spectrum and the fear of elite performance, high achievement at the other. Elite performance might be a betrayal of truly democratic principles. The middle class has always had a curious romance with the professed ordinariness midway between pastoral roots and wealth, primarily because ordinariness assured a certain predictable homogeneity in the social order, the status quo one required in order to feel secure. Security in the face of incipient chaos remained the central value for the middle class, for chaos almost always was thought to suggest "down."

The American middle class thus thrived from competition, making it a major voice in the preference for competition and games skills (prowess) over mass gymnastics for all. The "all" was too worrisome, as was "mass." "Mass" had too many lower class connotations which were inimical to the principle of selectivity through which one moved up the social and economic ladder. Baseball naturally became the preferred game: it was not violent, it was refined, desperately ordered, calm, in a team, with unassailable umpires. If there is a middle class neurosis, it might well lie in the attempt to combine nest and flight in a predictable location, the singularity of heroes and the ruled orderedness of teams. That was baseball, by 1912 America's most popular sport.[17] The combat violence of football and hockey would not gain favor until mid-century, for reasons I will discuss later on.

As informative as the paradoxes in middle class values are, any other element which might be conspicuous by its particular absence can be illuminating as well. The most significant example is the understanding of the purpose of the body itself. To be sure, we cannot fault a society for not knowing more than is available to it, as in the early decades of the twentieth century physiology but slowly extended its reach into the human interior. Yet we must note that regardless of its state of development, physiological concerns have never succeeded in becoming of primary influence in our attitudes toward sport in America, at least after the waning of the gymnastic movement in the period between 1865 and 1895.

The American definition of health in terms of fundamental physical qualities, social ideals, and corporate metaphor omitted the body as a physiological entity simply on whim or preference bred of fear, or pledge of allegiance to democracy. The result was to disallow the body the impetus and time needed to truly develop. This did not begin until the 20's and 30's, and then it originated primarily from sources in the arts and entertainment, as we will see.

The impatience of mobility itself created a frantic pace admired by all, but too overtly busy to support the body on its own terms. The goals remained focused toward productivity, speed, sweat, the daily demonstration of effort, the visible win, sales of self and product. Again the old Christian fear of the flesh conspired with democratic ideals to subordinate the body to economic and social benefits and to the tranquilizing effects of enervating daily, weekly, seasonal busy-ness and routine.

This was no longer work as the farmer or tradesman knew it. It mixed up the frenzy of mobility, upward mobility, with fear of both elitism and exclusion by those "above." Yet it was just as characterized by the need to exclude those "below" through selectivity defined by competition. In all of this lies, of course, the one thing the middle class man fears most: that he will not succeed, not be secure from chaos and uncertainty. Therefore work for the nest rather than the flight, of either body or mind. Strengthen the group and the two can be experienced at once. In its attitude toward physical culture the middle class becomes conservative, favoring the patterns of order and stability modeled by the upper class. That is accomplished best through competition and game skill prowess on the one end of the sport spectrum. On the other end the gymnastic and health culture loomed simply too big and uncontrollable, too inclusive of the working classes and thus too potentially disruptive to middle class sensitivity to social position.

## Between the World's Fairs of 1893 and 1904

By 1890 in the United States there were two basic philosophies of sport and fitness, each with its staunch and influential advocates. One favored broad health development through coordination and movement training and sought the social good in mass and progressively patterned gymnastic exercise. The other sought competition and accepted hierarchy as natural, with social selectivity (class) as inevitable, even necessary.

These differences are clearly delineated in a *Cosmopolitan* article on the 1904 World's Fair in St. Louis. Reporter John Brisben Walker bemoans the state of university sports (echoing Dudley Sargent's concerns at Harvard), extols the virtues of lifelong gymnastics-oriented health, and yet ultimately pays reluctant deference to the social and political, rather than individual, purposes of physical fitness.

> The difference between the year 1893 at Chicago and 1904 at St. Louis is perhaps more marked in the Department of Physical Culture than anywhere else. At the time of the Chicago World's Fair, physical culture was confined largely to the universities and colleges. Then the hysterical movement in college physical competition was at its height.[18]
>
> Its methods could not be explained upon any reasonable ground, and even very able and otherwise honest college presidents lent themselves to the fraud of advertising their colleges through athletic games ... the central idea running through it all is no longer the university; it is the public schools. The thought lying at the bottom of it all is how to take the public-school child and convert both him and her into strong-bodied, sane-minded citizens. ... But in the public-schools of 1904, the idea is not of competition, of hurrah and brag and display and school advertisement, but of truly bringing the child to an understanding of its body and advancing it in that physical training which will give it not skill in games, but a permanent stock of health and efficiency. As into everything in 1904, reason is being injected into physical training. "It is custom" is no longer sufficient to explain idiotic methods. Students themselves ask for the why and the wherefore, and get their answers from the health periodicals in such a way that old-fogey schoolmasters often expose themselves to ridicule ... university presidents ... instead of showing the force required to establish college athletics upon a basis of helping all — and most

of all the weak-bodied — to a thorough development of the body's possibilities.[19]

Walker's enthusiasm for gymnastic health and general physical fitness expresses his idealized and personal bias, however well-informed, more than a social or educational fact. And rather than proclaiming a new age of sports culture, the 1904 mass exercise demonstrations more accurately portray the swan song of a period of highly intelligent physical culture which had been in place in America, in one form or the other, since the late 1860's, where reason and understanding, as Walker says, were being injected into physical training. Dioclesian Lewis's *New Gymnastics for Men, Women and Children* (1862) went through ten editions and served as a standard text in schools, gyms, and home for 25 years. Home exercise equipment, for one's "parlor gymnasium," included rubber wands, pulley weights, and rowing devices and give us a picture of the long-forgotten prototype of our "modern" home gyms. German immigrants were significant enthusiasts and formed the same gymnastic societies *(Turnvereine)* which Friedrich Jahn had established in Germany.[20]

The ends of the physical culture seesaw are clearly defined. Competition sits on the one end, selectivity combined with organizational success to win and thus favorably advertise the productivity of its institution. On the other end sits non-selective mass sport as a means to insure life-long health and productivity for the public at large. These differing views had long been aspiring to the mantle of general wisdom, as they essentially still do. Ironically, mass gymnastics will turn out to possess the far greater potential for developing individual high performance, as European, Scandinavian, and Russian successes have demonstrated.

In the late 1880's the interest in so-called pedagogical gymnastics had grown to substantial proportions, even in the very period which the writer faults for emphasizing competition. In a book written in 1890 Claes Enebuske outlined a detailed progression of Swedish gymnastic exercises and their specific functions in training and stimulating the body to good health and mental alertness. He had given a demonstration in Boston in the spring of 1890, and that had resulted in a request that he write *Progressive Gymnastic Day's Orders* [21] which was then widely distributed.

Enebuske's book is startlingly modern in its intuition of the physiological principles of aerobic fitness:

> The functions of the heart and lungs are the fundamental functions of the body. Upon them the welfare of all the other functions depends. It is the aim of Swedish educational gymnastics to develop these fundamental functions,

and it endeavors to attain this end by a series of movements of the voluntary system which shall be arranged as executed as to bring about a healthy response between the muscles and the will. It does not strive to develop physical specialists [game skills], but only to train the different organs of the body in a manner that may serve the great double purpose of promoting the efficiency of the circulatory and respiratory functions and the increasing volitional control of the whole body.

Throughout its entire course the Swedish system of gymnastics proceeds upon the well-grounded theory that muscular strength must follow as the necessary consequence of a training so carried on as to promote the health and strength of these fundamental functions. Those who labor only to enrich the muscles often make piteous beggars of the heart and lungs. ... Get the heart right and the lungs right, and the muscles will meet every reasonable demand.[22]

Our contemporary distinction between central systems (heart and lungs) and peripheral systems (muscles) is thus over a hundred years old! Our loss of this approach to physical development and broad movement sophistication through emphasis on competition, specific skills, and muscle growth — social adjustment through games, productivity and power through might and winning — constitutes the major weaknesses in our endurance sports tradition, not to mention life-long fitness goals. Its presence in Europe accounts for the Europeans' continued dominance, particularly following its more sport specific awakening at the hands of Dr. Ernst Van Aaken (Germany) even before World War II, Arthur Lydiard (New Zealand) in the later 1940's and but a very few others in the 1950's.

Enebuske made another distinction which is even more enlightened. Speaking of the muscular resistance in the exercises, he says:

But whether the resistance be given by the hand of another person, by a machine, or by the leverage of another part of the body, the degree must always be commensurate with the individual conditions, and it should not be increased so as to call into operation the maximum or highest power of the pupil. The most favorable amount, or the optimum, is always somewhat lower, and the practical test for this optimum ... is that the movement must be performed with full, free breathing, and with accuracy, that is to say, without shaking or disturbing interference from other muscles. It is the purpose of training to gradually raise the optimum.[23]

This distinction between optimum and maximum reflects the modern notion, particularly since Italian physiologist Francesco Conconi's report in 1985 that endurance performance is improved most effectively by training just below anaerobic threshold rather than at race pace and that the primary goal of training is to raise anaerobic threshold, that is, the optimum level of physiological efficiency.[24] How sadly do generations of Americans know that training at maximum, however emotionally satisfying, is short-term at best and destructive in the long-run. We (and in this I include athletes, coaches, and too many of our physiologists) have been unusually slow to learn from the likes of Arthur Lydiard and the leading European, Scandinavian, and Russian physiologists.[25]

Americans have been particularly slow to learn this fundamental principle of physiological development because we learned another one too well: The body does not have laws unto itself; its growth is to be subordinated to social, industrial and political values. Organization begets stability begets productivity begets power and wealth: the application of this industrial-political ethos to sport is obvious in the case of the promoters of game skills and competition, as active in the late 1800's as they are today. Knowing what we know today, it is easy to agree with Walker in his 1904 review about the inherent value of life-long fitness. It is again particularly interesting that it was in fact the business world which would re-discover physical fitness as a key to industrial productivity beginning in the late 1920's. The current fitness boom really began in Elton Mayo's Fatigue Laboratory at Harvard Business School with research into the relationships between fitness levels, health, stress, and productivity in workers and management.[26] It took half a century for the business world to recover the wisdom of non-selective physical culture. The body, left to its own developmental principles, would turn out to be better for business than business could dictate itself. The educational world at the elementary and secondary levels has not yet even recognized the more productive change of perspective.

I speak in detail to the problem which arises from the educational system's bias toward competition and games skills, and its contrary effects on developmental physiology in young athletes, in my chapters "Letter to Parents" and "Training". Even in his World's Fair article, Walker must add to his fervor a note of more furtive recognition that the ideal of health alone is too singular to attract a restlessly progressive middle class for whom "middle" meant "up", foremost in social status and wealth.

I will close by ... a fundamental principle of government. "The maintenance of the health of the individual is a chief requirement of the healthy growth of the state." .... "All progress in the direction of health is synonymous with economic gain. On the other hand, health is the source of the nation's ability to defend itself."[27]

Writing in 1904, he also must have been aware of the overpowering image of Teddy Roosevelt, two months away from being elected President of the United States, and by that time well-established as a national hero. Roosevelt would propagate his own experience and resulting convictions about the decisive role of competition in personal and public life.

Indeed, one cannot but wonder if it might be the words of Teddy himself which echo in Walker's conclusion: 1) The body is a source of raw material for national defense. 2) Health is the means to an end rather than an end in itself. The end remains economic and political stability and progress. The point still is not the individual's well-being or level of personal performance; it is that there will be fewer weak links in the social-economic-political chain. Walker sees things in more humane and idealistic terms as he observes the mass gymnastics by the German Turners at the 1904 Fair: "Modern athletics for the development of the weak students as well as the robust."[28]

Theodore Roosevelt had long been nearly evangelical about this development of the weak, for he had been one of them. It will be useful to look more closely at Roosevelt and his decisive influence on Americans' ideas on physical fitness.

## *Stuck With Teddy*

Teddy Roosevelt was 13 years old at the time of Eastman Johnson's painting, *The Old Stagecoach,* 46 in 1904 when he was elected President (after 3 years in office following William McKinley's assassination). Formed in the years of Civil War, he embraced the spirit of reconstruction, personal and public. As the hero and rescuer of America's rightful and manly destiny he determined the sports culture of the 20th century.

Physically frail as a youngster, Theodore Roosevelt developed a rugged physique through a strenuous regimen of exercise. In his autobiography he recounts how "Having been a sickly boy, with no natural bodily prowess, and having lived much at home, I was at first quite unable to hold my own when thrown into contact with other boys of rougher antecedents." Sent to Moosehead Lake in Maine to recover from an asthma attack, he remembered being put upon by two stronger boys. "The experience taught me what probably no amount of good advice could have taught me. I made up my mind that I must try to learn so that I would not again be put in such a helpless position; and having become quickly and bitterly conscious that I did not have the natural process to hold my own, I decided that I would try to supply its place by training. Accordingly, with my father's hearty approval, I started to learn to box."[29]

The young Roosevelt thence learned privately from a boxing-master, as he also learned to ride with instruction. It is interesting that the autobiography, so clearly a paean to himself, is replete with self-deprecating statements about his lack of natural prowess, an obvious effort to descend from his privileged origins to the more humble hearts of the middle and working classes, a maneuver at which he became a master. Yet he almost naively emphasizes those origins when he notes that he was fit enough to join the hunt on Long Island.

It is undeniable, however, that he was truly buoyed by both his improved physical capabilities and resultant personal confidence, and he became a staunch lifelong advocate of vigorous activity. Thence the values which produced his physical reservoir became the source of two fundamental convictions about life: life is competition and life is public life, community and national service in politics. In 1876-80 Roosevelt came under the tutelage of Dudley Sargent, Harvard's first Professor of Physical Training. Sargent, who with others would form the American Association for the Advancement of Physical Education in 1885, believed fitness was best achieved by athletic contest rather than by gymnastic routine. And for him games were not just a physical matter but an ideological one as well. It is hard to estimate the force of Sargent's influence. Even though Roosevelt was enrolled in his course, he is not mentioned in Roosevelt's autobiography. It is clear nevertheless that Roosevelt knew Sargent and would have known his philosophy, so similar to Roosevelt's own. Whatever the effect, at age twenty-three Roosevelt leapt into the public fray, running for office in the New York State Assembly.

Competing and overcoming are continuous threads in Roosevelt's life, and overcoming oneself, he believed, the necessary prerequisite for competing successfully with others, be they people, situations, or nature, political rivals, nations, or the wilderness. He enjoyed the wilderness more because it preserved the opportunity for humans to realize their competitive relation to it rather than simply to exploit it. Exuding purpose and righteousness, he advocated war with Spain as Secretary of the

Navy, and once it was declared he left in 1898 to form the Rough Riders. His derring-do in Cuba, particularly in the Battle of Santiago in which he charged San Juan Hill, sounded out for decades since, as cry for Army officer and coach alike: "Charge the hill!" It rings out regularly on every running and ski course, just as another of Roosevelt's magic aphorisms, "Talk softly and carry a big stick." When not used at war, it worked just as powerfully on the playing field and locker room. Roosevelt reflected the very incarnation of self-contained power, the strong, stoic type who did not admit to pain under any circumstances. And even though Sargent had not intended winning itself to transcend the conditioning value of competition, winning became the inevitable goal, the display, the ritual of public validation so clearly central to Roosevelt's character.

As for Sargent, his more gentle aims were carried on by a disciple, Luther Gulick, who transformed the YMCA into a sport and fitness orgnaization. At the YMCA's training school in Springfield, Mass. he and his students promoted "muscular Christianity," believing a sound mind in a sound body would make for a saved soul.[30] It is interesting to note the difference between muscles viewed as a "big stick" and muscles as an element of "a saved soul." It is also interesting to record Gulick's early hint at dispelling the usual Christian dichotomy between soul and flesh.

But Roosevelt would galvanize the world around himself in a way far less reflective and much more rambunctious than Gulick. Robustness for him embodied total cultural and social mobility, and brought cowboys, prizefighters, explorers, and artists to the White House to hobnob with administrators from the educated elite. It was also characteristic that the use of power in public policy reigned over any potential excess in the exercise of democratic freedoms. Roosevelt emphasized that collective responsibility must govern individual freedom. Laissez-faire, by itself, was not to be his style, for he feared that uncompromising individual freedom was simply a sentimental excuse for personal greed, an invitation to abandon moral purpose. The result would be "a riot of lawless business individualism which would be quite as destructive to real civilization as the lawless military individualism of the Middle Ages."[31]

It is consistent with his state-above-individual principle that Roosevelt was ready to use the Army to break the miners' strike of 1902. When the larger public stability was at stake, he was ready with government intervention in business and labor affairs. Strong societies and countries survive and weak ones perish, so his experience of physical reality had taught him. The Union must hold, and this must apply to nations, states, communities, teams, and individuals as well.

Discipline and stability of the community would remain so overriding an American belief that if there were no threat to those values, we would imagine one in order to demonstrably defend them.

Just how potent these norms of life were for Roosevelt becomes clearer yet when we add his dismay over falling birth rates as "racial suicide" or his order to government printers to use a simplified spelling system. In the latter he fits precisely with the aims of the new educationists' curriculum of democratic social adjustment, civic "literacy" at the practical, non-mastery level. That he believes this despite his own elite classical education gives a good indication of the direction in which American notions of culture, be it physical culture, social, educational, or political culture, were evolving.

The galvanic nature of Roosevelt's power is unquestionable. Historian Mark Sullivan writing in the 1920's, described him as follows.

> And it is simple history to say that the relation Roosevelt had to America at his time, the power he was able to wield, the prestige he enjoyed, the affection he received, the contentment of the people with him. ... composed the lot of an exceptionally fortunate monarch during a particularly happy period of his reign.[32]

Sullivan's characterization continues with a mixture of reverence and zeal.

> Roosevelt in battle — which was Roosevelt most of the time — was a huge personality endowed with energy almost abnormal, directed by an acute intelligence, lightened by a grinning humor, engaged in incessant action. The spectacle, occupying the biggest headlines in the daily newspapers, gave to the life of that day a zest and stimulus and gaiety such that average Americans who lived through the period carried it as the ancient forty-niners remembered California, sighing "there'll never be another Roosevelt," and telling their grandchildren that once they saw a giant. *Anni memorabiles!*[33]

> Roosevelt's fighting was so much a part of the life of the period, was so tied up with the newspapers, so geared into popular literature, and even to the pulpit ... as to constitute, for the average man, not merely the high spectacle of the Presidency in the ordinary sense, but almost the whole of the passing show, the public's principal interest.[34]

This image of the man did not just happen. Roosevelt was able to arrange his permanent center-stage position by understanding that a headline, news dispatch, a cartoon were more powerful than editorial comment, however well-reasoned it might be. He deliberately used them as weapons in whatever crusade he undertook. From the Teddy Bears he inspired to the cartoons depicting him as a king, a cowboy in saddle rough-riding the world, or a centurion whose sword bore the inscription "Right Makes Might," Roosevelt was accorded an image little short of divine. So totally had he engaged the public imagination with his exploits and personality that in its December 27, 1906 issue *Life* would remark how his daily life was so vigorous, so emotional, so full of combative debate and dynamics that his ideas would "Make up a Daily Tale Which Those of Us Who Survive His Tenure of the Presidential Office Will Doubtless Miss, as We Might Miss Some Property of the Atmosphere We Breathe."[35] A cartoon at his death in 1919 depicted him as a rough-rider ascending through the clouds to what must be Mount Olympus itself.

Teddy would have found that quite appropriate, for he made no secret of the fact that his charge up San Juan Hill was not only the most satisfying personal experience of his life but even, as Sullivan puts it, "had high rank in the contemporary history of the world."[36]

These are but a few examples of the general apotheosis of the man. No one was more zealous than his sister, Corinne. Writing in the forward to a book about her brother, she quoted from a letter in which a major in the army in France expressed his feeling that Roosevelt "was the Jesus Christ of our day." She even adds to that her own experience in which a Japanese statesman had suggested Roosevelt seemed to embody the Shinto religion. "The word 'Shinto' means 'The Way' and 'Theodore Roosevelt' … was 'The Way' to be followed not only by the American people but by the nations of the world."[37]

The extravagance of such statements, even their naivete, does not detract from Roosevelt's many accomplishments or his truly powerful charisma. It is interesting to note, however, that he and those close to him did make conscious efforts to foster his stature into legend. Those efforts were amazingly successful, and they perpetuated the values he represented. Even today to be a real man is still to be "rough and ready," to "charge the hill," to "talk soft and carry a big stick," to be ready to do battle with all comers — wilderness, animal, nation, or rival. Witness any movie. Watch any athletic contest; listen to coaches. In sport in particular Teddy's values effect how we deal with the potentials and frailties of young bodies.

In Teddy Americans found the perfection of what they thought they were, ought to be, wished to be. He embodied their culture by both inclination and political purpose, and they worshipped him for it. "They" were our grandfathers, and they told their grandchildren the stories. We, my generation, we are those grandchildren; and we need to reflect seriously upon the values we have received.

If there is an American icon we recognize, it is Teddy, every value he embodied dressed in the eternal youth of his nickname. More than any American in the past century he established the ethos of exploring and conquering frontiers, be they natural, political, or personally physical. Big stick values still preside, however softly spoken, over most discussion of sport. As we will see, from industry to social values, from politics to education, in twentieth century America, despite temporary changes of emphasis, the impulse to compete has remained so strong, we seem implicitly needy to take on chaos itself, if no more concrete threat is at hand. The win proves dominance and equates to "harmony restored," the vision of natural hierarchy again preserved.

Our democracy came to prize homogeneity and homogenization, quantification (testing, scores for production or batting averages, GNP, wins and losses in play and fight). Conformity, social adjustment is elevated; the notion of the true individual is rendered comfortably blunt.[38] Divergence from the norm is suspect, frailty is cowardice, winning is the moral equivalent of noble character. The individual is strengthened not from within, by having unique potential or specific rights. The pure life of the soul is still the chastened life of the flesh, and that is best accomplished within the confines of playing field and scheduled competitions. Heroes reign, and the Union holds.

It will no longer surprise us that education, while radically "democratizing" its philosophy of the intellect in the interests of inclusiveness and social adjustment, would by way of contradiction leave out the body, leave it chastened, demonstrably in social and religious harness. How such an apparent contradiction entered and gained power in our educational institutions is of greatest importance for our understanding of the state of modern sport, so I turn briefly to the evolution of ideas in public education during the same watershed period, 1893-1911.

# Education and Individual Achievement

It isolates a person, anywhere, to think beyond a certain point.

—Rollo Walter Brown

A comparison of the National Education Association protocols of 1893 and 1911 gives a clear indication of the direction in which American thinking about education and physical culture had turned.

In 1893 the National Education Association Committee of Ten sought to describe and prescribe the goals and means of secondary education. The committee was comprised largely of university professors who advanced the traditional classical curriculum not only for students seeking college entry but also for all students for preparing them for the "duties of life." The goal of these intellectualists, as they came to be called pejoratively, was through "mastery" of subject matter[39] to train what they considered to be the essential "powers of mental growth and sensibility: observation, memory, expression, and reasoning, … an intellectual training that was good for college preparation or for life."[40]

In *Anti-Intellectualism in American Life* (1962) Richard Hofstadter describes the counterflow to such conservative and, many thought, elitist ideals.

> Even in the 1880's there had been a considerable efflorescence of programs of practical and vocational training. Increasingly, those primarily concerned with the management and curricula of high schools became restive about the continuing dominance of the academic ideal, which they considered arose from the schools' 'slavery' and 'subjugation' to the colleges. The high schools, they insisted, were meant to educate citizens in their public responsibilities and to train workers for industry, not to supply colleges with freshmen. Democratic principles, they thought, demanded much greater consideration for the needs of children who did not go to college. Regard for these needs and a due respect for the principles of child development demanded that the ideal of "mastery" be dropped.[41]

The choice of the popular bad word, "slavery," as well as the exaggeratedly egalitarian emphasis are unmistakable and continue to signal the intensity of Reconstruction ideals. Hofstadter remarks that two assumptions peculiar to American education distinguish it in particular from the practice of the rest of the world: its democratic assumptions and the universality of its aims.[42] To that ideal end students were "not meant to be separated either socially or academically, according to social class."[43] And regardless of the fact that "the realities of poverty and prejudice intervene to preserve most of the class selectivity that our democratic educational philosophy repudiates",[44] and even though those goals would be achieved at the admitted sacrifice of educational standards,[45] it was nevertheless viewed as a great accomplishment that "education could become the instrument of mass opportunity and social mobility."[46]

It should not be of only passing curiosity to us that our impatience to enjoy social mobility, our progressive notion of opportunity was so readily satisfied with lowering intellectual standards to achieve those goals, and in fact made them cornerstones of the new education as a conscious counter to intellectual capability. Many would argue that this educational-political strategy has been repeated in 1994 with what is euphemistically called a "re-centering" of SAT scores. The paradoxical quality of educational philosophy needs to be kept in mind when we attempt to understand the current situation in both academics and athletics in our schools: democratic all-inclusiveness achieved by disregarding high standards of content mastery. I would hazard the provisional observation that institutionalizing mediocrity rather than mastery in our educational system can hardly prepare students and athletes for mastery upon graduation.

Education in America thus went from voluntary and selective to compulsory and unselective for children up to the age of sixteen. On the positive side, mandatory schooling fit the new child labor laws. The problem of child labor had become acute in the U.S. after the Civil War. There were simply not enough available men. Child welfare was by no means a clear cut issue, however, for where federal labor laws were enacted they were then declared invalid in 1918 and 1922. The concern persisted nevertheless, as is clear from the Ohio Children's Code Commission of 1911 and the US Children's Bureau of 1912.

There was a shadow side of preventing the exploitation of youth, however, and that was the goal of protecting jobs for adults.[47] In either case, a much larger number of pupils was now increasingly unselected and unwilling, a captive audience, and the burden shifted to the educator to appeal to the broader "needs" of his charges. The old classical curriculum was out because

> as soon as public education included secondary education, it began to be more doubtful that everyone could be educated, and quite certain that not everyone could be educated in the same way.[48]

The 'mastery' of subject matter held by the intellectualists to be the goal of education fell more and more to the ideal of the 'needs' of children as they were, and those were most prominently social and civic, 'life adjustment' and 'citizenship.'[49]

In 1911 a new NEA Commission of Nine put in clear type what was already happening. Now comprised of only professional teachers (no professors or private school headmasters) and chaired by a teacher at the Manual Training School of Brooklyn, the goals were delineated in *Cardinal Principles of Secondary Education:* education should be training for good citizenship and choice of vocation. An edition of 130,000 copies was circulated by the US Bureau of Education, keying on the notion that "gift" no longer had to do with any intellectual capacity but rather was attached to the child's "dominant interest at the time."[50] It is interesting to compare "interest' as being both temporary in nature and superficial relative to the generalized goal of social adjustment through games. Perhaps this is the precursor to our public schools' seasonal approach to sport which so interrupts true development.

The *Principles* did not stop with the vague indignation of statements such as "By means of exclusively bookish curricula false ideals of culture are developed."[51] The imperative was forwarded that "New laws of learning must be brought to bear to test subject matter and teaching methods: they could no longer be judged primarily in terms of the demands of any subject as a logically organized science."[52] Thus the inner structure of the disciplines were demoted in favor of the "laws of learning" then being discovered, and the student was not to be understood as a mind to be developed but rather a citizen to be trained. The curriculum prescribed consisted of the following main objectives of education:

1. Health.
2. Command of fundamental processes [...the three R's...]
3. Worthy home membership.
4. Vocation.
5. Citizenship.
6. Worthy use of Leisure.
7. Ethical Character.[53]

Just how great a shift had taken place is clear by the grudging, single sentence concern for higher achievers: "Provision should be made also for those having distinctively academic interests and needs."[54] What this really amounted to, to use a crass term, was "dumbing down" for democracy.

Lest we see these changes as some bizarre conspiracy against the human brain, it is important to understand the context within which they were occurring. Whereas the immediate post-Civil War years may have been characterized by the desire and vision of a future soon to come which would be redolent of a more stable and idyllic past, America was in fact becoming anything but stable. Education was changing at a rate probably slower than the rest of the country's institutions, and it is in the face of what can only be described as the colossal ongoing chaos in American life that other changes, including those in education and sport, must be understood.

If we were to take Teddy Roosevelt's lifetime, 1858 to 1919, essentially from the beginning of the Civil War period to the end of WWI, this is a rough synopsis of what Americans would have witnessed.

> Three presidents were assassinated, a fourth impeached, a fifth stole his election. The Union admitted twelve new states, doubling its geography, making it the largest continental republic in the world by 1912. Ten constitutional amendments were voted on, seven of which were law by 1920. The country's population, number of foreign born, suicides, industrial laborers, divorces, gross national product, and white-collar workers all doubled.[55]

One decade alone, 1879 to 1889, has been described as "probably the most violent in American history in terms of civil disorders and labor-capital conflicts."[56]

A particularly telling figure for education was the 57.5% of the high school age children who in 1911 were of foreign born parents. Coupled with mandatory schooling through age sixteen, it may become more clear what the enormity of the educator's task really was. And it is here in particular that the peculiar universalist foundation of American education was put to a truly severe test, to deal with the radical heterogeneity of its pupils. It had a definite and desperate Union-preserving logic, therefore, when in 1916 John Dewey pronounced that democracy was the central issue of education.[57] That that goal was to be served by a leveling towards an all-encompassing middle ground is exemplified by the following statement in the same years by J.L. McBrien, Extension Specialist for the US Bureau of Education:

> The prime and vital service of amalgamation into one homogeneous body of children alike of those born here and those who come here from many different lands must be rendered this Republic by the school teachers of America.[58]

Of special interest to us in terms of how education would influence attitudes toward sport is the opposing view, articulated in the same period by Edward Lee Thorndike, that the issue of education was rather the "application of 'what science tells us'."[59] What is even more striking than the difference of opinion is the fact that nobody had heretofore believed any problem existed between the notions of democracy and science. People had generally basked in the Enlightenment notion that democracy and science lived together in some sort of pre-ordained harmony. Certainly the application of science would have been a useful goal in physical culture, as it had been in Europe for 50 years or more. That same application had in fact also been in the US as well in the period from 1865 to 1895, in the gymnastics movement imported with the Swedes and Germans, already mentioned with regard to Enebuske's *Progressive Gymnastic Day's Orders* of 1890 and the report of 1904 World's Fair.

With the power of "science" to test itself "overcome," the need for the advent of truly "educational" testing was soon firmly established. The new educationists simply ignored the elitist overtones of such testing in the sheer momentum born of the fervor for their own program.[60] They were not alone in their enthusiasm, of course. Such testing provided the upper class industrialists with a comforting rationale for their social position and purpose, combination of privilege validated by philanthropy, power masquerading as paternalism. Nobody exemplifies this more than Andrew Carnegie. Full of the "gospel of wealth" and the "morality of improvement," he had no qualms in brutally putting down the Homesteaders' Rebellion on July 4, 1892, and in doing so essentially ending "an era when skilled workers saw themselves as equal to their bosses, when they believed their rights of citizenship and the labor they invested in their work equaled the employer's property rights."[61] Unfortunately, educators have always seemed to be comfortably detached from the inequities of life, and their fervent belief in egalitarian democracy barely ever wavers from the conveniently simple.

The cultural trap represented by the only apparent inclusiveness (or rather placement, benign selection by the educational elect) of educational reform is an insidious one which still eludes our view today. Hofstadter notes of the pre-WW I years:

> It is impossible to stress too much the impetus given to the new educational creed by the moral atmosphere of Progressivism, for the new creed was developed in an atmosphere of warm philanthropy and breathless idealism in which the less gifted and underprivileged commanded a generous response.[62]

Idealism aside, testing confirmed the position in society and divine province of those already "placed" on top. In sport the notion of the "natural athlete" is the complement to the elitist view of talent as divine placement. Whatever the case, work as a means of upward mobility was clearly not seen as a factor in either society or sport but rather as successful adjustment and conformity to society as it was, i.e. was intended to be. Anything else would have rendered the body too dirt-tainted, too blue collar a means of success as it was supposed to appear in either religious or social terms.

Hofstadter concludes that the new educational 'science,' by destroying the validity of mental discipline [the classical notion of education], had destroyed the basic assumption upon which the ideal of a liberal education was based."[63] So fervently bent on reform as the new educators were, they would not even interpret objectively the results of experiments undertaken in pursuit of the possibility of transference - the applicability of skills gained in one mental discipline to another. In ignoring the clear evidence for transference, the dominant educational powers of the day preferred their own metaphor for the educational development of children to the indicators of science itself.[64]

There is already a haunting note of science validating the investigative devices and preferred theory rather than understanding more deeply the phenomenon or object of the investigation. It is a failing for confusing the finger pointing with the moon it points at. Chapter 10, The Limits of Visual Perception in Understanding Technique, will trace in some detail how cross-country ski "science" has suffered in particular from this confusion.

Even though advance and balance have informed certain elements of the public school curriculum since that time, the preference for social purpose, witting or unwitting, over the science of physiology has righteously persevered in our school systems. The will to inform and develop the bodies of our young people through the insights of physical culture barely existed. Self-development or self-discovery through sport remained within an ever-attendant social harness, and not just in an obligation to the world of economy (opportunity) but to business (wealth) as well. The old values do not move much; in fact, they seem to have become yet further entrenched in the face of continued growing social diversity and our fundamental fears of complexity in life. Not the least of these fears, of course, was that of the inherently chaotic human body. Fascination struggles constantly with anxiety and retreat.

Mrozek summarizes the change:

> The turn-of-the-century educator sought to ensure discipline and order inside the classroom and was more apt to use organized play and games to

regulate students, to sublimate their instinctive bursts of energy, and to harness them to the yoke of social obligation. After World War I, however, teachers were at least as apt to see the natural side of play as the more precious and fragile one. From elementary schools through universities, sports was a form of self-expression and a vehicle of 'getting along' with others.[65]

Sports, therefore, fulfilled the same aims as the other elements of education for social adjustment which Hofstadter describes.

The notion of directed freedom in education puts sport directly to use as social therapy and adjustment training. Elliot Eisner gives one of the clearest overviews:

> American psychology, particularly American educational psychology, has its intellectual roots in behaviorism. We have been mainly concerned with finding out how to shape behavior so that it approximates our goals. Our psychology has been primarily concerned with making learning efficient. As a result, it has been a psychology that has put invention, mind, and emotion on the conceptual back burner.[66]

Nowhere was this philosophy of shaping and adjustment more thoroughgoing than in our schools, and the particular vehemence with which it continues to reign has a great deal to do with our odd and contradictory compulsion to win, to gain through pain, and for our utter disregard for the elementary principles of human developmental physiology which would allow high-level success. "Adjustment" and "shaping" are in fact simply euphemisms for "control," either through distraction or the sublimation of excess physical energies. And control is justified on the basis that it fends off chaos.

It is also a characteristic of the desired healthful image that it is not so much fulfilled in the mass exercise so euphorically described at the 1904 World's Fair in St. Louis but rather is accomplished as a large team, a definable "package" of bodies, one might say. For the values of industrial organization preferred that the display (perhaps the window dressing) be not only cooperative but visibly corporate as well.

Still, it was important that mass gymnastics exercise was conspicuously democratic. The humane processes inherent in including the weak also should not hide the fact from us, however, that this form of sport was and is physiologically more sound — learning a grammar of movement is better for all sports. Nor are stronger, more talented athletes therein restrained from standing out. Whereas the homogeneous nature of the ideal social organization is emphasized, the age-old distrust of the body and the outstanding individual is also apparent. The stray hero is idolized, but for that to be readily possible, let alone encouraged, is not only undemocratic, it is to be feared as destabilizing. We are reminded here again of Roosevelt's worry about individualism as potentially chaotic.[67] The corporate group provides the collective harness required for a stable class society. Even ads of the day make the same point over and over again. A B.F. Goodrich ad shows baseball players, carbon copies of each other in a line, exercising in unison like a chorus line, something they never do in actual play. In a line, however, they can serve as the desired metaphor for the automobile and its balanced, safe tires.

The message is just as powerful the other way, of course. The automobile is a trusted metaphor for social organization, in this case sport. Goodyear thus connected its corporate status with health, team/social/industrial strength, and, thinly veiled, moral uprightness.

Among the few, William James would use the machinery metaphor for a different message.

> Official moralists advise us never to relax our strenuousness. 'Be vigilant night and day,' they adjure us; 'hold your passive tendencies in check; shrink from no effort; keep your will like a bow always bent.' ... The tense and voluntary attitude becomes in them a fever and torment. Their machinery refuses to run at all when the bearings are made so hot and the belts so tight.[69]

Despite the fact that social adjustment goals in education will retain a strong grip on the physical culture for the young, the 1920's and 30's would begin to take James' critique seriously, to both express more openly and loosen the tensions inherent in so tightly harnessed a body. At some point every horse kicks over the traces, at least once.

## The '20s and '30s, the Interwar Years: The Body Discovered and Contained

Indeed it is possible to stand with one foot on the inevitable "banana peel" of life with both eyes peering into the Great Beyond, and still be happy, comfortable, and serene — if we will even so much as smile.

—Douglas Fairbanks (1917)

This is the dead land
This is the cactus land
Here the stone images
Are raised, here they receive
Under the twinkle of a fading star
The supplication of the dead man's hand.

—T.S.Eliot (1925)

The Roaring Twenties and the Golden Age of the thirties would witness a significant loosening of the social harness in America; yet the release and self-discovery in physical experience at each turn met that persistent American unease with the body (Rollo May is equally precise when he calls it dis-ease). The urge to experience and discover was tempered by the urge to somehow defuse or at least distance physical expressiveness, to contain and package any experience of the physical pleasure in a socially acceptable, even redeeming, way. Certainly American culture was becoming both variegated and complex, compacted and wildly accelerated by technology. Fundamentally paradoxical varying expressions comingled: women danced in flapper dresses, and Prohibition raged; Calvin Coolidge fashioned a halo for business while the Lost Generation grew cynical and dark about culture itself. Codes of morality loosened precipitously. Woman could legally smoke, speakeasies were common.

Sex became an topic of open discussion.[69] A frank and free life of the emotions and senses was the response to pervasive hedonism.

How different it is when a nation wins a war rather than is torn apart by one. After WW1 Americans dared, deserved to be open, optimistic, to live for the moment. "Maroon him at a cross-roads, with five hours until train time," said an admirer of Douglas Fairbanks, "and he'd have the operator's first name in ten minutes and be learning the Morse alphabet, after which he would rush up to his new friend's house to see the babies or to pass judgment on a Holstein calf or a black Minorca brood." The harness was off. One could run in the pasture. In sport too there was intense enthusiasm, for its sensuality, emotional expressiveness, and good health. Joy and affirmation were possible for both body and feelings.[70] Fairbank's book, *Laugh and Live* (1917), might serve as an early edition of 20's popular culture. With much the same adoration which surrounded Roosevelt, George Creel described Fairbanks' "super-physical equipment":

> Fairbanks, in addition to being blessed with a strong, lithe body, has developed it by expert devotion to every form of athletic sport. He swims well, is a crack boxer, a good polo player, a splendid wrestler, a skillful acrobat, a fast runner, and an absolutely fearless rider.[71]

Possible, justifiable, yes, for a movie star. But how probable or successful would the experience of such frontiers be for the general public, given the powerful restraints of the previous generation? Fairbanks' unqualified exuberance for sport and physical activity, and not just on moralistic grounds but because that is what the body needs, is a significant new breath of fresh air. But will it reach young people yet in school, provide durable options for Americans' basic instincts?

It is a fascinating period in American history, one which challenges the very notion of cultural logic. It is more of a kaleidoscope with constantly shifting complex arrangements. For all the novelty and progressive attitudes, it is important to note that new behavior was the province of adults. What was good for adults was not considered so appropriate for children; and it is with children in their formative period of physical awareness and behavior that the dominant culture of public institutions is to be accurately measured, even though the avant-garde may be more creative, and certainly more interesting.

A clear picture of the general tension between freedom and control for children appears in the 1928 report of the Regional Plan Association of New York:

Careful checking ... shows that about 1/7 of the child population from 5 to 15 years of age may be found on these [play-]grounds. ... The lure of the street is a strong competitor. ... It must be a well administrated playground to compete successfully with the city streets, teeming with life and adventure. The ability to make the playground activity so compellingly attractive as to draw children from the streets and hold their interest from day to day is a rare faculty in play leadership, combining personality and technical skill of a high order.[72]

The same report deplores

the stubborn tendency of children to 'fool around' instead of playing 'recognized games.'[Recognized by whom?] This yearning for the Organization Child on the part of those who would incarcerate incidental play, and childrens' stubborn preference for fooling around on city streets, are both as characteristic today as they were in 1928.[73]

Sports and physical culture were evolving in varying ways simultaneously, for the older generation and the new, for adults and for children, each differently. Nevertheless, the motivating force in sport had always contained a fundamental reward which was difficult to quell within the individual (at least once he left the safe harbors of public education): feeling good, more powerful, better about oneself. Despite the reins so long sought for the body, the seeds of self-gratification and pleasure had always been present. Certainly even the more socially acceptable experience of feeling more intensely physical in team sports could hardly fail to make that same intensified experience available to individuals. Self-discipline as a frame of mind could hardly keep self-discovery outside the walls.[74]

Consider this summary of the continuing evolution of experience in the 20's and 30's:

In the first few decades of the twentieth century, the pursuit of enjoyment and the conscious quest for personal satisfaction were becoming legitimate goals in their own right. It was as if fun and personal gratification themselves were socially 'useful,' perhaps as individual efforts to construct the 'good society' and to fulfill the pursuit of public happiness by attaining it one person at a time. And by the 1930's, it was to become a virtual duty to 'have fun' and 'enjoy yourself.' Having fun meant using your body as a vehicle of gratification and pleasure. It meant caring less about personal health than about personal amusement. And it displaced the focus on national health and well-being as a purpose [so clearly articulated in Walker's article on the World Fairs] for an individual's pursuit of fitness and athletic accomplishment with a new turn toward health, fitness, and sportive engagement as their own reward. In decades past, virtue was the reward of one's disciplining athletic pursuits, but by the 1920's and 1930's, the athletic quest and the cultivation of the body were themselves increasingly taken as intrinsically virtuous. Personal fulfillment took on the air of public virtue.[75]

Not the least among the factors in this change for Americans, of course, was not only winning *the* war but winning *a* war, and the resulting combination of righteousness and just reward: "I deserve this for our or my sacrifices. It was our bodies which survived and were superior in this blood ritual of men. They are worthy of honor and the pleasures of victory." Winning WW I after the Civil War might well have been experienced in much the same manner as we experienced winning WW II after the deep uncertainties and struggle of the Depression, or as winning the Gulf War after the national contortions over Vietnam.

At the same time it should be recognized that the social results of a war won are not always universally seen as positive. Shaking loose the social and cultural harness in the confidence and euphoria of winning was in some ways as disturbing to the older generation as it was exhilarating to the younger. One generation cedes its ways to the next only grudgingly, if at all, despite what the following generation might accomplish. I would even assert that cultural values require at least three generations to truly evolve to something definably new or broadly experienced. I say this only to reiterate the non-linear evolution of attitudes in any one period and to suggest that sport too was a phenomenon which was becoming much more complex; or at least its inherent complexity was becoming more public, for both individual Americans and the community. The belief remained that athletic performance, even when its rewards included personal pleasure, was primarily validated as a demonstration of moral and social values, what is good for us, whether the values in question were old or new.

By beginning this historical review with Johnson's painting, *The Old Stagecoach,* I was suggesting that art, and the arts, provide reliable comment on the period in which they appear. Among the distinctly new artistic aspects in the interwar period from 1920-1940 was the resurgence of dance, both in ballet and in the advent of modern dance. Perhaps physical expression in America could thrive more easily in the realm of the aesthetic or artistic because there at least people had always expected and granted unusual freedoms.

To be sure, a stage might have been provided. But that it was indeed a stage had a way of keeping new experiences of the body in a somewhat antiseptic environment, as we will see. The stage, just as the field, even though it is the essence of play, still presumes a strict limiting structure and very few actors, dancers, players, heroes. Their movements remain at a distance, beyond the masses orderly seated, spectators only, not participants except in the vicarious sense. The romance of a performance is witnessed rather than experienced directly or spontaneously. The body still remained spectator more than participant. The body seen as a source of experience and insight in itself remained in harness to the body seen as the proper servant of other, more noble ideals and values.

Dance in particular, however, showed itself to be especially articulate in overcoming these conflicts. Jamake Highwater describes how "Modern dancers ... do not simply perform the movements of the choreographer — they become the movements."[76] Rudolf Arnheim had given that distinction an earlier phrase: "The dancer does not act upon the world, but behaves in it."[77] The dancer simply enters the tension as natural to life and movement and thus may exemplify the manner of release from the dualism of mind and body which so strangles Western culture.

> Twentieth century people are products of their gradual withdrawal from an awareness of nature and their place in it. They believe that nature serves them and that divine intention makes them the dominant being of the world.[78]

No one was more visionary in resolving this notion of culture as conflict than Isadora Duncan. By 1905 she had rejected the idea of ballet as art in the service of ideas, norms, or wealth. Dance was not to be an exercise in facile ceremony or entertaining decoration. "Instead, Duncan envisioned dance as a personal ritual capable of supporting both ideas and feelings" in the dancer.[79]

The most fundamental source for her convictions was her physiological comprehension of dancing:

> Duncan was concerned with the inner, kinetic motivation of dancing, the motor intelligence that provided the dancer with an articulate body. She envisioned motion as an activity which commenced in the solar plexus and then undulated muscularly into the rest of the body. Duncan's inclination to talk about 'the science of movement' was entirely new.[80]

It is clear to me that such ideas make dance much more the true ancestor to modern performance sport than the science of sports mechanics itself. Modern biomechanics has just barely caught up in the last ten years. And the institutions of education have not made physiological comprehension of movement or notions of the body's motor intelligence the basis for athletic performance. Certainly in the 1920's the broad American public would hardly have connected with Duncan's performances — dancers were as rare and distant as other stage performers. Nor would it have been significantly influenced by the esoteric nature of her ideas.

Another of the ancestors of modern performance sport also worked outside the mainstream and within the spirit of tolerance and curiosity which so characterized the avantgarde culture of the 20's and 30's. Elton Mayo and L.J. Henderson established the Fatigue Laboratory in the basement of the Harvard Business School in 1927. For the first time researchers would undertake a "competent investigation of the physiological changes induced in the human organism by the conditions of its daily work."[81] As with Duncan in dance, here the body would finally begin to receive its due consideration, free of subordination to religious, social, or economic norms.

Neither the physiology of dance nor of industrial production would ever penetrate the minds of educators in America's public schools, where the main populace was institutionalized. It is much more the fact that precisely in our schools was where the older generation had the most powerful hold over the new and younger and could chose what values were thought best for them. Schools were not considered the place for such things as tolerance and curiosity. The norm would derive from the conviction and wish that things would stay the same as when the parent was a child, or as the educator sought to guide and protect the young from the forever incipient chaos of life and body.

Whatever was happening in the minds and bodies of the American artistic or social avantgarde, therefore, the children in the 20's and 30's were still not far removed from the values of Teddy and his post Civil War generation. Storybook characters like Dick Merriwell had appeared serialized in a legion of magazines. "Dick Merriwell's Determination or In the Game to Do or Die," or "Dick Merriwell Up Against It" portray epic moments of character in football games in *Tip Top Weekly: An Ideal Publication for American Youth*. On the back of each magazine Frank Merriwell's *Book of Athletic Development* is advertised as containing "directions for a thorough course of Athletic [sic] training, which, if followed faithfully, cannot fail to aid all young men of the present day."[82] Drawings of three young men featuring muscular biceps and chests suggest the promise of success. This is 1901.

The themes and tone had not changed much by the 20's and 30's, when a never ending flow of books appeared for young people, all with specific edifying purpose. In one example, *Down the Ice* by Harold M. Sherman,[83] a series of short stories set forth the rituals of sports combat still trusted and well-loved. In "The Ski Battle," for example, a young Georgia boy comes to private school in the North, experiences both the snow and the derision of his classmates, quietly perseveres with the ski jumping coach until, to the amazement of all, of course, he defeats the school champion. This is 1937.

The power of identifying with stage performer, actor, or sports hero could hardly avoid planting the seeds of individual impulse in the spectator. It is even reasonable to consider that the fervor of a young boy reading about ski jumping might well lead him to a sense of possibility for himself quite beyond any socially redeeming value intended by the story.

In America those with progressive attitudes toward such an individualization of physical experience in these early decades of the century found an ally in the theater and, even more profoundly, in the movies. Physical expression, even abandon, could enjoy the protective cloak of artistic grace, both a socially redeeming intent and a freedom in aesthetic experience. Models from theater and movies, every bit as lithe and sensuous, even partly naked, as the art deco standards of the day allowed and exalted, opened a new door through which to value physical culture, from nubile sculpture to the animal litheness of hood ornaments to the muscular grace of automobiles.

One need only think of a flamboyant Douglas Fairbanks, or Johnny Weissmuller's innocent, primitive, naked, and above all virtuous Tarzan, or even the utterly graceful athleticism of Fred Astaire, to comprehend the new possibilities presented to the physical side of Americans' experience. The mass presentation of these new models of refined physical movement as socially positive action, particularly in movies (most obvious before sound — body movements, gestures become articulate communication) made the change all the more pervasive. Movie stars quickly became icons in their own right and were admired specifically for their physical capabilities.

Weissmuller, of course, Olympic swimmer and Tarzan, links ideal sport with film and celebrity entertainment. A golden age of athletic achievement stirred a frenzy of enthusiasm for physical performance and an outright adoration of the body itself. "The rush to sport showed a positive embrace of something quite new as a pivotal element in society — the unabashed love of the human body and the quest to bring it to its highest fulfillment as an act of personal and social joy."[84]

Movies in particular moved popular celebrity culture into a vastly more influential position within American culture in general. To be sure, it was also more superficial; but paradoxically the less serious, entertainment aspects of this culture made it possible for play and sport activities to become more acceptable for their own inherent value, without any further justification than that they made one feel good, more energetic, inspired, and competent. Douglas ("Dougie") Fairbanks was the model of the day, Teddy Roosevelt reincarnated, albeit in somewhat facile rendering. Where Teddy rode astraddle the globe, Fairbanks posed at a lunch of prickly pear cactus. The message is similar: Take on the elements, all of them, with zest and confidence (key words in Teddy's catechism). Even Teddy's imperious didacticism breathes in Fairbank's airy prose.

> Health is synonymous with action. The healthy man does things, the unhealthy man hesitates. And when we get ready to act we will act with the air of a conqueror. We must supply from our own store our atmosphere of confidence in order to win confidence. The successful man is the one who knows he is right and makes us realize it.[85]

The spirit dominates, natural and ever-smiling, as any of Fairbank's films, however amusing today, would demonstrate. In *The Lamb* he set an early example of things to come. "He let a rattlesnake crawl over him, tackled a mountain lion, jiu-jitsued a bunch of Yaqui Indians until they bellowed, and operated a machine gun."[86] If you needed to heal up a few days from such adventures, Fairbanks recommended reading as a means of "keeping in touch with the big visions."[87] Having a library meant Shakespeare, Emerson, and Teddy Roosevelt, in that order, followed by Sir Walter Scott and James Fenimore Cooper.

Following one step forward in the evolution of this complex and varied period in American culture there will be those forces which pull back, or nudge to the side. The new freedom was contained in two ways: First, the theater was a powerful forum of expression, but it was also essentially comfortably removed from everyday real life. The individualism in such expression was communicated through roles played rather than life actually lived. Character remained separate from person, therefore, and the power of the person was transformed into celebrity.[88] And secondly, the possibility of identifying personally with the enlarged role the movie star plays remains implicitly cancelled by the distance the celebrity remains from the population at large. Admiring is one thing, being or doing is another.

Thus it fell to neither the leaders of American education, so ostensibly committed to democratic social goals, nor to the fine arts nor to industry to provide models of personal physical experience, but rather to sports heroes and movie stars. They were most universally available in the country and all the more easy to accept because they were socially and politically neutral. Neutrality above all soothed middle-class ambivalence towards physical culture, physical work, physical performance, physical expression, in short, to the body. On the one hand, models like Johnny Weissmuller and Douglas Fairbanks were free of the anti-individualist forces of industry, church, or education, with their institutionalized grip on younger people. On the other hand, Tarzan was fantasy, Babe Ruth a hero, the objects of imagination and worship, even motivation, but hardly functional models of real life engagement for ordinary people.[89]

It must be observed, in fact, that such celebrities were almost totally detached from any challenge, even implied, to the existing social order. Like actors, athletes were seen in their "theater of play" and its unthreatening variety of assigned and ephemeral roles. They provided relief from social and class tensions, therefore, rather than insights into class or community. And outside the more complex and demanding process of education, they could function more freely in determining mass taste and values through simple entertainment. Perhaps the ritualistic character of boxing (the most popular American sport before baseball) demonstrates most clearly the mixture of gladiator and God invested in the sports character, in which the winner might then be vested with moral superiority, or at least whose struggle might be cathartic for the viewer — The Great White Hope or the Brown Bomber. The vicarious experience of physical, sensual violence inherent in these contests should not go unnoticed, nor the repression which was sublimated in the spectator in the process.

Such popular culture, however apparently facile, had complex power. It both stimulated interest in sports, and it divided the rare hero from the masses of spectators. For the latter it was ritual and theater, not sport alone. That disconnecting distance from personal physical fulfillment is the negative side. The spectrum of experience might have Douglas Fairbanks's *Laugh and Live* (1917) at one end and T.S.Eliot's *Wasteland* (1922) on the other, or F. Scott Fitzgerald's *All the Sad Young Men* (1926). Fairbanks' notion that a simple smile will overcome any discrepancy between the banana peel of life and the Great Beyond seems simply silly. Nevertheless, his heroic popularity produced a major stimulus to physical fitness and athletics. He also expressed a view of efficiency through physical fitness which would in fact be validated later by the research at the Harvard Business School's Fatigue Laboratory in the few years following its establishment in 1927.

Perhaps Ernest Hemingway best portrays the vastly complex way in which the new freedoms in physical experience contained both welcome expressive energy and deeply discomforting repression in America. Hemingway published *The Sun Also Rises* in 1927. Though set in France and Spain, the characters are American and British. One is a repressed, woman-dominated ex-collegiate boxer looking for friends and female conquests, one is an over-sexed, nurturing English woman, another an alcoholic aristocrat gone broke, two are reporters, one rendered impotent by a war wound. Nothing could expose more completely the struggles and ambivalence of that generation to experience of the body. The centerpiece of their gathering are the bull-fights, in which the bullfighter transforms violence into dance and a ritual which combines love, noble combat, and blood-letting. A mixture of sexual sublimation and emotional catharsis results in the viewers. Fascination, suffering, athletic refinement, beauty, and insight all become ingredients of a finer passion, *aficion.* The bullfighter, of course, is the god figure, and the only truly attractive character; but he is too fine a ritual treasure, and he must be given up. The ideal is seen, even touched, but the experience remains apart.

Compared to Hemingway's matador, the gleam surrounding Tarzan, the noble savage, was thin indeed, though for its superficiality all the more approachable. Add this quality of comic book myth to the sweat and blood of boxing, and the attractions are obvious: a simple social and psychological vent for the experience of struggle and conflict in both daily experience and values, and particularly in the rosy balm of pure fantasy.

It had always been the case in America that this purified, otherworldly realm of sports heroes, perfect beyond general knowledge or experience, was what in fact made them particularly attractive. They are not attractive because they are accessible but precisely because they are not. For whatever powerful effect they might have on cultural values, they offered a comfortably antiseptic model in terms of social challenge. They were, after all, perfect gentlemen, leopard skin loincloth aside. It is interesting to note how these model heroes of the 20th century actually follow in Teddy Roosevelt's footsteps. Intent upon down-playing his aristocratic origins, he surrounded himself with actors, cowboys, and sports heroes at White House occasions as he consciously worked his own legendary stature as a middle class Greystoke (the proto-Tarzan) in his many wilderness and jungle exploits. The difference is that his autobiography is replete with the details of challenges, the overpowering of nature and beast. Notions of respect and acceptance of Nature's governance do not appear as they do with the later Tarzan, Lord of the Jungle, whatever violence or jungle cries it might have cost him, the aristocrat savage, perhaps even a white Indian.

This absence of social challenge — a hero just does not do that — in fact was not totally neutral. It actually facilitated submission to that very social order and left the field in predictably noble arrangement, even if it was the jungle.[90] That status quo implied Paradise and innocence defended, a belief which was the ultimate palliative for any social or moral tension. Wide unquestioning acceptance was easy for that very reason, and not at a serious enough level to have compelling influence on educational philosophy. Popular culture was considered too rude, like the body itself, for that.

It was actually a positive sign that the particular evolution of sports culture was neither the work of the moralistic middle class, nor corporate lions, nor even individual physical culturists like Bernard McFadden in the early 20's. As isolated a figure to physical culture as Isadora Duncan to classical dance in the 1890's, McFadden had succeeded in creating something of a culture of his own with his magazine, *Physical Culture,* by the more liberal 20's. Sports did begin to borrow a constraining command structure from the scientific and corporate realms, but now it did so with its own stronger self-informing sense of identity, outside the mainstream of education and society. Individual physical culture was maturing into more institutional practice.

> The accommodations undertaken to accept the body — its sensuality and sexuality, its beauties, and its physical accomplishments — gave conscious support to the principles of hierarchy and authority. To rely on coaches, trainers, nutritionists, and others was to submit oneself to the control of experts, deferring to their judgment.[91]

It is only fair to recognize that this particular deference to authority at least was an appropriate source of interest and support. To be sure, the science of the body quickly merged with the newer science of sport itself to create its own particular doctrinaire pathways to the highest goals. But here at least the body was being represented on its own physical terms, was finally receiving its own sort of "government." The strengthened sense of identity in sport itself is indicative both of the advent of sports physiology and its determination to be a science on its own terms rather than a chattel of social norms of status or contemporary education theory. That tension between the two views of sport in the 20's was vividly portrayed in the movie, *Chariots of Fire* (1980). One athlete runs for his religion, another, an aristocrat, trains casually by practicing hurdles set up on his expansive lawn and made precarious with glasses filled with champagne, while the lower class Abraham hires an Italian trainer and is roundly reproved for it by indignant officials.

By the 1920's, therefore, new attitudes did make it possible to accept joy and enthusiasm in sport, rather than self-denial and physical suffering. It is perhaps symptomatic of the restraint still present in the period that physical culturists shared the preference for a smooth, lithe Tarzan of Weissmuller in a way which contrasts starkly with the rippling bulk of a Charles Atlas. Atlas, born in 1903, was a weakling in his youth, and his manner of overcoming it closely matched Theodore Roosevelt's experience.[92] Following McFadden's program he ultimately won McFadden's "World's Most Beautiful Man" contest in 1921 and set the stage for our contemporary body builders. Even more obvious is the manner in which Weissmuller's grace and athletic prowess also contrasts with the exaggerated, even caricatured form, the rude violence and destruction of Arnold Schwarzenegger's popular movie roles in the 1980's and 90's.

Fairbanks stated the preference clearly:

> Physical exercise is something which can be carried to extremes. We can go at work so intensely that we become muscle-bound and develop some structural enlargements that we do not need. This happens very often among athletes. The ordinary man should fight shy of such plans. Superfluous strength is only for those who have need of it. What we really want is strength enough to carry us through our daily rounds with comfort and a feeling of efficiency.[93]

There are indeed elements of a serious physical culture here, even if one still senses a note of restraint, a warning against excess. Boundless enthusiasm for sports and physical activity is valued in its own right, and that is new. "We must recognize the wants, the needs of the physical system and see they are supplied." In 1917 Fairbanks is speaking in his usual categorical manner, and points again to Teddy Roosevelt as the Olympian example. But he does emphasize mental and bodily morale rather than morality, and thus indicates a shift from external imperatives to secular and personal interests. Instead of being physically active in sport because it is right, it is right simply to be physically fit, active in sports, healthy.

Johnny Weissmuller's natural creature image of the 1920's and 30's carried this attitude a step further by rejecting pain, that most elevating of Calvinist tonics, as the essential component of gain. In doing so he helped realign Americans' view of how divine promise was to be realized and fostered our love affair with the idea of God-given talent as being the source of the particular promise we will achieve, the manifest destiny of the American body in all its myth and romance.

It is odd how Americans warmed to this fundamentally conservative, aristocratic view of physical and spiritual capabilities: we are beautiful by virtue of what we have inherited, not by what we might make of ourselves. The general mass of people seemed only too ready to ignore the most salient feature of that romance: although he does extraordinary deeds, and we feel gratefully vicariously rescued, the hero remains both singular and a fantasy, inspiring but not real, a doll wearing a simple moral label of virtue.

The shadow side of movie heroes thus appears: entertainment which actually anesthetizes the viewer from any sort of serious reflection on real life. As an aesthetic expression of his time Weismuller might be said to relate to Schwarzenegger as Fred Astaire to John Travolta. The more modern types may originate more surely from the working classes, but none of them would inform a viewer in any serious way about the real lives of an athlete like Jim Thorpe, Tommy Smith, or Butch Reynolds. Where there is a clear evolution of attitudes in this comparison, it is toward sexuality. In Schwarzenegger and Travolta it squirms, barely contained, just beneath the surface of their movements; in Weissmuller and Astaire in the 30's it remains totally sublimated. The body remains an object of fantasy and aesthetic delight but also a budding source of personal physical experience.

Whether in sports or dance or the movies, therefore, by the 1920's the body was finding new locations of authority. American personal experience and development began to include the notion of physical movement and sport not just as the satisfaction of discipline but the pleasure in release. Mrozek cites the contemporary psychologist, Stanley Hall, who "exhibited a devotion to principle and strenuous living that reflected the older value structure, but he assumed that human instincts were essentially positive, requiring release and development — a clear anticipation of the twentieth century's enormous emphasis on personality and 'getting along.'"[94] This emphasis on personality (psychology, psychoanalysis, Freud, Adler, Jung and others) was able to link getting along with letting go.

The notions of release, of positive abandon and letting go clearly redefined the power of both the individual and the body for Americans. Fear of that tilt toward chaos was especially acute in two groups, the cultural elite and the middle class, for different reasons.

First, the cultural elite worried: "such people did not trust the unguided choice of the common, working class American. Without the promptings of the experts and the elitists, the ordinary mass of Americans might degenerate into a mere mob, feeding its whims and drives without discrimination."[95]

This reminds again of Teddy Roosevelt's fear of "a riot of lawless business individualism which would be quite as destructive to real civilization as the lawless military individualism of the Dark Ages."[96] His misgivings about the totally individual individual remained powerfully engrained in the American sensibility. The fear of chaos, of the loss of the Union and the promise of America itself were irrevocably bound together with anxiety over what might happen if the physical self were truly released. For the broad public, for which public education was the stabilizing institution, the flesh expressed in abandon was tantamount to abandoning social order and productivity, to consorting with the powers of evil and destruction themselves. If this attitude seems extreme, it is helpful to remember that in the interwar years (1920-40) we were still few enough generations removed from the Civil War for its horrors to be still vivid, particularly among fathers and grandfathers.

Though the pleasures and uses of letting go were easily established, therefore, guidance was reapplied just as quickly. After WW I, Army authorities supported sports activities, even a "Military Olympics," as a way of keeping troops occupied with things they simply enjoyed doing. The criterion became less health and toughness of soldiers than in simply defusing rebellion out of boredom and pent up energy.[97] Sexual energy was, of course, a prime ingredient of this overfull reservoir. Sport became an exercise in directed freedom, that euphemism for behavior control which still in the year 2000 remains the cornerstone of sports philosophy in education. Directed freedom also makes a public which feels stable and homogeneous particularly fertile ground for mass-market advertising. This is where education tacitly strikes a deal with the business world.

Second, the middle class also found reason to be fearful, for its love of freedom seemed only matched by its fear of the masses, its love of direction and mission forever tempered by its faith in proceeding only in definable groups. Heroes were admired not just for their lofty (aristocratic) standards but just as specifically because achieving those standards might remain by no means available to all those "below". Thus the celebrity and "theater" aspect of the hero. The aesthetic halo of the artist elevates him above the lower class, sub-cultural "performer". Of course that lower class performer would ultimately move the stage virtually into the audience, create jazz and freely expressive forms of dance. The American was learning to enjoy not being in harness, not so separate from himself. There seemed to be something of the gladiator and slave which was simply going to come out.

The 30's, with an explosion of athletic accomplishments, came to be known as the "Golden Age." The turn of interest and value to the individual self, to perfect body — not just creating it but releasing it from within — was a significant step in the evolution of physical consciousness. This development was in no small measure facilitated through experts and expertise, as well as the aesthetic of the 20's and 30's, At a time of pervasive corporate values, in which the "democracy of teamwork" never quite masked the dehumanizing effects of workplace homogenization, the body became both a release and the subject of outright adoration, either in participatory sport or in theatrical sublimation with sports heroes. We think of Weissmuller not as Tarzan but as Olympic champion; newsreel after newsreel at the Saturday matinee featured Jessie Owens, Babe Didrickson Zaharias, Buster Crabbe, and of course the whole pantheon of baseball greats.

Even where new ideas were simply tolerated, that at least provided mental space for physical culturists to pursue a perfecting way of individual life - physical, sensual, emotional. There was enough freedom from the pressure of external mores not only to be healthy but, with the breathing room, to feel more healthy. The athlete could discover himself for a time, so to speak, out of harm's way, and with the blessing of being included in a positive aesthetic of the body, even in the exaltation of the lonely fighter or runner modeled for him in either sports figures or movie stars.[98]

The potential importance in America of such individual feeling for energy and motivation was not lost on either the social or the business world. Being good at recognizing trends is the first step toward learning how to manipulate them for marketing aims. Trend receptivity itself had long been supported by the notion of directed freedom. And almost anything good for business has had a way of finding a way into social, if not religious, imperatives. Moves toward affirmation of individual confidence and self-reliance espoused by Norman Vincent Peale and Dale Carnegie, however, did much to relieve the guilt traditionally attendant to any non-utilitarian pursuits of the body. Self-development of mind and body urged one to take greater charge from within. That step is very significant, even though it is expressed in terms of another public responsibility. It is almost as if instinctively these early preachers of self-improvement realized that an idea would always sell better to Americans with the label of obligation attached to it.[99] Though the stage is the 1930's, therefore, not far behind the curtains seems to lie an earnestness and urgency not much different from the concerns of the post-Civil War generation: humans are perfectible — that is not just possible; that is an American obligation. The difference is that the obligation is centered in the individual rather than in external social codes.

This is perhaps the most fundamentally new and progressive element in the 20's and 30's which is relevant to American athletes:

Rather than being the source of temptation that violated moral precept, the body became much more a vehicle for relationships and a means of gratification — not a matter of fear, but a matter of fact. The physical side of humanity was not a regrettable accident but an essential instrument of identity.[100]

It followed that success might thus also be experienced on a quite strictly personal and physical basis.

This recognition of the physical self as a resource available in a more complex way to the outside world rather than necessarily only to be subdued by that world marks a significant step forward in both respect and interest in the body. It also reflects the research which Harvard Business School was doing after 1927 into the relationships between industrial productivity and physical well-being and whose positive results set off the fitness culture we have known since the 1970's.

In such an atmosphere of diversity, invention, rapid communication, and change, culture itself was becoming the frontier by 1940. That presented new levels of possibility for the individual: jazz and technology, dance and art and sport, each with its geniuses and dizzying array of sham experts and authorities — fads, nostrums, philosophies. With novelty comes curiosity and excitement, but also anxiety and the need to join a definable, reliable stream of common values. This not only reflects the presence of social harness; it demonstrates the personal response to a dramatically more complex culture. The middleness of middle class attitudes becomes more demanding and problematical: how does one find the external imperative to restrain and balance one's original individual impulses? From the point of view of the athlete, however, one can say that he could finally rejoice in the imperatives of his own world. This too was a step forward, as the tales of these legendary athletes, all curiously individual, demonstrated — Ruth and Weissmuller, Red Grange, Owens, DeMar, Nurmi, Babe Didrikson, Glenn Cunnigham.

The power of the group remained telling, however, and continually laid a conservative rein on the individual in America at the same time that it maintained an utterly progressive view of itself as a group. Team and organization reflect the ideals of stability, harmony and government; extraordinary individual performance threatens at least unpredictability (the antithesis of planning) and tension, if not chaos itself. This priority was institutionalized, of course, in public education, where administrative efficiency and citizen-building masqueraded as cognitive and physical development. The paradox of simultaneous conservative and progressive views explains the "mixture of acclaim and hostility faced by those various proponents of physical culture and sport whose love of the body was so ambivalent."[101] Douglas Fairbanks notwithstanding, in America the joy of athletic movement has never been able to totally jettison guilt, and the tension arising from the struggle continues to account for our American urge to say that harder is always better. For Americans simple mortification of the flesh has always been a tempting solution to uncertainty and paradox, not to mention ignorance, particularly for a middle class which had always rowed with religion in one oar, industrial gain in the other.

Nor have the problems inherent in such divergent attitudes ever been really resolved. Long-term individual development has been paid lip service but still never been given the credence of team sports and their alloted seasons of the year. The opportunities, even expectations afforded artists and musicians have yet to be granted athletes in any broad sense.

Mrozek reviews:

> Where late nineteenth century imagery drew on the objectivity of science, the photographs and films of the interwar years abounded with the rich personality of star performers and other celebrities. Where the older iconography extolled discipline, the newer one was rich in action. If the image of decades past drew strongly on the tradition of self-denial, the 'new era' fostered visions of joy.[102]

Where the individual might thrive and express some joy in himself "in character" on stage or esoterically in the arts, as artist or participant in music or dancing, among the masses team was the more conservative standard, particularly as an expression of extended family. In the 20's and 30's, right up to the time before WW II the coach would direct his players as a father figure, a kindly friend to his athletes in the joy of their collective effort. The legendary Knut Rockne rendered teamwork, the ability to cooperate, the winning power of building warm personal relationships into a catechism he later preached for Studebaker in 1928. However benign the notion of fatherhood, however, authority still remained the most salient characteristic of team leadership.

Despite the virtues of teamwork, therefore, the emphasis on group rather than individual hardly disguises some basic American fears. Personal perfection is an inspiring myth, lacking in any of the sense of fatality or tragedy present in most European myth and experience. It is also widely seen in America as a socially destabilizing one. It is one thing for the hero to be selected by authority or elected by the masses, another for him or her to self-select, either into or out of an activity.

That negative side of the authoritarian sports philosophy was tested in the movie *College Coach* (1933). A domineering coach's single-mindedness of purpose is not shared by his star athlete, who is interested in education. How many hundreds of times this scenario has been played out over the years is hard to guess. One such typical scene is remembered by former U.S.Surgeon General, Everett Koop, from his football days at Dartmouth in 1934. Told by his doctor that further shock to his head might cost him his eyesight, and firmly committed to studying medicine, Koop informed the legendary Earl "Red" Blaik that he would have to leave the team. Blaik, who had recently arrived at Dartmouth from West Point, responded, "So, in other words, you're a coward."[103]

Wounds for such coaches and their athletes were but those of a hero, a decent man's reward. Regard for frailty was simply unmanly. That the body might be inherently valuable for itself remained apparently a demeaning consideration, a view still seen all too often today.

Team, and sacrifice for it, mirrors the old worry about upsetting the Union. That worry endures. Witness the outrage over the ultimate protest of Tommy Smith and Lee Evans in Mexico City in 1968. On the other hand, the perfection of power through the accumulation of wealth takes place in a circuitous enough manner to render it somehow antiseptic, unthreatening and permissible. One need not expose the flesh, raise a defiant fist in the air. Nobody is openly injured or publicly defeated. Storming Mount Olympus with physical culture, however, amounts still to disrespect for both the working man and authority, a secular blasphemy in America, and decidedly undemocratic at that. For in doing so one both betrays one's personal origins and sets oneself above the masses. If one presumes to heights at one's own directives, that challenges both order and fundamental principles of humility.

In the latter idea the American middle class simultaneously identified with the upper class' fear of the working class. The middle class had to work hard, but it was bad form to show it. The middle class was always the place where the harness was tightest. The ultimate was to "get along," was to join in defeating, taming the wilderness or jungle, all the while mourning its loss, and rescuing paradise from the tensions profane and unsettling to middle class notions of certainty. Only the common cause could bring true joy.

That all-sobering common cause appeared in the rapid succession of the Depression and World War II. National crises quickly dampen people's enthusiasm, and pocket book, for experiential frontiers, innovative behaviors, out-of-mainstream research like that of Harvard's Fatigue Laboratory. Whenever the Union is threatened, conservative forces soon re-assert themselves. The military model for sports mirrors the dictates of social discipline and industrial productivity which must join hands to render evil defeated; and there will follow a powerful re-assertion of grandfather's notions of physical culture.

## World War II to the Present

If World War I was a war which Americans needed to win in order to confirm their confidence in the Union, WW II was *the* war. And whereas WW I released a culture of joy, enthusiasm, of lush sensuality and graceful physical line and movement, the Golden Age of the Roaring Twenties, WW II was another story altogether. For the children of the Depression and adult soldiers who won WWII the promise of physical and moral high ground had been convincingly attained. The flag was planted, and pain and privation had been both suffered and fused into myth by victory. Pain became the new nectar. Hurt and agony were now the smithies of a youth robust in both body and character, the guarantors of progress and the measure of "informed" physical training. The notion was accepted that the flesh is best toughened by being beaten into shape, as if the body were a damaged fender to start with. For all the joy and triumph of winning the war, the years following in the late 1940's and 50's were a revival time for old Calvinist values.

If ever the Calvinist fiber of American culture had been tested, it was in the Depression. Few men worked at what they chose, or wished. Work took on the definition which would last into the 60's: doing something you don't like to do, and doing it in order to survive. Self-denial once again came to the rescue as the abiding source of human energy and social balance. (By that same definition, working by wish or with pleasure became suspect as not truly worthwhile or productive work.) Victory in WW II deepened and confirmed such convictions. It is not surprising then that in sport as well "Pain was not shown as a mere accident of training but as its very core … sport was life, and life was war."[104]

The problem for American sports culture was not in winning the war, of course, but in applying its codes of soldiering to the science and social setting in which human physical development is optimally achieved. Confusing politics with physiology has created innumerable casualties in sport, and almost no winners. Put another way, soldiering may save your life in battle, but it kills our youth on the tracks and playing fields. In the 1960's Arthur Lydiard, the visionary New Zealand coach, would express this so clearly in mocking the "gain through pain" approach. In training in Tokyo for the 1964 Olympics Bruce Kidd of Canada had come to the track and run 20 times 400 meters in 62 seconds. Swelling with adoration, the Canadian press asked the New Zealander what he thought about that. His reply was, "I'm very pleased about that. He put the last nail in his coffin."[105]

We must admit that a belief in gain through pain is understandable in the euphoria of victory. And there is nothing quite as convincing and comforting as winning a war to sweep away doubts about national social values or destiny, and to reduce nagging ambivalence, to a few comfortably simple denominators. Michael Blowen described it as follows:

> Years ago my father, who spent the war in the Seabees, would tell World War II stories — tales from the South Pacific that emphasized teamwork, camaraderie and the victory of life, liberty and the pursuit of happiness over death, totalitarianism and tyranny. There were romantic allegories with good guys and bad guys and nothing in between.

> For reasons as complicated as the war, it remained for him a time and place where heroes gathered — men who needn't worry about bills, delivering office furniture or collecting tolls on a bridge over the Connecticut River. The war was larger than any of their lives.[106]

Clearly one of victory's chief attractions is that it no longer needs to be relativized by its position within a complicated world. It seems simply natural: first an example is set, then it becomes a right deserved (as was the right to pleasure after WW I), then a social duty and moral rite, finally the announced goal of education. As Vince Lombardi's turn of phrase had it, "Winning is not the main thing; it's the only thing."

Doubt of such a maxim when moral victory has been won in a war becomes heresy, if not treason as well. In more sober moments we know that doubt need not show a weakness, anxiety, or readiness to submit. In the broad perspective over the generations since the Civil War it would be doubt and questioning which had become a prime source of renewed curiosity, ideas, and experience in this country. And as attitudes evolved, the process was never linear, as handy as that might be for our efforts to understand them. The positive and negative shades of doubt would appear both in unpredictable sequence as well as simultaneously, often the difference determined by which generation happened to be speaking. Each new attitude usually represented synthesis rather than categorical change. It is also important to keep in mind that not all segments of any society change attitudes at the same time, or in a similar way. Thus, where adults may change their views, compulsory education could and did keep a more conservative hold of children with its own preferred version of American ideals, its own interpretation of the meaning and lessons of major historical events.

The experience of WW II affirmed two attitudes in America toward the human physique which form a curiously American combination. Where Americans preferred to think of victory in war as a demonstration of individual natural superiority, the attitude towards athletes as superior by virtue of "natural talent" was deepened. Conversely, the imperatives of preparation and training were played down. Because the nation had won, the price in pain was recognized and justifiably exalted. The harnessing of the flesh was re-affirmed. Oddly, power was defined both by the mortification of the flesh and the conspicuousness of that exercise. The battle is clearly more profound in the seeing. Teddy Roosevelt's example is renewed in its combination of derring-do and stern physical regimen. The two attitudes still form the pillars of educational philosophy and athletic morale in the United States today.

By contrast, Weissmuller's Tarzan of the 1930's, with his smooth, understated sensuality, presented a natural, untouched image of the body which rejected pain as the essential component in gain. This image had supported the American attraction for the idea of God-given talent as the source of our promised achievements. I have noted how the romance in this attitude depends upon the hero being singular and a harmless fantasy, a doll wearing a simple moral label. Winning the war, however, suggested that the fantasy of being divinely talented was real, the fantasy of herodom truly powerful, and the simple moral label apt.

In the United States the "natural talent" attitude remains very much alive today in an age of would-be over-achievers for whom native brain and body power defines paths of education as well as social and professional success. In American sports culture it is the "natural athlete" who need not train so hard. Perhaps, it is reasoned, he should not, gifted as he is; it might be like painting a diamond. Certainly this notion pleases the elite and genteel, and those who would imitate them, providing the perfect combination of both ground for winning and an excuse for falling short. If I did not do well, it was because I was not serious about it. And then, working at it was beneath me (it's only sport), too lower class. If I do well, it was no great effort for one divinely blessed. (cf. Ch. 3, "Affirming the Flesh")

Heroes themselves have a way of forgetting the "blue collar" sources of success, the hours and hours of hard work they put in training, often quietly and alone, and prefer to emphasize, with requisite and appealing modesty, how Fortune has smiled on them. Thus, they affirm their gift, their godliness. Teddy Roosevelt is again the curiously American example, for he took pains to forget his social blessings as an aristocrat and to deify the middle class values of talent and mobility towards success (perfection) through competition with self and thence with all. Mortifying the flesh prepares oneself to conquer all. Personal ruggedness borne of strenuous challenge is godly. Of such ideals Teddy remained the prophet. He made sure to romanticize his middle class talent, his humble herodom. He ignored the pain in pain in order to make it seem simply part of the daily routine, of a normal life. In doing so he re-established pain itself as the ultimate method of success. The romantic delusion that pain is not really pain but the transcendent sacrifice of self on the way to the greater good is essential to the American belief in its divine promise.

Extremes borne of this delusion are close at hand. All too often young athletes labeled "talented" become the focus of parents', coaches' and schools' hopes and are then overchallenged: the greater the pain, the greater the hero-to-be. He or she is then squandered under the guise of that very "promise" which stays with us Americans forever, so particularly fired by the middle class imperative of vertical mobility.

The victorious American athlete may also soon believe himself to be the muscle culture, in both the literal and figurative sense. The elite young body is "helped" out of its initial weakness (i.e. imperfection, like Teddy or Charles Atlas,) and blown up like a balloon with premature weight training and body-building. The imperative to attain "bigness" floods every adolescent boy's consciousness, with early esteem and social acceptance the rewards. We might again compare the different attitudes: one seeks to join and release natural physical elements, the other to challenge and subdue them. Weissmuller compares to Atlas and Schwarzenegger as Astaire to Travolta, grace to muscle.

In the post-WW II period the ethos of sport was enticingly simple: we can and should win: it is our American destiny. We must win at sports like we won at war. And this attitude lives on powerfully in this country, regardless of whether we listen more to father or grandfather. It is an endorsement of the militaristic approach: winning is patriotic duty. Therefore, discipline the body, toughen it, beat it into shape, shape its behavior through training.

Broader implications follow. A nation blessed with victory in war has elevated herodom and victory to both a personal and civic imperative. Winning on such simple and compellingly moral terms ironically then requires that the "war" go on. Nothing less is worthy of the memory of "the boys over there." This means both uniform and uniforms, the "boys in blue" and the local team. If there is no war, we play our opponents into the role of enemy, our sporting bodies into battle hardware. We seem to miss the point that this does not raise sport to the significance of real war but rather distorts competition and athletic performance, not to mention war itself, into adolescent role playing. The theater of war becomes plain theater. Simplistic notions of patriotism become more important than informed interest and development of individual physical performance. At this point, as the Dutch cultural historian Johan Huizinga put it, sport and play have receded to a state of "adolescent puerilism."[107]

Questioning or relativizing the importance of victory at every appearance has always been a major problem for Americans. It seems we have forever confused victory with success, and anybody's victory with America's success. Patriotism blinds as often as it informs when it comes to sport. It tends to make competition the only mode of improvement and winning the only indicator of successful preparation.

The need to win every event, of course, is to assume that finding the right answer, winning, is the same thing as understanding the problem. Winning explains and validates retroactively any process which precedes it. It is an error, of course, which over and over produces experts of information with little knowledge about the diverse and long-term nature of physiological development or athletic performance. The limitations of experts nevertheless too often establish the pretense to authority and abet the confusion of authority with actual knowledge. Those in positions of administrative power thence give orders, assuming those orders contain the requisite wisdom. Patient collaboration is simply too slow. The military model is present again.

Perhaps our trust in answers rather than patient, disciplined solutions is part of our American cultural heritage of wholesale movement, bustle, change, of incessant transformation and innovation, all of which make patience virtually a sin. Too patiently dwelling upon process itself threatens anarchy. Perhaps that is inherent in the nature of our 20th century, with its explosive technological innovations, kaleidoscopic cultural diversity, all bent upon accelerating somewhere. This has not changed since 1900, the turn of the last century. Perhaps it is our way of dealing with the Christian doubts which inevitably accompany each further discovery about the body, the physical self. Yet WW II should have made us see most clearly that winning at all costs can quickly become fatal. That war, any war, has precious little to do with the survival and healthy development of young bodies.

What has happened to the Golden Age of sport of the 20's and 30's, with its values of individual expression, self-fulfillment, performance as a value in itself? Certainly the Depression made success seem a frail notion, and thus in the 1930's victory became less important than the process of strengthening the identity of individuals on a team or in a club.[108] In America at that time the focus of interest had finally discovered the importance of the person whose body was involved. "It was the individual whose needs and desires set the standard of what made activities worthwhile."[109]

But the balance between individual and group needs was maintained in a particularly American way. As Donald Mrozek has described it, "The final belief that what must be good for the individual must benefit society seems the ultimate in presumptuousness, but it is the integral premise of twentieth century sport."[110] The powerful American paradox remains in place: sport links personal joy with social duty. "Mastery of one's body, then, allowed a curious mastery of one's self and one's place in society."[111] In other words, individual performance was not to be understood so much as a matter of free choices but rather of requisite decision, not so much a matter of personal discovery and expression as mastery of self according to accepted norm.

Beneath the surface of new freedoms and change in the 20's and 30's, the tradition of subordinating the body to other social and religious values never really faltered much. Everett Koop's experience played on, unquestioned in the 1940's and after. The powers discovered in free physical development were always quickly co-opted by moral and social aims. In 1939 Johnny Burns boxed one more time to save the farm in the movie, *They Made Me a Criminal*. The martyrdom of body to idea remained. It is interesting to reflect how Johnny Burns prefigures the lower class heroism of Rocky Balboa, and how that heroism is quickly exploited as a political theme in *Rocky II,* a truly gross romance of a bipolar struggle of flags, an understandable if hapless propagandistic remnant of the Cold War years. The progression from *Rocky* to *Rocky II* further demonstrates how quickly "mastery of self" can become "elevated" to moral or political soldiering for the superior society.

The 1920's and 30's idea of individual self-discovery and self-fulfillment through health and sport did not return to the American consciousness really until the 1960's, after the long sleep through the euphoria and conceits of victory in WWII, and through the reign of the soldier athlete. Three groups which had traditionally been most conservative and culture-bound in this process — educators, physiologists and the medical profession itself — resurface in their responses to the evolution of modern physiology. Theory abounded in the mid- to late 60's from American's preference for laboratory experiment, but there were still very few coaches and doctors in the U.S. who persisted in their research of applied training science in the field. Among the foremost internationally was Arthur Lydiard of New Zealand, who began his seminal experiments with training right after the war and who can be considered the legitimate father of modern endurance training. His training theories produced gold medals in Tokyo in 1964. Invited to visit Finland with his ideas in 1968, and reinvited after stormy dissension over them had sent him home, his methods were critical to Finland's gold medals in the Munich Olympics in 1972: Lasse Viren's in 5000 meters and 10,000 meters and Pekka Vasalla's in 1500 meters.

In those same Olympics American Frank Shorter won the marathon. In the early 60's Shorter was in high school, watching Bob Schull and Billy Mills win 3000 and 10,000 in Tokyo. A new Golden Age of sport in this country? What was happening? It is not by coincidence perhaps that it was the age of the flower people as well, a time of openness and free critique of our deepest cultural values. It was also a time which saw renewed research into the effects of physical stress on workplace performance at Harvard Business School. Clearly a new physical culture and the fitness boom had begun.

In the 1960's and 70's (during which time Lydiard made a number of visits to the U.S.) a few leading American coaches had also been listening to another international prophet of modern training, the German, Dr. Ernst Van Aaken, by then in his 70's. His rule of 20:1 — the relation of distance work to speed in training — is still valid today.

But even into the 1980's most physiologists and MD's in America still clung to the essentially romantic and Calvinist notion that the body could (because it should) adapt to any work load, and level of exercise, any physical challenge. Harder was still better, the only really trustworthy way to improve performance. (In Chapter 10 I give extended examples of this traditional training culture in examining the history of U.S. ski science.) The mechanical principles of industry coupled with the old Calvinist dicta on the rudeness of the flesh, stronger yet following the necessary regimentation and sacrifices of WW II, still held the floor in our American schools and universities, even when physiology and the all too few informed coaches were telling us differently.

Modern professional sport provides examples of a change in focus and therein expresses the modern connection between individual health fitness and business productivity. It is not mere circumstance that *The Harvard Business Review* would interview Bill Walsh, San Fransisco 49ers coach in the 80's and later coach at Stanford.

Walsh embodies in many regards the latest point in the evolution of attitudes to toward sport. He refines the notion of victory by working towards a winning program over the years rather than the necessity of victory in every game. He speaks of informed, patient preparation and the development of each individual's potential over time, his "arc of utility." Winning will be the result of a complex set of talents, efforts, and processes, not the cause of success produced by regimentation or simple moral fervor. He balances business values and player development, professional entertainment with personal growth of the athlete.[111]

Today any fifteen minutes in front of a television set will re-affirm how powerfully notions of personal fulfillment through sport govern contemporary American advertising. "With it" ads promoting health, beer or automobiles are sold with healthy bodies, not much different from the past when roller bearings were sold with a baseball player.

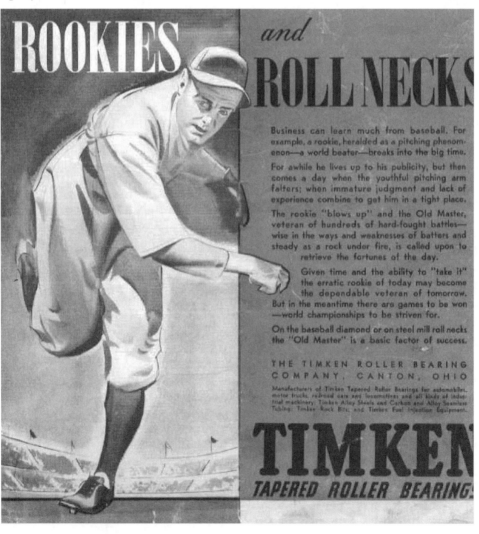

Still, with the new ads, the hero is finally presented as an everyday possibility for the average citizen. Marketing in the meantime, well-understanding the fundamental urge of the middle class to rise, has found its greatest power of persuasion by attaching elitist qualities to products. It is worth noting in this regard that marketing, whatever its goals, has had a positive effect on the public interest in sport by making physical activity itself the source of personal and social good rather making social good the rationale for sport.

This model, according to which personal physical development *precedes* social good rather than responds to its call, still remains conspicuously absent in primary and secondary education. The conservative forces which direct education have seldom considered youth worthy of adult wisdom and practice, righteous protestations to the contrary notwithstanding. Americans have forever idealized youth in order to claim youth's promise, but have chastened youth in practice and pedagogy in order to harness the profane flesh and fend off incipient anarchy.

The single most important factor in allowing the physical self to come into its own, on its own terms, is physiology. It is the link between ideals and the powers of the flesh and is essential for human physical performance of any kind. Exercise physiology has taken strong root in America really only since WW II. Sports physiology changed not only our practice of physical and sports development, it changed our attitudes toward the body, however slowly. It some ways it took the war to accomplish those changes. Above all, a huge number of war wounded provided the laboratory for research into various rehabilitation protocols which would soon become the basis of modern strength training for athletes. What went into physical medicine as clinical rehabilitation was quickly recognized for its athletic performance enhancing potential.

Physiology changed the culture of sport in America in ways which, subtle at first and then more compelling, made us uneasy and cling to older notions for a time. Physiological insights not only take us out of the constraints of social class but beyond all conventional notions of authority. In this its hearkens back in a curious and nostalgic way to the interest in sports and health science in the gymnastics era of the late 1800's. Physiology goes beyond the physical culturist and his external rationales and fancies. Deference to authority thus becomes deference to one's own fundamental phyiological processes, with or without the "expert," be he MD or coach. Nothing else makes sense.

Nevertheless, the two most powerful strains in American sports education persist: the militaristic and the Calvinist, the powerful and the righteous in "muscular Christianity." They match well and simply, even when fundamentally misinformed about the internal processes of the body. Gain through pain is a credo common to both. The goals are also similar: mortifying the flesh for the moral liberation of the spirit. The serenity of the body-politic craves such chastening, as does the requisite calm of "character." As Teddy had said, "With soul of flame and temper of steel we must act as our coolest judgment bids us."[112]

We judge youth to be the ideal and the beautiful, but its flesh in real life is to be feared and controlled. And there we are stuck with Theodore Roosevelt, in adoration yet of his robust physical stature, of competition as the basic mode of human affairs, of the joy in conspicuous challenge of self, wilderness, or enemy. They are basically all the same object. His banner still waves: "Charge the hill!" And he leads on, the middle class ghost Rough Rider of every American man's billowing sky.

We still hear it on every ski course and at every foot race. In our youth ski league and in age group track, our budding athletes compete regularly but train little. The three-season format in our schools creates and insures fractured preparation at best and schedules of competition from the first week of each new season on. This is the foundation of the early destruction of our American kids. Their physical development compromised systematically, our skiers cannot reach international levels. The training culture in their schools has in fact made sure of it. The attrition we observe in the teenage years, therefore, cannot simply be attributed to the normal and explosive diversions of teenage life. The attrition is equally to be attributed to the very design of the sports education in our schools. Competition has been confused with training, and physiological development has been unwittingly inhibited. As ironic as it seems, that is how we have been educating our children.

None of this, mind you, lacks for a sense of personal fulfillment, good feeling, health, and camaraderie. But we must take the body seriously enough to take physiology at its own word. We must gain the sense to revere and rejoice in the body's own dance in sport. If we do not, then our performance levels as adults and the sound physical development of our children will remain resistantly short of our potential and our hopes. A leap of faith does not equal a leap in performance, unless it is faith in validated physiological principles of training and performance rather than the handy buzz-words of religion, industry, or education. Only then will our American athletes begin to achieve the level of awareness of the musician who studies music on his instrument's terms. For the athlete this requires both simplicity and discipline, for he is instrument and player at the same time. Mistreat either, and there will be no music.

# Part Three

# Developing
# High Performance:
# Ingredients and Recipes

# 5

# *Putting Miles By: Training*

It is necessary to know the inner structure of man.
—Leonardo da Vinci

Training provides the body with the various means of adapting to progressively higher levels of work. In cross-country skiing these higher levels are characterized by a combination of speed and endurance. The body will adapt in the manner in which we stimulate it to adapt.

However, adaptation, and thus training fitness, does not take place as a linear response to a linear increase in loading. Rather it is characterized by a sporadic process of uneven improvements and plateaus. Furthermore, linear loading past the point of anaerobic threshold can have effects which might still be considered a type of fitness but which actually work against speed-endurance performance in cross-country skiing. Misunderstanding of the nature of developmental physiology and the ways in which the various components of training interact in terms of both amounts and timing is largely responsible for our very limited success in cross-country ski competition.

In general it can be said that the most effective modes of training are those which most closely approximate the movements and physical demands of skiing. In practical terms this will mean training on skis and training in hills. The principle of specificity of training is certainly one of the most reliable ones. It determines our choices most often.

On the other hand, there is the adage: Race to your strengths; train to your weaknesses. The wisdom in this notion is that it reminds us that doing only what we already do well may be limiting our development. When we reckon, for example, than an increase of half an inch per stride in running gains us 60 yards a mile or from 8 to 10 seconds, depending on the pace, we realize that the smallest of improvements yield very significant rewards. Developing our strengths will always be the dominant source of reward, of course, as Anikin has said in his description of Nikolai Zimjatov's development.

> When a child he was not distinguished for a strong physical development among his age group but was noticeably superior in running events. ... Major efforts were made to develop the boy's advantage in long-distance abilities and endurance. Gradually his insufficient strength qualities improved, without excessive intensive training.[1]

But we need also to recognize clearly all the necessary elements in development and, knowing each of us is somewhat lopsided in his growth, not neglect any of them.

For example, Americans remain 1–1.5 seconds behind every 100 meters in international competition. That accumulates with mathematical deadliness to finish results. Until that deficit is eliminated, we will remain behind, no matter how well we do our other training. One way to add that speed is to concentrate on skill speed work in the spring, working at 50 to 100 meters, then keep track of it throughout the summer and fall. It is not anaerobic speed so much as it is neuromuscular coordination work and natural power training. It is surely not the sole way to add speed; that is done with the whole recipe. But when I see a skier who cannot ski 100 meters in under 17 seconds, fully rested, then that skier clearly will not ski any 100 meters of a 5 or 10 kilometer race in 17 seconds, even when fully trained, and that means he cannot place among the top skiers. He or she will have to do some long-term raw speed work in order to fill in the blank.

I don't call it working on weaknesses, therefore, but rather simply recognizing a requisite other dimension and working on the possibilities available in it.

We do no different throughout the year's training as we monitor the skier's training speeds. And we know what goal speeds are for the early season races. We always adjust training to gain the added dimension we want most. That comes in our final two months of race preparation. Now we need to go back to the beginning.

# *Ingredients in the Recipe*

## Training Zones

Training remains quite simple at the lowest level of intensity. If we train at base or special endurance levels, we develop the body's peripheral system. If we train at anaerobic threshold, we will improve our speed more quickly, but that will be complicated by the fact that then the full development of the peripheral systems will be somewhat slighted. Since they comprise the transport and recovery mechanisms, the heavier loading at threshold will not enjoy the long-term support level of those systems. Threshold loading will therefore fatigue the body faster (transport-run out of gas) and longer (recovery time needed before next session). The amount one would like to do at threshold would then itself be too limited. We do recognize the need for speed, however. How is this to work? The task becomes more complicated yet by the requirement to adapt to race speeds at heartrates even above anaerobic threshold. That is also the place where our desire to achieve most logically locates itself. It is also the place where we discover that the body has its own peculiar, even perverse, form of government. We find then that we cannot simply legislate a linear improvement curve by wanting to very much or by working harder.

The body is a conservative organism, as I have said before, resistantly mysterious, taciturn, cryptic in its manner of "speaking" to us. That both bedevils and fascinates us. But it is clear that anaerobic work is so high-cost (in simple terms, getting 2 ATP's per glucose molecule as opposed to 36 ATP's with aerobic work) that the body can only afford a little of it. Even in order to endure that and adapt to it in terms of improved performance it must be preceded by the massive investment of base capital which we started off with at the lowest levels.

It is fundamental to endurance training, therefore, that the body is governed not from the top down but from the bottom up.

Another way of looking at the relation of top level performance to base level training is to distinguish between LOAD and CAPACITY.

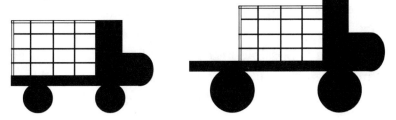

The truck with the smaller capacity is easy to load up, and that full load gives the sensation of maximum work being accomplished. And it seems to make sense to load it to capacity because you want to complete the job as quickly as possible. The truck soon wears, however, if maximally loaded all the time. Run too much "overaxle," and it weakens quickly as the miles lengthen and speeds are pushed. Fatigue is reached sooner, for the stress level of the load-to-capacity ratio remains at peak. Wheels wear and blow more often, springs break, repairs and down time mount. You must either unload, slow down, or travel shorter distances to continue .... or buy a new truck.

But that truck is our body, and we don't get to buy a new one.

Without increasing capacity, overloading — the key to training effect — is not possible. Even adding a bigger engine (central system) through high intensity training will simply add stress to the frame and only create a momentary (year or two) illusion of increased ability. This is often what happens with early teenagers.

We have increased the capacity in the second truck. The same load can be carried both longer and more swiftly, more easily... because it is a lower percentage of peak capacity or energy demand. Further loading (training effect) is now possible as well.

The body is not a truck, of course, but it is a very conservative adapting organism. The truck analogy makes clear how additional capacity must precede further loading if early breakdown is to be avoided. We enlarge and strengthen the structure, the holding and carrying capacity. That is why base or special endurance work dominates the year and precedes all other kinds of training. Later in each year only, and later in one's teens, greater loading becomes rational, and can be sustained through a steady improvement curve for many years.

It is also important to understand when we speak of enlarging capacity that we are not speaking about adding muscle size. We are enhancing muscle chemistry and circulatory structure.

Physiology speaks much about capacitance as a process critical to efficiency. Metabolic capacitance, for example, is described as a "more economical energy delivery system to any cell that has a peak energy demand that is in excess of its average energy demand."[2]

The distinction between capacity and load may apply to technique and race tactics as well. In technique one must create space in one's movement patterns before additional loading is possible in the form of speed accepted and carried. The space is gained through greater range of motion, a more open and thus more responsive flight attitude in gliding, and certainly tension release, the most critical of all.

Applied to race tactics, recognition of the constantly varying limits of capacity is the key to allowing a given climb, for example, to load the skier's capacity only to the level at which he can avoid a damaging stress level, one from which he must either unload or slow down following the climb in order to return to some level of homeostasis (maximal lactate steady state). If he loads too heavily in charging the hill, that level of homeostasis simply will not return to earlier higher levels at which he was still competitive with the field. A wonderful and praiseworthy maximal effort in the climb will have simply damaged his overall course speed.

I once heard a coach complain that the American skiers' problem was that they did not know how to go fast when they were tired. So he prescribed hard training when they were tired as a solution. He missed the point of the distinction between capacity and load: they did not go fast *because* they were too tired. So the skiers trained bravely on when they were tired, and it should not have surprised anyone that they became slower yet. Only increased capacity will allow for the loads of high level race speeds.

Another factor determines this direction of the flow of power. Human anaerobic capacity appears to be finite. And that capacity can be achieved in 4 to 5 weeks of 3 anaerobic bouts of training a week. Working longer or harder at anaerobic training will not improve that capacity, nor will it improve speed. It will simply exhaust the body and ultimately slow it down. We will also learn that **anaerobic work yields anaerobic endurance at the speed you have now; it does not produce speed itself.** If we wish to elevate performance, therefore, we must do so from below, by building a larger and larger foundation.

The question goes on in scholarly circles about which of the systems, peripheral or central, is most influential in determining performance. I will go into some detail about each of those systems shortly. For the moment I would only say that, as is usual it is not a case of either/or, vegetables or grains, but of proportions and timing in the best recipe for ultimate speed and endurance. The very essence of this process lies in establishing the highest level of speed or load at which an efficient cost can be sustained, thus allowing the advantages of base work, peripheral systems development (the working muscles), to join with those of highest speed and effort, central system development (the heart and lungs).

In conventional terms that level is called anaerobic threshold. It is the point where the anaerobic metabolism of glucose in the muscles begins to mix into the aerobic metabolic process, like a drop or two of red mixed into a bucket of white paint. Lactate begins the climb at a rate steeper than we can totally recycle or remove it through oxygen intake, and we begin to feel a slightly different "tint" inside.

Just short of that point, however, we feel the most buoyant, comfortably swelled up like a balloon, but with no sensation of stretch or stress. Accurate identification of threshold is essential since we would like to know and feel where we can reach the highest velocity-stimulus possible to recruit fast twitch muscle fibers. We also need to recruit them for long enough for those fast twitch fibers which are capable of adapting to aerobic/oxidative metabolism to do so. For duration, we know, is the key to adaptation. Should the effort exceed actual threshold, and anaerobic/glycolytic metabolism begin to play a larger role, then duration must shorten and with it the desired aerobic bio-chemical adaptations.

These processes are neither linear nor mathematical, as is quite clear from the following figure. The farther to the right one moves the greater the cost, predictably for a while, until at anaerobic threshold it climbs too steeply to maintain for long.

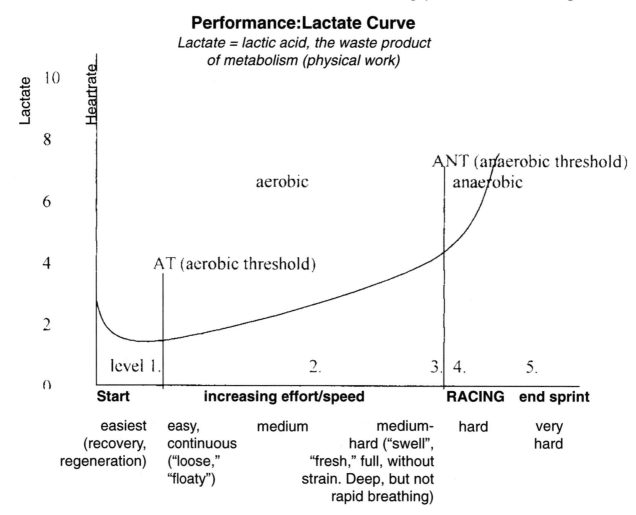

**Base/special endurance (Level 1):** the easy level at which lactate is either removed more rapidly than it accumulates (as in recovery/regeneration) or can be accommodated with gently rising oxygen intake. The easiness is critical because it allows a training session to last a long enough time to facilitate gains in metabolic efficiency, the foundation of all other aspects of training. 80% of year's hours.

**Threshold (Level 3):** The highest aerobic level of effort. The level at which the fast twitch oxidative muscle fibers are given enough activation time to adapt optimally to the high aerobic demands of near racing velocities. 10% of year's hours.

**Race Pace (Level 4):** Playing for the slight increase in speed just beyond threshold. 10% of year's hours. Little time at all is spent at either level 2 (which is mentioned only to define the area between 1 and 3 where so many athletes become stuck while forcing base pace too much) or level 5 (which is sprint speed seen only at the ends of races but is not a functional part of training).

"But couldn't we just train at racing level longer, until we could just take it?" we ask wistfully. It is a question we have asked for years, and many a physiologist, athlete, and coach still does. The answer is No; because our body's anaerobic capacity is finite, based upon the particular nature of its bio-chemical balance and the particular quality of anaerobic metabolism. It is perhaps the body's most maddening paradox, the prohibitive price at the height of the performance curve. But that is the body's instinct for survival at work. It knows that aerobic metabolism is eighteen times more efficient than anaerobic metabolism. We might think of it as too low an octane fuel for the engine we have. Or we might compare the body's response curve to the friction curve of the ski on the snow. The glide lasts briefly, then the friction increases, and at an increasing rate. Dreams of prolonging the glide thence drive the energy costs so dramatically upward that efficiency is lost in fatigue. At the same time amplitude and frequency of the total movement are lost.

Given those increasing and ultimately prohibitive costs, it is also clear that increases in the intensity levels of training cannot be assigned the same effect. An increase at threshold per minute is clearly of greater added loading than the same added time at base levels. An increase at race pace per minute is monumentally more influential yet than increases at threshold. Thus we must always adjust our thoughts and plans to balance each intensity level as the critical multiplier in any quantitative increase.

It was for this reason that Dr. Ernst Van Aaken first suggested a 20:1 ratio of endurance to speed work as early as the 1920's, a ratio remarkably close to the 18:1 between aerobic and anaerobic metabolism (36 ATPs:2 ATPs). That has never seemed correct to us Americans, for did not greater productivity, not to mention superior character, come from working as hard as you could, all the time?

It is clear we can only proceed sensibly with a knowledge of the various intensity levels in which subjective feelings and objective measurements match. We need, in a word, to face reality squarely and with our most daring intelligence. Only then will it be possible to stimulate the systems necessary to truly improve performance with the most rational mix of amount and sequence of efforts and training types.

## Training Zones

### Level  Physiological Purpose

**1**
*1-3 hours*

a. Recovery, regeneration from work in zones 3, 4, and 5.

b. Basic endurance, distance work, peripheral systems (circulatory system, muscles).

c. Capillarization: the body builds/opens up additional blood pathways, a new network of capillaries, microscopic blood vessels, so that oxygen and fuels can be brought to the muscle cells in greater quantity. The capillaries respond to increased blood flow pressure by building new vessels to ease the friction. Thus increased blood flow pressure must be sustained and continuous in order to elicit this capillarization response: the primary purpose of zone 1.

**2**

Generally to be avoided, a sort of "no-man's land" between base endurance work (capacity building) and more specific threshold work (performance readiness). Stimulus by both load and duration at this level is not discrete enough to facilitate either.

**3**
*3-20 min.*

Speed/strength endurance, a balance of capillarization and power, the highest level of aerobic endurance/velocity.

**4**
*20 secs.- 2 mins.*

Race pace, a balance of all the systems, aerobic and anaerobic. Psychological adaptation to racing environments. Zone 4 is zone 3 + 2-4 heartbeats per minute (bpm), up to 6-8 bpm at the tops (not in the middle!) of longer hills. At the top end, and in zone 5, greatest loading of the central system (heart and lungs).

**5**
*8-20secs*

Sprinting speed and movements. Used for short (50-100 meters or 15-30 flexions) distances for the development of power through speed (strength/power gains through increased neural activation of the muscles more than hypertrophy of muscle mass, though some hypertrophy will occur).

## How to Find the Zones

There is an easy way to locate these intensity levels or training zones. I have tried several protocols and digested the theory behind others. This one is as accurate as any other and more accurate than most. I conducted it with several National Team members, and the training zones matched well with a more sophisticated test involving roller skiing or ski walking on a treadmill with increases in load and lactate sampling every three minutes (Finnish protocol).

It is not appropriate to discuss various test protocols here. Theories and practices abound, as well as rationales. I will only note that protocols in which the load is increased every minute will likely produce an anaerobic threshold figure of about 5 beats per minute too high. It takes close to three minutes for the body to reach homeostasis (biochemical balance) at each new load level. If increases are made every minute, for example, for the sake of convenience in the lab, the heartrate piles on itself, "races" to any extent, as if in anticipation, to catch up. It seems to overreact. Whatever the mechanisms are, Conconi found his 1000m protocol (approx. 3 minutes) to produce the greatest concurrence of the "knee" in the curves of the various indicators, lactate, carbon dioxide, volume of oxygen, etc., the lactate curve being the most accurate.[3] One National Team man was tested with both one minute and three minute protocols. He used the result of the one minute protocol until early fall, when with the agreement of his coach he dropped his threshold level five beats. The three minute protocol indicated that is where it belonged in the first place.

The test I use is comprised of 8 laps (1600m) on a track. Asphalt allows for roller skis as well, as long as the roller skis are slow enough, the same as snow friction. The test can be done running or roller skiing. So long as the athlete moves as efficiently on roller skis as on foot, there will be only slight differences between the two. I prefer roller skiing because it is specific and involves more of the body simultaneously.

The skier passes the starting point with a flying start. From that position I record times per lap and the heartrate which he/she reports by glancing at the wrist heartrate monitor as he/she passes by. The idea is to find the highest heartrate which the skier can sustain for 12 minutes or so. I chose 12 minutes because it has been ascertained that that length of time will give figures reliable for longer periods of effort without depleting the athlete in an exhaustion test. It is "middle distance" time, an effort and speed-of-movement environment characteristic of cross-country ski racing.[4] And it turns out to correspond closely with Dr. Jack Daniel's measure: "$vVO_2$ max is the velocity of running which coincides with $VO_2$ max. This velocity of running is the one which the runner could keep up for about 10-15 minutes in a race situation, under current level of fitness."[5]

The skier's heartrate will level by the second or third lap. He/she may try to hold it a bit higher, but my experience for ten years is that that will not be more than a beat or two, and then the result can be mixed. Sometimes the velocity will increase, but usually only for a single lap. Then it will return to the optimal levels of the sustainable heartrate. Or the velocity may drop off right away in the lap in which the extra couple of beats per minute were achieved. Loss of efficiency of movement and poorer fuel supply are invariably the reasons. Both the sustainable heartrate and the velocity per lap at that heartrate are usually very easy to see.

That highest sustainable heartrate is what I call racing heartrate, RHR = zone 4
(Maximum all-out end sprint = zone 5)
RHR – [10-12]bpm = ANT (anaerobic threshold) zone 3
ANT – [20-30]bpm = AT (aerobic threshold) zone 1

Zone 1 is primarily for recovery and regeneration types of distance skiing at its low end, base endurance at its higher end.

As the specific race preparation (some call it anaerobic buildup) period nears, anaerobic threshold may move 2–3bpm closer to RHR. That is an excellent sign, of course, and can signal upcoming improvements in performance. Short of regular lactate testing in training, however, I have discovered no practical measure. With most skiers I rely upon a quality level of long-term communication and can then judge from their subjective responses to training that threshold has risen a little. In any case, the increase will seem too small to be significant. That small rise, however, is just as crucial as a small change of gears might be in a racing car or bicycle, or the change from regular to high-test fuel.

An equally important part of this test is the velocity achieved at RHR. Although we have monitored effort well over the past years in this country (we have a cultural, religious bond to the nobility and productivity of work, and tend to praise effort regardless of outcome), we have paid less attention to actual speeds, not just at RHR but at all the other training zones as well.* If training is going well, velocities at all levels will improve, across the durations of each level. Requisite speeds at each level are just as significant as requisite hours. Executing all levels of training, in the right

---

*Among the few notable exceptions to this has been Steve Gaskill.

order, is the only reasonable way that those velocities will rise evenly, and that is the only hope that the velocity achieved at actual RHR will ultimately put your skier with the leaders. Otherwise the gap between the training types and zones will be too great and the resulting stress will block the achievement of the necessary race speed at the goal point of the year's preparations.

Adjustments are made in relation to the main training purpose of a given period. If the goal is base endurance, as in the summer, then one would emphasize distance rather than speed. If the skier begins to fatigue, he cuts the speed in order to maintain the distance. In the fall, and particularly early winter, speed monitoring becomes more precise. In those seasons, depending upon the speeds the skier is going naturally, it is usually better to keep the speeds and cut the distances. Ultimate goal speeds determine the rate of change in either distance or speed.

Furthermore, in any skill speed session, if the skier cannot maintain past speed or the speed of earlier runs, then the coach must immediately cut back from 100's to 50's and increase rest intervals. The goal purpose of every session needs to be assured in terms of real speeds and real distances in proper balance.

## Patterning and Periodization

The keys to seeing improvement at all training levels lie in two fundamental principles: patterning and periodization.

Patterning informs many aspects of our lives, from eating and sleeping at certain times, to work schedules and domestic routines. It is our instinctive approach to time and stress management: work, rest, work, rest, in a given pattern of loading and relief which allows us to adapt to and accomplish the most over the long haul. It is our instinct for both survival and the basics of happiness which has taught us the recipe in which work is tempered by both rest and by variety, changes of pace, we say. We also know from the most basic of biology experiments (stimulated frog's leg) that doing only a single activity without rest or the relief of varying it fatigues us more quickly and permanently. Variety, on the other hand, allows equally productive activities to complement each other and stimulate growth beyond any single routine, both physically and mentally. This, of course, complicates our lives as well, and those of our employers. The factory model, after all, is so marvelously convenient, the human machine, the industrial version of the military regiment.

But either the fact or the metaphor get the body into deep trouble, early decline and lowering productivity. Certainly it is death to athletes. A training week thus looks as follows:

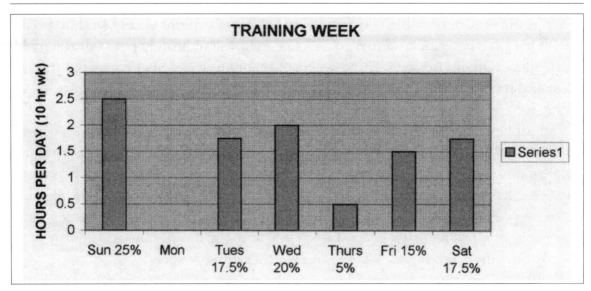

The two easy days, Monday and Thursday, fall two and three days before the largest days. Our bodies seem to operate in units of 48 hours. The effects of a workout or rest will be felt accordingly 2 days later. The body is thus rested best for Wednesday and Saturday (a usual race day) or Sunday, depending on adjustments and schedule. This may vary slightly from training periods to competition periods, where races may fall on both Saturday and Sunday. In this latter case it is often wise to move Wednesday's harder session back to Tuesday. I do this only in the competition season, however, in situations where back-to-back races are coming or if I get a message of fatigue from the skier.

In general the four day period preceding a race on Saturday runs as follows:

**Wed.** 1/2-1/3 distance time trial
**Thurs.** very easy or rest
**Fri.** easy for 20 minutes or so,
then 8-10 minutes at threshold,
followed by 5 minutes at race pace.
The 5 can be a mix of shorter fast runs. I call this session 20-10-5.
**Sat.** **RACE**

Of particular importance again is the general 48 hour rule for body response. If you do hard training on Thursday, you will pretty predictably be flat on race day. Knowing that, some skiers do not train but work on their equipment or do errands all day. Nothing could be worse for your legs than standing or walking on hard surfaces.

If you do not get going some on Friday, on the other hand, it will take you half the race to get warmed up, for your body is still in rest mode. Perhaps it is like an airplane: the engines must rev up for a few moments before the plane begins to climb again. That is what Friday's session accomplishes. I speak more about race day itself in a separate section.

In training periods it is also most rational to do any time trialing you wish on either Wednesday or Saturday. Following such a pattern will provide both the most satisfying and reliable trial and keep the skier well set up for predictable race-day performances in winter. The 2-day rule also applies generally to the effects of loading. The skier will feel most tired 2 days after a tough workout.

That is why it happens that one frequently feels wonderful the day after, senses a new level of fitness, and joyfully goes hard the next day … .only to have the bottom fall out for an additional two day period 2 days later. In essence he has "poisoned" the remainder of the week by not staying in the pattern. Manshasov records Russian research according to which exceeding volume or intensity in a workout by 12–15% will require a two day rest.[6] Optimally one does something very light following a long, hard day, something regenerative to remove lactate from the muscles and simply "freshen" the body. This kind of a session allows the body to rest even better than sudden total cessation of activity following a big session.

There are various forms of period patterns. A period may be comprised of four weeks or three weeks. Some athletes like to use a 10-day "week" rather than a 7-day week. The success of any pattern depends first and foremost upon its execution, both in terms of content and duration. By duration here I specifically mean months and years of the same pattern. It takes at least two years of the same training plan for it to begin to show real results. If the athlete or coach becomes impatient and keeps changing the plan, the body will remain in a haphazard environment, with little predictability or control, and only spotty success, if any. "By feel" training is whimsical at best and turns your body into the equivalent of a third grade classroom, each member shouting or raising his hand at random, unpredictable occasions. If the teacher or athlete begins to respond to every expressed feeling, little "syllabus" will be accomplished. (By analogy, the constantly changing, three-season high school sports schedule in itself explains much of why high school programs fundamentally fail our young athletes.)

I am personally most comfortable with a 4-week period in which the first three weeks increase and the fourth is essentially an "active rest" week.

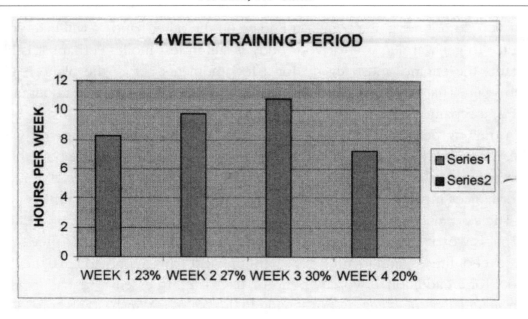

As in the week's pattern, rest is built in to the 4-week pattern. And as with the week's plan, so also in the 4-week period: the damage done by exceeding the target hours per day or week or period by very much, or jumbling the pattern of training types may not appear for a few days, or even sometimes a few weeks. It will appear, however, and all the more inexplicably because any notion of cause is lost in the month or so delay in the body's response. Any crash is accompanied by great confusion. A comparison of actual training times with the planned targets will almost always show the error, or pattern of error.

**Periodization**

Periodization is really only an extension of the principle of patterning. It characterizes the pattern of the whole year and the order in which the year's recipe is put together. The "year" need not be 12 months necessarily, particularly for younger juniors who are still wisely engaged in a number of other sports activities. But the minimum preparation time for a truly interested skier is six months. This does not mean he or she must totally specialize all training activities. But a plan is necessary for any optimal development into which the variety of activities can be located and sensibly added up. Instead of just being one diversion or activity after another, each activity can be added on top of a general plan, like bricks in a rising wall. Knowledge of this integrated process only increases the sense of worth and confident growth a young athlete feels in his love of sport.

Periodization is the way to state how the various types of training may enter the optimal sequence in the long-term recipe. As any of us knows, the cook does not simply throw all the ingredients into a bowl, stir vigorously and bake. Periodization thus gives the optimum time to each activity in each of the training zones to have its greatest positive effect on the athlete's development.

That effect also prepares the foundation for the next higher level of loading, and that sequence is the sole manner in which the subsequent training becomes effective in its own right. It is like tilling the earth first, then waiting until the ground is warm before planting, then weeding and cultivating the dirt regularly after planting. The planting itself, like anaerobic work, is actually the smallest part of the process. With proper timing, sequence, and balance you will have growth and harvest. There is no way to hasten the process, no trick, gimmick, or extra effort which can contravert periodization and the time it takes. The process must remain very gradual and progressive over the years.

Nor can the "season" of training be rearranged or reversed. That should be obvious, once we consider any living organism other than ourselves. So patience and a sense for detail are the most necessary, attention to the smaller as well as the larger obvious things. Raw desire, simple want, is unrealistic, childish, ever dangerous. The year's schedule appears as follows:

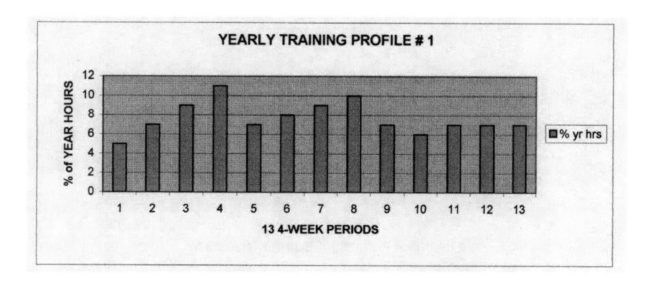

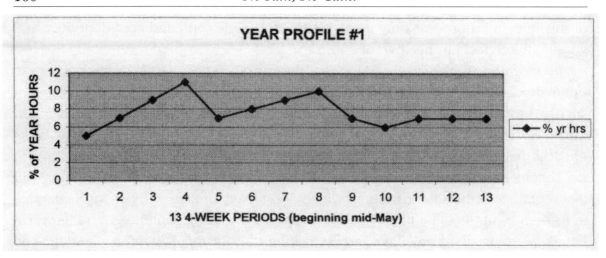

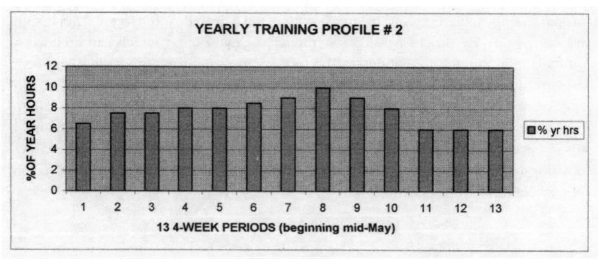

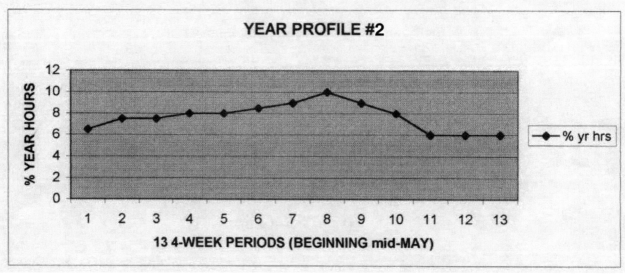

Profile #2 follows a gradual volume buildup through November, with careful progressive addition of threshold work from July or August on. Profile #1, which I have come to prefer, reaches a volume peak in late August, then begins a new climb, emphasizing threshold work leading into early competitions. It has the advantage of high volumes in the summer when there the days are both longer (more sunlight) and more free of school time constraints. The second peak's beginning fits naturally with the beginning of school in September. It is a profile generally used in both Italy and Norway.[7] What the year's recipe of training types and intensities adds the next level of planning. The following example shows a version of the double peak profile shown above.[8]

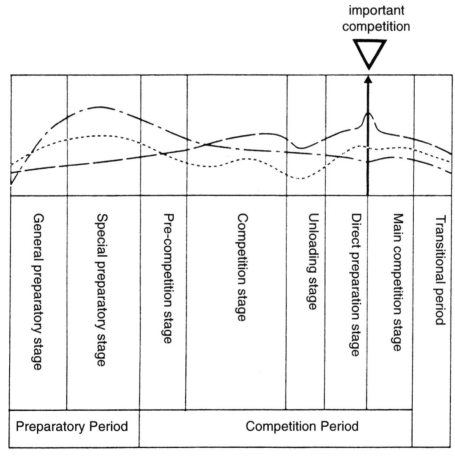

Source: N.G. Ozolin, *Sovremennaya sistema sportivnoy trenirovki* (Moscow, 1970), p. 384

The arrangement of daily time targets and loads is easily accomplished with a simple spreadsheet. That assures that distribution of a yearly training load will be both systematic and even. Changes in yearly hours can be instantly recalculated, compared in advance, and adjusted according to individual circumstances. Each skier has a plan for himself, his experience, his age. He never gets caught then just imitating what others, usually older, are doing, or trying to make the team by keeping up with the older skiers. Such bravery is admirable but ill-advised, as the discussion here should have made clear.

Although the variables remain numerous in the most planned of situations, such a spread sheet assures that the variables themselves will not become haphazard, in other words variable variables, which is chaos, whim. If adjustment is needed, identifiable variables can be altered. Then at least results can be tracked to the variables which most likely caused them.

Such a schedule provides particular support for the injured or sick athlete. It is so easy just to retreat 25 or 50 hours, spread over the year. The overall stress is dramatically reduced, while the athlete still maintains all of the other training variables, according to familiar pattern. Without such a plan the athlete and coach will usually decide to rest totally for the short term, then jump back into the old plan too rapidly. They want to forget the break in training. They may, but the body cannot. Even short-term illness or injury can be handled most rationally, and thus supportively, with a plan in hand. Drop to a lower hour plan for a period, or three weeks at least. Five to eight weeks may make even better sense. The patterns stay the same. With recovery the athlete may return to his original plan with the smallest loss of hours and the least amount of psychological discomfort, for throughout the down time he or she will have been able to remain "at home" in the plan.

## Basic Spreadsheet of Year-Hours Distribution

| | 13-May | 10-Jun | 8-Jul | 5-Aug | 2-Sep | 1-Oct | 29-Oct | 25-Nov | 23-Dec | 20-Jan | 17-Feb | 17-Mar | 14-Apr |
|---|---|---|---|---|---|---|---|---|---|---|---|---|---|
| yr hrs | 500.0 | 500.0 | 500.0 | 500.0 | 500.0 | 500.0 | 500.0 | 500.0 | 500.0 | 500.0 | 500.0 | 500.0 | 500.0 |
| % yr hrs | 0.05 | 0.07 | 0.09 | 0.11 | 0.07 | 0.08 | 0.09 | 0.1 | 0.07 | 0.09 | 0.06 | 0.06 | 0.06 |
| period hrs | 25 | 35 | 45 | 55 | 35 | 40 | 45.0 | 50.0 | 35.0 | 45.0 | 30.0 | 30.0 | 30.0 |
| week 1 | 5.8 | 8.1 | 10.4 | 12.7 | 8.1 | 9.2 | 10.4 | 11.5 | 8.1 | 10.4 | 6.9 | 6.9 | 6.9 |
| week 2 | 6.8 | 9.5 | 12.2 | 14.9 | 9.5 | 10.8 | 12.2 | 13.5 | 9.5 | 12.2 | 8.1 | 8.1 | 8.1 |
| week 3 | 7.5 | 10.5 | 13.5 | 16.5 | 10.5 | 12.0 | 13.5 | 15.0 | 10.5 | 13.5 | 9.0 | 9.0 | 9.0 |
| week 4 | 5.0 | 7.0 | 9.0 | 11.0 | 7.0 | 8.0 | 9.0 | 10.0 | 7.0 | 9.0 | 6.0 | 6.0 | 6.0 |
| Sun 25% | 1.4 | 2.0 | 2.6 | 3.2 | 2.0 | 2.3 | 2.6 | 2.9 | 2.0 | 2.6 | 1.7 | 1.7 | 1.7 |
| Mon | | | | | | | | | 0.1 | | | | |
| Tues 17.5 | 1.0 | 1.4 | 1.8 | 2.2 | 1.4 | 1.6 | 1.8 | 2.0 | 1.4 | 1.8 | 1.2 | 1.2 | 1.2 |
| Wed 20 | 1.2 | 1.6 | 2.1 | 2.5 | 1.6 | 1.8 | 2.1 | 2.3 | 1.6 | 2.1 | 1.4 | 1.4 | 1.4 |
| Thurs 5 | 0.3 | 0.4 | 0.5 | 0.6 | 0.4 | 0.5 | 0.5 | 0.6 | 0.4 | 0.5 | 0.3 | 0.3 | 0.3 |
| Fri 15 | 0.9 | 1.2 | 1.6 | 1.9 | 1.2 | 1.4 | 1.6 | 1.7 | 1.2 | 1.6 | 1.0 | 1.0 | 1.0 |
| Sat 17.5 | 1.0 | 1.4 | 1.8 | 2.2 | 1.4 | 1.6 | 1.8 | 2.0 | 1.4 | 1.8 | 1.2 | 1.2 | 1.2 |
| Sun | 1.7 | 2.4 | 3.0 | 3.7 | 2.4 | 2.7 | 3.0 | 3.4 | 2.4 | 3.0 | 2.0 | 2.0 | 2.0 |
| Mon | | | | | | | | 0.5 | | | | | |
| Tues | 1.2 | 1.7 | 2.1 | 2.6 | 1.7 | 1.9 | 2.1 | 2.4 | 1.7 | 2.1 | 1.4 | 1.4 | 1.4 |
| Wed | 1.4 | 1.9 | 2.4 | 3.0 | 1.9 | 2.2 | 2.4 | 2.7 | 1.9 | 2.4 | 1.6 | 1.6 | 1.6 |
| Thurs | 0.3 | 0.5 | 0.6 | 0.7 | 0.5 | 0.5 | 0.6 | 0.7 | 0.5 | 0.6 | 0.4 | 0.4 | 0.4 |
| Fri | 1.0 | 1.4 | 1.8 | 2.2 | 1.4 | 1.6 | 1.8 | 2.0 | 1.4 | 1.8 | 1.2 | 1.2 | 1.2 |
| Sat | 1.2 | 1.7 | 2.1 | 2.6 | 1.7 | 1.9 | 2.1 | | 1.7 | 2.1 | 1.4 | 1.4 | 1.4 |
| Sun | 1.9 | 2.6 | 3.4 | 4.1 | 2.6 | 3.0 | 3.4 | 3.6 | 2.6 | 3.4 | 2.3 | 2.3 | 2.3 |
| Mon | | | | | | | | | | | | | |
| Tues | 1.3 | 1.8 | 2.4 | 2.9 | 1.8 | 2.1 | 2.4 | 2.6 | 1.8 | 2.4 | 1.6 | 1.6 | 1.6 |
| Wed | 1.5 | 2.1 | 2.7 | 3.3 | 2.1 | 2.4 | 2.7 | 3.0 | 2.1 | 2.7 | 1.8 | 1.8 | 1.8 |
| Thurs | 0.4 | 0.5 | 0.7 | 0.8 | 0.5 | 0.6 | 0.7 | 0.8 | 0.5 | 0.7 | 0.5 | 0.5 | 0.4 |
| Fri | 1.1 | 1.6 | 2.0 | 2.5 | 1.6 | 1.8 | 2.0 | 2.3 | 1.6 | 2.0 | 1.4 | 1.4 | 1.2 |
| Sat | 1.3 | 1.8 | 2.4 | 2.9 | 1.8 | 2.1 | 2.4 | 2.6 | 1.8 | 2.4 | 1.6 | 1.6 | 1.4 |
| Sun | 1.3 | 1.8 | 2.3 | 2.8 | 1.8 | 2.0 | 2.3 | 2.5 | 1.8 | 2.3 | 1.5 | 1.5 | 1.5 |
| Mon | | | | | | | | | | | | | |
| Tues | 0.9 | 1.2 | 1.6 | 1.9 | 1.2 | 1.4 | 1.6 | 1.8 | 1.2 | 1.6 | 1.1 | 1.1 | 1.1 |
| Wed | 1.0 | 1.4 | 1.8 | 2.2 | 1.4 | 1.6 | 1.8 | 2.0 | 1.4 | 1.8 | 1.2 | 1.2 | 1.2 |
| Thurs | 0.3 | 0.4 | 0.5 | 0.6 | 0.4 | 0.4 | 0.5 | 0.5 | 0.4 | 0.5 | 0.3 | 0.3 | 0.3 |
| Fri | 0.8 | 1.1 | 1.4 | 1.7 | 1.1 | 1.2 | 1.4 | 1.5 | 1.1 | 1.4 | 0.9 | 0.9 | 0.9 |
| Sat | 0.9 | 1.2 | 1.6 | 1.9 | 1.2 | 1.4 | 1.6 | 1.8 | 1.2 | 1.6 | 1.1 | 1.1 | 1.1 |

## Modes of Training

As we begin training, there are also decisions to make about the most effective means.

*Running in hills and in the woods, with poles.* That is ski imitation. Hiking with poles is excellent base training also. Even where the hiking trail is rocky, if you carry poles with you all the time, pretty soon they will have a way of finding where there is a firm place to push from. Just having them along builds strength and the habits of the upper body. Soon they are just other limbs. You have become a four-legged animal; that is what cross-country skiers are.

*Running* is basic as well, and particularly good for foot speed, quickness work. But it is not as good as running with poles. It is also true that running with poles needs to be approached as ski imitation, with active engagement of the poles with each stride, not just running with poles in hand.

*Roller skiing* suggests itself most obviously, of course. Along with ski imitation it is the most effective mode of training. The roller skis must have good resistance, however, as close to that of snow as possible. It is well documented now that in the early years of roller skis, they were somewhat heavy, and the results remained good. With technological improvements, however, the resistance went down, and it is now known that the majority of even the top world cup skiers actually suffered from detraining as a result of using roller skis which were too fast.[9]

Resistance provides not only the loading specific to skiing. The type of friction curve provided is that of snow and produces the correct sequence of eccentric loading-coil-recoil response in the muscles which produces the best kick. I have experienced two athletes who skied 100m as fast as possible on the faster skis, several times, with rest between. Another time they used the "slow" skis, and their times for the 100m were lower! So we must not consider loading only but also the particular loading-unloading impulse "curve" which characterizes the most effective kick and thus the greatest velocity.[10] I speak further to this topic and the relevant research in Chapter 8, Technique, in the section on Classic Technique.

How much classic and how much skating technique? The ratio remains 60:40 for older kids, with less skating for younger juniors. The amount of skating ultimately should be determined, however, by the level of mastery of the movement, specifically the absence of stressful torque or twisting in the hip and knee joints. We also remember the rationale: at the same heartrate and perceived effort, skating results in a level higher intensity than classic, for reasons, it is assumed, of greater simultaneous involvement of the total body mass and resultant unavailability of relaxing limbs/muscle groups and circulatory areas to remove lactate. We remember the Russians' experiments before the Calgary Olympics as well: the high percentage classic skiing group performed better in both classic and skating competitions.

When roller skis first appeared, we noticed what we thought was a deterioration in ski technique. Some thought that ski technique was evolving; I thought it was worsening as a result of the skiers adapting their technique to roller skis rather than roller skis to skiing. The same phenomenon has taken place with the use of roller skis which are too fast. This a yet another example of how the body will adapt to almost anything we present it. It also confirms the point that just because it feels alright or is available as an type of training, it does not necessarily mean it is good training. We can also extend this conclusion to remind ourselves that there will usually be a theory available for everything, training or training device. Without lengthy and collaborative testing in experience that theory remains purely speculative and as such worthy of healthy suspicion. Certainly we do not race to our athletes with it and change their training.

*In-line skates* are not appropriate. They are too fast to approximate the resistances encountered in skiing. They also immobilize the ankle, a joint whose freedom and flexibility are critical to the power of the kick, both in classic technique and in skating. The importance of free, rapid plantar flexion has, in fact, been a goal of speed skaters for some time, at the very time skiers were imitating the fixed ankle pushing motion of the skaters. The new klap-skate allows skaters this flexion, and with it a host of new world records. Skiers must exercise a similar range of motion.[11]

*Rowing* is excellent training for general strength and endurance. It is a favorite of the Russians. Especially the sculls with sliding seats and outriggered oar locks are excellent training devices. They provide a welcome change of environment, particularly in hot weather. Some, including the Alden Ocean single and double, are very stable in the water. The double can be rowed in pairs, of course, and that makes partner training pleasurable. Any level of work can be accomplished in a shell, from overdistance to threshold to speed skills. It is one of the places where the arms and shoulders can thoroughly indulge in threshold and speed work and where the whole body can work in concert. There is even the elliptical force-glide motion of skiing.

For upper body workouts, particularly for diagonal poling simulation, *kayaking* is excellent.

The most specific device available for poling/upper body work is a Concept 2 rowing machine mounted at a steep slant and equipped with a TaylorBar to allow the arms to pendle past the body line as in skiing (see illustration on following page).

Upright Concept2 rowing machine with a double-pole bar which allows the hands to pass the body line as in skiing. *(Upright arrangement, double-pole bar adaptation and design by the author, 1999, patent pending)*

1. extend up and forward    2. hands head for the knees! ...    3. ... past body as legs rise

Bar shape   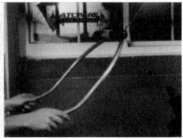 Means of attachment

It has many advantages. It is simple and portable. It displays heartrate readout, stroke rate (42-45 strokes/min.!), velocity, time exercised and distance covered. It thus gives immediate feedback to govern the athlete's training levels and biomechanical efficiency/effectiveness. The resistance can also be set low enough to allow for real distance/base training for just the upper body (which actually begins at the knees!). I have young skiers who do 10km (sometimes as 2 x 5km) three times a week. There need be no concerns that diagonal poling cannot be done on the device. Particularly with the advent of skating and the ascendant importance of double-poling, it became clear than single-poling and double-poling were not such separate movements. It was in fact rational to approach single-poling (diagonal) as simply half of a double-pole.

*Biking* on the road is little used now, except for long overdistance work. Even with a heartrate similar to other modes, the work load is not of a type which produces the lactate responses of skiing. Biking, particularly mountain biking, can be effective in steep hill work if the rider stands in the pedals, long enough, and avoids the everpresent temptation to sprint, other than for very short spurts. But mountain biking is excellent for coordination and responsiveness to terrain and speed. I recommend biking only as variety training, and as a substitute for times when an athlete has been injured. Even in that case, my first choice would be rowing.

# First Elements of Training

## Special Endurance or Base Training

The basis of endurance performance is oxygen transport. This fundamental principle of physical fitness has been known for a hundred years in Europe. Americans learned it in the late 1800's, then gave it up for other cultural priorities. I traced the evolution of those preferred values which have been so counterproductive for endurance sport in Chapter 4.

We must recover this first principle again and let it work. We begin with the persistence and patience known to every man of the land: each activity in its amount, time, and sequence. Timing is of the essence, hurry the greatest danger.

Long before the choice and planting of seeds, longer yet before the harvest, it is in May and June that the fields are turned, harrowed, and dunged, all the base materials of growth and ground worked and worked in.

The human body is similar ground, it takes that long to make itself ready, and the early, patient working of its systems provides both the most critical and secure preparation for speed in the coming winter and the dominant training activity, up to 80%, of the athlete's yearly training hours. Like the farmer, he spends most of his time caring for the ground rather than the plant itself. Unhurried and meticulous he works, assuring growth by enhancing the ground.

Perhaps it would be more precise to say that base endurance training prepares the body for training itself, so that it can train at a higher level for racing later. The body is prone to growth but a fundamentally conservative organism. It is the slow expanding of all the body's capacities, accustoming them to work, to toughening and to an untroubled, lean elasticity of movement which will allow the higher intensity, specific race training to not only be tolerated but to take strong and durable root.

At the very beginning, therefore, we have made a distinction between *capacity* and *load*. We must build capacity first, before we can adapt to progressively higher loads or speeds. I have used the analogy of two sizes of truck to explain this distinction.

Short of long years of base endurance training — as with farming the least dramatic, inspiring, or fun — the more dynamic, speedier, flamboyant forms of race training will fall like seeds thrown onto an untilled meadow. They take delayed and shallow root, then bear momentary and poor fruit.

Even if the ground is well-prepared, the temptation to test for progress too early will be like the young boy with his first garden who cannot resist the need to see if his seeds have sprouted, so lifts up the dirt to find roots. The young athlete who tests his progress early, not to mention continuously, with excursions into hard summer speed or regular fall competition is like that youthful gardener. He does not help the growth and may well in fact inhibit it, regardless of what he sees.

What is base endurance training? To start with, I like the Russian term, special endurance, for it avoids our instinct to connect "base" with "low, less quality, rude". Special endurance suggests more accurately the critical stature of this initial and fundamental training activity in the overall training-performance recipe. We will ask just how it is so fundamental to performance, why must so much of it be done, what are its particular joys?

Special endurance base training is the process of gently but continuously stirring the body's systems to motion, forming its physical and mental habits to work. The loads are light, but they are carried long, and then longer. There is nothing boisterous or dramatic about it. There is little sense of immediate reward, except for the feelings usually 5 to 6 weeks after starting that one is more mobile, can go further, with little effort. The first rewards will not be proof of speed but rather a sense of physical range, of freedom. The task takes a majority of the training work hours of the year, and it will take from 5 to 7 years before the skier will have a truly reliable indication of his growth and its translation into speed.

The pace is rhythmical but restrained. The breathing is perceptible only as a presence rather than a pressure, like a light hand on one's shoulder, the nudge of a breeze against high grass. The bow is strong, even as you begin; but you touch the string for initial flex and suppleness —   no thought of power or aim. You can converse with training companions while you are underway together, your heartrate somewhere between 120 and 145 beats per minute (bpm), but not higher. You slow on the hills, even to a walk. Even, continuous effort is the key. The work to be done is reckoned in hours, not speed. And there is too much of it to be done to allow anything faster. It is like practicing the piano. A session is two hours. Playing twice as fast for one hour does not work. The goal is the time spent, not the intensity of the work.

Nor lower than 120 bpm. Thus in base/special endurance training the most difficult challenges are often on easy terrain, particularly downhills, where the pulse easily drops beneath the training effect zone of 120. Especially for beginning athletes there is the inclination to stop and chat. Boredom is the arch enemy of us all, but to experience the reward of overdistance, you must maintain the effort through the entire period of time set out, from 45 minutes for beginners to 3 hours plus for mature athletes.

So the goals of base endurance, stamina training are specifically factors of time spent, not the intensity of the load. These goals mainly involve increasing the capacity of the body's peripheral systems.

To most Americans the idea of de-emphasizing intensity and prescribing easy to moderate continuous training seems antithetical to the very nature of productive work. Psychologically we tend to be a little unnerved by it; it seems frivolous, undignified, unathletic. It is the ingredient in the recipe almost always left out, especially when coaches or athletes are in a hurry, the short season does not give them time, or they are easily bored. Special endurance training, however, is the very foundation of physiological development, the very flour in the recipe, so to speak. Its unavoidable importance becomes more clear when we understand a fundamental distinction made in exercise physiology between the central system and the peripheral system.

The central system is the heart and lungs, the cardiopulmonary system. It is stimulated primarily by more intense loading, although because heart and lungs are also muscles of a type, they also require easier, continuous levels of stimulation in order to become durable and efficient at their tasks.

The peripheral system is comprised of the exercising muscles, the local supply and distribution of blood and the metabolic processes involved in muscular work. It requires the easy-continuous stimulation of repetitive movement order to develop both neuromuscular and metabolic efficiency. You can have a large pump, but you also need a wide, refined net of vessels and subtle mechanisms at their ends for the pump to be of any major use. Discussion in exercise physiology has varied between ascribing greater importance for performance to one or to the other. Suslov helps the either/or problem by speaking of "links," and thus is able to explain how the systems are not so much discrete as interconnected and overlapping, particularly at the ends of the peripheral-central spectrum. (The spectrum is circular, therefore, not linear.) Speaking of performance as stemming from "a highly organized functional system," he explains, "This system consists of three harmoniously developed links: an 'executing' link — the muscular apparatus; a 'supply' link — the oxygen transport system; and a 'regulating-controlling' link —the central nervous system and the endocrine system."[12] I will relate the various types of training to these "links" as I proceed with the discussion.

To return to base endurance training, the capacity of the body's peripheral system is enhanced in the following ways:

1. capillarization of the blood vessels,
2. enhanced oxidative enzyme activity,
3. basic toughening through increased neural activation of muscles, and
4. psychological adaptation to work itself.

The last is complex, to be sure, but at the outset it is important to suggest the positive as well as tougher side. Whereas boredom and the discipline of staying out for long periods of time is trying, it is also a positive experience in providing release from all sorts of daily tensions, as is the rapid realization that the body soon works very well by itself, and this quickly becomes a source of confidence and sense of power.

## Capillarization

Capillarization takes place at the muscle (peripheral) end of the cardiovascular continuum.

> From the cardiological point of view [peripheral adaptation] is often underestimated. The haemodynamic and metabolic processes in exercising muscle are decisive for the end performance capacity achieved … Local blood supply and oxygen utilization (oxidation capacity) correspond directly with total distribution of blood in organism in limiting performance.[13] Muscle biopsy studies have shown a mean increase in capillary area of 36% due to endurance training.[14]

As with training in general, the enhancement of one capacity tends to have collateral effects. In the case of capillarization increased blood flow also results in more efficient intramuscular blood distribution.

Christopher Koch describes the process as follows:

> So the body begins building additional blood pathways. With training, the muscle tissue develops a new network of capillaries, the microscopic blood vessels that are smaller than the diameter of a single red blood cell, so that oxygen and fuels can be brought to the muscle cells in greater quantity … the capillaries respond [to increased flow pressure) by building new vessels to ease the friction.[15]

In medical science the jury is in fact still out as to whether additional vessels are actually formed or whether the capacity of those already present is enhanced. In either case, the increase in the efficiency of blood transport to the working muscles is dramatic, in the manner perhaps of fuel injection to a conventional engine.

*The Olympic Book of Sports Medicine* describes the results:

The resultant peripheral metabolic adaptations are:
1. Increase of number and size of mitochondria.
2. Enlargement of the activity of some aerobic and anaerobic enzymes.
3. Augmentation of myoglobin.
4. Increase of intramuscular glycogen content....
The sum of the peripheral adaptations causes a reduction of the sympathetic drive of the heart.[16]

Put another way, the increased efficiency of the peripheral end of the vascular transport and distribution system is the basis for the heart and lungs (central system) being able to accomplish increasing loads/speeds without damaging or otherwise limiting stress levels. It comprises the "tilled earth" part of improving performance, in which the "seeds" or loads are accommodated naturally into the dynamics of healthy growth, rather than simply shocking the "ground"/ body with sudden increased demands for which it has not been prepared. Growth is achieved through the process of response and adaptation, not shock and repair.

How is capillarization stimulated in training? The answer is a matter of both training quality and training time. Both factors, the aerobic quality and the long duration, are suggested by the body's essentially conservative nature. It changes very slowly, even though it is marvelously flexible and responsive. The stimulus to enhance capillarization — and thus oxygen transport — must therefore be repetitive to an astounding degree, both in a given continuous workout and over several years. [17] That is made possible through low enough intensity training to allow for the necessary repetitions/ duration to stimulate the desired response in the capillary beds.

It cannot take place through anaerobic training because anaerobic training does not stimulate oxygen transport but rather the supply of energy (ATP) through the breakdown of creatine phosphate and glycogen in the relative absence of oxygen.

It does not take place in the weight room because the number of repetitions is not large enough and because the pressure on the heart/blood flow is too uneven and too low. Seldom, and then only in the third set of a very active weight circuit, have I have documented anything close to an aerobically effective pulse level (120 + bpm). Compared to effective endurance work like rowing, for example, even 3 sets of 30 (isolated limb) repetitions in a weight session hardly compare with the 700–800 (whole body) repetitions experienced in 30 minutes of rowing. And we know that 45 minutes to 2–3 hours is even more desirable for effective endurance adaptations. Another comparison: skating up a gradual two minute long hill requires roughly 100 steps on each leg. A session of 15 to 20 climbs thus accumulates some 1500–2000 repetitions. No weight session will ever approximate these numbers. Experience has validated the research finding that weight training may help stabilize joints and help in other small ancillary ways, but it does not affect endurance positively in any profound way. I discuss this topic in greater detail in a subchapter on strength.

Field sports, unless the level of skill is high enough to allow for continuous play, are not generally effective in endurance base fitness for the same reason: the load level/speed is too short and discontinuous to stimulate the necessary capillarization or enzyme activity.

**Enhanced oxidative enzyme activity.** Ulf Bergh, the prominent Swedish physiologist, reviews the important aspects of enzyme activity in cross-country skiing in *Physiology of Cross-Country Skiing.*

> For proficient cross-country ski racers, the activity of oxidizing enzymes in muscles of greatest importance in cross-country skiing is approximately double that in the same muscles of untrained persons; in other muscles the activity is only slightly higher for trained persons. The activity of those enzymes which function in the breakdown of glycogen seem relatively equal in trained and untrained persons.
>
> Other studies indicate that (1) enzyme activity decreases rapidly when training stops, and (2) it takes a long period of training to build up to this level of activity. *[One season of training is thus not enough.]*
>
> A study made during the Lindingoloppet (30km foot race) showed that those individuals with the greatest percentage of slow muscle fibers as a rule also could maintain the highest average tempo.
>
> The activity of oxidizing enzymes is greater in trained than in untrained persons, even for the fast fibers. The fast fibers of a trained person have approximately the same oxidizing activity as the slow fibers of untrained persons, which implies that even fast fibers are affected by endurance training, and therefore are significant in the capability for prolonged work.
>
> How can fast fibers be engaged in an activity in which they normally do not participate? Apparently, endurance training at an intensity corresponding to 70–90% of maximum oxygen uptake first engages the slow fibers, which subsequently are depleted of their glycogen. Thereafter (1–2 hours), the muscles must

engage more fast fibers, which have retained their glycogen stores unchanged. In this manner, even the fast fibers are affected by endurance training.[18]

**Increased strength through increased neural activation of the muscles.** Enhanced blood flow and enzyme activity do not improve performance by themselves. Base endurance training also improves actual muscle strength. The strength is gained not through muscle hypertrophy (increased cross-section), however, but through increased neural activation. This process can be a puzzling one to both athlete and coach, for whom, as the adage goes, seeing is believing. We like to see strength in the form of increased muscle size, not just feel it.

To quote again from the *The Olympic Book of Sports Medicine:*

> Strength increase is not synonymous with hypertrophy. In fact it is possible, especially in untrained subjects, a major part of the strength increase can often be attributed to an increase in neuromotoric activation of the muscle... there are a number of reports which have shown force increases without appreciable increase in muscle circumference or individual muscle fiber size. ... There seems to be an appreciable activation reserve, which can be mobilized with appropriate training. There are several ways in which the training can change activation: (a) more activation to the prime movers; (b) an improved co-contraction of synergists; and (c) increased inhibition of antagonist muscles.[19]

Each of these factors speaks to the critical importance of specificity of movement and natural, "whole-movement" activity. "More" must be understood as "more often" and "repetitive", since the body must become comfortable with the activity in order to achieve either effective synchrony, the muscles acting in concert, or inhibition of the antagonist muscles, which takes place through habituation, tension release (relaxation), and improving flexibility.

Even to the extent to which increase in explosive power is achieved through some increased muscle size, particularly in more mature athletes, that power can be improved in easy concert with base endurance work. A recent Norwegian study, for example, found that "explosive strength training at 10% of 1RM [repetition of maximum] is able to stimulate muscle hypertrophy, and that the hypertrophy is of the same magnitude as after training at 90% of 1RM."[20] In a study conducted with women skiers, another Norwegian group found that more general, racing-specific endurance could be enhanced through a protocol of 3 sessions a week of 6x85%1RM for 6 weeks.[21] We need to add the comment here that whereas this six week program had positive results, we should not therefore conclude that continuing the program would continue to help, any more than continuing to add any ingredient will improve the recipe further.

In an interesting related study done by a Finnish-Italian team, it was found that extra-loading with only 5–8% of body weight was sufficient to stimulate improved mechanical performance of muscles. The aim again was not hypertrophy of the muscle, but rather that

> an enhancement of the activation of the phasic motor units had occurred during extra-loading conditioning. An analysis of the F-V [force-velocity] relationship of the leg muscles ... has shown that the maximal level of electromyographic activity is recorded regardless of the tension or speed developed. Because the F-V curve shifted to the right, it is believed that an enhancement of neural activation (firing rate and/or synchronization) had occurred to satisfy the altered requirements.[22]

"Altered requirements" were the extra loading. What may seem surprising is that the "extra" was relatively small, falling within the relatively low additional loading of base endurance work. The point I would make is that muscular strength is significantly improved by base endurance training, as supported by the fact that maximal electromyographic activity is not necessarily dependent upon tension/load or speed but upon the duration of simple repeated stimulation. Neural activation, therefore, similar to increased blood flow and distribution in the muscles, is most optimally achieved through continuous special/base endurance activity.

Anecdotal evidence is compelling as well. In the summer of 1987 National Team skier Dorcas Denhartog clearly needed upper body strength. We began double pole sessions on roller skis of 2 hours + (22 miles) once a week as a special emphasis within her general training. With no visible change in muscle size she had our best placing in Calgary (23rd) and reported "no problem at all" with upper body strength. Having engaged the following summer in a major weight lifting supplement to her training, her results plummeted the following winter.[23] (Further specific discussions of the role and character of strength training follow in subsequent sections.)

I reiterate the distinction between capacity and load in physiological development. Building capacity, with all the time and patience which that requires, must precede specific training for high performance in competition. That is a fundamental principle which has not been well understood in American sports education and will doubtless remain puzzling in a society in love with muscle and overt competition.

Yet the evidence could hardly be more compelling that a majority of endurance training must aim at increasing capacity, and that it must precede, both in time and magnitude, any successful or long-term adjustment to higher loading. Again I am reminded of the time spent working the soil, weeding and stirring the ground, before planting, and then the patience before attempts at harvest.

At the simplest and absolutely necessary levels of understanding, thinking not only of adults but particularly junior developing athletes, it is logical that 80% of training must be aerobic. Only under aerobic conditions will the duration of the training stimuli be possible which is required to bring about the physiological growth changes which enhance the capacity for work. The comparison of aerobic and anaerobic metabolism itself provides the clearest perspective. A molecule of muscle glucose, metabolized with oxygen (aerobically), produces 36 ATP's (adenosine triphosphate) of energy at the site of the working muscle. The same molecule of glucose, metabolized without oxygen (anaerobically, beyond the body's ability to match load with oxygen intake), produces only 2 ATP's. It is aerobic work, therefore, which expands capacity and raises performance. Anaerobic work can put the final touches on racing fitness, but if it becomes routine or too early in the training cycle, it in fact limits improvement. The best proof of this can be seen even within a season, as regular competition causes levels of oxygen transport — max $VO_2$ — to drop.

How does base endurance training at the low/continuous end of the intensity spectrum relate ultimately to race performance?

It is known that cross-country ski performance is most prominently related to raising the level of anaerobic threshold relative to maximum heart rate. In the next section I discuss threshold training in greater detail. Here I would only briefly support my theme by citing Francesco Conconi's initial discovery that the training level most effective in elevating ANT (anaerobic threshold) corresponded to a level within 5 bpm below ANT. The minimum time required to adjust and reach homeostasis at this level was 3 minutes. Duration of work at this level may go up to an hour, but are most effectively maintained between 3 and 20 minutes, depending on the training age of the athlete. Longer times tend to become an actual time trial and are too long to allow for the recovery needed to continue interval fashion beyond 30 minutes.[24]

Conconi essentially validated and specified what was understood earlier: "As interval training mostly aims to load the oxygen transport system, it is unnecessary to select a training tempo that requires a large anaerobic contribution. ... Running 'hard' can result in paying the price for excess tempo: high lactic acid buildup."[25]

It is not surprising that the successful ski nations mark training intensities even lower for juniors than for more mature athletes. High, maximal loading is supplanted by the notion of optimal loading for the capacity at hand. And that is not achieved through exhaustive training or incessant competition. Competition is not a training program; if it becomes one, it will only soon "overload the truck," "throw seeds on unprepared ground," "start too many plants too close together, which thus choke each other and remain small."

If there is any obvious reason for the failure of American endurance athletes, it is in high school sports programs which are comprised of three seasons of competition, fall, winter, and spring, in which competition begins immediately, often twice a week, and little if any time is given to preparation. In other nations, by age 15–16 most teenagers have chosen a preferred sport, and although they may continue to play other sports, those are subordinated to the goals of the major interest. For that major sport 4 to 9 months of preparation precede 3 months of competition. In the US little preparation, if any, precedes 9 months of competition. The latter schedule would become clearly illogical, even abusive, if only the distinction between capacity and load were understood.

Bergh's "price of excess tempo" is not only momentary, in a given training session, but applies as well to longer-term success. The Russians showed early on how training at optimum-plus level elicits rapid early improvement, but then soon a plateau, followed by persistent lowering of performance levels.[26] The trap for Americans is that any training at all, regardless of type, elicits this early, and quite rapid, improvement. With it follows a natural sense of justified effort, wisdom, and accomplishment. But the predictable long-term, higher-level performance is being lost in the process. The pattern of 4–6 weeks of improvement followed by a flattening and then decline in performance (often accompanied by sickness or injury) is all too routine in the seasonal approach to sport in American schools.

The wisdom of horse racing, where people ironically are much more careful with animals than with our children in school, applies with equal precision to human athletes. *The Fit Racehorse,* by Tom Ivers, describes the necessity of working on capacity prior to loading:

> Every mile of LSD [long slow distance] is money in the bank. The mild stresses cause ... bones to remodel, expanding in diameter and becoming denser. Tendons and ligaments thicken and become more stretch resistant. Joint capsules and tendon and ligament bursas become more stable while cartilage pads between bones thicken like calluses on a working man's hands. ... Perhaps most important, the horse gradually builds a daily workload which

will form the foundation for him to perform the stressful stages of conditioning with quicker recovery and more safety. Later, he can do more speed work, more cardiovascular work, setting up speed and endurance on the racetrack. ...

Warning: All the structural changes we're talking about here take place far more slowly than specific muscle conditioning for speed. Without background mileage, the quick-prepped Thoroughbred quickly leaves the structural remodeling of his body behind and his muscles quickly adapt for speed, setting up the possibilities for a multitude of injuries due to lack of structural development. He gets fast, but the wheels drop off. And he won't get near his peak racing fitness because he can't do enough speed work to bring him to that level of fitness.[27]

Intelligent human athletes know as well. Siri Halle, a Norwegian girl who won two gold medals at the 1992 World Junior Championships, explains her training approach.

I believe in training that is steady and enjoyable. I have increased gradually as I have gotten better but have not tried to train twice as much to get twice as good. You cannot stress yourself to peak performances! Excess energy disappears with lack of enjoyment! I added up my hours from last season from April to April and found that of the 550 hours trained only 10 were of real hard training with interval and *spenst* [hill bounding]. Most of the 10 to 15 hours I train per week is spent on non-stressed jogging, fast walking or ski-running. I am satisfied as long as I stress myself to a pulse of about 120.[28]

I have seen the joy on my own athletes' faces who have trained this way. With a year of only base endurance work, a few threshold sessions and a few races (no hard race pace training!), three of my skiers repeated a two mile level-of-fitness trial on a quarter mile track. (They tell me their pulse each lap; I record the time.) In this second trial, with the same pulse rates and perceived level of effort as the first trial, they improved between 9 and 12 seconds a lap. They were stunned, and very pleased. They had been patient, and now had more confidence than ever.

Base endurance training works. It is the foundation of growth and long-term success, of the later joys of performances far beyond the win of a week, a season, or a given year.

# *6*

# *Linking Base Training to Racing*

## Level 3 - Threshold Training ANT +/-2 (Anaerobic Threshold)

The ways in which base/special endurance training is ultimately linked to highest levels of performance in racing clearly comprise the more complex elements of an athlete's understanding and discipline. Whereas base work takes up 80% of his time, threshold training and speed work usually dominate 80% of his thinking. The most fundamental relationship between endurance and speed can be seen in this performance pyramid.

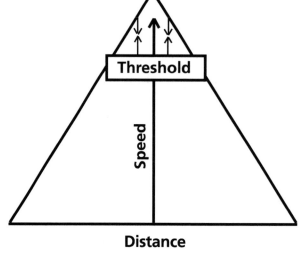

The need to grasp and apply those complexities of ultimate performance places huge demands not only on the athlete's physical capacities but on his intellectual and psychological sensitivities as well. Russian analysts stated the problem with wonderful simplicity in *Ski Sport* in 1975.

## Linking Base Training to Racing

Sports demand above all high indexes or showings in competition. For the skier this is high movement speed. But of course rather than moving at high speed only on some sections, it is important to be able to show medium high speed on the whole distance. For this it is not enough to simply go fast; one must also go thriftily and economically. Thriftily means not losing more strength than necessary in a given moment, saving it so that it can be properly spread out toward the finish.[1]

Threshold training is where we learn these necessary economies in mixing speed with endurance, where tenacity finds the uses of restraint, thrift the possibilities of velocity. Threshold is the area of the box in the pyramid, and it represents the highest velocity sustainable through aerobic metabolism. It is comprised of a variety of pace work and has the particular practical purpose of adapting muscle to movement closest to race speed but without incurring the lactic acid debt associated with anaerobic metabolism. With an adequate oxygen supply, muscles, in particular the adaptive type fast twitch fibers, are stimulated to adapt to higher velocities in a full but "friendly" demand environment.

Threshold work is not hard-as-possible training, or maximal sprint speed. It is 92%-95% loading. The point is not exhaustion but adaptation. Thus if the speed is around 95% of race pace, fairly long intervals are made possible. If we are doing strides or other quickness work, we keep them very short in order that the cumulative effects of the effort again does not exceed threshold. Thus the organs and muscles learn to breathe well at progressively higher velocities over long distance precisely because they are given enough time in that environment for adaptation (learning) to take place. It should be obvious that we will not accomplish that if we are gasping for air or in significant pain. If we keep the muscles well supplied with fuel, on the other hand, they will remain bright and responsive to the stimuli we provide, much like school children. And we know well that pooped children do not learn much, as our bodies in general do not. We may feel brave, adult, manly, and morally upright for ruggedly sacrificing the body in the service of our sport, town or country, but that has little to do with intelligent physical growth or high athletic performance.

On the other hand, once one has a broad training base, subsequent work at or close to anaerobic threshold does have the effect of moving the threshold curve to the right, allowing greater speed to be accomplished aerobically. Racing fitness is in fact ultimately achieved each racing season to the extent that anaerobic threshold rises with respect to racing heartrate. The higher the velocity which can be sustained aerobically, the faster the race times will be. An elevation of ANT by even 2-4 bpm will result in significantly improved performance. No amount of anaerobic work can match the gains of even a small elevation of one's anaerobic threshold. We do not pull ANT up from above; we nudge it up from below.

Threshold training is perhaps the most subtle of all the types, as its name suggest. Being at threshold is something like riding the crest of a wave which swells but does not break over. For this reason I call threshold intervals "swells". Some coaches call them tempo runs, or speed endurance. Whatever the name, the purpose is to move full and swiftly but without breaking into anaerobic metabolism. This work is therefore perceptibly short of race pace, although for its relative ease surprisingly close, 92.5% – 95%. And although threshold intervals do not feel "all out," a threshold session of 4 x 10 minutes or, for an older skier, 6 x 15 minutes, is very, very hard work. Given the fact that races, even 5 km, are 90%+ aerobic, threshold work is very effective. It is, as I say, how fast you are going — how fast your body runs at its optimum at the moment — not how fast you can go — driving it to its maximum single, momentary effort. Races, we know so well, are anything but momentary.

I ask athletes and coaches to try this experiment with threshold work. I have run a ski trail 6+ kilometers long on foot at my highest sustainable heartrate, 168 bpm. Another week, rested, I ran it again at ANT up to 6-7bpm lower. It felt too easy, but my time was 1:20 faster! I have done this same trial a number of times. The results are always the same. Americans need to understand a fundamental paradox of human performance: **effort does not by itself produce speed, efficiency does.** The sense for speed means the optimum effort for all the body's systems, not the maximum of one or two.

Whereas the initial prescription for elevating threshold was to train as close as possible to ANT while remaining below it, subsequent research has been less doctrinaire. The reasons for allowing a plus or minus 2 bpm (my preference; others allow a wider span) are that ANT for different training modes and individual daily physical states will vary some, and that, given that variance, even if one is slightly over ANT, the dominant energy supply mechanism will remain aerobic. I still believe that through mid-fall it is best to be at or slightly under ANT rather than over. The key is the execution of "slightly". That is what takes great restraint, calm, subtlety of feeling. You must become a speedometer, not a scale, a thermostat, not a thermometer.

Level 3 training occurs in intervals of 3–15 minutes and up to steady state sessions of 20 minutes or more. At 3 minutes one has reached an established marker for the time needed for the organism to adapt to an increased load and for the heartrate to

*Linking Base Training to Racing*                                                                          181

level out at that load/speed. At 15 minutes and beyond one is entering race length periods of adaptation (particularly for women).

I therefore like to keep level 3 hill intervals to at least 3 minutes, even if that requires linking two hills. Level 3 sections on flat and rolling begin at 10 minute lengths in August, 15 minute lengths in October.

The deciding factor in choosing the length of a threshold interval, however, is how fast you want to be moving. Americans are notoriously slow at their highest speeds. I often opt for shorter L3 lengths and greater numbers, especially with juniors, in order to maintain the highest velocity without exceeding threshold heartrate.

There is a good available link between race pace and threshold sessions. I call them 15/15's — 15 seconds at speed followed by 15 seconds rest. I begin with 2 minutes of these in June, just to alert the system. My session would be written thus: 2–3x2(15/15's)/5–8 @ANT. That reads: two to three times 2 minutes of 15/15's at anaerobic threshold with 5 to 8 minutes of rest (jogging, easy skiing) in between. In July I go to 3 minutes of 15/15's and thus reach the base threshold adaptation time. 100–150 meter strides at best kilometer pace with full recovery (3–400m jog, walk) provide an analogous means of doing fast paced training within the friendly threshold environment.

As I will note in the chapter on speed, 15 seconds has the advantage of eliciting maximum oxygen uptake for the speed but is short enough not to exceed threshold heartrate. That is because through 15 seconds the fuel supply originates in the breakdown of creatine phosphate, not yet the anaerobic metabolism of glucose (glycolysis) with its accompanying lactate buildup. There is therefore high stimulus for low cost, with good speed benefits both in terms of raw speed and speed endurance.

If these sessions take place in hills, which I also like, I reduce the lengths: Tuesday and Friday are hill days (2–3x1(10/10's)/5–8 @ANT … if speed is what we wish to emphasize. If I have a skier with great natural speed, then I will do the 2 or 3 plus minutes continuously and work on endurance.

Level 3 is also reached in speed sessions, by the end of each of the sprints and also in the strength stations. Though the pulse drops again rapidly, the linking of 3 or 4 circuits of 3 stations each amounts to an accumulation of ANT time. For the moment I judge that time to be 6–10 minutes per session. It would be easy, of course, to keep one's pulse near threshold more continuously simply by jogging from station to station a little more rapidly, but then in both sprints and strength stations the pulse would begin to pile on and the goal of recovering well between circuits would be lost. The success of the sprint work for speed/power gain is that ANT not be exceeded over the 100 meters. One could go a little more easily in the sprint, of course, in order not to exceed ANT, but then the specific speed/power goals of the session would have been compromised.

The manner in which threshold work should be structured into the year's plan is as follows.

1.  L3 comprises about 10% of the total hours, depending upon the age and training maturity of the skier.

2.  L3 work begins with two or three sessions in July, at 3 minute intervals, to wake up the chemistry and coordination. In August it becomes once a week. The volume of L3 training peaks in late November and early December. I have special endurance peak in late August, for L3 work begins in earnest in September. Because the volumes of L3 work become quite sizeable themselves, another, lower overall volume peak occurs in early November.

The top of the L3 curve cannot coincide with the top of the overall volume curve, as it used to in many of our programs of the single peak #2 type (Ch. 5, p. 162). The cumulative load becomes simply too severe, even with the volume peak in mid-November. A number of years ago in Labrador City my 4 skiers worked on L3 intervals of 10–20 minutes. They were whipped in late December. Being tired is expected; being exhausted is counterproductive. Their fatigue could also have resulted from too steady a diet of too intense level 2 base work throughout the summer. The long, very long term effects of even slightly overintense training behavior are difficult to overestimate. The effects of training a certain way are felt many months later. Even racing one's training a little bit here and there will result in a lowered capacity to adapt to higher levels of intensity as the racing season approaches.

The athlete's and coach's desire to learn, improve and think further is by its very nature intense, of course, as each of us tries to more thoroughly understand and optimize the training development recipe. The goal forever remains to discover the missing ingredient and add it in just the proper quantity and timing to the winning mix. Americans have historically turned to strength training (or at least our version of strength training) for that ultimate ingredient. We see top international skiers and seldom say, "Wow! He's quick and light in the feet!" Almost always we respond, "Wow! He's so awesome strong!" That is the American cultural bias at work: solve physical challenges by means of more power and a better mechanism, in a word: get bigger and stronger. As the results show, however, this approach has not brought our athletes success.

The topics of endurance, strength and speed clearly need to be sorted out (or rather re-sorted) and made more useful to us. What we will find is that the cause and effect relationship between each of them and high performance is somewhat different than we might have assumed. What will be clear above all is that the optimal training applications of each will further underline the pivotal role of threshold training in its various forms.

## *Strength and Endurance Training: How They Fit Together*

An understanding of the relationships between strength and endurance in training and racing is essential, perhaps most of all because the experience, the feeling of strength (or lack of it) is often confused and misleading.

You have reached the 3/4 point of a race, for example, and feel weakness. You want to touch the accelerator a little more, but there is not enough there to dash over the hill and be away. What is it you feel? Lack of strength. The muscles are tired; therefore they are not strong enough, so we reason. "I need bigger muscles!" you repeat (and not just for the race but for the mirror as well).

More often than not athlete and coach meet with similar mind and solution in the weight room, or in extended strength sessions of some kind. The weight room, however, is the location of many benefits but also many misconceptions and false hopes. We undertake what is considered a good strength-endurance routine: 3 sets or circuits of 5 or 6 exercise stations, 2 for lower body, 2 for torso, 2 for upper body, 20 repetitions each, each set increasing the weight 10 pounds.

We could do fewer repetitions, 5–10, in order to build greater bulk, reasoning with the basic physiological principle that contractile force is directly related to muscle cross-section. This approach has been tried many times, including by a group of Swedish women, and by Gunde Svan himself. It was rejected because the increase in muscle size/weight reduced the effectiveness of the cardiovascular system and resulted in poorer performance, despite strength gains. Performance is a matter of efficiency, and efficiency is defined by a positive relationship between the cardiovascular system and muscle on the one hand and body weight on the other. With the added weight of muscle bulk, max $VO_2$ figures had dropped.

More important for endurance athletes is the notion that increased strength can be achieved not only through added muscle cross-section or size but also by increased neural activation. The principle involved here is that "the more intense and more frequent a stimulus, the more motor units and therefore the more fibers are activated and the stronger the contraction."[2] Speed and frequency of movement in strength work thus can be used as resistances and produce improved strength, in a way therefore which supports both efficiency and natural balanced physical development in a young athlete. Twenty repetitions may emphasize the strength-endurance principle, particularly when we reckon we will ultimately have done 60 at each station; but we will see that this strength training version is really a rather meek supporting activity when compared to what is required in endurance sport.

If we do any regular weight training, it is in the spring. I call it "watering the flowers". It is a way to generalize training again, identify weak areas, stretch and strengthen generally, particularly in the torso, before endurance work dominates from June on.

What are the gains from weight training (or a mix of weights, plyometrics and paired resistance)? Primarily joints seem to gain in stability and movements may feel more free and powerful. Such strength sessions last from 30 to 45 minutes, and done 3 times a week, increased strength will begin to show in the 5th or 6th week. There are three main purposes, and I believe in them:

1. injury rehabilitation and balancing of specific strength deficit areas;
2. as warmup and warmdown to other endurance sessions;
3. for improving endurance (while never being a substitute for it) by improving joint stability.

Improved stability/balance facilitates tension release, and thus flexibility, which in turn facilitates motor unit synchronization, a key factor in physiological efficiency.

So many high school athletes head for the weight room saying, "I need to get strong, so I can get ready for ski season." They may indeed get a little stronger, but seldom faster and almost never more truly fit. Why cannot strength work be a workout in itself?

On the way to an answer some comparisons are instructive. Whereas a strength session may involve 60 repetitions or more, and thus seem impressive and tiring enough (and you feel hungry afterwards), a rowing session at an aerobic rate of 20-25 strokes per minute, for only 30 minutes requires 600–800 repetitions! And most endurance sessions will be longer than that, 45 minutes to 1 hour plus. An hour of base level ski imitation running (70 strides/minute) produces 4200 repetitions!

It is clear that strength endurance work by itself can only be supplemental. Despite the feelings and appearance of more strength, there will be little improvement in performance if strength training becomes either separate or a substitute for any part of the overall aerobic development regimen.

Why are 60 plus repetitions not an effective endurance factor? Wearing a heart rate monitor during a weight session tells the tale. One circuit brings the pulse up only to around 90 bpm, the second circuit to around 110 bpm, and the third to around 110–125. Only the third circuit even approaches a minor aerobic effect.

Following a 6 week stretch of weight training with 3 younger skiers (I was rehabilitating a knee), we all noticed that despite noticeable gains in strength, our running/ roller skiing endurance was no better.

There are two main reasons for this experience. It was spring, and we had cut out much of our mileage for the usual "down time" before summer. More compellingly, we validated for ourselves that fact that weight training simply does not stimulate the blood vessel capillarization process at the muscles which is the very cornerstone of endurance sport. Only continuous aerobic activity (heart rate sustained above 120–125) accomplishes that.

Strength stations mixed into an aerobic session work much better. Once the heart rate is firmly in the aerobic zone, strength stations, done resolutely and without hesitation, maintain the heart rate level well.

As a warmup and warmdown they are equally useful, for they facilitate both strength work and the stretching which is too often neglected (Stretching and strength together have been shown to give better strength gains than strength work alone.). In this case I divide the strength/stretching into halves, 15–20 minutes at the beginning, 15–20 minutes to finish off.


After enumerating the limitations of weight/strength training, I want to return to some benefits, however secondary.

The first is simply the improved strength, the sensation of greater stability, which, if it is in combination with thorough capillarization, and thus improved oxygen transport, will help carry you over that hill at the 3/4 point of the race. In this case I am again not talking about improvement in bulk/cross-section/weight but in the level of neural activation. It should be clear by now that when strength "dies" in a race, it is almost never a case of pure strength, muscle power. It is a matter of the loss of both coordination (motor unit synchronization) and the capacity of the strength available to endure further (both because of dwindling glycogen supplies and lactic acid buildup). So it is skill and endurance work which gives you your strength late in the race, not more strength work alone.

The second reason for improved endurance performance through added strength has to do with the interplay between muscle contraction and blood flow. When a muscle contracts, blood flow is occluded, oxygen transport is momentarily slowed. We know, of course, that in aerobic performance only a given fraction of maximal force is used, perhaps 40%.[3] Thus blood flow is not totally occluded. But it will be occluded to a smaller percentage yet if total muscle strength is greater to begin with. The necessary speed will be achieved at a lower percentage of peak torque. The transfer of oxygen from the air to the muscles throughout endurance activity is thus enhanced through strength training.

Now we should have an explanation of the nature of strength and strength training in ski racing. Strength can be maintained at its highest available level through an entire race only by means of efficient blood flow/oxygen transport, which in turn is dependent both upon the thorough capillarization effect of long aerobic endurance work and the lessened level of blood flow occlusion gained from greater strength.

Strength training by itself, even strength-endurance circuit training, cannot therefore produce the aerobic fitness which is the basis for endurance sport performance. The necessary sustained heart rate levels are lacking, and capillarization does not take place. Knowing what we do, we also conclude: there is more strength gained in endurance training than there is endurance in strength training. It is not by chance that skiers report that it is the threshold intervals which make them feel stronger and stronger.

These phenomena may also explain why field sports (like soccer, field hockey and lacrosse, which rely on short bursts, even many times repeated) do not enhance or even maintain aerobic endurance levels, unless the skill levels of the group are unusually high. In fact, greater emphasis on aerobic endurance might very well enhance the ability levels of these field athletes to both perform better late in their games and maintain greater skills and power throughout their training and competitions. For young skiers who wish to become better skiers, therefore, fall soccer and field hockey must be supplemented by significant doses of aerobic endurance training, threshold work in particular. Recent Norwegian research on a group of elite junior male soccer players in fact comes to this precise conclusion.[4]

The question of how we counsel young athletes toward making informed decisions on their own behalf about which sports are complementary to each other is implicitly answered here. Implicit also are ways in which various sports can be trained in ways which are more mutually supportive to the overall physiological development of the younger athlete. For it is the physiological bases of development which must govern the use that coaches, parents, and schools may rightfully make of young people. Given the fact that the years 15-19 are the most significant in terms of cardiovascular development, the need for young cross-country skiers to sacrifice soccer or fieldhockey in favor of more aerobic sports in the fall is both real and a delicate emotional point of counsel. The years 15-16 are the years of first major decision and responsibility for the requirements of higher performance, reward, and pleasure in sport.

## *The Relationship Between Strength and Speed*

In America the relationship in athletic performance between strength and speed is perhaps the least well understood of all the physiological connections.

In our preference for added power and mechanics the assumption has been widely accepted that greater strength would automatically result in greater speed, as it does in cars. American skiers have in fact shown good strength development, however, yet their speed has not improved commensurately, if at all.

Based on that assumption of speed naturally deriving from power, most often the formula for translating strength or force into work has been adduced to describe the source of greater speed, or the connection between simple strength and dynamic movement. Thus, if you lengthen the time of the application of force, you travel further. That is work. You accomplish more.

$$FORCE \times DISTANCE = WORK$$

This has been the prescription for improving kick in ski technique since 1979, and it remains prescriptive for both classic and skating.

But that formula confuses the fundamental factor in racing, speed. The initial assumptions seem to be that distance covered is the same as time spent, and that work done is the equivalent of speed achieved. But time spent is not racing time, for racing time by definition is always shortening. Thus in the actual formula for power,

$$\frac{FORCE \times DISTANCE}{TIME} = POWER$$

If we concentrate our attention on the time multiple, for that is the only direct way to consider speed, it becomes clear what the error in thinking has been. **TIME is not a multiple, it is a divisor.** If you want more work, a greater total muscle impulse, you can indeed increase the time of application. Somehow it has been overlooked that in order to increase speed, the time of application must rather decrease.

- Work therefore increases impulse area.
- Power defines impulse shape/speed.
- Under conditions of increasing speed, work must actually decrease in order for speed to be attained and supported.

I will point out the implications of this observation in a number of settings throughout my book. I note here only briefly that the Russians were aware of it by the mid-70's. Some biomechanists noted its applicability for runners in a study after the 1984 Olympics, stating the principle that speed is inversely proportional to the length of time spent on the stopped support foot. The notion of longer kicking time has persisted, however, in American skiing, beginning in 1979 with the Penn State biomechanical study of classic technique. What has been overlooked is that increasing the time of application must necessarily slow the speed of application.

This is best visualized by looking at the force - velocity curve.[5]

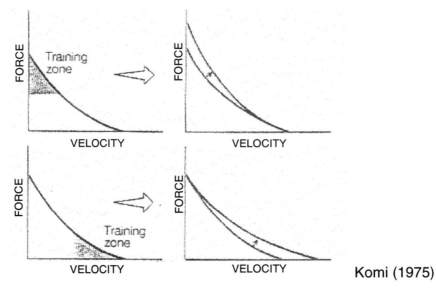

Komi (1975)

If we add to the force, we naturally slow the velocity of application. If we emphasize one, we de-emphasize the other.

A second proof can be derived from registering just how fast a skiing kick is. The Russians measured it at between .09 and .24 seconds, or less than the blink of an eye.[6] Thus, as they observed, greater time is not available, any more than it is to speed up the blinking of an eye. Only on a steep climb perhaps does the speed slow enough to fall within the time available for greater force application, and even in that case the shape of the application is more critical than the simple increase in force itself.

A third proof is available in the form of a simple demonstration. We turn a bicycle upside down on its handlebars and seat. We experiment by moving the wheel by hand. How do we maintain or increase the spin velocity of a bicycle wheel? Greater force may start it, but from that moment on it becomes quickly apparent that any increased time of force application will be accompanied by a slowing of the wheel in order to accommodate that greater time. The sensation of force applied is greater, but an increase in speed does not follow.

And how many times have we worked to tighten or loosen a screw whose slot is worn. No matter how much heavy force you apply, the screwdriver still slips out of the slot. Then you sort of pounce on the screw driver with a very rapid push, and the screw turns.

What do these considerations mean for strength training for cross-country skiers?
1. It includes weight training only for core/torso stabilization work and as part of the larger, more important mix of general strength training with medicine balls, plyometrics, flexibility work, and general training itself. Many texts support this approach, among them *Rowing* by Dr. Ernst Herberger, et al., the bible of oarsmanship from the former East Germany,[7] and *From Childhood to Champion Athlete,* by Tudor Bompa, whose four basic laws of strength training are instructive:

   ◆ Before developing muscle strength, develop joint flexibility. This is the key to both range of motion and protection against injury from later higher levels of loading.

   ◆ Before developing muscle strength, develop the muscles' attachments to the bone (tendons). Muscle strength improves faster than the tendons' and ligaments' abilities to withstand tension and cushion the bones forming the joints. Because of faulty utilization of the principle of specificity and the lack of a long-term vision, many training specialists and coaches constantly stress just the specific exercises of a given sport.

   ◆ Before developing the limbs, develop the core of the body. Although it is true that legs and arms should be viewed as the performers of athletic skills, it should not be forgotten that the trunk represents the link between them. The legs and arms are only as strong as the trunk is. A poorly developed trunk will lead to a weak support for the hard working arms and legs. The abdominal and back musculatures provide the trunk with an array of muscles whose bundles run in different directions surrounding the core area of the body with a tight and powerful support for a wide range of physical moves.

♦ Before developing the prime movers, develop the stabilizers. Prime movers, the muscles primarily responsible for performing a technical move, work more efficiently when the stabilizers or fixator muscles are stronger.[8]

2. Weight training is particularly helpful in cases of clinical rehabilitation or specific muscle imbalance.

3. Particularly for junior coaches, who often must train skiers who do both alpine and cross-country, or who must train both groups of specialists at once, it is important to recognize fundamental differences in the motions and speeds between cross-country and alpine skiing, and thus their radically different requirements and capacities for strength training, especially with weights.

We need to expand this point in order to understand the differences. In alpine skiing the contractions are largely slow and characterized by extended eccentric resistance to gravity. There are relatively few quick movements.[9] In cross-country the contractions are very brief eccentric loadings (in the glide, just before the kick) and primarily very quick eccentric and concentric contractions.[10]

Whereas relatively high resistance training with weights is appropriate to the slower movements of alpine, it is inappropriate for cross-country. Anecdotal evidence shows that although some top skiers have done some weight training, the majority do not. The validation has been broadly researched.

Ulf Bergh argued for this conclusion in Sweden as early as 1974. His statement of the basic principle runs simply: "The effect of training is greatest at the load used and considerably less for other loads."[11] The force-velocity curve graphs this principle. It also suggests that speeds at and slightly above threshold will stimulate the responses in strength which are specific to those speeds. Without training habitually enough at those speeds, we will lack both the neuromuscular coordination and the particular strength we need for successful racing.

More recent re-assertion of the value of weight training for cross-country skiers is not persuasive. Bergh is adduced as well in a recent pro-weight training study for his article in which it is shown that heavier skiers may have the advantage on flats and shallow climbs, whereas lighter skiers have the advantage on steeper climbs. Presumably the argument is that it is not such a disadvantage as we might have thought to carry the extra weight gained by weight work. Bergh's study, however, does not suggest that conclusion. Neither does it attempt to consider either the speed-of-movement-to-weight factor or the cardiovascular capacity-to-weight factor. Both go to the heart of skier efficiency, and neither relationship is aided by weight training.

4. For cross-country skiers, therefore, speed itself is the most reliable resistance to produce speed. Strength/power work provides some stability to accept that resistance, but it does not produce the speed itself.

We have come to learn all too well that it is possible to be very strong at slower speeds and weak at higher speeds. Komi's force-velocity curve documents this principle. I give several American examples of this in the next section on Tempo/Speed Training which follows. Two examples can make it clear here.

I have pulled skiers behind a snow machine at speeds over race pace to observe the results of their responses. Although they supplied none of the propulsion, within 500 meters they were at highest race pace heartrates and deeply muscle tired. That fatigue was still present the following day. The same responses accompanied two top skiers running on foot leap-frog style with a 12 foot long stretch cord of half-inch surgical tubing. Both jog. The lead runner then runs faster until the cord is stretched, at which point the following runner allows himself to be slingshotted forward at a velocity which quickly exceeds race speed. Pat Cote and Dave Chamberlain did this session for 5 kilometers (with numerous rest pauses) once a week during the fall of 2000. Though their cumulative heartrates did not exceed threshold (except on occasion), the workout was very hard overall, and they routinely felt muscle tired the following day. Most importantly, their speed improved and the strength to sustain it.

Both examples illustrate recent research to the effect that higher speeds produce higher vertical ground forces in the runner. The reactive quality of muscular activity is emphasized throughout.

Although muscular activity likely varied with skiing mode, it appears that the musculoskeletal system meets the mechanical requirements of increasing skiing speed through equivalent muscular activity simply by modulating the recruited muscle to perform the same task more rapidly.[12]

The critical relationship between speed and muscle impulse is further described in research connecting higher speeds with greater ground forces:

Fast and slow runners achieved equivalent impulses with different combinations of effective force and foot-ground contact times. Faster runners applied greater ground forces during briefer contact periods, whereas slower runners applied lesser ground forces during longer periods.[13]

But the critical initiating role of speed itself has never been clearly stated until test trials connecting leg power and hopping stiffness with sprint performance. The description runs as follows:

"The vertical release velocity and impact velocity are equal in a harmonic jump."[14]

"The eventual beneficial effect of the leg stiffness on maximal running velocity is a new finding in teenage runners."[15]

"The eccentric apparent spring constant [resistance to impact speed/force] increases with increasing running velocity, whereas the concentric apparent spring constant remains constant."[16]

"A group of top male sprinters had higher apparent spring constants during the eccentric phase than did less skilled sprinters."[17]

*"This reactive power is involved in each stride to maintain the high running velocity."*[18] (Italics mine)

Further initiating effects of eccentric loading responses to increasing speeds are described in research analyzing leg stiffness and mechanical energetic processes during jumping. Stiffness is understood not as rigidity but as a measure of elasticity, much in the manner of a stiffer or more supple bow or flyrod, tighter or looser shock absorbers. Countermovement jumps were carried out with ever decreasing ground-contact time.

Leg stiffness, ankle stiffness, and knee stiffness were influenced by the duration of the ground contact. Shorter ground contact times caused higher leg stiffness values. Leg stiffness influenced the vertical ground reaction force as well as the lowering of the subject's center of mass. Leg stiffness also had the effect on the amount of energy transmitted to the sprung surface. Higher leg stiffness values caused an increase in the amount of energy transmitted to the sprung surface. Conversely, an increase in leg stiffness caused a decrease in the energy absorbed by the subjects [and thus lost] during the negative phase of the jumps.[19])

The authors summarize:

This higher muscle activation caused changes in the stiffness of the lower extremities, and this way also caused higher maximal ground forces and lower vertical downward displacement of the center of masses during ground contact, as well as shorter contact times.[20]

Along with the many insights for training and technique as well in these remarks, there is only one mistake in this summary, a not unusual confusion of cause and effect: **Higher muscle activation did not cause shorter contact times. Shorter contact times caused higher muscle activation,** as the trials actually demonstrated.

*Conclusion:* The strength a cross-country skier requires will be achieved optimally at the speeds of movement at which he must race. This speed is the origin and primary stimulus to the strength which that speed requires in order to be sustained throughout an endurance event. Speed will not necessarily improve with increasing strength work.

It should now be possible to interpret and execute speed training more rationally in terms of developing not just higher physiological thresholds but also the higher speed thresholds to go with them.

With these ideas in mind, it is possible to talk with a fresh perspective about pure speed training, its benefits and when and how much to plan into a training year.

## Speed/Tempo Training

We wish after all to race, and as a National Team we remain frustrated in our efforts to gain the 10 to 15 seconds a kilometer (1.0 to 1.5 seconds per 100 meters) which still separate us from world class skiers, those same seconds which, with the rarest of exceptions, have always barred us from the elite.

What does this mean? It means that no matter how much we train, we will never catch up without improving our raw, basic speed. The relationship between raw speed and endurance speed may seem a little astonishing at first look. Comparing test results over 100 meters and 3200 meters, I have found a close correlation. One skier could roller ski 100 meters 1.3 seconds faster than the other. In a 3200 meter racing heartrate test as I have described earlier the former was 5 seconds a lap faster. That computes very closely to 1.3 seconds per 100 meters.

I made a similar test years ago at an Olympic Trials in Lake Placid. At the far end of the stadium, within the first 400 meters of the race, I timed a number of the top women through a 100 meter trap. With one exception their finish order for 5 kilometers reflected their order of speed in the trap.

Our notion of speed training has evolved haltingly over the years. For our years of training it would seem we have sufficient endurance. Bill Koch won Olympic silver in 30 kilometers. Less well known is that John Mike Downey placed second in the Norwegian Birkebeiner that same year. Later Wendy Reeves won the 60 kilometer Russian Murmansk Marathon, and Kerrin Petty won the 80 kilometer Swedish Vasaloppet. Jesse Gallagher had a fine 30 km in the World Junior Championships. His observation about the race was telling: the conditions were tough and the pace slower than normal. In that situation he could stay closer to the pace. All these examples, with the exception of Bill Koch perhaps, document Americans' strength at slower speed.

We have also done skill speed work: yet we are still not going fast enough to be world class. We know the goal must be to have the greatest power at the highest aerobic heart rate. Yet either doing increased training at ANT generally or adding race pace work later in the specific preparation period just prior to racing has not delivered the improvements we would all most like to see. Clearly something has been missing in our understanding.

I think we Americans have been caught in the middle of the high and low ends of training. Uncomfortable with easy training, we have routinely tried to nudge our base training levels up and slipped into level 2. But that is too high, a sort of no man's land between base work and threshold. Recent reviews of European and Scandinavian programs report 80% level 1, 10% each for level 3 (threshold) and level 4 (racing). Virtually no time at all is spent in levels 2 or 5.[21] Training base, however, is raised through volume, not intensity. And though we have finally shied away from too much work at racing intensity in the training period, we have been tempted into lots of tempo work and time trialing.

It is within this context that speed needs to be understood. For in order for us to do more effective speed work we must first get the base work at the low intensity where it belongs. Remember the distinction between building capacity and building load. Base or special endurance training builds capacity. If we do not take care that it be easy and thorough, we will never carry the loads we need later. Only on this basis will we develop enough peripheral system capacity to adapt optimally to the higher intensity work, the various higher speeds.

We want to go faster at base endurance level as well, of course. But that will not happen by adding intensity; it will happen by building pure speed, speed skill, natural swiftness. We approach speed then with great patience, and with a couple of essential notions.

First, **speed is an environment**. We go where it is and adapt to it. It is either how fast we are going (as I have described threshold intervals) or faster: flats or shallow downgrades where there is more speed that we are accustomed to, where we have to paddle faster to keep up with the current.

We will accomplish that adaptation through ease and swiftness of movement, not through power. Power will result from the swiftness, for it takes significant power to tolerate speed. And without the first principle — ease — the movements learned will be useless.

Test this principle of speed on the bicycle wheel as I have already described, or on the potter's wheel which applies more to skating. Swiftness of movement keeps you up with the speed already present in the wheel, and wears you out after a while. Application of power slows you down and wears you out even sooner.

The second fundamental notion follows from this first one: **Hard, breathless or painful interval training is not speed training.** It is anaerobic endurance training. It does not give you more speed; it rather allows you to maintain anaerobically the speed you already have. It prepares you for racing; it does not give you the speed in the first place.

American skiers and coaches have also long assumed that speed would result from increases in strength and power. It hasn't. First we need to turn the relationship around: power develops from speed. Second, and just as important, we need to structure speed work by distance covered and by intensity in such a way that it does not simply degenerate into anaerobic work. Anaerobic work, as I have just noted, primarily develops anaerobic endurance, not the speed we usually associate with going at speeds which become anaerobic if sustained over an extended distance.

Our first aim must be to stimulate the neuromuscular development which brings our coordination into a skill and comfort level at higher rates of speed. In these sessions we run or ski as fast as possible (FAP) without breaking up good form. In fact we achieve that speed through maintaining optimal form. The swiftness has grace and light springiness to it. That is *speed training*.

Our second aim is to spend enough time at higher speeds around anaerobic threshold to stimulate the fast-oxidative muscle fibers to adapt to aerobic metabolism. That is essential to achieving real speed endurance. In these sessions we move at anaerobic threshold (ANT), 80-90% of our top velocity. This is pace or *tempo training*.

Our third aim is to continually rehearse the optimally efficient movements we need by repeating somewhat long speed distances. We lower the velocity slightly in order to have a little longer time in which to concentrate on our movements and to begin to accustom our muscles to maintaining higher speeds at greater comfort, relaxation, and flexible range of motion. This is also pace or *tempo training..*

In essence we are using speed itself as the stimulus to power and endurance rather than weight or gravity (hills). Thus we train wherever speed is already most available, flats with good even footing, even slight downs, and, where we have the chance, with the wind at our backs.

By converting meters divided by two into steps or strokes in rowing we can just as well perform the workouts in any training mode just by counting strides or strokes, without having to measure everything. Measuring does clearly give the best indicator of change, however.

In this process we need to constantly remind ourselves how slowly the body changes and that the smallest of changes is enormously significant. Be patient and tenacious. It is critical to understand that all seven weeks in the example program given in Appendix 1 must be done faithfully in order to achieve the benefits of it. With a regular schedule, changes will begin to appear, usually in the fifth week, first in muscle tone, then in speed improvement. If you just dabble in the speed work, the overall recipe is compromised, and there will really be no way to predict what the result will be, if any. The sample program in Appendix 1 is derived from "Develop a Fall Conditioning Program for Sprinters" by Jim Hiserman.[22] It mirrors in a systematic way the suggestions of other research. It also exhibits the extreme care and thoroughness with which sprinters and their coaches work on speed development, something endurance athletes, particularly skiers, need to take seriously to heart.

In Appendix II I give another, simpler version of speed work which can be easily maintained throughout the year, sort of a little pepper an athlete can sprinkle into the easy distance days. It comes from Joe Rubio's article, "Acceleration Training for Distance Runners."[23] In Appendix III I give some examples of a basic strength and flexibility routine I have taken from Dr. Remi Korchenny's video, *Speed Improvement*.[24] I have tested both the speed development program and exercises with several skiers and had good results.

Above all, it is clear from that true speed work will be short in duration, very short.

We will continue to do good amounts of ANT or threshold speed work (speed endurance), 10 to 12% of our total volume. It can be a mix of slightly over and under

ANT, for ANT is not a single number; it is a narrow range, but a range nevertheless. Research has shown that slavishly remaining specifically sub-threshold does not yield better results. Threshold for different modes of training will differ slightly anyway, and the Russian description of level 3 as a "mix"[25] is mirrored by American research[26]. My description of threshold is: Racing Heartrate minus 12bpm +/-2. Plus or minus 2, no more, and the minus is as important as the plus.

Sprint work cannot just begin haphazardly, of course. It must be preceded, prepared for, by base speed work in the form of extensive and intensive tempo training throughout the summer and fall, as I will explain shortly.

In pure speed work we go from aerobic skill speeds, "floats," as I have called them since 1979, to plain sprints or FAP (fast as possible) runs over 50–100 meters on the flat (50-80 running, 75–100 roller skiing or skiing). 4 to 8 runs are done from a flying start with 4-8 minutes of jogging, flexibility, and strength work (paired resistance double poling and torso work) in between. To the coordination, quickness, and power effects of skill speeds we thus add general strength work as warmup and regeneration.

The rationale is as follows.

Our aim is to gain speed power, or specifically the kind of power required to increase our speed. Speed in this scenario becomes synonymous with strength training, for the resistance is neither weight nor hills but speed itself. Working on the force-velocity spectrum, we are training to achieve the highest force but also specifically what is necessary by training at the highest velocity. The goal is not to hypertrophy the muscle fibers (as with weights or slower movements) but rather to improve power through enhanced neural activation of the muscle. This is accomplished by moving as rapidly as possible through the optimal range of motion. Progress in functional athletic strength is not gained by hypertrophy of the slow twitch fibers anyway, as Kuznezow and Counsilman individually suggested some years ago.[27] The practical strength we are after is based upon the combination of this greater neural stimulation and the capillarization gained from long-term base endurance work.

We started talking about speed and have apparently only been discussing power. What happened to speed? That is precisely the point. Skill speed alone has supplied some quickness but obviously not produced times faster enough to be competitive. To overcome the deficit we increase the speed in order to get the power effect.

Informed execution of this training is critical, however, as it has perhaps been the most misunderstood and abused form of training over the years.

In saying I intend to add this ingredient of speed right from the beginning as part of general strength training, I begin with a historical perspective. Like some others, I have worried about FAP muscle work being too anaerobic to fit with the aims of high volume endurance programming. Still, the possibility of both achieving greater speed/power and of shifting the impulse curve of the movement to a span earlier in the arc of each movement seems to me a notion which we have not tested well enough. In fact we have spent so much time working on strength that the impulse has sagged to even later points in the pendulum arcs.

I have been relieved of my worry by an interesting Finnish article which reports that in a 400 meter sprint the energy source (ATP) through roughly the first 100m is the breakdown of creatine phosphate (CP) and that the role of glycolysis is small. That means to me that true anaerobic metabolism can be avoided if the sprints we do remain under 100m and if the rest between sprints is long enough to insure that lactate does not build up. Lactate levels were measured after 100m: 3.6–5.4 mmol1/1 are not so high as to add a destructive stress to an aerobic program. At the general removal rate for lactate of .5–.6 mmol1/min., 4–6 minutes of recovery would be more than ample enough to return the muscles to a fully fueled aerobic state prior to the next sprint.[28]

What remains of central importance is the finding that the lactate values built rapidly following the first 100m (we can assume more rapidly yet for athletes at earlier training levels). We need therefore to remain within that distance, not exceeding a time of 15 seconds (for running on foot that time should remain closer to 10 seconds, on roller skis or snow skis 15–20).

Eight seconds has long been used by runners as an optimum speed time, and this has once again been backed up by *Trainingslehre* (1986, East Germany)

> Studies by Soviet researchers have shown that elite 100 meter sprinters reach top speed between the fifth and sixth second, while athletes of lower ability reach top speed earlier. … Thus, the optimal training distance ranges from 35 to 80 meters for the elite sprinters, and from 20 to 60 meters for junior athletes.[29]

The added distance for such pure speed work for roller skis and skis is necessary because the rate of acceleration is slower than running. The time of the effort still must remain under the 15 second mark identified as the boundary for pre-lactate speed training.[30]

If the number of sprints goes past 5, then a lengthened rest interval should take place before the next set of sprints which have only 4–6 minutes rest between them. It is central to speed training that the stimulus is made to fresh muscles. Despite the fact that the degree of neural activation might remain large, a fatigued muscle is simply less "irritable" and responds to stimulus with both less force and slower speed. Where we might accept this response level in an endurance session, it is inconsistent with either speed or power training. We should not confuse the types of training or their specific methods of execution. It is characteristic of both the tempo work which prepares the base for sprint work and the sprint work itself that full recovery take place between all sets and repetitions.

Even so, it is further interesting to note that it takes approximately 25–30 strides to cover 80-100m. This means that each leg performs roughly 25–30 repetitions at maximum speed for maximum power. If we chose to sprint that far in a given session, 20–30 repetitions represents also a strength endurance component in this exercise. But I would advise staying on the shorter side at least until fall, for we are doing lots of endurance work already, and we want this part to build pure, raw speed and the strength it takes to respond to it. Research has shown that strength training can also enhance endurance performance, even though this takes place independently of increases of $VO_2$ max.

The most important notion here is the speed perspective. We *start with* speed, which then begets strength which then can enhance endurance (even though it is not the predominant training mechanism for doing so). Increased strength was associated with elevating lactate threshold, and both were thus factors in extended endurance time. The precise means through which these factors might be responsible for improved endurance performance, however, is as yet unknown. Speculation includes the notion that a change in fiber type recruitment improved the time to exhaustion (on a bicycle) by reducing the percentage of peak tension required for each push (of the pedal). Also, since blood flow during contraction is known to be inversely related to the force of the contraction, less occlusion of blood flow (and thus more efficient $O_2$ supply/La removal) should result from a reduced percentage of peak pedal force.[31]

Looking at the reverse scenario, it would be logical to speculate (and unfortunately it is only that) that if we do not train our speed at peak tension, the increased speed of racing will constitute enough of an increase beyond our levels of adaptation to speed that blood flow would be occluded all the more. No matter what our levels of endurance and strength, therefore, they will not be optimally functional for racing without being able to operate at a lower than peak level of muscle tension. Skill speed work may help some in this regard, but clearly it has not helped enough.

Warning: Do not be confused — achieving peak speed is the result of releasing peak tension in the muscles, not through tightening up or "driving hard". Skill speed work is excellent for this, and even sprint speed is best gained through total elastic looseness. Endurance or speed movements all depend upon releasing tension everywhere possible. Think of the slingshot principle.

Of further interest for the relationship between speed and endurance training is the finding that sprint training stimulates that same level of cardio-respiratory output as endurance training (8 seconds to $VO_2$ max).[32] While endurance at that level is not provided by sprint training (which means that sprint training cannot become a substitute for endurance work), there is a hint here of how to maintain full output levels during periods of recovery, just as it is necessary to do just one hard workout a week in a recovery period to maintain racing fitness.

Finally: it will be critical to train upper bodies in this 30 reps/best speed manner as well as legs. Despite logistical hassles, double-pole sprints must be done as well, either on roller skis, snow skis, or a double-pole machine (pictured on p. 166). Tension release, full range of motion and elastic quickness are the key factors in such speed work. Any shortening, tensing or lowering of the body's center of mass works counter to all the purposes of speed work. As with toeing down/"kicking" early, the effort in poling must be to move the major impulse span to the earliest possible span in the poling arc.

One approach is to have this session account for 2 workouts of the week. Such sprints (15 +/- seconds (30 complete strides, or 60 steps: international stride frequency for skiers is only slightly less than 2 strides per second), 3 or 4 sets with 8–10 minutes rest) may be "salted in" to not more than one other (distance or hill) session a week as well. It is important to remember the number of sprint sections remains between 3 and 5, even in the more specific circuit workouts. To do more than that number is both inappropriate to speed/power goals (too many and the speed and peak muscle force falls) and to endurance (the endurance would be anaerobic, which is only added in peaking periods). To quote a Soviet source:

> Exercises directed toward the development of speed, such as 10 X 100m run, were formerly used as a part of the general physical fitness training process. This anaerobic mode of working out at high cadence and significant expenditure of effort has little in common with ski racing, so that these training methods have now been abandoned.[33]

From our discussion it is clear, however, that the problem is not in the sprint work itself but it how it is executed. The key lies in long-term preparation for speed work, at distances shorter than 100 meters, through regular tempo work (90% +/-of maximum speed), and through adequate rest within the sessions themselves. Rest is particularly difficult because speed sessions tend to get the athlete revved up and high-strung. Long rests are irritating, boring. It is here where athletes and coaches need to become inventive in supplying interim activities as diversions and fun.

We have seen 8–10 and 15 seconds before, in the section on threshold training. Their reappearance in speaking of speed suggests the link we hope to achieve between the two types of training. 15/15's can bring a significant speed component to training each week, two in more gently rolling terrain (Sunday and Wednesday) and one or two in hills (Tuesday and Friday). 15/15s is read "15 seconds fast, 15 seconds walk or slow jog". It appears in a training schedule as, for example, "4–6x2(15/15s)/ 8–10". That translates into 4 to 6 times 2 minutes of 15 seconds fast, 15 seconds rest (walk/stretch or light jog) with 4 to 6 minutes or longer very easy between each 2 minute set.

Knowing that 8–10 seconds on foot or 15 seconds on roller skis or skis attains full speed and maximum oxygen uptake without going anaerobic demonstrates the link. Even some minutes of on-and-off 15/15's on roller skis will not exceed ANT. These will have close to the same speed effects of sprinting as well. It is important to repeat that in hills these become 10/10's. An easy way to execute these short on/off sections is to count steps, 15 steps for 10 seconds, 20 for 15 seconds.Not surprisingly, 15–30 seconds on and off appear in Joe Rubio's speed maintenance program as well.

Speed development and maintenance can be done on foot or skis, in the summer, fall and again in early winter until the goal velocities are achieved. The only difference in the winter version is that the FAP or acceleration gradations are built up of stride numbers and reach up to 50. This larger number reflects the specific race preparation character of the period which of necessity contains higher intensity and an enlarged anaerobic component.

The kind of speed training described here provides not only speed; swiftness begets power, which in turn accommodates the demands of higher velocities, wherever they occur in training. Such regular "pepper" in training further aids in maintaining the good muscle tone/skeletal muscle support required to tolerate the amount and variety of loads/stresses throughout extended periods of increasing fitness.

**Reviewing Basic Principles**

With these considerations planted and rooted in our minds, we can look back over the whole year's patterns and periodization and understand the rationale for each of the ingredients in the training development recipe.

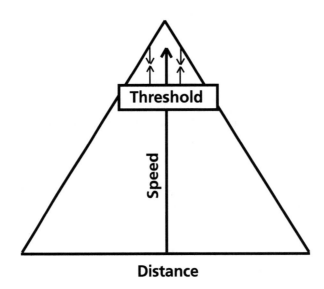

Overdistance is quite straightforward. The goal is time spent, not effort or speed. Each session needs to be continuous and long. It may be uncomfortable at first to go as slowly as you must in order to stay out as long as necessary, but you can learn not to feel either guilty or bored. Going out with others is best. You don't have to do the same thing the entire time. You may combine activities, which can relieve the tedium sometimes. If you do mix activities, however, be organized enough ahead of time, so that there is little or no break in the switch over.

We start with the basic elements gained in endurance work, the essential development of the peripheral systems. With that well established, as the year moves up the pyramid we progressively add resistance in two basic ways. The first is speed. Short speed transforms strength into power by quickening neuromuscular response. Long speed extends the duration and economy of that speed through progressive pace work at and slightly above anaerobic threshold. That economy is made up by combining physiological capacities with sensory/perceptual acuity (quiet balance in moving faster, freedom from tension, confidence).

The second form of increasing resistance is hills. Hills contribute specific power and cardiovascular loading

1. by stimulating/recruiting a greater proportion of fast twitch muscle fibers near anaerobic threshold, which helps those "speed" fibers adapt to aerobic metabolism and thus their highest economy;
2. by enlisting the forces of gravity to overload the heart and lungs; and
3. by narrowing the angles of body to ground to stretch the muscles and improve their range of motion and elasticity/stiffness.

## *Terrain and Execution*

When we are seeking to develop better speed, we remain in easy terrain, for there is where speed is most available. With the fewest hindrances to speed, we can find balance and comfort in it most readily. Like listening best to music where there is no noise, we "listen" best to speed where we can move swiftly without distraction or tension.

When we are seeking specific power and sharper cardiovascular loading, we go to the hills. And one thing is certain: our event will always be in hills. So we naturally train in hills, for pleasure, for purpose. That is our instinct. Trust it. Any differences will be in amount, steepness, and length, depending on the goals of a session and the time of year. Varying sorts of hills make up the skier's particular "playing field." They form the natural "intelligence" with which the terrain informs and thus forms him. That collective intelligence moves progressively from the specific endurance end of the training spectrum to the power/speed end, from base (AT) training to threshold (ANT) to racing.

There is a place for flats and gentle rolling terrain in training, to be sure. Flats are for easy regeneration work or raw speed sessions. Raw speed, or base speed, as I have called it, is another of the more undeveloped aspects of American cross-country ski training, and I have spoken to that issue in a previous chapter. Here I would only reiterate the fundamental notion that **speed begets power;** power does not necessarily beget speed. Power may make speed possible, but it does not install the neuromuscular "gearing" or perceptual acuity which allow us to actually go faster.If we do not grasp this notion, we will continue to "go fast only at slow speeds" and never achieve the racing parity with the world's best.

Flats can also be used for strength or range of motion work as well, if we can run in shallow water at the shore, in high grass or sage, or through Alaskan type muskeag (spongy, springy tundra). But this is general conditioning rather than specific to cross-country skiing. Research has shown that all of the body's systems adapt in an amazingly discrete and specific way to the terrain used.

Ultimately then, it is less the type of training which counts so much as the particular use you make of it at the various times of the training year. You control that. From June on we hike and run and roller ski in the hills, with continuous, easy movement. These are aerobic hills. In mid-July threshold hills (ANT hills!) begin with bounding on Tuesdays and Fridays. In the later fall they become more extensive.Here are some types of hill workouts. They can be done virtually in any of the modes, if you understand the physiological processes you are trying to stimulate. (For example, you can do hill work on a flat by bounding, or by putting resistors on your roller skis, or by rowing, in the earlier summer. Ultimately, however, we have to get specific, for the lactate response at the same heartrate will differ on hills from flats. Specificity remains the most decisive principle.)

**Hill workouts**
♦ even effort, continuous — hiking, running, ski running (ski imitation), rowing (power strokes), mountain biking.
♦ ANT-hills: 3+ minutes — it takes 3 minutes for the body to reach homeostasis, the higher chemical balance, at the new level of loading. (It is essential that these remain aerobic in order to maintain the pace for 3+ minutes. Later, in the race preparation/speed endurance period in November and December, when the best pace speed must be maintained, hills should not exceed 2 1/2 minutes because you simply cannot hold your form, and thus efficient speed, longer than that.[34]

**Bounding**
The Norwegians call it *spenst,* or "springiness" training. It derives from Arthur Lydiard's hill bounding routine for runners and adapts well for skiers:
♦ verticals ("Pogos"). The extreme vertical motion is necessary to approximate the

demands for both power and quickness at the highest horizontal velocity. (In other words, the faster you go, the more vertically you must kick or lift off in order to stay on top of the speed.) Going for height.

- arcs: going for distance (like a horse leaping a bar).
- short sprints with or without poles.
- "poles only": double-pole every other step, approximates kick-double pole and skating.
- side-up's: facing to the side, the lower leg pushes off and crosses in front and up the hill (with or without poles).
- back-up's: back facing up the hill, push-off left between 10 and 12 o'clock,right between 12 and 2 o'clock.

**In all movements straighten the leg completely from hip thrust to toe-down, be active in the shoulder/arm lift in front and behind.**

### Bounding with skill speeds in between

- Loops comprised of a hill (2 x 10, 20, or 30 seconds of varying bounding types with a walk/stride recovery between) with 2 or 3 x 10-20s acceleration on a flat or gentle down, to the bottom of the hill again, or next hill.
- Additional loading in hills can be by either length of time or speed, for power or quickness afoot, again depending on the skier's particular needs. We remember that these needs must be identified early enough. It will require 4-6 weeks minimum to accomplish physiological changes by the time of the most important races.

### Summing Up

- Adding length gives you endurance.

- Speed with long rests gives you speed, with short rests anaerobic endurance.

- Hills give you power. But they can also fool you. It can become too easy to get in a hard and satisfying workout if your speed is comfortably slow, but you cannot afford to let such slow speed become the dominant gear. Otherwise, even when you are in terrain where you have the air to go faster, you will remain stuck in your hill gear. You also do not need many of them too close to the important races because they are too tiring, otherwise you will leave your best racing effort in the training session rather than the race. "Fresh" and "sharp" remain your cues, the feeling of being a little "overamped".

- Flats and easy rolling terrain, in short sections, give you skill speed and quickness and are good for firming up fast pace work. Shallow downhills are good to include for this as well.

- Little if any hard hill work is done in the competition season, when threshold (which is rising) intervals up to one kilometer are the choice if the athlete needs other speed/pace work beyond the week's racing. I like 1 kilometer because it not only allows you to go fast, it will show you the best speed you can actually strive to maintain in a race. Too often shorter all-out intervals are excursions into brave hard work but delusions of race speed. Race course terrain is used, but hills are not emphasized. Certainly very short foot speed and technique exercises continue to include hills, however.

Returning to the training seasons, it is important to understand hill bounding as ski imitation in order to remain technically specific to skiing motions. Reaching too far forward up the hill with the foot, for example, results in the hips dropping as the pole pushes. Simply walking with poles has a similar effect. In skiing the hips rise as the pole pushes, however, so particular attention must be paid to achieve that movement. It is most easily accomplished by starting off at an easy jog with poles, then slowing with each step to a gently bounding pace but without changing anything in the lift-off at the ankle/foot or general rhythm.

# Linking Base Training to Racing

Poling hand down
hips/heel drop (not like ski stride)

Start

Poling hand down
hip rise with lift off ball of foot (imitates ski stride)

## Peaking

In reality the entire year's schedule is a peaking schedule. That is the most fundamental nature of periodization and patterning. Most people think of peaking, however, as the process of sharpening leading up to an important race or race series. This area which includes threshold and racing zones is the most delicate. The key is to encourage continued aerobic capacity at the highest level of speed while adding the anaerobic capacity specifically needed.

The stress levels involved in the final race preparation and peaking periods are great, so it must be re-emphasized that the primary components of peaking are tapering, early rest, and then reloading. That in itself provides the best basis for choosing the final peaking types of workouts. We want the best speeds, we plan to stimulate the optimal responses in terms of both speed and endurance, but without such sustained loading that anything is drawn off the larger base aquifer of fitness.

That is particularly true in the last 10 days to 2 weeks leading up to the first important race. In that final period the taper balances the final intense anaerobic work (for athletes 18 and older!) when volume drops by 30% or so, and in the final 7 days by 50%. These final 6 weeks are a delicate balance of refining the body's processes and rest, and requires close monitoring and communication between coach and skier. There are some basic guidelines.

The first is to plan backwards from the race at least 8 weeks. That can be done by mid-fall, or as soon as the winter's race schedule is known, and figured into the year's plan. In rough outline peaking requires 5–6 weeks of race preparation. These are the early trials, intervals, and races in later November and December.

Note the phrase "race preparation". That is different than racing the big races. These early races are run in the service of the athlete's specific development. They serve him; he does not need to serve them, achieve any particular result. They are training races only. In combination with his other training they serve a period of intense maximal aerobic endurance, anaerobic buildup and final sharpening. He will doubtless become quite tired, and the training hours drop markedly. He becomes progressively more edgy, partly from having so much time on his hands, partly from the sharpening process itself, from its effects on his chemistry. He is "amping up". He is about to shed his cocoon.

In the final 6 weeks anaerobic work is added to the mix in order to gain the tolerance for race pace, which is usually 4–10 bpm above anaerobic threshold (ANT

— itself higher by 2–3bpm than mid-fall, if training has been effective). With 3–4 anaerobic bouts a week, of varying kinds and lengths, including very short sprints as well as time trials just over ANT, anaerobic capacity can be achieved and enhanced within the six weeks.

Since even the shortest races are 90% or more aerobic in nature, it is important to remember that anaerobic capacity is a required but not the major factor in racing. It is most critical to maintain all the aerobic fitness gained up to this point. In that light it makes sense that the goal of anaerobic work is to stimulate body chemistry, not batter the body with 11th hour toughening. Anaerobic sessions are thus conducted at a very fast pace but at optimal or "best" speed, at desired race speed or only slightly faster, not frenzied sprinting. One finishes tired, not beaten down.

A Norwegian study from 1990 confirms this by concluding, "a significant improvement in anaerobic capacity was found although the training load was far from exhausting."[35] The idea is to gain just a *little bit* more, and that is difficult enough, but that little bit will make a significant difference in the results. Another study showed a 3% improvement in 5km running time after 7 days of taper (85% drop in volume!) and drastically increased intensity work.[36]

Efforts to precisely determine the best distances/times for anaerobic intervals have been somewhat inconclusive and basically depend upon the fitness level of the athlete and his/her years of training. One rule of thumb, however, is that it takes roughly 2 minutes at full speed to exhaust anaerobic capacity.[37] That length interval promotes capacity. Shorter intervals (10–30 secs.) improve the rate of energy release. Both improve performance, their systems closely linked. Knowing that, the coach's choice must made based upon his athlete's specific training state.

One interval session might be 5x5 minutes/5 rest. That is for a mature skier with good natural speed and a substantial base in years of training. Beyond such speed endurance intervals (ANT+2–3bpm), I alternate max $VO_2$ work in a week between sessions of 2 minutes and 1 minute. Beginning with 4–8x2 minutes/5–10 rest, I cut the rest by 30–60 seconds a week. With 8–15x1minute/1 rest the rest drops 15 seconds each week. I would do these on Tuesdays and Fridays if the races were on Saturdays. Both the number and rest intervals are determined by the skier's responses. If the skier cannot repeat the interval without losing speed, the rest must be lengthened or the number of repeats reduced, or both. Two-minute intervals in particular are very intense, especially for younger athletes. Depending on age, training state, and the needs of individuals, I do the alternation between 1 minute intervals and 30 second intervals (begining with 1 minute rest and reducing it 15 seconds each week).

**Under no circumstances may speed be compromised at this time of year!**

For short "pocket" sessions I also like 10secs/10secs or 15secs/15secs for 5–10 minutes or so, 2–4 times over to spark speed and lightness afoot. These also have the effect of toning the muscles: speed begets power.

What is most essential for both athlete and coach is to observant and honest about the athlete's ongoing condition these final weeks and adjust training based on the knowledge of what each training type can provide and how the early races are proceeding.

Early races are for two main purposes. The first is to re-adjust to the psychological environment of public competition. The second is to make final training adjustments. The early races provide the insights into what you need more of, endurance or speed. If you are fast or faster than goal speed but are dying a little too early, late in the race, you need endurance. Keep or lessen the speed slightly and lengthen the intervals, from 3 minutes at ANT+ 2–3bpm to10 minutes, or even 15–20 minutes, using only 3 or 4. The ever so slightly reduced speed of these longer intervals may feel too easy, but believe in it. It is faster than it feels, and it is speed you can use. Remember, if your training has been effective, your anaerobic threshold will be 2–3bpm higher than in mid-fall. A slightly reduced perceived effort now could very well elicit equal or even improved speed from what you have come to expect. It is time to measure progress by actual speeds, not by mere effort or feeling.

What you cannot do is simply add more of the short intervals at the highest speed, or simply lengthen them; that will exhaust you, not help you adapt to optimal speed endurance. Training stimuli do not "take" in a tired body. What you need is not anaerobic endurance in the hopes of better tolerating your level of fatigue (rising lactate concentrations) but aerobic or threshold endurance, so you can remain efficient at that speed and not go anaerobic in the first place.

If you finish the race with everything you have in you and still are a little slow, or not tired, deep in the muscles, it means you have good endurance but need speed. Shorten the intervals, to something between 20 and 60 seconds, and add repetitions. Ample rest in between is crucial. If you decide to simply work harder and strangle the rest intervals, you may gain a little anaerobic endurance, but you will tire quickly and lose the neuromuscular coordination (motor unit synchronization) element which is so essential to gaining speed.

In general, the more hours per years an athlete trains, the longer his peaking taper will be, as much as three weeks for a skier doing 6-800 hours. Two weeks is a good place to begin. The final 10–14 days, however, are the most critical. 10 days is

*Linking Base Training to Racing* 211

the minimum tapering time necessary because it takes 10 days for the body to get rid of the residual fatigue resulting from the buildup period. Very fast, interval work, shorter and fewer, are balanced by very easy distance, but not overdistance, sessions. Threshold work goes on, reduced dramatically in amount. Of course you cannot accomplish any drastic adjustments on whim or out of nowhere in the last 6 to 8 weeks. The body is that conservative organism that likes only gradual changes. We have to monitor the speeds in each of the training zones all year in order to make the final tuning process possible.

The die is cast. There is really nothing you can do better at this point than stick to the plan. Make no last minute decisions. By no means do the extra interval or workout you might itch to do. The itch means you are ready to race, not to train more. Do not waste it a day or two before the day you want it. After all, the whole point of the year's training has been done according to plan. It takes the last bit of patience, confidence, inner calm to wait. Think of it this way. Waiting, resting now is just pulling the sling shot further back.

After the maximal aerobic/anaerobic build-up period, the race preparation portion of the year, there need be no further additional loading. You have done what the body can do; further loading will only tire you out, not improve you racing fitness. What you want to do is preserve the precise racing chemistry, speed, and rest by counting back the rest interval and by giving your whole fitness aquifer time to re-fill. You want to sharpen the knife edge, not file the blade away.[38]

In the final preparation period more effort to increase speed simply adds tension. Even if you can get it, it will not be specific race speed, and thus it is not usable. Overspeed at this point simply strains the muscles, which suffer a loss of elasticity and response quickness through excessive lactate loading. We are reminded of Ulf Bergh's fundamental principle: The training effect is greatest at the load used and far less at all other loads. In the final peaking period we need to administer just those loads in just the way to maintain what race requires without becoming overzealous or greedy. Greed simply begets fatigue. Paul Garvey sums up the task nicely:

> During the peaking period, the athlete's volume drops drastically, and the intensity increases or is maintained. This allows the athlete to maintain his increased level of fitness while at the same time promoting recovery from the work done in the training season.

> A coach must not forget the basic principles of peaking. If the athlete has not experienced enough stress, he will not reach a peak. If the athlete has experienced too much stress, he will not recover and will not reach a peak.

Regeneration is the key to successful competition.[39]

If additional speed is still needed, think of it as sharpening, not as loading. You are trying to free up what you have through tension release and finer movements. So you do it where it is easy to find, on the flats. Though it is easy to develop the loading on hills, the speed achieved at that load will be slow, relatively speaking. Americans, I among them, have often made this mistake.

I remember a conversation with a somewhat dispirited Allison Kiesel after the first race of the 1980 Olympics. She was bewildered by not having enough speed, though she felt strong. I asked her what kind of sharpening intervals she had done in her final training. She said natural intervals, where the hills occurred in her training courses. Loading is indeed natural there, but will add power rather than the specific speed one wants to add. The force-velocity spectrum graph is once again the key to understanding the precise effects of different kinds of loading.

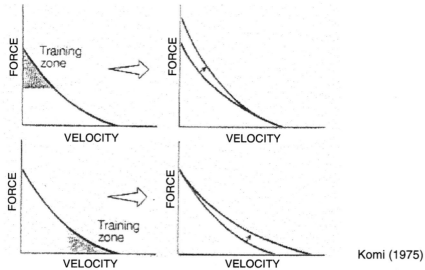
Komi (1975)

So hills can fool you. They are an inviting and easy way to get high load training session in, and one has the satisfaction of having worked nobly and hard. Yet for all the power and quickness of movement involved, the actual velocity is relatively slow. That works to the detriment of your sensory-perceptual comfort and coordination at higher velocities, the very goal of your peaking process.

So we finish speaking about peaking with this graph both to explain the limitations of hill work in final racing preparations and to direct the orientation of our training when we want final speed.

**How fast you are is how fast you will go.** That seems an almost silly truism. That speed, however, has not happened for Americans yet. It can, however, if we refocus on speed, in both concept and execution.

# 7

# *Racing: Farewell to "Charge the Hill!"*

The race is nothing new. I do not mean to deny the race its significance, for after all it is the performance for which we have prepared the entire year. It is also the most compact and public presentation of that preparation, and that is perhaps the decisive difference: there can be no secrets now, no explanations, only a present, a course, and what we do. It is the scene in which we see not only who has trained diligently but more importantly who really loves to go fast, to race. In very real ways it will be a statement about what the athlete has done and, by extension, display the level of personhood to which his complex physical and mental development has brought him. The question "What is he made of?" cedes more precisely to "What has he made of himself?"

In the reckless abandon of the race, the slingshot let loose, the graceful violence, every athlete is fired by the deepest of curiosities: "How perfected are my insides?" "What will I feel of their strange powers?" "I will try my skill at flying!"

If there is an extra thing about race day, it is perhaps that unusual excitement — urge mixed with uncertainty, an odd fear mixed with the passion to leap, a dive but upward — an excitement in our own incipient perfection, or its possibility, approximation, in which the potential to excel, to perform our best, even slightly beyond, compacts and plays every ounce and fiber of our physical and mental vitality. Like the artist in recital, there is really nothing new, except the unerring presence of this time in which to show and measure oneself.

But racing is different, we say. How can you say it is not? For a very practical reason: by making a stranger out of race day, by making race day an alien experience, we are led to make mistakes in training preparation, in goal setting, in tactics. Our desire to do well, to excel, perhaps to win, leads us to believe we must and can overcome all obstacles and go beyond ourselves. We will want to believe that because we have worked long and hard and are good people, and wish it so sincerely, that a miracle will occur to give us flight and the power to excel above all others.

We cannot go beyond ourselves. We may well discover more of ourselves than we knew though, if we are calm and alert, have prepared intelligently and learned specifically to race. Then we will race with a clear, uncluttered head, focused only on the possibilities at hand, today, now, between Start and where the track first disappears into the woods.

There will be no miracles, however, no strange and sudden magic, no divine intervention. Truly strange and alien elements seldom if ever accompany great human performances. This truism leads to several fundamental principles of racing.

The foremost is that racing is not a contest with the terrain. As long as Americans view nature as something to be dominated, just as the body is something to be beaten into shape, then racing will remain combat, the skier will remain stuck in an adversarial relationship to the terrain through which he races. There will be little success and little joy in that, for in any such contest the terrain will win, every time, regardless of who might win the race. The scene is not a battle, the cry is not "Charge the hill!" Say goodbye to Teddy.

There are no enemies, no strangers. Just as racing is the perfection of training, no desire for an outcome can be different from the patience and detailed execution of each training session. Such a desire is both wasteful of psychological reserves and time spent in training as well as simple folly, assigning to faith and hope, even charity, what the body and mind and senses have ample capacity to achieve by themselves. After all, they have been practicing!

Racing is using that practice best. So a second principle: Nothing will happen in a race which has not happened in training. You can count on it; your body is ready. Now let it run.

Well, maybe something new. In the vastly complicated mix of physical and mental development over a long period of preparation there can be no absolute certainty of the optimal mix of factors for each individual. In some respects that unknown quality is what is most distinctly human about competition and why racing is, in the best of cases, so humanizing. It is perhaps, we might say, the very insistent imperfection of our will to higher performance which makes the whole game so fascinating, so magnetic, perhaps even heroic.

But you cannot dream of miracles or magic removing that imperfection, nor will it work to presume you can remove it yourself. That kind of confidence is posturing rather than real power. On a given day, however, everything may go together perfectly. That will be a gift, and you will ride it with an exhilaration and joy which is magical itself, an unforgettable perfection of yourself and landscape, and utterly momentary. If you dream of it and become greedy, you will only cause its continued absence, as if it were a shy spirit. You will overlook too many other things you can do which set up the circumstances of your best performance in which that extra element might, by chance, enter. As B.F. Skinner remarked, "The task is not to think of new forms of behavior but to create an environment in which they are likely to occur."[1]

Zen goes him one better, in the "art of controlling circumstance." That is accomplished by being sensitive to the rhythm in the way things go together, to the natural balance and creative tensions which suggest both harmony and flight. It is the basis upon which gracefulness and efficiency become the same thing. Just by being in a state of heightened awareness to one's surroundings improves the possibilities of going fast, with it, responding early to changes in terrain, adjusting instinctively to track and movement rhythms, accepting the speed available everywhere. You are aware not so much to this or that specific, single objective but rather more "off center". The whole environment acts simultaneously upon one's peripheral vision and proprioception. That is when you will go with the terrain best, lifted by it, going with the grain, like the grain in wood, in the fibers of your muscle.[2]

So there can be no new mental sets, no new words or metaphors, on race day. There is no way an athlete will perform well the first time with a new instrument. If you have traveled well by compass, you do not cast it aside on race day for a sextant. The critical element is the highest degree of acceptance of what you are, now. There will always be enough of bravery and alertness in that for any hero, and that is what we want, the ultimate graceful human being. That, whether you know it or not, is what you have decided to be.

Think of the circumstances of racing. We can draw the simplest of tactics from them, and they will be all we need. We know:

1. Everything we do is part of going with the terrain, not against it. We enter into its speed and character, avoiding any adversary role. We want to ride it like the swells of the sea, always just ahead of the crest, of the swell of the wave, never just behind.

2. The body is an absolutely marvelous system of levers and elastic bands, fuel supply and delivery. There is more speed in those systems and in the terrain itself than you can force out of them. So get into them, go where they are, with them.

## Preparing Yourself to Race on Race Day

I consider the final preparation for the race to begin forty-five minutes before the Start time and be complete within the first kilometer of the race. Why the odd frame?

The forty-five minute warmup is standard. Some skiers, particularly mature skiers on very high hours, use up to an hour. But forty-five minutes gives you the 20-10-5 routine which is so effective: 20 minutes in zone 1 (easy), 10 minutes in zone 3 (medium hard, ANT, threshold), and 5 minutes in zone 4 (race pace). The last piece can be done a variety of ways, depending on preference and state of mind: they can be 1x5 minutes, 2x2:30 with 2-3 minutes rest in between, or 5x1 minute with 3 in between. You might even do a mix, to include 3 or 4x:30. The speed in these final minute is just 2 or 3 beats above threshold, but quick, elastic, loose. Some skiers staying at threshold itself, feeling warmer, less "wound up." There are a few minutes left before you start: stretch, run in place or in a small circle with a few quick movements — butt kicks, knee lifts, springs off the toes, spinning the arms and shoulders — and quietly review your mental cues. If you suddenly feel drowsy, don't worry; it is not fatigue. It is the signal you are warmed up and totally relaxed, combined with the attendant shots of pre-race adrenaline.

You will have to experiment with the last five minutes. It is extremely important, for it tops off warming up all the systems. Those at highest speed need good warming too — all chemistries and movements rehearsed — but not taxing. You want to tickle your chemistry, I say, not challenge it.

There you have just about the 40-45 minutes, which puts you at start time with just enough time to mark skis, perhaps adjust wax, your body heated up, sweating and ready. You might even say you are already 45 minutes into your race. It is precisely the routine you did yesterday, the training for the day-before-race. So you are in the race already on familiar terms. Nothing different here.

One thing about the last five minutes of warmup is unusually important: part should be done in the first kilometer of the race course, from as close to the actual starting line as possible, certainly yesterday, today again if possible. Think of the customary training session. You drift off pleasantly, down the trail a ways, getting warm, and train out there in the woods somewhere at random. You become quite familiar with the course … except you have never skied the first kilometer either warm or fast. It is still a stranger, the door into the race, and you have not even checked to see how it opens, and opens best! That is like not having practiced the first bars of a musical piece you will play in concert. No matter if the instrument is tuned; you have to have done the music the way it goes, from the start.

I have a maxim: **No race is won in the first kilometer, but many are lost.** It is often the strangest and most anxiety-filled kilometer, because of adrenaline, race hype, eagerness to get on with it. Even many good racers start too fast because they have not experienced that first kilometer at fair race speed. If they are anything short of "cooking" all over with warmth, that added speed will be more disastrous yet. They will carry an early lactate load through the race like a cannonball in the stomach. Thus it is most helpful to check your warmup closely a few times with a heartrate monitor. I have watched young athletes warm up well according to time but, not being in the actual race situation, not accurately in terms of zones, especially that last 5 minutes. They still began the race cold.

All you usually get from that initial extra effort is just that anyway, effort, not speed. So you need to know your speed and use it, no other speed. With the first kilometer well done with good but easy speed, you have the race in hand; you own it for yourself.

I like the 20-10-5 sequence because it solves a major task at the race: the general wandering around, waiting, without plan except to more or less tolerate the time until you get to do what you have come to do, to race. If this time is spent in chatting, last minute arrangements, finding the right clothing, going to the toilet, a visit to parents, then you will participate but you will not race. You did not train, I don't think, just to participate.

A National Team woman whom I coached made an interesting discovery. If she warmed up thirty minutes, her heartrate would not reach racing levels until about kilometer three. In a 5 kilometer race her race was about cast, done. She could race in as fast as she could, with great effort. Unfortunately, it was not that particular last 2 kilometers which appeared in the results. We knew then that for her a thirty minute warmup would put her somewhere in places 6 to 10. With a 45 minute warmup she reached racing heartrate levels already early in the first kilometer and could expect to finish in the top 5. The equation was as simple as that.

There is therefore a principle in this: **The body will take the necessary time to warm itself up fully, whether that happens to be in the race or before it.** And a truism: **We get no credit for parts of races,** a notion which has other applications, as I will describe shortly.

## Hills and Flats

A number of years ago, in National Team trials at West Yellowstone we made another discovery while using heartrate monitors. Heartrates tended to dip well below threshold on the flats and easier sections of the course. We were reasoning at that time that since more than half the race time was spent on hills, that was where the greatest effort needed to be made. So we pursued the dictum of "Charge the hills" with even greater fervor and bravery ... but then had to recover or "take a nap" on the easier sections.

So we set about staying in the race on those easier sections as well, without much improved success. It never occurred to anyone that the flats were underdone precisely as a result of the hills being overdone. We continued to deal with the course as a series of isolated pieces rather than a single integrally related whole. Our way of combining the pieces was what made no sense. Speed is cheaper on the easier sections, while charging the hills makes you feel rugged and righteous but costs so much you cannot continue well over the top and beyond. You are forced to take sometime to recover.

Assume for discussion's sake that anaerobic threshold amounts to 4 mmols of lactate. If you drive full bore up a longish hill that figure would rise to 6-8 at least. Lactate is generally removed from the blood stream at the rate of .5-.6 mmol per minute, that is 2 minutes per mmol. In order to get back to an operable level of aerobic efficiency in peak form, you would need to return to something like 4-5 mmol. Where will you find that minute or two? You won't. There are no free minutes on a race course. Skiing more easily will help, as in relaxing a little on the easier sections. But that is why our skiers raced the flats poorly; they were too pooped from putting on a good show on the hills. That costs us too dearly on the easier sections, where it is cheapest to be going really fast! The misconceived understanding of racing and tactics is obvious. It's the old American adage: anything worth doing is worth overdoing.

Tales run forever of our skiers following Europeans up a hill, staying with them, only to have them vanish in the 200 meters following the hill. I talk more about this "mystery" in the next chapter, Technique, and in Chapter 10 I discuss the misconceived notion of racing as a series of power intervals. It is another case where something did not work, so we just did it harder. And since we did it so hard, we also went so far as to redefine the race to match our approach. A cross-country race, so the definition went, is a series of power intervals. It never occurred to us that our concept and tactics were wrong in the first place. We forgot to consider that the only place you get when you charge the hill is the top of the hill, that hill. At that point, for those who have not died along the way, the battle is over, yours included.

One of my favorite racing mental sets has been "Float the hills, race the flats." Athletes love it and have done well with it. Heartrates have remained more evenly in the racing zone. The race feels "easier" but is really only more evenly spread out in terms of effort, that is, it is more efficient and thus faster overall. At the end the racers have felt utterly exhausted but exhilarated at not feeling beaten up. They feel less immediate punishment from the race, but are dead asleep on the couch two hours later. They invariably have done better, top five. They have used the terrain, gone with it, rather than attempted to assert themselves and beat it into submission.

One of the main reasons hills had been so difficult before was in fact the way we were doing them. Rather than try something else, we tried harder, got stronger, did strength work (I heard one coach say 7 days a week), and were absolutely noble in the task. The anaerobic nature of hills assumed, that training increased. Our definition emblazoned on our minds, we had succeeded unfortunately only in defining our sport to match our limited understanding and experience of it. We were in fact culture-bound, and thus naive. Like Icarus, we thought to fly a little too close to the sun, and our wings have melted, again and again.

Had we stood further back, we would have remembered that from the body's perspective the most efficient, and thus fastest, way to get from start to finish is with the most even effort through this most hilly of events. The devil in that for the hard-charging racer is to accept the notion of allowing his speed to drop a little on hills in order to have the even effort over the top and beyond where it becomes cheaper again, rather than bounding the hills at maximum power and then, as he for some reason hoped, holding the speed through anaerobic endurance past the top. Touching back the effort a little will allow the hill to be taken at threshold at the bottom and not too painfully out of reach over the top. The drop in speed is in fact rather small. Threshold velocity is still between 92.5 and 95 percent of full race pace.

This approach has persisted in eluding us as a possibility. The terrain does indeed present a series of hills, and we need great strength, flexibility, and endurance to race through them. But the greatest speed throughout (ANT+2-4) will result from the most even, best continuing effort. The lore of Thomas Wassberg's late "charges," or Torgny Mogren's World Championship 50 km should have taught us something. One thing is that those were not "charges" at all but examples of refined pacing, against which faster starters suffered too great an attrition of their energies too soon in the race.

What is the right, the optimum effort? We cannot rely on pain to tell us we are doing our best, what are the other measures? Maximum is less efficient, we know. To seek pain as a guarantee of speed is therefore folly, the "no pain, no gain" slogan uninforming and simplistic.

What that slogan does, as I have noted elsewhere, is simply confuse Calvinist morality with physical performance. It mistakenly equates physical discomfort, mortifying the flesh, with the cause of an inspired and productive spirit; where in fact discomfort is rather the natural result of great and intelligent exertion in high-performance. In the next section on tactics I will speak of a number of ways in which maximum effort does not serve the skier with the speed he expects. He is being simply righteous, it turns out, rather than right. For a moment we should clarify this idea of pain, before we get to the hills.

The distinctions in approach to optimum rather than maximum effort and where pain fits in to our measurement of that distinction has been neatly formulated by Jeff Simons, Ph.D. in his article, "No Pain, Your Gain."[3]

> First, there is 'injury pain,' what you feel when you touch a hot stove or severely twist your ankle. This pain is a signal of real danger and possible physical damage. The second type of pain is 'fatigue pain.' This is pain arising from cardiorespiratory and muscular distress during physical exertion. It is natural, not typically dangerous, and is to be expected in hard training and racing. ... We want to moderate and control fatigue pain to achieve optimal race performance.[4]

> Realize that the reality of intense physical performance is that your sensory organs are bombarding the brain with information that the body is not comfortably at rest. That is fine. ... High performance is by nature outside of physical comfort zones. The reason that one can experience less pain in exceptional races is due to clear association without fear. ... Learn to read and understand the signals without fear or anxiety. You will feel far less pain.[5]

How do you proceed with learning how to do this? Simon continues:

> Practice directing attention to the elements of racing that you can control and that will optimize your performance. Train yourself to redirect your attention to technique, strategy, efficiency, and immediate goals. By paying atten-

tion to what you can do at the moment, you can enhance control over your race and reduce any perception of pain.[6]

I speak to the subject of positive association cues, mental sets in racing, self-communication loops and tactics in my chapters on technique and coaching. In the next section on hills I offer some further tactics which allow the racer to focus on overall speed and control pain in the process — a double gain.

## Hill Tactics

♦ Cut the power and increase frequency a stride and a half before the hill starts up.

♦ The arms and shoulder make little adjustment, while the steps quicken decisively.

♦ Look to the top of the hill, and then just over it, release all tension in your joints ("empty out"), be light, free, and quick in the feet, and take whatever glide comes to you. It will be more than you get by forcing it.

♦ Looking to the side, anywhere but at the ground in front of you, has a way of letting your body adjust its position automatically relative to the pitch of the climb.

The rationale is this. You cannot carry the stride length from the flat up the hill. Prescriptions to the contrary from the National Team and Penn State's biomechanical studies from 1979 were misguided (see Ch. 10, "The Limitations of Visual Perception in Understanding Ski Technique"), for the cost of maintaining that glide length, that way, was simply ignored, like the young driver who wants to stay in fourth gear and soon luggers the engine dead. It was assumed the foreigners were just tougher. They may have been, because of their training, but they were smarter and better scientists as well. If the shifting response comes late, speed comes to a virtual halt and must restart in the new gear. Much of the momentum is lost and efficiency disappears. That is why I say shift before the hill begins. That is even good driving technique.

The high anaerobic cost of maintaining long glide itself is exacerbated if the body is not given time to adjust to the new load level presented by the climb. That physiological response requires roughly 10-20 seconds. Maintaining flat glide length (the wrong gear) or attacking the hill (using accelerator only, adding power) ignores that necessary response time and thus compounds the anaerobic loading.

It is worth reiterating another misconception about hill training which may lead to ineffective tactics in racing: it is good for speed. It is, but as the power foundation needed to sustain speed, not to produce or sharpen the speed itself. So hill work belongs in the buildup period, not the peaking period. At the Lake Placid Olympics in 1980 our skiers were terribly disheartened by their performances. 1976 had witnessed Bill Koch's silver medal, and 1980 was to prove American skiing had arrived. It clearly had not, and we searched together for reasons. I had one conversation with our top woman, Alison Kiesel, and asked her about her final preparations. Were there intervals? Yes. What kind? Natural intervals wherever there were hills.

There is no doubt it is easiest to load up on hills, but the speed is also slower on hills than it needs to be on flatter and rolling sections. You may quicken in the feet, but it is like second gear — high rpm's but slow velocity. The fifth gear, overdrive, the one you need to keep you going fast once you have achieved good speed, never gets installed because you have not spent enough time adapting specifically to speed. That takes going where high speed is most available, and that is on the "easier" parts of the course. If we do not train in such terrain, we will not have the coordination, the neural and perceptual responses to take the speed, even if it is available.

## Technique Factors

A related mistake is made in technique: reaching as far as possible up the hill with the foot, in both classic and skating. That is the part of the leg most visible of course, seen most readily and accordingly most prescribed. Where the foot lands, however, is the result of how high the hips are at any given speed and pitch of the hill. If the foot is reached forward, the hips tend to drop behind its point of contact with the snow. This may even feel powerful, but it is biomechanically inefficient and thus squanderously expensive of energy, most particularly because it depends upon chemical energy sources in stabilizing and working the quadriceps muscles rather than the freer elastic energy which can play the dominant role when bone support (balance and high hips) is maintained.

If the foot is reached far forward in ski walking or hill bounding, the motion achieved also becomes non-specific to skiing. I have videoed this phenomenon, and skiers, including National Team members, were startled by how different this incorrect ski walking appeared from actual skiing, hips going down with the poling push rather than up.

The hips gain their height, and flight, in response to the kick, and keep that height by however often the kick must be repeated. That is a function of gearing, instinctive response, turn-over rate, which in hills must be significantly faster (as in high rpm in second gear) even with somewhat reducing speed, to keep momentum loss to a minimum. This is what you accomplish in hills. You assure it by responding to the hill early, getting the requisite movement pattern comfortably stabilized, so it can take you up the whole hill and beyond.

For it is really the top third of the hill which is more critical than the bottom. You must have energy left at that point in order to continue with good speed. If you "surrender," "go to zero" at the bottom, you will be OK at the two-third point. Everybody is tired there, but you will have spared yourself the higher lactate load which will kill the others by the top. There you will do the vanishing act, while the others will be "out the back door." Go over the top by acting as if the hill has not begun to crest yet. That keeps you in the same gear long enough for the speed to come back to you before thinking to lengthen your stride again. If you lengthen too soon, you again "lugger the engine." If the price is not apparent at the moment, it will be soon. If you stay in the same gear, with quick steps free of tension, the speed will just run back to you. When the flat comes, you will already be at full speed again, flying along, while others are paying for their bravery, or bravado, back on the hill.

It is hard to believe at first that a higher stride rate could be more speed efficient than a slower rate, longer glide. But it is. Constantly compare stride length and rate to actual speed, as opposed to how it may appear, particularly on hills, and you will see. Stride length, as I often point out, is often confused with step length instead of flight distance and velocity. A stride, launched into flight by the natural compression rebound in the legs, and though it appears less extended, is fast. The step, which looks more extended, and thus more ski-like, is actually slower.

We do well to remember the discussion in the section on "The Relationship Between Strength and Speed." The ground force required to set the ski on the hill and maintain momentum in the face of increased gravitational resistance(shorter glide distance/time) can only be produced by a combination of very rapid and repeated application (short contact times). These short contact times combine with leg/shoulder stiffness to reactively produce the most optimal and efficient speed for the terrain. The speed here, as in faster terrain, is thus best able to "feed on itself."

Attempts to maintain long strides result in lowering of the center of mass, the hips fall behind the point of contact with the snow, and the knees, bent too deeply, have simply absorbed the braking forces of friction and gravity rather than stored them eccentrically and returned them as lift for the next stride, however short. Again, what we have would have is what appears to be a long step which feels powerful but is actually unnecessarily slow. The quicker, shorter, higher technique appears less glide-like perhaps, but the glide is actually just as long and it possesses a higher flight velocity. The best analogy might be a truck again: staying in high gear until the truck luggers on the hill and then shifting gears is both hard on the machine and suffers loss of momentum/efficiency. Any experienced driver knows you downshift just before the hill to pick up the rpm's and do not upshift again until most of the speed returns over the crest of the climb.

The following diagram sets out the tactics for hills.

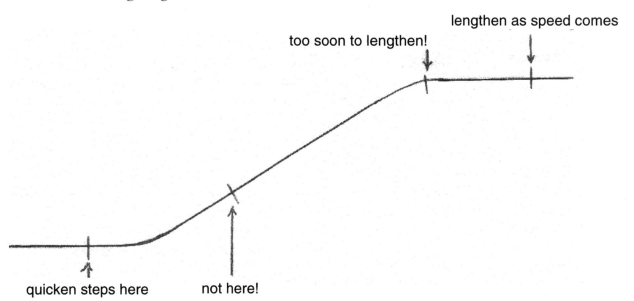

Must you keep the whole race in mind for the whole race in order to maintain optimum speed? No. That is too large and vague to hold on to. You approach the race as a sequence of parts. The section training you do during the week, skiing through various combinations of terrain in order to learn responsiveness to transitions and changes of direction, converts immediately to racing. The parts present themselves; you simply respond.

Focus your eyes on the track from where you are to where it disappears from view, even beyond if you can see through the trees. Find a half a second. No more. If you get greedy, you will start to over-ski, gain one second here but lose two soon after.

How do you do that? Tension release largely and an accompanying tempo a touch faster. Tension release alone is usually enough because it cleans up motions, moves the hips up and lightens the feet. In running, for example, an increase in stride length of a half inch amounts to 65 yards in a mile, or 8-10 seconds. Considering that gain, it is also clear that any attempt to get more than that will be too much. The same goes for skiing. Small, very small changes bring significant gains. And what is nice is that that makes them thoroughly doable; and you should know, of course, that not doing them starts the small losses in the other direction. So don't wait! Start at the start, finding the half seconds which are there for you, in the track, in your body.

How do you go about that? There is a self-communication loop which works very well. I call it simply "zero - minus - plus" (I see it 0 - +). Zero means a stride or two of complete tension release, "surrender" to whatever flow pattern you are in. I have mentioned it before in terms of communication: the tension runs from your fingers and toes like water from the holes in a bucket.

The next step is Minus, to let up on the power, the accelerator. Remember the bottom-of-the-hill situation in terms of charging the hill and over-skiing. You cannot simply add tempo to the same energy output you are in. That is charging, better understood as overcharging your body. If you want to add tempo(quickness), the Plus, you need to make a space for it first. Thus the sequence: 0 - +

Output in fact will remain close to the same, but efficiency will dramatically improve. The net effect will be that you float the bottom with little or no loss of speed, and you keep on flying over the top and beyond. On a long hill you might do 0 - + two or three times. Every time it will feel like you are giving in; in fact you will be holding or gaining.

0 - + is an effective sequence for any place on the course, with any change of terrain, when any situation arises. It simply is a good way to shift gears as often as you need. It is even a good sequence for passing other skiers without getting caught up in the hurry and tension of a head-to-head situation. You can stay in your own race.

What you have really done with this is set your body up to respond quickly and naturally to terrain and situation. It removes the psychological burden, above all, of wondering what you should do here, there, if or now.

Another situation: in mid-race you are going as fast as you can. You begin to feel a little bit tired, a little dull. What can you do? Just hang on? That will only add to your current state. Chances are your stride length is a little long, as it gets when you use a lot of power. This is wonderful so long as you remain efficient. But if you begin to hurt a little, you cannot simply go on. What is a response?

Go through 0 - + to check for efficiency and re-gear. Your stride length will doubtless be only slightly changed, if at all, but you will have lowered the effort and improved the speed.

Responsive — the magic word. Remember it from the chapters on technique and communication? Technique is a response to speed, terrain and snow. That kind of spontaneity characterizes good racers. Whenever I have asked our skiers their impressions of a first international race, they have said two things: the Europeans race all the time, every bit of the course; and they are constantly changing techniques, responding to the course in whatever the terrain, track, snow suggests.

There are thus two keys to good racing speed.

1. We race best at optimum speed, not maximum; and thinking of even effort allows you to race the whole course the fastest.
2. A high state of responsiveness, a fluid, tension-released range of responses.

Can you do anything to help yourself keep lively mentally on the course? Yes. More tactics in self-communication, again particularly in situations where you are going as fast as you can but do not seem to be able to stay light and quick. You begin to wish the end would come. You sense yourself "going into the heels" a little, or feel your elbows getting a bit heavy. It is getting monotonous; you are beginning to daydream.

It is fairly easy actually to "go to sleep" in a race if your mind is blank and you have no sensory anchors planned for the day. Even unrelieved concentration on the track itself can induce tension and mental deadness if it is not varied and relieved somehow, waked up with cues and tactics. It is the constant change in responses itself which maintains relief and sharpness that is physiologically so efficient, even apart from terrain changes.

So it is good tactics to keep going back to your sensory anchors, the cues which return the physical and technical responses and responsiveness that keep you finding that half second just ahead. Then every section adds to your success, one short one after the other. You know then that with every moment you are executing your best, yet free in your movements, uncluttered, businesslike but loose, carefree. You respond to each change as if it were a possibility; you make possibilities for yourself.

That is what racing is all about. It is not about being powerful, about being a hero or goddess who can bury the course. Manifest Destiny has no efficacy in ski racing. You just cannot go fast enough thinking you can power through. If you do, your tactics will be those of the club and the stone wheel. You may even win a race or two on your strength, particularly in your early teens, particularly in America — but never in international competition. There is a simple reason. If you are trying to produce the most power, you will take time to make sure and feel it. That puts your efforts at the force end of the force-velocity spectrum. The greatest force is produced at the slowest speed — not good tactics or mental set for racing on skis.

That is where training communications come in. Just as you go 0 - + physically, you have learned also to go to zero, clear, then cue the senses from your technique and imagery index. The mental and physical loops create simple overlapping responses to an astounding degree. I have had skiers make technique corrections on course to a cue they do not remember hearing after the race. They just remember things going better. Such responses keep you alert, constantly re-focusing, fascinated.... and what is most interesting, more powerful and fast than you would be if you set out directly to be powerful. The results will show you, for you will have controlled the circumstances in your favor one section after the other and been given the extra speed you could not have forced in being.

Can this be learned? Of course. First, think back on your best races. They were bewildering in their apparent ease often enough that, if you consider that, what seemed exception can in fact be made the rule. So often athletes say to me after a race, "I felt so easy, I could have gone harder." My response is, "Had you gone harder, just that little extra, you would have broken the subtle efficiency and soon gone slower."

Try it in training first. A 3-5 kilometer loop is enough. Race as hard as you can one loop. Then, after 20 minutes or so recovery, do it again 4-6 bpm lower. A 5 kilometer loop is better, more reliable, only because you can bash your way around 3 kilometers and perhaps avoid the penalties of over-skiing having to be paid on course. But even a short course, even a single kilometer, can provide illuminating comparisons of tactics and communication. Wherever ease and efficiency are gained, speed will follow, because of movement refinement, responsiveness to terrain, and fuel supply economy.

I also tell athletes to try skiing or running such a loop as gracefully as they can. That also invariably improves speed.

The Russians call it ease. "The demand for easiness denotes the search for the means of the best use of moving forces, of the lowering of breaking forces, the use of elastic and inertial forces, and high economy in the use of one's muscle strength."[7]

3-5 bpm below your measured RHR may in fact give you better speed for the same effort in a long race. This is the difference between optimum and maximum. Optimum gives the speed that lasts the race, Maximum is the body's greatest effort for as long as it can last, which as any of us knows is not long. Yet once we had defined the race as a series of power intervals, these intervals seemed short enough for us to "max out on" and then recover on the easy parts. I have suggested already how that strategy double-crosses us by forcing us into a lowered effort profile on the parts of the course where the speed is most available.

Optimum suggests we should be thinking "speed" rather than "effort" when we train and race. We have shown how harder is by no means necessarily faster, for it may create tension and actually slow and belabor the kick.

Try it in a race. Not all races are equally important, particularly the early winter races. They are for training and learning to race. Run what I call a "throw-away race" to try the different approach. It takes this carefree frame of mind to get rid of the instinctive competitive urge long enough to do a whole race "inside yourself." When I have asked afterwards how they felt, skiers have regularly responded "I don't know. I felt sort of asleep. I could have gone a lot faster." Just as often the same skiers mention in an off-hand way that they went by some others sometime after the mid-point of the race; or someone passed them early, then they passed them back later. And just as regularly these races have turned out to be excellent performances, high on the result sheet.

What about power then? Yes, it is there, but it is the last of the elements you add. To quote the Russian approach again: "At first strive for stride ease, then add the requirement of swiftness and only on this basis shift to power of stride."[8] That power in itself will be best applied through increased swiftness of movement, and not by lengthening of kick time (which gives the feeling but not the speed of power).

How much power? Not much. You will get all the power your body can generate, and more, but never by forcing it. Hold your index finger a quarter inch from your thumb. That much. Or hold your hands in front of you like holding the reins. Release the tension in your fingers; they might move forward an inch. That much. And each time you release that little bit, no more.

These are good images to think of. Each athlete will find those which are most clear and which evoke the responses he wishes. Coaches have others as well. Particularly the thumb and forefinger is of a sort which is very effective because it shows by touch and feeling that power is a release, not a push, a slingshot depending on quickness of foot, not raw push. All push does is punish the snow. Release creates flight. Trying to feel powerful only makes you feel powerful. If the tension is constantly released, you will feel less but be going faster. You will experience some discomfort in a tough race, to be sure, but total release of muscle tension, keeping your joints "empty," racing at zero, will guarantee than it is the result of the best possible speed.

As with 0 - +, keep each speed for 3 or 4 minutes to see if it holds. Then do it again by repeating a cue or image. You will inch forward easily into new speeds, but never in so far you cannot touch the speed back a little and go forward again. That is learning to race; it is intelligence, daring, playing for speed.

# 8

# *Technique*

"To you," the old man said, "the apple is a very, very complicated and mysterious thing. But for the apple tree it is easy."
—Jamake Highwater[1]

## *Basic Notions*

I define technique as the body's response to gliding, to terrain, and to speed. This perspective allows us to join the terrain and speed, to be lifted over the snow.

At the outset I must say that there is so much information about technique available, I hesitate to present my own version. We have already produced too much information and tested it too little. Americans love whatever is new and naively assume that if information is generated by advanced technology, then the information must be unassailable. But information becomes knowledge only when it has demonstrably moved us. It is like stones in the skier's pockets: it must truly carry more than its own weight, if it is going to be included in an athlete's and coach's store. But what do we keep? What do we throw away? For we cannot simply keep on adding more ideas without overloading the athlete with thoughts instead of speed. How do we learn to comb and trim it all?

It is one of the terrible ironies of any sport that the sheer fascination and boundless good will which its participants bring to it conspire to produce informational clutter just as often as enlightenment. And because we are not inclined to become less interested, we have not cared well to discriminate between reliable scientific test, with disciplined reflection on the one hand, and coffee shop folklore on the other. For the reliable and haphazard are equals in the lore of the sport we love.

I also recognize that there is some hypocrisy in my writing yet more. My hope, however, is to explain how fairly radical simplification is as possible as it is necessary. I will speak of "learning by subtraction" as a means of unloading the athlete's mind and freeing the body into its own most natural and efficient devices. I will talk less about doing movements than about letting them happen.

This is a different attitude toward technique and toward teaching it. I want to take the adversary relationship out of both; the body performs better when we collaborate with it than when we compete with it for dominance and control. I have had a gut feeling about this for years. But I find my approach is not unique; dancers came to it sooner than athletes and coaches. Erick Hawkins remarked: "The spirit of Western man ... made him think he had to work, to exert effort or force, and to conquer nature. Therefore dance teachers have passed on this erroneous notion about human movement — that you must 'make' the movement happen, or dominate the movement through your will, or through 'hard work.' Hawkins has turned away from this mechanistic approach and seeks "natural movement," like the movement of most animals: "They are always concentric, effortless; they have never been taught ... that man should glory in being excentered, filled with effort and striving and subtle Puritanism."[2]

One is reminded of the Russian approach to ski technique: first easiness, then swiftness, and only after these have been thoroughly achieved is power added.

A final question may arise: if movement is that natural to the body, is learning necessary? Doesn't it just come down to "going for it"?

No. Sound patterns of movement need to be freed from the blocks the body sets for itself. Imprecise movements create too much internal stress, add needlessly to its load, and thus prevent it from reaching its physiological optimums. In his book on cross-country ski training, Manshosov describes the limit of developing load as the moment when speed, pulse, and steps become uncoordinated.[3] Technique plays a significant role in raising that limit. One of my best young skiers is a good example. She could run at a heartrate of 196 but ski and roller ski only at 182. After a year of technique work she skied at 187. After two years she was able to ski at 196. Her ski movements had become clean and naturally integrated enough to allow her body to work to its full potential.

A final note on the perils of imitation. There will always be an urge to imitate the latest hero's technique, whether or not all aspects of it are in fact the biomechanical optimum. Everyone, from kids to masters skiers, imitated Gunde Svan's skating technique, most obviously in the upper body and arms, until, some years later, it was recognized that Torgny Mogren was the better model. More recently, Bjorn Daehlie became the model. Like Svan, his many medals were very persuasive. And as with Svan, as we imitated the obvious we missed some critical essentials. It seemed as if everybody suddenly transformed his technique into his personal image of Daehlie. The finish of the relay in Lillehammer was instructive, however: Daehlie was beaten by Silvio Fauner's superior poling motions. Daehlie himself remarked on several occasions on technical improvements which he was trying to make.

Warning: knowledge of technique comes from a thorough understanding of biomechanical models, not from hero worship. The Russians recognized this already twenty-five years ago.

> Earlier the technique of the best skier was the model, but even the best did not always have entirely perfect technique. For example, D.H. Vasiliev was always in reality the best on the track, and an ideal example of technique, perfect for that period. But 10-15 years later some champions of the U.S.S.R had gross errors in technique and the youth studiously copied them.[4]

# Classic Technique
# (Traditional, Diagonal)

Diagonal skiing is as natural as walking down the sidewalk, running through the woods. It is different, of course, because the foot you step onto does not stop; it glides on. What is important, however, is to accept that difference and recognize that it is the glide which makes skiing different from walking or running, not the kick; the flight, not the launch mechanism. Stated this way, saying "glide makes the difference", it rings as an almost infantile truism. The sad fact is, however, that it needs to be stated, for we have forever been so impressed with the mechanics of power, we have become distinctly mediocre gliders. We get off the ground with the best, but have learned little about flying.

If fact, if we approach speed on skis from gliding rather than kicking, we will produce a quicker, more natural and effective kick! As a result the term itself, "kick," will prove inaccurate and misleading — like kicking a ball or like a horse kicking back. What we will have is a natural, elastic springing from one gliding ski onto the next. The sound of the words we use themselves, we know, are powerful communicators of concept and movement. I believe we must make this fundamental change of both word and approach if we are to recover the level of technical mastery which we once saw in Bill Koch and Alison Kiesel in the later 1970's and which we have not seen since.

I begin with glide, therefore, and examine the elements of that movement which we need to question and understand.

What then are the needed responses to a gliding support leg? In order to stay balanced on top of the gliding leg something must be done to help the upper body keep up with the speed forward of the ski. Those things which accomplish this are:

1. Let the hand-arm-shoulder pendulum swing more forward through its native relaxed arc;

2. Let the entire torso curve up and over the support leg forward, comfortably but more than at first might seem either necessary or possible.

Both of these responses maintain the body's balance easily and high over a glide ski moving forward.

Now re-sequence these responses to gliding. "Over in the shoulders" and "full swing forward and back with the arm-shoulder" ("half-moon poling"), and suddenly you have accelerated dramatically.

A hundred times a year I will say "up in the legs, over in the shoulders." Have any skier ski easily and upright. Then cue him or her to "over in the shoulders — more" and let your arms swing forward as a unit, flexed comfortably but 'no elbows'." You will see the skier's speed increase immediately and without effort. It is as if the body needs the basic pitch of a wing to plane on the air, much as a ski jumper.

**Maxim 1:** If you want to fly, you have to move your body in a "flight attitude," and continue it well, moving your wings fully, otherwise you stall out and will too quickly have to re-lift.

Given the fact that flight velocity is not constant but is a factor of the friction curve which attends each glide, this flight attitude is not a single position but rather a continuous "curving over" of the upper body through the apex of the glide. A look at simple biomechanics shows how the body responds to speed, particularly decelerating speed, a topic little considered, never written about, to my knowledge, and of critical importance to the skier's ability to continue his glide efficiently. The nature of this response is determined by the manner in which the body in motion counters the friction curve of the glide, namely through strategies of unweighting the ski, particularly towards the end of the glide when the ski is "dying" most rapidly.

The weighting-unweighting continuum proceeds as follows. From the point of greatest flexion in the knees (shallow in the knees, deeper in the ankles) the downward push of the leg and foot launches the body mass upward at a steep angle forward (57–63 degrees). This angle must steepen with increasing track speed. If the skier's arm and pole were the long hand in the plane of a clock face, the pole would point up to 1 o'clock. Down weighting occurs as the body accelerates upwards. Unweighting begins as soon as that acceleration slows, then ceases, and the body "tops out" in free flight, like an airplane leveling out at cruising altitude.

If there is free flight, however, it is momentary at best. Given the friction curve in skiing, in which friction increases at an increasing rate, there can be no hesitation in a flight "position". The cessation of lift acceleration must be extended, or "curved over" through a downward acceleration of the upper body mass. This movement combines sharp down unweighting of the ski, at the steepest and final section of the friction curve, with the application of that same weight/force to the poling motion. The best skiers will most subtly match the friction curve of a given terrain and snow condition with the upward acceleration-deceleration-downward acceleration curve of their general body mass. They have, as we say, that elusive and masterful instinct, "feel," for snow and speed.

Perhaps what we mean is more like "touch," a grace of movement in which it is difficult to distinguish between what is generated by the skier and what seems so oddly to come to the skier from the ground itself. Certainly such skiers as Nikolai Zimjatov, of whom the Finnish coach said, "How can you beat him? He never touches the snow," mock the presumptions of plain power. Unbalanced additions of power or extra motion at any point will be of little help and most often increase friction forces on the ski rather than increase speed. The best flight or gliding will be initiated if the ski is already flying, or gliding, before it touches the snow. The cue is "glide before the snow".

**Maxim 2:** Our problem is not to produce speed; it is to accept the speed already there — in the snow, our skis, our body as a marvelous system of levers and elastic bands.

I have said nothing about pushing yet, about power or kick — purposely. We live in an age of motors and cars, and terms like "engine" and "machine" are words of great athletic praise. Too bad; the human body is not a car, not something you get into, shift, and press the accelerator. The metaphor is both inexact and especially misbegotten, for it leads us to the wrong perspective on movement. With such words in our ears, we think to "power up" and overcome the terrain. In any adversary relationship with terrain, however, the body will lose, every time. It may even feel the conqueror, but the speed will be slow.

*Technique* 235

On the other hand, look at the creature who skis by, upper body comfortably but significantly arched forward, arms and poles pendling fully and rhythmically. What do we see? A four-legged animal.

**Maxim 3:** Cross-country skiers are four-legged animals.

**Maxim 4:** All limbs are created equal.

I know; I still have not spoken of kick. American skiers are so biased toward legs and leg strength, we seldom see even a top skier who uses his or her upper body fully and in synchrony with the legs. Yet very often I have told skiers to screen off their legs by imagining a cardboard skirt around their waists and just ski with the upper body. Immediately the legs and feet pick up the needed rhythm and tempo.

In many respects, the less time we spend thinking about kick, the less time it will take to do it. Since velocity is inversely proportional to the length of time the support ski must remain stopped, the relaxed coil/recoil of the leg/ankle/foot needs to be as rapid as possible. Intellect and thought are too slow to be of help. The Russians have measured the time of stasis to lift-off to be between .09 and .23 seconds, roughly the blink of an eye. You cannot improve that by trying harder — only by releasing tension more.[5]

**Maxim 5:** The best way to improve speed and technique is to get out of our own way. That is best accomplished by releasing tensions through the whole body and by reducing the quantity of thought we carry with us.

**Maxim 6:** The ground is not to stand on.

It has been widely suggested, fallaciously, that a longer kicking time (conceived as pushing against the snow) can generate more total kicking force and thus greater speed. I address this and other false conclusions in our skiing "science" in a chapter on the recent history of cross-country ski science. Here I would only note that extension in kick time may feel better, mainly because it is therefore identifiable as motion at all. But even if more force is in fact generated because of the longer time it is applied, that greater force will be located more towards the force end of the force-velocity spectrum. (fig. next page).[6]

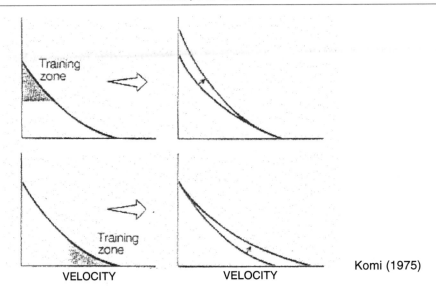
Komi (1975)

The speed at which the force is delivered will actually be slower than either the available or necessary velocity for racing successfully. In the mid-70's the Russians explained how their experts had changed their thinking.

It was considered that lengthening the time of pushing raises the impulse of force (the production of the size of force). But they overlooked the fact that the increase of the impulse of the force at the cost of an increase in time gives a speed increase only if the path of the application of force is unlimited or sufficiently large. With a limited path of the action of force (a swing of the straightening of the leg) the more the time the less the speed of the straightening of the leg on this course.[7]

In racing, it should be obvious, time is in short supply. If we take time to kick harder, we will indeed become more powerful, but by no means necessarily faster. That has been the story of American cross-country skiing, with two or three notable exceptions, for as long as I can remember.

That short supply goes right to the crux of our problem. Power and its application are simple to understand, so long as there is sufficient or unlimited time available. As soon as we start going fast, however, that time or "window" of application narrows, thus changing the whole quality of power. That requires some re-thinking. I have already discussed this topic with respect to training for speed. I review it briefly here. We must think of it in terms of neuromuscular adaptation as well, for that is the very essence of technique, coordination, motor unit synchrony, efficiency of movement.

The formula most often given to explain the relationship between speed and power is: FORCE x TIME = Work. Work defined as impulse would then accumulate as work accomplished, in our game, we assume, speed. The assumption has been that greater work automatically produced greater stride length and thus greater speed. That has been a pillar of American morality, but it leads us astray in thinking about speed on skis.

The Russians early on clearly saw how racing velocities severely limit the time variable. Since power is speed-specific, the power required has little or "no" time to build an impulse by adding raw force, which is, as we have seen, most effectively done at the slower end of the force-velocity spectrum.

More directly, we might say that in the formula FORCE x DISTANCE / TIME = POWER it is critical to recognize that the time multiple must be decreased in order to gain speed. If one decreases the time of application, while maintaining the distance (stride length) the force over the distance is also reduced, with an accompanying reshaping of the power impulse to one characterized by less force but with greater accelerative effectiveness, given the speed at hand. Still, the speed increases. Plain power is not, after all, what we are looking for. The notion of power alone in fact does not provide us with adequate insight into kicking for speed. I have as often improved a skier's kick by taking away power as I have by adding it.

A basic confusion about the dynamics of kicking has been so tenacious in American technique teaching that we need to look for a more appropriate explanation. Everyone knows how to get started. The trick is to go faster once you are already going fast. As with my example from track, the biomechanics of leaving the blocks (greater impulse from greater time against the blocks[8] are qualitatively different from those of the strides following the initial acceleration, where speed becomes inversely proportional to time spent on the support leg.[9]

A physics teacher friend suggested another model, a bicycle wheel. A bike turned upside down will do. Starting the first wheel rolling may allow for a fairly long and forceful push with the hand-arm-body. Further acceleration, even the maintenance of current velocity requires a fundamentally different approach. The experimenter cannot apply great force because the wheel is spinning too fast. He cannot rely on simple added frequency of pushes of the same force because, again, the wheel is going faster that that as well. Many, many strikes, grabs, or pushes at the wheel create only tension in your arm, and it quickly wears out and falls away.

There is only one way to add acceleration to a spinning wheel: a totally lengthened shoulder/arm/hand must accelerate to a speed slightly greater than the wheel and strike it lightly but with extreme rapidity. And then let the wheel spin free until the limb has recovered, re-lengthened, pre-loaded, and is loose and elastic enough for another strike. A potter's wheel provides another analogy to foot strike, particularly for skating.

The wheel-kick analogy is not exact, of course, for the skier's or runner's support leg/foot has no alternative to stopping momentarily. In a study of 1984 Olympic sprinters the authors documented a distinct compromise in the lift-off due to unavoidable braking effects — the foot's rearward motion slows to less than average velocity.[10] They do reckon, however, with the necessary eccentric loading forces generated by just that momentary braking. The braking is in fact a necessary phase in maintaining (re-generating) lift-off power and speed. What we call kick, therefore is not so much a push as it is the release/rebound of an eccentrically loaded leg/foot, a springing therefore.

This has helpful analogies to gliding long rapidly and kicking with speed rather than force. The optimum necessary force will develop out of the swiftness of its application. (You will find it takes great power just to keep up with speed which is already present, let alone increase it.) Speed is the dominant player: keep up or be left behind, even when it is your own speed. Paradoxically, therefore, if you try to kick with greater force, you will probably glide longer but it may well be without greater velocity, just as a more forceful, conscious blink of your eye.

Other evidence supports our notion of kicking more swiftly rather than forcefully. In a study of three types of drop jumps the greatest movement (springing force) was developed around the knee and ankle joints by bounce drop jumping in which the rebound upward followed elastically and without hesitation upon a natural, only moderate flexion. Efforts to deepen the angles of flexion before rebounding, in order to create more time of force application, in fact failed to do so *(see next page)*.[11]

Viewed yet another way: since "the highest force is produced closer to the lowest than to the highest speed,"[12] any major effort to increase force output will require an increase in both muscle tension and the time needed to accomplish the flexion. Both factors are inimical to the production of speed. If in the effort the knee angle goes too deep, the drop jump comparisons even show a lower output for the lower speed. The same holds true for skiing. Perhaps this phenomenon is best explained by the loss of mechanical advantage and elastic force in the deep angle of flexion, and with it the loss of efficiency. The feeling of greater force in fact signifies greater cost of causing the force rather than greater speed resulting from it.

Thus a different notion applies: "It seems the actual speed is decisive for the force output and not the manner in which it is reached."[13]

So blink your eye and think of kick, then spring — the less you feel, the faster you are going. This is a hard one to put your faith in, but it works. It helps some to recognize that much of what makes us feel is tension, and that is the skier's arch enemy. There is also an alternative: we cannot make our kick motion faster, but we can let it be faster.

**Maxim 7:** Speed and power come not from an increase in muscle tension but from the release of tension. We do not push a slingshot forward.

Now let us talk briefly about kick, and call it spring. The spring can only be brief. That is its nature. Beyond that, the ground is not to stand on.

1. Stand on foot or skis, poles comfortably in front in the ground or snow for support. Release all the tension from every joint up and down your body until you feel nothing, like water running out of your fingers and toes. The skeleton

*best*

seems to settle into itself, in what we have learned is bad posture, the joints become jelly rather than hinges. I call this position/emptiness of tension and feeling "zero". "Zero" is the most important thing a skier needs to know. The more he trains and races "at zero," the faster he will go.

2.  Now … jump up as fast as you can. Relax a bit more, lift off quickly and float up a fraction longer, supported by your poles, the flight as if in slow motion. That is how to kick. Do it running on a hill, do it kick double poling, skiing diagonal. It will feel as if you are starting your kick even in front of yourself, very soft on the ground or snow, like slipper feet, but then toed-down- sprung-into-flight faster than you can even sense what has happened. It will not take much sensation of power to effect instant grip and a very forceful launch. We have already seen how the natural flex and rebound spring from a shallow knee angle elicited the greatest force (down-jumping studies on previous page) Eliminating the time required to flex more deeply also naturally shortens the time of the movement, thus improving its speed.

It was the Russians who carried out the first extensive studies of the relationship between friction/gliding and ski movement, and in doing so formed the most reliable theoretical basis for our sport. My own explanation may seem too complicated in its own right, the Russians' perhaps more so yet. But the simple, practical application we need as athletes and coaches must be derived from thorough reflection, and that process is important to review. We must improve our understanding of what we are talking about to our athletes. We simply must think more profoundly in order to speak more accurately and simply.

The Russians had discovered by the mid-70's that the older vector models of the kick were misguided. Observing the angle of the kicking leg at its extension, a 45 degree launch angle seemed to fit nicely with the geometric mean between vertical and horizontal.[14] Oddly, the presence of speed as well as friction factors were little considered. For its part, speed is more easily considered the result of movement rather than its co-defining cause. But because we do not see the speed, of course, does not mean it is not powerfully present. The increased track speed of contemporary ski racing makes the lift response of the kick even more vertical than it might have been in the days of wooden skis.

Arthur Lydiard recognized this early on when he included vertical springing in his hill bounding regimen for runners. He saw that the faster the runner was moving, the more vertically he would have to lift in order to stay "on top of the speed," which is to say in order to maintain one's center of mass high enough ("high hips") to allow full swing and extension space for the legs (greatest forward swing speed at the periphery of the arc, greatest speed of lift towards the end of the extension). Although the vertical springing, what I call "pogos," seem at first to have little in common visually with forward movement of the body, Lydiard pointed out early on that the faster the runner was moving, the more vertically he would have to lift in order simply to keep up with the momentum demands of the speed already there. (Thus my maxim: our task is not to produce speed but rather to accept it.) Since power is speed-specific, the power and type of motion required while going fast can only be produced effectively by a more vertical springing motion. Otherwise the natural elastic lift-off degenerates into a simple shuffle beneath the weight of the body. It is not by chance that Lydiard's hill-bounding routines re-appeared prominently in Norwegian hill springing, what they call *spenst*.

The Russians found the optimal lift-off angle to be 63'30", in practical description, very steep indeed, and steeper yet than the 57 degrees Maier and Reiter observed some years later, in 1980.[15] The authors conclude: "Along with this the body will receive an acceleration for 'take-off'; in this way a completed push-off with the foot is made. No other way of increasing horizontal force is possible."[16]

Two further notes are of critical interest.

1. "Toward the moment of ski lift-off from the snow the force of pressure falls to nil. Therefore there is no point in increasing the pressure on the ski back at the end of the push-off, as has been recommended earlier."[17] We could add as well that at that point the shear forces against the holding power of the snow are also greatest. Still, longer kicks, holding the heel down, have remained a staple of American technique teaching, from our own biomechanical studies in 1979 to as recently as 1991.

2. "But if force is to be applied, striving not to move the ski back, but to make a movement backward with the knee, then precisely in the final moments of the push-off it is possible to obtain the large necessary force, directed along the hip 'for flight'."[18]

For all the persuasiveness of their theoretical models, the authors hasten to list a number of variables in terrain, waxing, snow type, and others, which cannot be figured into the model. After all the physics and biomechanics are said and learned, they say, racing a course depends ultimately upon the instinctive responsiveness of the skier. That puts us back at my beginning definition: technique is the body's response to gliding, terrain, and speed.

## Learning Naturally

Two learning sequences and then some additional helpful details to make us better four-legged animals. The details, I should caution at the outset, are not meant to stockpile more information, on the theory that more information will help you ski better. To the contrary, I never let my skiers train with more than two cues a day (toe-down early and knee back, for example). If one's total inventory of things to work on goes beyond four to six items, I say you cannot add anything new until you eliminate something or re-group to keep the items at six maximum. For again words are like stones in your pockets. They must carry their own weight and more, or you are just weighting yourself down with gratuitous thought-junk. Keep the few, very few precious ones; throw the rest away, far away. It is worth reminding ourselves that as skiers your goal is not to amass a collection of information but to go fast. Coaches amass information but parcel it out sparingly, differently to different individuals. Otherwise, like a fuel mixture too rich, he will literally "over-choke" his athlete.

Finally, I know it is a paradox: it takes a lot of thought to teach us not to think too much.

The word "re-group" gives the best hint as to how any of us best proceeds, namely through looking not at positions or motions but at movements-in-relation.[19] Movements are never individual, positions never a goal. If one looked at a strip of movie film, which frame would represent the goal? What point in the movement do we seek when we pause a video tape? The extended positions are the most pleasing and dramatic, but everything in between is just as key, and most often receives no attention at all.

Movement is an unbroken, rhythmical continuum, and each point is determined by the totality of the movement as systems of responses to terrain and speed, and the desire to go fast. Many a skier looks wonderful, achieves lovely individual positions and movements, but cannot go fast over the snow. That skier is carrying too much information, looking from the outside at himself, and imitating the images he has of other skiers. He is posing. That kind of exercise can be helpful, initially. Ultimately this sort of information will remain too fragmented. Athletes are not catalogues, nor can they be actors assuming the shapes of others. Each must become his or her own model, an animal whose movements are whole, totally integrated and involving,

*Technique* 243

and, in the best of cases, beyond particular awareness. Then the information will be of the type which groups individual pieces and thus reduces their numbers. I call this "learning by subtraction." The less the skier is thinking about, the better he or she will be able to race with a clear mind and uncluttered senses. Only then will his or her responses be quick, simple, and released enough to go truly fast. Skiing must become a combination of easy precision and reckless abandon.

It is very helpful to regularly free ourselves from cues for isolated elements of technique. "Whole body" types of cues can provide the image or feeling to "put things together." I often tell skiers simply to ski "gracefully," as if they were dancing. Another cue I use is "clean it with speed." Sometimes we become so thoughtful and deliberate, we jam our own movements with thought. Going fast homogenizes things and smoothes out edges. At the opposite end of imaging, I sometimes have skiers move "rough." These skiers have becomes so smooth, they have become either powerless or tense, or both. Skiing as if they were returning a punt breaks through that tension and adds a note of craziness and reckless responsiveness to their movements. I also use the Yoga images of "breathing into your joints," or "move as a skeleton, the muscles are passive, weightless." Both these cues have a way of lightening the movements and releasing tension. The result is invariably increased swiftness and ease of movement.

"Technique," as we call it, is in fact the body's natural, instinctive way of propelling itself. The cues we use are some visual, auditory, and kinesthetic triggers to help it be itself. It knew how to move long before we came along, and our greatest challenge is to restrain ourselves from either owning those instincts or thinking only we can help the body do right. There are only a few sequences of movements needed to gain a feeling for how natural skiing is.

Jog easily and with graceful springiness. Gradually swing the arms more fully forward and lifting loosely behind. Follow the hands over forward in the shoulders. The further forward the shoulders are curved, the longer the glide.

How do you take the glide? Simply by rising easily and continuously up over the lead leg (to ride on bone-support rather than muscle tension) and going over in the shoulders, almost like a shallow porpoise dive, to let the ski run on through its natural glide … before quickly stopping and re-launching.

That is the sequence from the bottom up. Skiing differs from running, of course, in that the support leg does not remain stationary but glides forward. That gliding creates all and the obvious difference. But the launching mechanics are the same or nearly so. Certainly skiing is closer to light bounding, being an elliptical motion where running is more circular. Yet the body propels itself in a basic way, whether running or jumping or gliding. And to the extent this same subtle spring, however subtle, is kept in a walking step, you will have ski imitation in ski walking with poles.

Thus whether on roller skis or snow skis, I ask even top-notch skiers to jog with a nice springy toe-down for a distance of 30 or 40 yards to their skis. I ask them to put their skis on but to disregard them, to continue to sense the running but to add the forwarding emphasis in the arm swing and upper body attitude. It is an excellent, natural review of kick dynamics as well as an effective corrective when technique becomes too hinged and mechanical, for as in language, a review of the grammar of human locomotive has a way of making various movements more articulate, more trim and graceful, in a word, more efficient.

I also teach all my skiers how to run on foot. A very few points make all the difference in their feel and efficiency, and thus natural speed, in running, not to mention pleasure. I would say that only one in twenty athletes runs with natural efficiency, and many of those, not surprisingly, do not enjoy running. Once they learn, it becomes a whole new experience. They also quickly realize the practical benefits which Arthur Lydiard described years ago: if you increase your stride length by a half an inch, you gain 60-80 yards a mile or 8-10 seconds. That half inch is easily available with a little technique work, and then imagine the multiplied distance per hour of training time in a year. It is not difficult to imagine the salutary effects on both the skier's base speed and the quality of his movements.

Then I use the same familiar cues for skiing technique. As one Norwegian exchange student/skier (4th in NCAA ladies 10km) remarked after doing a short running technique routine with me and noting her improvement in both speed and ease, "Every time we go out skiing we think about technique; when we go running, we never think about technique. That really doesn't make much sense." On the other hand, Europeans have long since made the connection between running and skiing. Many of the top skiers are nearly national class runners, with times in the 14's for 5000 meters, and once or twice a year the Norwegians do running time trials over 3000 meters as one of the ways to estimate the relative status and potential of their best skiers. *(See running-skiing comparison photos on following page.)*

It does happen that when the correct running motions are transferred to skis, initially a bobbing or pogo sticking motion may result. It should be understood, however, that this vertical up and down is not the result of too much bounce in the legs but of being too upright in the upper body. Once it curves over forward naturally, the "bob" will disappear. If you "smooth out" the kicking motion, you will give

# Technique

Vegard Ulvang *(above)*, Oddvar Brå *(directly below)*

*Note:* Runner and skier have similar body positions throughout.

up the main source of your power, which lies in the rapid and elastic flexing and rebounding extension of the legs.

There is another danger, particularly with young skiers, that this jogging/light bounding brings with it a "bicycling" recovery motion which we do not want in skiing, for it tends to raise the shoulders (or result from the shoulders coming up) and thus stalls the easy flight over the glide ski. The corrective is to emphasize a total extension of the leg beneath the hip joints. Walking with emphatic toe-down is sometimes helpful, or remembering to push the knee cap straight back. So the exercise is very useful, but its execution takes some care.

The best way is to think "glide before touching the snow" and "touch the snow at the decal on the other ski". The springing leg will automatically and rapidly straighten just in the process of gliding.

Yet another effective means of refining kick or lift I have found in elementary ballet exercises, in the *tendu* forward, to the side (for skating) and to the rear for classic.

**Torgny Mogren**

If we examine the classic pictures, we also note the outward rotation of the hip joint in the *tendu* to the rear. As the shoulder-arm-hand is a single unit, so is the hip-leg-foot. As the kick/lift is completed, the hip has "opened," rotating slightly to the rear center and rising. This movement is both a corrective demonstrator for kicking and a very effective follow-through refinement which facilitates weight transfer and supports longer natural balance on the gliding ski. Most skiers are in too much of a hurry, too "busy," to complete this total range of motion and thus waste available free glide time.

# Technique

Jochen Behle

Julia Tschepelova

PHOTOS: FISCHER SKIS

**Maxim 8:** The swing point of the hip-leg-foot is the center of the lower back, not the hip joint.

(2) Another sequence runs just as naturally from the top down. It is a fundamental and elementary way of propulsion to simply stand on the skis and double-pole oneself forward, almost as if one were practicing the butterfly stroke in swimming.

Now add the spring as I have described earlier, the quickest way to leave the ground, but on one foot followed by headfirst poling. Now you have a double-pole with kick. Kick with one foot and then the other.

Now, without changing the basic forward curve of the body or kick mechanism, simply go from two-pole pushing to alternating or single-poling.

**Maxim 9:** Diagonal stride, single-poling is half of a kick double-pole.

Let us emphasize glide again. It is helpful to think of glide as the propulsion force. It takes place in front of the kick, which is stationary. If we think too much about kick, we will imagine it traveling backwards. That creates a subtle but significant hindrance to getting up onto and over the gliding ski, mainly by dropping the hips. There is progressive opening of the knee throughout the glide. Most skiers just launch onto the glide ski and then wait as the stride "dies." Or they drive the knee forward, thinking it more dynamic. That too is an illusion, however: because you feel strong does not mean you are necessarily fast. But it does usually indicate that you are tense, and tension and speed are mutually exclusive.

Speed takes place in front of where we are, not behind. The glide elongates by means of free glide time in front, not by elongating the kick backwards. Be reminded again of "gliding before the snow," "touching at the other decal" (sweeps). Once again compare for yourself. If the forward-swinging ski touches the snow near the other foot, you will indeed have to drop down behind it and push the ski forward as if on a scooter. And it will feel like a long push out the back. That is a 1 – 2 motion, down, then forward. That is how I first learned it in the 50's, but it is old style. If you sweep forward, touching beside the decal, you will be there almost at the instant of your kick/springing. You have eliminated the "1" and fly along higher, with vastly greater quickness and lightness, 2 – 2 – 2! After having a skier feel his 1– 2, 1 – 2, then 2 – 2 – 2 is a marvelous and easy lesson in speed and relaxed flight over the snow.

Another demonstration can graphically illustrate the difference in approach. You can take a long step and feel powerful and extended like the picture of a great skier. Measure the length you have traveled. Then, starting from the same point, take a relaxed running-type spring forward. You will feel shorter (less consciously extended), but when you measure you will see you have actually flown further by some inches, and it is a flight which has been more rapid.

And, like the slingshot, we do not push it, we let it go. As the arms/shoulders swing fully through their arc, so the legs swing fully forward through their natural arc. Each is spring, swing, follow-through. And glide is as dependent on the last two as on the first, for without swing and follow-through, any spring loses that optimizing force of momentum. Hurried, or blocked by a shortened pendulum, the stride

Step length (top) vs. running bound length (bottom). Note the gain in distance past the pole handle in the bottom, the higher and more forward position of the hips.

dies. Trying to extend momentum beyond its natural swing, particularly by over-reaching with the lead foot, looks and feels powerful, but that only extends step length, not gliding/flight speed nor optimum body movement.

It is the slingshot approach. It is reckless abandon, follow through, momentum, freedom of movement.

Some analogies from other sports are often illuminating. In *The Shotgunner,* Bob Nichols observes that many of us "use our two good hands and two good feet to hinder us in our wingshooting as much as we use them to help" and wonders why a certain one-armed shooter could be so good. He concludes that the one-armed shooter is never able to stop the momentum of his gun and thus has unimpeded follow-through.[20] He compares this man to the normal two-handed gunner who, otherwise dextrous in the use of both hands, "is often led to employ left-hand control excessively at the instant of the shot. When he does so, his stopped gun-swing is the basic reason for an otherwise 'mysterious' miss."[21] Nichols again finds too much control as the reason behind flinching: the gunner is simply holding his weapon too tightly.[22] He is trying too hard and blocking his body's natural attitude and momentum. In a final example, which reminds me of the efforts some make to kick harder, he speaks of the shooter whose fingers are wrapped around the stock so tightly that the trigger finger is actually "frozen."[23] Sometimes skiers try so hard to kick that the attendant tension makes the kick both start late and then be too powerful. It has the effect of flooring the accelerator all at once, with the result that the "wheels simply spin" rather than accelerating the body forward. It is a jerked instead of an aimed shot. In skiing, thinking always about gliding, flight over the snow, will ultimately make each spring of the body into natural and instantaneous flight. It will be as the dancers say: dancers do not do the movements; they become the movements.

> You can practice shooting eight hours a day, but if your technique
> is wrong, then all you become is very good at shooting the wrong way.
> — Michael Jordan[24]

## *Poling*

Some notes on poling. First, it is in many respects the most pronounced general weakness in American skiers, so much so that I would almost begin any exercise of technique with poling and let the legs follow. American skiers are still largely two-legged. We need to be four-legged.

Once again, the biomechanics are fairly simple. It is of first importance to understand that the poling mechanism consists of a linked muscular skeletal system beginning at the knees (hip flexors), connected at the stomach (torso), and ending at the hands. Once the pole touches the snow, force is first applied by lowering the upper body, or curling it down over the pole. You pole "head-first" and "start from the belly button."

The push downward of the arm follows rapidly, then is complete as soon as the elbow passes the body line. Further active extension of the forearm backwards is counterproductive, since there is little or no remaining force available at this point in the triceps extensors. Rather the rear pendulum continues upward with the shoulder-elbow-hand totally released. In following through it thus provides additional lift from simple kinetic energy. The arc described by the hand in poling is a half-circle, the flat part of the half circle more or less parallel to the ground. I call this half-moon poling.

It is important to understand the shoulder-arm-hand as a single unit. The shoulder functions therefore not just as the swing joint of the pendulum arm-hand but is a part of the pendulum itself as well. Absence of this shoulder activity, which in moving ("dislocating") forward results in the natural rotation of the shoulder axis forward, up, and to the center, is one of the most characteristic weaknesses of technique among Americans, particularly juniors. The shoulder-arm-hand pendulum also plays a significant role in weight transfer from ski to ski (as I have earlier noted with hip rotation).

**Maxim 9:** The swing point of the shoulder-arm-hand is the center of the upper back, between the shoulder blades, not at the shoulder joint.

(Cf. Maxim 7. The swing point of the hip-leg-foot is the center of the low back, not the hip joint.)

What do we look for in the arm itself? It remains slightly flexed throughout, relaxed but "rigid," "with no elbow." In reality the angle at the elbow changes in response to changing speeds. Critical to the lift in front and behind is the elbow, not the hand. If the elbow raises in front the muscles through the latissimus dorsi will pre-load. The whole system then may rebound elastically to the center when the pole makes contact with the ground.

The forearm angle responds to speed, more extended as the speed increases, somewhat less as it slows. It has been suggested that the arm be carried at a right angle, the elbow close to the pole. There is no biomechanical basis for this sugges-

*Top:* Oddvar Brå   *Bottom:* Thomas Wassberg

tion; to the contrary. All that does is to shorten the functional length of the pole and give the sensation of faster movement. It is helpful to think of the elbow more as pointing 45 degrees (or more) out rather than vertical, more in the manner of a butterfly swimmer. The chest thus remains comfortably open, the arms naturally more rigidly flexed and firmly linked to the torso and hip flexors. When the elbows drop, "crack," behind a planted pole, it is usually a sign of a weak torso/shoulder/arm system. Lengthening the arm may seem to slow the movement, but lengthening the radius of the swing is able to increase the speed of the push at the periphery, thus keeping up with the skier's present speed, if it is great, and offering the opportunity to propel himself forward more effectively "at that speed." To push more forcefully at that greater radius length requires that speed of movement and only slightly more, not more raw strength. Success in doing so is not a matter of more muscle bulk but rather of better linking to the torso lever system (cf. pivot point in kayaking.)

Postcard:
Lake Placid, New York, 1921

Frode Estil

Olga Danilova

PHOTOS: ARND HEMMERSBACH /
*Ski Langlau / Triathlon / Marathon Magazine*

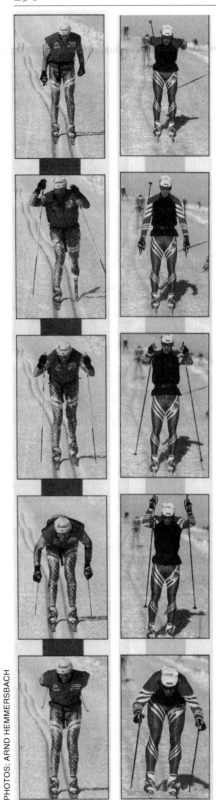

Mikhail Botvinov

Alexei Prokurorov

The hand follows a full, natural path, therefore, which begins in front of the eye, passes by the knee, and rises behind, as if floating loose from the elbow. Only on steep climbs does the hand pass a little more above the knee and the elbow does not finish its pendulum as fully behind. As with automotive gearing, the cycles must shorten to keep contact with a speed the terrain needs.

It is essential to keep the hands in the plane of motion and the palms generally facing the center. This is the natural manner in which they hang at one's sides, and swinging them without poles gives a feeling for how little the hands turn around the wrist throughout the poling motion. Turning the hand outward to the rear at the end of the poling motion produces no further power and only serves to roll the shoulder down and forward, at the very moment it wants to be rising and curling easily in behind the butt (or at least if the skier thinks of it this way, the arms will follow through more straight back, in a plane parallel with the direction of the ski, rather than flaring to the side).

Preserving the arms' natural flex is also essential. The elbows should not be pinched in order to line up (for some reason) with the shaft of the pole. The arms/elbows rise in front as naturally as a swimmer's, elbows comfortably outside the axis of poling. In that attitude they also more readily avoid hinging at the onset of poling, one of the prominent mechanical faults particularly among younger skiers.

Consideration has been given to where the pole should be planted beside the ski relative to the skier's foot. The concern is idle. The poles follow the movements of the skier, as do the skis, and land wherever they do depending upon pole length (the choice of which relates to the skier's body type, skiing style, and strength), terrain, and fitness.

# Technique

**Raisa Smetanina**

The notion that the pole is only effective to the extent that it is pushing back is too narrow. So is saying it simply keeps the ski moving. As with all segments of the body, the insertion of the pole initially aids unweighting in concert with the downward acceleration of the upper body. Only as the movement continues does the role of the poling motion turn predominantly to pushing, or, more exactly, pulling the body through.

Let's consider this last statement. The poles, of course, do not move backwards, for they are fixed in the snow. They essentially fashion a slingshot, the skier's torso and arms being the elastic sling. The sling is stretched by moving the poles forward. Once they are fixed and the ski is unweighted, the poling motion is effected by a release of the stretched muscles, as if toward the center of mass, the middle. The poling motion thus combines unweighting of the ski (initially) with the sling effect of the body forward through the poles.

Extra push with the poles after the body has passed the poles forward is then of little use. That only pulls the shoulders back and down when they should be rising in follow-through and moving with the torso forward through the height and flight of the gliding ski. What appears as a dynamic whip-like movement at the end of the poling arc is rather the final unloading of the motion which began when the poles first touched the snow, much in the manner in which a fly rod appears to fling the line from its tip rather than its base.

*Cues for poling*

1. half-moon poling
2. no-elbows/ pole with shoulders (deltoids, like epaulettes) — smaller, less distance to go
3. from moment of touch, hands head straight for the knee and past
4. elbows lift behind (or finish up, providing lift)
5. hand at eye level or above in front (poling motion is initiated head-first, arms/ torso accelerate downward as a unit)
6. hand stays in plane of motion, palms to the center
7. hand swings slightly to center in front, curls around slightly behind (facilitates weight transfer, most critical factor in continuing glide)

*Cues for torso*

1. over in the shoulders — more!
2. shoulders "dislocate" forward (slightly to center)
3. shoulders stay over after poling
4. hip releases, opens to rear (follow-through) after kick
5. shoulders open slightly to the rear and up as part of poling finish

*Cues for legs/feet*

1. sweep = whole leg pendles through. Stand on it only when it has passed the decal on the other ski, or the lead wheel of the roller ski
2. place hip bone out over gliding ski (achieves same thing as no. 1)
3. toe extends down totally within 12"-16" of other foot passing forward
4. early toe-down (collapse/lift power/speed greatest if only shallow flex at knee)
5. kick timing is improved by increasing the speed of the hand pendling forward from the knee up, letting it "whip" towards its foremost extent. I call this "kicking with your hands."
6. glide before the snow.
7. "slipper feet": as ski touches the snow, the ankle opens softly forward, touching first with the back of the ball of the foot, then the heel, like a ballet walk or sneaking to the refrigerator when others are sleeping.
8. "slipper feet" has another application. Particularly in softer tracks, too hard a kick results in shear/slip rather than grip and propulsion. Change the learning sequence jogging to walking, stepping more and more quickly, toeing off suddenly but always lightly. Accelerating the arm swing forward naturally lifts the flight onto the gliding ski. The swiftness of the movements then creates the delicate power appropriate to the conditions.

# *9*

# *Skating*

Get the fundamentals down and the level of everything you do will rise.
— Michael Jordan[1]

Skating on skis is based on double-poling, the most elementary means of propelling oneself over the snow. That may seem an odd statement, given our bias toward viewing the more powerful leg movements as dominant in skiing, and given the apparent similarities between ski skating and ice skating. But what is true of classic skiing is even more true for skating: in cross-country skiing we become four-legged animals. For us all limbs are created equal, or at least we need to think of them that way. In skating in particular it falls to the arms and upper body in general to coordinate and direct the motion of the whole body over the snow.

It is important at the outset to get over the notion that ski skating and ice skating are similar. Though similarities are initially apparent, they are in fact superficial. The fact that cross-country skiers are de facto four-legged creatures should make it clear enough that a qualitatively different set of dynamics is at work. Beyond that, the friction curve on snow, not to mention the presence of drastically varying terrain, is fundamentally different than on ice. There is a vastly wider spectrum of velocities both with each stride (the ice skate is freer, particularly towards the end of the stride) and from stride to stride (terrain factors). Furthermore, snow, no matter how compacted, is much softer, and thus penalizes edging more than ice. The fact that the ski is wider also increases the effects of edging on snow in excess of that of a skate on ice.

The comparison with speed skating, especially in its recent developments, in fact instructs us in quite a different way. The introduction of the new Klap-skate suddenly allowed plantar flexion to become fully part of the skater's propulsion. The results were an increase in speed, a run of new world records, and, of particular interest for skiers, a somewhat higher body position. This result confirms the findings from drop jumping (p. 238) in which going deeper into knee flexion in fact produced less propulsive force around the knee and ankle joints, at a slower speed, than going less deep. In a word, the future for skating is in flexible ankle flexion and a higher position, not in rigid ankles and a lower body position.[2]

Skating is one-legged double-poling. The arms/shoulders pendle naturally and fully forward, up in the elbows to assure pre-loading of the larger back muscles. They operate optimally as a unit, parallel, as little offset as possible, and as little staggered in the time of striking the snow. (In the beginning of skating we mimicked the stagger, then exaggerated it in a sort of elongated gallop. We did not see what we were looking at, however, and soon athletes recognized closer together was better. Biomechanists had already noted that the fastest race horses had the shortest time between the strikes of their forward hooves.)

One of the best learning sequences for skating proceeds "from the top down." Begin double-poling, elbows up, comfortably stretched forward in the reach of the hands, over the ski (not back towards the ear or held at 90 degrees), and at the end of this stretch yet up over a "bump" (reaching for a jar of jam one shelf a bit higher), then descending "head first," leading the arms with the upper body through the pendulum down (remember downwards acceleration of the upper body mass creates unweighting of the skis as well as maximal poling force) and then up to the rear. The arms do not thrust back and down (for there is no mechanical advantage left at this point) but rather always finish by rising behind, lifting with the shoulders.

The generation of force is of elastic bands toward the center. It starts with the muscles stretched from stomach (even knees) to hands and is released toward the belly button just after the upper body mass (head first) starts down. That stretch seems to emanate outward through the hands like a whip. And like the end of a whip or fly rod, the hands/elbows float free, up behind through the completion of the force pendulum and resultant longest possible unweighting of the skis. The shoulders remain over; they do not rise in this "finishing out." Upward acceleration of the body mass creates weighting of the skis.

Then, without changing anything in this full double-pole motion, begin skating from ski to ski. The poles will touch the snow free of the skis if they are simply canted in the hands, making the appearance of a parallelogram. (Spreading the hands to keep the poles away from the skis sacrifices most of the potential power of the poling.) There is no biomechanical basis for distinguishing between a "hang pole" and a "push pole." Because of the angling direction of the skating motion there will be a natural angling or asymmetry in the poles. This is the result of the overall motion, not its cause. The overall force effectiveness of the motion will be the greatest to the extent that both arms/shoulders generate body force against the ground and kinetic energy through the push back and swing forward as a unit in parallel.

The poling needs to complete itself through the direction of glide on this poling side before the poling side foot pushes off to the other ski.

The upper body does not consciously turn to face the new direction of glide. If it does, the knee of the poling side turns in to follow it. The leg is twisted like a wrung towel, and the ski edges, damaging the glide. Furthermore, it is both weaker and highly stressful on the joints to push off a twisted limb.

Ballet dancers have a helpful cue which prevents the knees from twisting inward from their base of support in a *plié*. They say, "Keep the little toe on the floor." If skiers push off the little (outside) toe, the knee has less tendency to twist or kink toward the center.

Using another cue, the best weight transfer from ski to ski is accomplished when the non-poling side is simply "curtained off," erased from the skier's perception and concern. Without concern for facing a new direction, anticipation is avoided, and the skier remains comfortable in completing the poling motion and full glide on the poling side, loads that leg eccentrically to a more complete degree, and then will unload more powerfully and rapidly onto the other ski. Since under these conditions the hips tend to remain higher, the distance necessary for weight transfer will also be shorter, the direction of weight transfer typically more forward than to the side. In this regard the V1 stride approaches marathon skating more. Greater flight speed over a shorter weight transfer distance is a true formula for more efficient race speed. (I have been working with this for some years now. Among the best who have demonstrated it are Terje Langli, Torgny Mogren, Jari Isometsa, and Thomas Alsgaard.)

As with the way the arms appear somewhat asymmetrical in skating, as a result of the constant change of flow in the direction of the motion, so the upper body will turn somewhat to follow the shift of weight to the new ski. But this is the result of the weight transfer from the foot and leg, not its cause. Weight transfer is optimally accomplished by a sharp, quick push with the foot, not by turning the upper body. Turning the upper body to "help" the weight transfer only weakens the force of the kick by fading toward the other ski too soon. Even the thinking itself about weight transfer results more often than not in fading too soon in that direction out of anticipation, much in the same manner as looking at oncoming headlights causes us to steer into them.

I began with a learning sequence "from the top down". The same efficient movements are achieved through another sequence, this time "from the bottom up". We begin by diagonal skating. The skis are skating forward while the arms swing in alternating fashion, the arms crossing parallel to the opposite gliding ski. The arms thus swing across in front of the body, while the other pendles freely up behind, as in diagonal skiing. In fact it is most effective to be thinking about diagonal striding while diagonal skating. The arms seem to flow better with this in mind, and there is the benefit that the skier learns to think of skating and classic movements as progressively more similar, each in its way basic to the body's natural instincts for self-propulsion.

Continue diagonal skating for some minutes. In gliding on one ski and then the other, each ski goes through a similar pattern: glide ... then push off, glide ... push off. Each glide comes with a rise in the legs, to a very shallow angle in the knee. It feels almost straight but is not. The important point is to achieve bone support quickly. A pronounced quick drop follows, and rebound to the other ski. After this pattern of "glide ... push off" is secure and even on both sides, do not change anything in the feet. Simply switch from diagonal poling to double poling on one side. After the change in poling the feet continue to do exactly as they had while diagonal skating. Rarely do we see skiers who glide on both skis fully and then push lightly but sharply from both skis.

Important: the legs/feet do not care what side you are poling on. Whatever the side, both legs and feet do the same "glide ... push off." With subtle variations and syncopations in response to terrain and speed, both feet always both glide and kick. This notion was validated in Penn State's biomechanical study of skating in which the distinct fluctuation in toe velocities was measured, on both sides, not just the poling/strong side: "As the thrust from skating on the weak side begins, velocity again increases up to nearly average velocity. The other skiers do not exhibit this distinctive velocity fluctuation, perhaps as a result of ski angles and skating push."[3]

I tend to the latter cause, namely in the quick toeing-down of the push off, rhythmical but whip-like, shooting the feet which creates the spiking effect of the kick, rapid deceleration/eccentric loading followed by dramatic reacceleration/unloading. Svan's graph shows that pattern in both center-of-mass acceleration and vertical position of center-of-mass above surface level. We will see it in toe velocities as well.

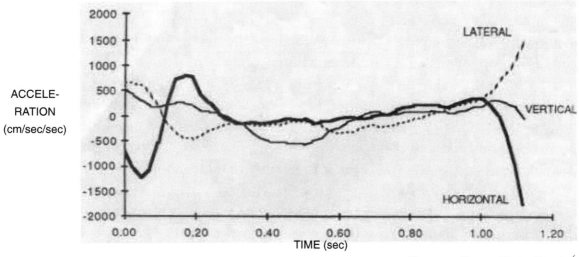

Source: Penn State Study[4]

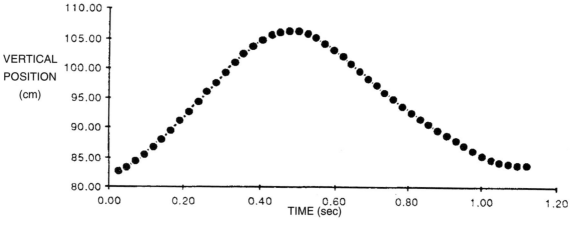

Source: Penn State Study[5]

I have found the sequence "from the bottom up" the most effective of all for teaching skating and reviewing the basics even with National Team skiers. Skiers should not hesitate to diagonal skate for as much as an hour at a time, uphill, across the flats, downhill. It is the best way to teach skaters that they need to let the ski run, glide freely first, before they kick. They will soon recognize that the initial glide is in fact essential to a forceful, swift, well-timed kick because they are totally on top of the ski first. Throughout the latter phases of the glide, eccentric loading builds and thus naturally adds to the natural recoil or explosive rebound force of the kick.

A third teaching sequence separates the arms from the legs, then adds the arms in phases. I take the arms out at first because sometimes I see an oddness or confusion in the rhythm of a skater and cannot locate the source of the problem. More often than not (as with classic) it is in the movements of the arms: they are moving too fast to allow for the entire glide ... push off rhythm. The timing in the legs is hurried, the glide is not optimized because the legs hurry to keep up with the arms.

As many others do, I begin skating, like a speed skater, curving over at the waist, hands clasped easily behind on the rump. Glide ... push off, glide ... push off.

Then with one pole. The reason for one pole is that many skiers have one arm which either wanders or curls out wide in front or flies to the side in back. Put the pole in the good hand. It is easier for the empty hand/arm to follow it in a parallel, even pattern of movement.

Once the arms are working smoothly together and in the rhythm of the legs, add the second pole. Repeat the sequence as often as needed. Usually it succeeds in slowing the poles down enough to allow the legs/feet to complete their motions.

## *Poling*

These are the checkpoints of clean, swift, powerful poling.

1. Arms/shoulders working parallel, as closely as is natural and unstrained (shoulder width) and in the direction of the poling side, ski through the entire poling motion. This will begin to deviate toward the finish of the motion, with natural following; but most skiers turn much too early.

Larissa Lazutina

2. Elbows lift well in front, gently flexing but "relaxed rigid." I also say the arms work "without elbows" to keep the elbows from collapsing into the motion. Dropping in the elbows almost always signals fatigue. The pole push is engaged "head first," or "from the belly button outwards," the extended hands moving rapidly toward the knees.

Lubov Egorova

3. The arms then swing up loosely behind, rising with the body. "Finish out behind" is one of the most effective technique cues I have ever used, with beginners and top skiers alike. With younger skiers I call it "putting a tail on the kite" to keep it flying and stable in its direction. I also cue this essential finishing with "friendly hands," as if they almost wanted to clap behind.

Thomas Wassberg

Maurilio De Zolt

4. The shoulders go up and over the poles in an arc, starting the head-first acceleration downward and through. As the arms/elbows finish, and the new glide leg straightens, the shoulders stay over, i.e. throughout the entire weight transfer. Both arms/shoulders push in unison, so there is no sensation of pulling harder on one side of the torso than the other. I say, "Pull straight down the warm-up zipper."

Bente Skari

Olga Danilova

5. The shoulders remain as "flat to the ground" as possible. Looking at the skier from front or rear, particularly the poling side shoulder has a tendency to dip. If it does, the hip below it "pinches" to the center, the ski rolls inward onto its edge, and the outside arm will be blocked from finishing up. Some tip of the shoulders does take place, but again it is the result of the overall motion, not the cause or source of velocity.

6. A final note on shoulders. There is a strong tendency for the non-poling side shoulder to "fade" towards the inside before fully engaging in the poling motion. That whole side of the poling is simply lost. That loss is particularly abetted by distinguishing between a "hang pole" and a "push pole". Before skating was analyzed it was interesting to watch the older skiers like Ove Aunli and Oddvar Brå learning to skate on the Dachstein glacier. Both skiers were learning through their instincts for movement rather than through instruction in technique, and both were

leading forward with both arms in unison. Over five years later a study of Olympic skiers concluded: "The most successful competitors were able to maintain a higher race velocity by achieving a substantially longer cycle length, which was accomplished in part by more extensive involvement of the weak side leg and trunk."[6] It stands to reason that this conclusion applies to the use of the arms and shoulders as well.

Loss of velocity due to fading of the shoulders to the center needs to be countered by cueing to "lead well" with that inside shoulder toward the poling side ski, in order to remain "square" to the direction of flow as well as "flat to the ground."

Both "dip" in the outside shoulder and "fade" to the center by the inside shoulder result in the upper body loading all to the outside half of the torso muscles. Half is not enough. Poling square and flat engages all the torso muscles along a center line, "down the zipper."

One of the best cues for staying to the side, besides thinking about the motion itself, is simply to "look past your ski tip to the side of the trail," as opposed to looking straight ahead down the trail. Our bodies go where we are looking.

## The Kick/Push/Liftoff

It is helpful to begin a discussion of the kick, in skating or classic style, by first noting what happens to the legs during poling: they open up at the knee. Aside from cushioning and shallow flexion for a split second just before lift off, the knee joint feels as if it essentially is always and progressively opening throughout the glide (it does not straighten totally). As a result the hips are always rising, as the poling motion goes down and through in its arc or pendulum. This allows for the greatest unweighting of the skis due to downward acceleration of the upper body mass and the highest hip position (bone-supported rather than muscle supported) prior to pushing off. Greater and more rapid force can be generated from a shallow knee angle than from a deep angle. (I have reviewed the science behind this conclusion with regard to drop-jump comparisons in the traditional/classic technique Chapter 8.) It is important to remember that a deeper flexion may feel more powerful. What it feels, however, is more feeling only, and that by no means necessarily translates into more speed. We tend to equate more movement generally with greater speed, sensing more muscle activity and overall dynamism throughout the body. Once again this is illusory: what we feel is feeling. Refinement of movement is what produces speed, and that may seem even like a reduction of general activity in technique, less feeling.

I have an adage: The less you feel, the faster you are going. Feeling is most often created by tension, and some types of rhythmical, elastic tension are good. But speed results most often from the release of tension. Thus the adage. I often tell my skiers, after doing a few minutes of tension release mental sets: "Now ski for an hour and feel as little as possible."

It is further helpful to think of the kick in the following way. Hold your two poles in one hand at the top of the grips. The baskets are as far apart as your shoulders, perhaps a little less. Visualize the grips as your hips, the baskets your feet. Imagine the kick/weight transfer not so much as pushing the baskets out, in which case the grips/hips drop, but rather as the baskets remaining more or less in place and the grips/hips moving a short distance back and forth above them in an easy swaying motion.

The whole body thus sways from ski to ski together, as a unit. From the point of view of the whole body swaying, we might also visualize the back and forth of a metronome, rocking rhythmically above the changing points of contact with the snow. It cannot be remembered too often that technique is whole-body movement rather than a sequential aggregate of individual movements. The latter impression is easily given, but we should understand that that is only because language itself is sequential. Human movement is much more simultaneous.

After the poling arc is complete and the knee quite open, the kick is accomplished simply by collapsing down on the flattest ski possible (it well never be absolutely flat, it will only feel flat, even on the snow) and rebounding, like a shock absorber, to the other ski. All the leg levers and muscles release at once, rhythmically but with great swiftness, and swiftness more than power. It is like a graceful pounce or springing, like a cat, toeing down or "pointing" (as the Swedes say) from the ball of the foot.

The direction of this push with the foot is obliquely forward, not to the side, to between 1 and 2 o'clock, not to 3. Why? Skating is faster than classic style because the motion forward is more continuous. As a result, if the push is to the side, by the time the impulse is greatest, the body's center of mass will have already moved ahead of it. The result is that the push will actually finish up behind the skier, at 4 or 5 o'clock, or at 7 or 8, and the leg will have to be lifted or stepped forward to its next point of glide. Even some top skiers make this mistake and pay dearly for it.

The toe-down of the kick (the kick does not take place through the heel), beginning at it earliest point, is directed forward, along the ski, and slightly out. I call this "shooting your feet." As a result, as the kick/push reaches its greatest impulse it is still functionally beside/beneath the center of mass. It stays caught up rather than behind, and rebounds naturally to the center and forward, landing in precisely the optimal next spot rather than having to be consciously stepped forward from behind. So the toe-down shoots toward 10 or 11, 1 or 2.

It is characteristic of this foot movement that it is very rapid, short in duration, and only therefore powerful. That is then not just power; it is the appropriate power for the speed at hand. A long, slower push may feel smooth and powerful, but that is an illusion. If we feel something longer, we assume that there is more of it. Not true. The biomechanical studies done by Penn State have shown the best skaters kick with a definite punctuated foot flexion, more precisely plantar flexion. It is not round and even but rather "spiked" (much like classic style), showing at the moment of push a rapid deceleration and subsequent immediate re-acceleration or rebound through which weight transfer to the other ski is achieved, at the greatest flight speed in the shortest time. The Penn State study states: "Svan and Ostlund exhibited toe velocities of greater fluctuation [than the slower skiers]. The drop off of velocity in the later part of both skating phases (for Svan and Ostlund) might be attributed to a greater skating thrust with associated decreased ski velocity (but greater CM [center of mass] velocity)."[7] A longer, more evenly rounded skating push is thus less effec-

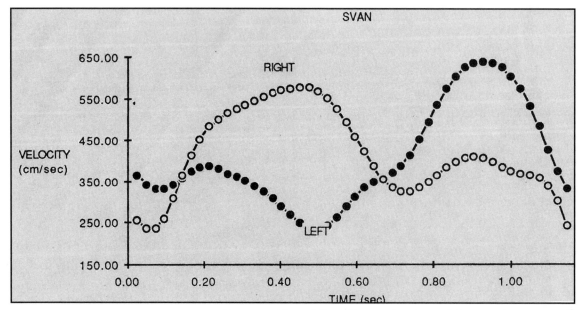

Source: Hay, *The Biomechanics of Sports Technique*[8]

tive. As Torgny Mogren expressed it, giving his reason for not skating on roller skis: it didn't feel right; the wheels left "bananas" on the pavement.

This movement, once mastered, may feel too dainty, too light and dance-like. So much the better, for as dancers know, just that is very powerful and the most efficient. Dancers too were the first athletes to know that body movement is generated through curves, is ballistic rather than geometric. Dancers had learned that in the 20's. Most ski coaches were still describing technique in terms of geometric force vectors in the 70's. The body, however, just does not move in straight lines without soon "disappearing" into the ground.

Perhaps the best test of the power inherent in toe-down, or *tendu,* as the dancer would call it, pointing (or plantar flexion, as the kinesiologist would say) is the fact that it is the first part of technique to go when the racer becomes fatigued. He or she "goes into the heels." An easier proof yet is simply to compare: jump off your heels. It is like having peg legs. Now jump with toe-down. See how much higher you go.

Understanding this toe-down from seeing it is admittedly puzzling, for it appears at the end, greatest extension, of the push-off. Early biomechanical study described it as following at the end of the push off by the larger leg muscles, as a sort of finishing flick. Not so, for what we see is the result of significant loading much earlier. We learn that from electromyography. Using a simpler analogy, think of the blink of an eye. We notice the blink when the eye is closed. Of course, that is the end result of the blink. The blink is the whole movement.

I have mentioned that the other thing to go when the racer becomes fatigues are the elbows. They hinge deeply and drop lower. It is good advice almost anytime to say, "shoot your feet!" or "elbows up!" or "no elbows." That means remain relaxed but comfortably sprung, like a bow.

I would note here that one of the most inhibiting factors to effective toe-down and natural rebound to the center and forward has been the stiffness of some of the skating boots. Boots which totally immobilize the ankle tend to inhibit both lower leg flexion and plantar flexion and work at cross-purposes to full utilization of the body movements available to propel us over the snow swiftly. I advise boots which, while having good lateral stability, also allow ample flexion both forward and to the rear of vertical to the ski. If the kick is completed through plantar flexion, the ski will seem to almost snap free of the snow and land naturally in front again.

## Skating: V2

At a certain point of track speed another movement response is required to either maintain one's velocity or increase it further. In classic skiing one goes from diagonal to kick double-pole. In skating one goes from V1 — one pole push for two glide pushes — to V2 - a pole push with each glide push. Whereas in V1 the rhythm runs pole … push/lift from the foot, the rhythm of V2 is more compact.

Most obviously, in order to return to a forward position in time to pole with the next foot push-off, the recovery of the arms forward must be more immediate. The movement is further quickened by the pole push taking place simultaneously with each foot push.

The quick recovery of the arms/shoulders forward is the easiest new movement to accomplish to get into V2's particular rhythm.

Here are two learning sequences.

1. Double-pole a ways. In the recovery phase of the arms/shoulder coming forward, rise alternately on one foot, then the other. This will be done more easily by quickening that arm/shoulder recovery speed. (A smaller, lighter limb can always be moved more quickly. Thus, almost any desired increase in quickness can be initiated from the arms better than the legs.)

The rising on the one foot becomes more crisp at the same time as a result. Quickness and rhythm are always gained through tension release. Pushing with foot and pole in synchrony will be the natural overall result.

2. Some may find marathon skating a good way not only to skate in a track but to become comfortable with pushing with poles and foot simultaneously. Then without a track, marathon skate 3 strokes to one side, 3 to the other, then 2 strokes and 2, then one to each, and you have V2.

This sequence has the added advantage that it tends naturally to keep the skis as straight forward as possible. There must be an angle to the skate, to be sure, but the main pressure on the pushing ski is not outwards, away from the body, but rather more up and down, underneath the body, an elastic compression-rebound rhythm not unlike diagonal skiing. (The difference is, of course, that in diagonal style the toe-off is down, in skating it is obliquely forward, "shooting the feet".)

These quickening movements very often cause a quickening of the entire movement cycle. This can create too much movement above and on the snow to allow for good glide over the snow. The skier is too busy to be effective. Like second gear in a car, the rpm's go up but the speed remains limited.

Three key cues release the glide and thus real speed of V2. "Finish out" each poling arc behind. This will actually snap the arms forward more rapidly and easily because they have been pre-stretched behind. "Finish out" the reach in front before setting the poles is likewise critical.

Sometimes I say "dislocate the shoulders" up and forward. This pre-loads the arm/shoulder/torso muscles as well and thus quickens the application of forces in the poling push.

"Shoot the feet" assures that each kick is completed with subtlety and snap, like a rapidly uncoiling whip. Without it you will be pushing off through your heels, as if you had a peg leg.

**V2 Alternate or Waltz.** Begin with V2, then simply drop out every other pole push. It is that simple. Instead of another poling motion, the arms "miss" and sweep forward, up and across to the other side.

In all the skating steps the greatest and fastest glide will be achieved not by pushing more often but by following each glide more fully with one's whole body. That maintains momemtum most efficiently. It is done by keeping the shoulders over and rocking the whole body — in line from head to toe, sort of like a metronome — back and forth over each succeeding gliding ski. No amount of twisting in the torso and shoulders will help at all; that only agitates the ski needlessly on the snow, creating more friction and dispersal of directional forces. It may feel more energetic and active, but as I have said before what we are feeling then is simply feeling and energy, not necessarily efficiency and speed. Efficiency is most often characterized by feeling less, not more. Furthermore, the feeling for effort is an unreliable guide to speed. Think about speed, not effort!

## Index of Cues

1. Finish out behind, reach comfortably stretched in front, like double-poling.

2. Both hands together behind — tail on a kite — friendly hands.

3. Reach forward one shelf higher for the jar of jam.

4. Think of the hand/arms swinging forward and back parallel to the poling side ski, in a sort of long rectangular box the width of the shoulders, the length of the ski.

5. Move hip joint forward as follow-through to kick (rotates slightly rearward in classic, forward in skating).

6. Lifting the knee a little, in recovery from the push-off/kick loosens, stretches the gluteus muscles, especially on hills.

7. Avoid letting outside shoulder drop — causes hip to pinch inward, edge the gliding ski. Shoulders stay "flat to the ground."

   *Corrective:* Exaggerate follow-through with outside arms/shoulder.

   From point of pole contact with the snow inside hand moves directly towards inside knee.

8. Avoid letting inside shoulder "fade" down and away from the poling side motion. This halves poling effectiveness.

   *Corrective:* Lead to poling side with inside shoulder, see hands directly in front, feel them move through to the rear in parallel.

9. Pinching, kinking, twisting result in general from trying to go too fast around one's weaknesses, avoiding them rather than correcting. Finish poling in the direction of the strong side ski before kicking off. Push off the little toe.

10. Shoot the feet to near 1 or 11 o'clock.

11. Hip kick: initiate the push-off with the butt muscles rather than the foot. This will help the whole hip-to-toe unit open up at once and make even the toe-off more effective.

12. Glide before the snow!


## General Images

1. Fish swimming up rapids (for hills).

2. How do fish propel themselves? Not only with fins but by curve of body mass against water, curve of skier against flow of movement itself.

3. Potter's wheel for skating, swift movement, the right touch, gives the right power. Power does not necessarily give swiftness, and may even slow you down.


Nothing is more revealing than movement.

— Martha Graham (b.1894)
*American choreographer*

# Some Ideas on Teaching

With this understanding and these many cues in mind, it may be helpful to consider briefly how to evaluate a skier's technique and how to approach making adjustments.

**Teaching principle #1: No movement takes place in isolation;** no one movement is discrete unto itself. Arms, legs, and torso always act in combinations with each other.

The whole body participates in any of its movements. The corrective for a mistake is thus almost never at the point at which the mistake is observed. Try making corrections in the big joints, basic movements first; the extremities will tend to follow like the end of a whip. Simply changing the positions of the extremities tends to result in superficial, more "cosmetic" changes without moving the body's overall movement patterns in the direction you wish.

**Teaching principle #2: Look two times.**

First you must bring your eyes together in front so you can see each droplet of rain on the grass, so you can see the smoke rising from an anthill in the sunshine. Nothing should escape your notice. But you must learn to look again, with your eyes on the very edge of what is visible. Now you must see dimly if you wish to see things that are dim — visions, mist, and cloud-people … animals which hurry past you in the dark. You must learn to look at the world twice if you wish to see all that there is to see.[9]

In watching what a skier is doing you have to look both at him and then past him, making him dim and his surroundings and general rhythm more apparent. As in looking to the side of a shadowy shape at night, called "off-center vision," one's peripheral vision picks up a sharp outline where it will fade to the iris. Highwater gives an example from dance.

In watching a ritual, or a dance, you do not see what is physically before you. What you see is an interaction of forces by which something else arises. Those who only see what is before them are blind.[10]

For the ski coach that something else is movement and the essence of technique. Only from that standpoint is it then possible to accurately understand the specific movements the skier makes. It also explains why it is possible to see a skier in one's peripheral vision only and yet feel precisely whether he is free of tension and moving efficiently, gracefully; and it explains the paradox that a great skier may seem to be moving slowly but is going very fast. Freedom from tension always will feel slow to the eyes and body.

This perspective profoundly effects the nature of communication. (I discuss communication more thoroughly in Chapter 2, "Coaches and Coaching.") Selection, type, and the particular words chosen to communicate are what matter. Too much information is one thing. Use of information is another thing upon which to reflect, in advance. We often feel we are not doing our job if we are not talking, repeating explanations, adding further information. In this, however, we are thinking more of our own satisfaction than of our athletes' improvement. There are many ways to make information more reliably convert to speed, usually through reduction in quantity and selection of type.

For the moment I only suggest the following: Balance two notions:

1. Be patient; take time: keep using the same couple of cues; don't run to new information just because you don't get instant results.
2. But if it clearly isn't working, try something else. Then don't tinker with your original cues. Clear the blackboard, and start over with a fresh set of cues.

And we remind ourselves again finally that the body already knows how to do this and that we will do best to think about it from the inside, how the skier feels it.

> Modern dancers … do not simply perform the movements of the choreographer — they become the movements.
>
> —Jamake Highwater[11]

# Part Four

# A Critique of
# Recent American Ski Science

# *10*

# *The Limitations of Visual Perception in Understanding Ski Technique*

You see, but you do not observe.
—*Sherlock Holmes*

At the 1979 USST spring training camp at Targhee, Wyoming the latest, state-of-the-art biomechanical study of diagonal cross-country ski technique was introduced. Billed as the essence of new scientific insight, anticipation was high. The films were technically dazzling, the explanation by one of Dr. Charles Dillman's assistants from Penn State thorough. He had omitted only one thing from his description of technique, on the advice of the Ski Team Staff. They warned against his use of the term, "late knee straightening." That would lead to a late kick, a traditionally well-known fault.

After the presentation, Judy Rabinowitz mused, "I don't see all that." And Stan Dunklee concluded, "I don't think we see what we're seeing." Nevertheless, the staff put the study to text and the gospel was spread.

Our skiers did not go faster. Why?

The answer goes to the heart of a fundamental problem, shared by the USST, with our American approach to gathering and evaluating information in support of our athletes' development. At this point in our sport's history any discussion of technique must be preceded by a review of the principles according to which it is even possible to draw conclusions and claim insight. Just looking and deciding has been woefully short of adequate, as we will see.

In the biomechanical study of ski technique a premium was placed on long glide. Stride rate among skiers of all ability was nearly the same; stride length made the difference in speed (already documented in Toni Reiter's book, *Skilanglauf Heute*).

All efforts were directed toward maximizing glide rather than tempo, and this dictum stuck until some notice was paid to the varying tempos by different skiers in the Penn State skating studies of 1986. But in 1979/80 the word was firmly "stride length."

At the Olympics at Lake Placid, I watched Bill Koch, Jim Galanes, and Tim Caldwell in training. Something was odd in their movements. Their hips were dropping markedly between strides. So elongated had their strides become, their kicks slower and more deliberate for more power, or so the reasoning had prescribed.

The over-emphasized stride length burned our skiers up. They looked fine; they always did. But they were not fine, as the results showed. The increased energy costs of such deliberate movements were clearly ineffectively high. And no amount of strength training done since has been able to tolerate that cost. Koch died, Allison Kiesel died; there was great disappointment. Skiing with Allison the following November in West Yellowstone, the overuse of muscle energy and the resultant loss of more natural elasticity and light-footed quickness was only too clear.

Koch was a particularly interesting case at Lake Placid. He buried himself in the early races, to the despair of himself and others. There was even indignation in response to his pulling out of the 30 km. But as I stood in the stadium in the 50 km and he skied by, something was now wonderfully different. Light again, high over his skis, flowing easily and fast, it was the old Koch as he had been skiing in November, 1975 in Cooke City, Montana and right through his Olympics which followed. In Lake Placid he was still in 6th place at 35 km. I do not know what happened after that. Did he "put the hammer down" at that point? Did he go for the new stride length concept and run the cost up again at so inopportune a point in the race? Only Bill knows, perhaps.

Doug Peterson was also in the race. Certainly one of our most intelligent and curious skiers, he had eagerly taken to the recent science of it. The report over the radios from 32km was only too graphic: "Doug's coming up the hill, and he's carrying a piano." He dropped out by us in the stadium, in deep anguish.

These are among the best cross-country skiers we have ever had. Our attitudes about science as well as the resultant science itself did not serve them well. We saw but were too impatient to observe? Partly. Perhaps it is more precise to say we did not understand the nature of perception itself. That we confused the technology of the investigative method (technology is not yet science) with the physical human realities to which we were applying it was (and remains) only part of the problem.

Let us follow how this played out. To say the cost per unit of glide distance was too high suggests the problem was not too little of anything, talent, training, motivation, coaching efforts, human concerns, goals, or kindness. It was a problem of too much, and that more is not always better is an ecological insight to which even contemporary society and science are still only reluctantly coming. Too much energy output for the velocity achieved; in fact, the extra deliberateness probably actually slowed the speed. In a word, we faulted on the principle of efficiency, the name of the endurance game.

How did we arrive at this "too much?" The limited perspective of competitive academics. No electromyography was overlaid on the biomechanical measurements. The claim was that biomechanics was sufficient in itself. But viewing film alone, quantifying the motions of the body in space and time, the impression is that all movements are actions, things consciously done. It seems simple enough, except we then have everything to think about and do, and that is both unnatural and burdensome. Movements are not all individual actions, their own point of origin. As many, in fact, are results of others, responses, effects, reactions.

Electromyography helps distinguish actions from reactions. The Swedes had done it already, with helpful results.[1] A few of our skiers and perhaps two or three coaches felt that "something was missing" in the biomechanical study in 1979. Their hesitations were perfunctorily brushed aside. But it was not long before researchers themselves were questioning conservative biomechanic practice. E. C. Frederick wrote in 1985:

> As evidenced by the predominance of descriptive analytical papers in the literature, one can argue that sports biomechanics suffers from a particular shortage of strong synthesis and theory. We have mastered the application of mechanics to describing the characteristics of structures and the kinetics and kinematics of movements, but we have contributed little to the understanding of the theoretical meaning of these findings.[2]

He goes on:

> First, an emphasis on synthesis involving improved mathematical models that incorporate electromyographic data might help us predict what kinematic adjustments in movement will cause the greatest transfer of energy between and within the segments.[3]

Earlier than that the Norwegian theoretician and coach, Haldor Skaard had remarked: "The traditional biomechanical methods do therefore not give a clear picture of the efficiency of a technique."[4] "We must try to enter into the spirit of the movement and feel what is right."[5] W. Baumann echoed Skaard's sentiment at the same conference in a presentation entitled: "On Technical Training in Cross-Country Skiing under Special Consideration of the Roller Ski": "The film analysis alone does not yield sufficient information about the technique."[6]

Our American program persisted in its reverence for that 1979 study, and, for all its insights, probably set back our progress 5 years.

Now electromyography supplements biomechanics at Penn State, and segmental analysis (body segments in terms of both active force application and passive kinetic energy) supplements simple center of mass measurements, thus moving the understanding of movement from geometric vectors of force around the body's center of gravity to the ballistic complex which dancers have understood for some years. Peter Cavanaugh of Penn State himself would later suggest (1990) the problem which some athletes and only a few coaches sensed when this first study appeared in 1979, when we asked for electromyography in relation to the diagonal technique study and were refused in the euphoria of new confidence. Cavanaugh reviews the earlier conservative state of biomechanics in its extravagant claims for kinematics. "Kinematics," he defines for us, is "the description of the movements of segments of the body in space without regard to the forces and moments which caused that movement to occur."[7]

"Yet the critical question of what to do with kinematic data," he goes on, "has sometimes been ignored in the face of fascination with the data collection process."[8] He then concludes: "Quantitative electromyography provides the final link which is needed to establish the details of muscle action."[9] Without that link, the typical behaviorist bias was pursued: technique is simply a matter of shaping body movement, without regard for internal (unobserved) processes, so that it approximates the desired visual model. This manner of thinking and drawing conclusions is painfully widespread in American education, as Eliot Eisner has observed.[10]

What would have been the difference in perspective with these additions?

On film the analysts saw the lead foot gliding forward up the hill. They reasoned that it was being done actively.

Result: if the foot is pushed forward by itself, the hips drop low and behind, necessitating greater muscle (thigh) power for stabilization, the use of chemical energy rather than "free" energy from balance (bone support) and elasticity (natural pre-load and release).

Had the analysts been more patient and added electromyography, they would have discovered that the leg-foot pendles forward as a unit (group!) under any circumstance from the hip joint. If the hip joint is maintained in a high position, a fundamental principle of human locomotion, the leg pendles freely and lands naturally at the optimal point on the ground in front in terms of the attendant speed and terrain. High hip positioning is the result in turn of the lift from the kick of the opposite leg-foot. Only the last of these motions is actively done, the remainder are effects of that action.

## *The Limitations of Perception, Visual and Technological*

The location of the stride, its point of appearance, therefore, was where it appeared on film. Its origin was not there, however, but "hidden" in the power of the lift off of the other leg.

There are two problems to describe here:

1. a problem of perception, which is to say that the eyes work sometimes in imperfect ways; and

2. the confusion of simple method of quantification with the physiological reality of movement, without reckoning with the integrated nature of internal processes. We will see how one problem leads into the next.

The first problem arises most often when we see a top athlete, assume we "see" what he/she is doing, and imitate it. In cross-country skiing this tends most often to happen with motions at the periphery of the movement, because that it where the greatest range of motion makes an element of technique most obvious. Arm movement is a good example. In the beginning years of skating it appeared Gunde Svann began his poling with his hand back in the plane of his ear. That was easy to imitate, and many a beginning skier still does. Few noticed that by the time his poles touched the ground his arms were extended more forward. Torgny Mogren, even Maurilio DeZolt, began the motion more forward, were thus better to imitate, but of course were not Gunde. A moment of Gunde's style was taken to be biomechanically correct technique. A 90 degree elbow position represents a similar case. Seeing it once, some experts assumed, unreasonably, that it was the principle for all situations.(cf. Poling, p. 252.[11]

Conversely, motions not seen immediately were assumed not to be present at all. In the biomechanical study of classic technique in 1979 the analysts prescribed kicking with the whole foot, with the toe pointing down as follow-through at the end of the push. Just from my feel for technique movements there seemed something missing in this explanation. I also knew that the neural activation of a muscle group starts well before it appears obvious in the movement of the athlete. Operating out of the behaviorist faith that observable behavior accurately encompasses the truth of a phenomenon, early toe-down (plantar flexion) was simply denied importance.

Five years later, however, the same researchers put transducers on skiers' feet and found that great pressure was indeed applied early on to the ball of the foot. I took the author of the study skiing, and ran him through a technique session. At the end of it he was skiing quite well, and even said it felt wonderful. "It feels right," he remarked," but its not what I think I see in the film." He had made my point: we cannot always see what we feel in movement; we cannot always see what makes a movement what it is. We dare not leap from simple description to prescription. (cf. my article, "Plantar Flexion" in *PSIA Journal*).[12]

How does this happen? Can we really not trust our eyes? Is seeing not believing? In a moment I will talk about the nature of perception.

Here I turn for example to Bob Nichol's discussion of "The Gunner's Eyes." Keep a moving skier in mind when he speaks about "the optical illusion where the target may not always be doing what it appears to be doing."[13] "If you are a newcomer to this gorgeous sport [jump-shooting mallards] … the natural tendency is to under-shoot." The shooter expects the duck to move in the direction of his head, but he really "hits the surface of the water a tremendous blow with his wings and actually leaps high into the air. The jumped mallard thus rises, or 'towers', much faster than he moves forward."[14] A crow provides a different trick. "With wings spread to catch the wind, and only moving his wings slowly to keep his balance, the escaping crow simply 'fell away' with the wind, that is, he actually moved backward.... and was not traveling in the direction his head was pointed in at all."[15]

I was amused and enlightened to read this, for I have often said that good skiers as often disguise what they are doing as show it clearly to us. And not because they mean to but because their style of movement in general is somehow distracting. I think of Thomas Magnusson, who seemed to ski so roughly, almost like a punt return specialist, or Maurilio DeZolt, whose blur of activity over the snow almost totally hid the soundness of his biomechanics, the actual austerity of his technique. (DeZolt sets up another problem: how can he wind up the tempo so? One answer: cutting the power, tension release.)

Even Thomas Wassberg, the ultimate "long-strider," partly disguised what he was doing. We saw his long legs, but then we knew that glide was independent of leg length. On the other hand, I skied for a ways behind him one day when he was skiing easily between the races at the Lake Placid Olympics, and I was startled by the dance-like spring in his kick, something which was hard to find again visually in the swiftness and more dramatic overall activity of racing movements.

If we are particularly driven by the need to add details to our knowledge of technique, and many of us find ourselves in that description, another point is necessary, of critical practical value. You cannot work with too many points at once, split from each other mosaic fashion. Nichols has another example for us, shooting quail. He recommends a single shot weapon at first. Too many shells in the chamber or "If we 'get too many birds in our eyes,' a miss will usually result."[16] Concentrate on the first bird, and the others will come in the right number.

Biomechanics can accurately describe flight, of course, locate the shape of its curve and direction. But without electromyography it will not know enough to prescribe just how the bird or the skier did it. It will find appearance and assume, too often incorrectly, that it is fact.

The Penn State skating study provides another example. There it notes: "The fastest skier had velocity angles directed more nearly up the track than did the slower skiers," and then concludes: "Thus it is important the CM [center of mass] motion not be directed along the ski glide direction but rather aimed in the track direction, as much as possible."[17]

Wrong conclusion! First off, we cannot say whether the velocity angles resulted from speed or speed from angles. And secondly, good speed results from the body going well with the glide direction, on both sides.

Were we perceptually better trained, we would recognize this as a case of the illusion inherent in stroboscopic effect. A light flashing first at one side and then on another will appear as a line of light between both. The body does not aim up the track between the angles of glide, it flows rhythmically back and forth with them. Separating the directions of aim of the center of mass from the angles of glides simply creates tension and loss of momentum. The body is sort of drawing and quartering itself.

A fish does not keep its body in the middle and push it with its fins. Its whole body curves against the water, back and forth, and thus generates forward motion.

In the conservative, exclusivist biomechanics of the time the belief reigned that observability and measurement provided adequate proof of the truth of a phenomenon. Quantifiability confirmed it. I was told the biomechanists could tell us how to do it without electromyography. So without it to separate cause from effect, we in essence doubled the task for our skiers. We gave them more to do and feel, and with greater feeling the sense of greater power. But we slowed them down in the process!

It is a pitfall close by in any exaggerated use of methods of quantification. Our pitfall is that we love numbers so much, their mystery and finality. As Richard Hofstadter remarks," The American mind seems extremely vulnerable to the belief that any alleged knowledge which can be expressed in figures is in fact as final and exact as the figures in which it is expressed."[18] He is talking about educational intelligence testing, but the same problem haunts the scientific community as well.

It had taken five years to add electromyography to the classic technique study and to validate the powerful forces of plantar flexion in the kick. To that point its presence had been denied, even defied. As the USST undertook a study of skating with Penn State and the collaboration of the Norwegian Haldor Skaard, plantar flexion was again denied, because Haldor did not see it, and he was the invited guru. But it was there, as powerfully as ever, but for USST staff it took too long to truly observe what they were seeing. Meantime the Europeans, knowing about human movement from long traditions of gymnastics, improved much faster than we did with our own American innovation. Among other examples, a Finnish film on skating which appeared the same winter clearly showed a springy and pronounced plantar flexion.

We were not only beaten by training, therefore, but by superior capacity to learn. We had severely incapacitated ourselves by denying the existence of what we personally could not see, and we had confused the method of analysis with reality. We had not found a valid reality; we had simply validated the consistency of the test protocol and equipment.

This has been the case, and remains so, with the terms for analyzing stride characteristics: length and rate. With only those two simple concepts, the distinctions which could be made about the relationship between kick rate and glide length simply do not catch the essence of skiing. Forced to think of skiing in terms of the two has severely limited our sense for what we are doing.

For human propulsion is much more complex. In the first place, the presumption that greater glide length derives from the application of greater power is wrong. It derives from a kick which has a different impulse shape, not simply power. At higher speeds (glide length) the beginning of the kick is softer in order not to interrupt the flow. Because of that initial softness and easy flexing it can be more swift. Only when a kick is swift, swift beyond thinking, can it both keep up with speed and improve it. The general impulse shape of the kick is therefore more elliptical and less even or circular (even application of force throughout the kicking time). Part of the motion is longer, then, part more swift.

The question is not rate or length but then relationships between the two within every total stride. Understanding of this would allow us to recognize that added power does not necessarily make either a better kick or a longer glide, any more than slamming the accelerator and holding it down produces optimal acceleration in a car. More often than not skiers go faster if they reduce the power applied and are more subtle and swift in the feet. I speak further to this critical point in a few moments.

A final example of deficient understanding has plagued our grasp of strength training and the relationship between speed and power. In my chapter on traditional technique I have talked much about power being speed-specific and the fact that the speed of many movements had both speed and impulse shape characteristics which exceeded the speed of conscious deliberation. Recent study has confirmed that most athletic movements in fact combine concentric and eccentric contractions at speeds beyond the capabilities of current instruments to measure. Early on in *The Olympic Book of Sports Medicine* the problem is recognized:

> The primary reason for the small amount of valid research in this area is probably due to the lack of available dynamometers that can load the muscles through the entire physiological range of contraction speeds. The maximum speed of most of the commercially available instruments can cover only 20-30% of the different physiological maxima. As Goldspink (1978) has demonstrated, the peak efficiencies of isolated fast and slow twitch fibers occur at completely different contraction speeds. Therefore, it is possible that in measurements of the force-velocity curve, when the maximum angular velocity reaches the value of 3-4 rad/s, only the efficient contraction speed of STF [slow twitch fibers] will be reached. The peak power of fast twitch-type muscle may occur at angular velocities more than three time greater than our present measurement systems allow.[19]

We have invariably concerned ourselves with what we could see and measure, logically enough. But we have regarded what we could not see as if it were not there, and that has included movements whose speed and impulse character exceeded our powers of observation, movements which are clearly decisive to speed. If we disregard what we cannot see or measure, that makes us comfortable with training the muscles at measurable speeds with measurable resistances, most often with weights. And it seems totally logical to do what we can rather than admit to a standoff with a stubborn mystery. And bringing in scientists, we cannot expect them not to prescribe whatever it is they know.

But it is wrong. In not being able to observe and measure speeds beyond our eyes or instruments, we have assumed that no results meant negative results — a fatal mistake. We have done great amounts of strength training at loads which we could quantify and which seemed to approximate the movements we could observe. But as the force-velocity curve makes clear, as does its early application in the Russian technique timing studies, the addition of force, by itself, does not support an increase in speed; it may as well slow speed down in order to accommodate that force.

This is another case of confusing the moon with the finger pointing at it, validating the eye and instruments of measure rather than identifying the phenomenon of skiing movement for what it truly is.

## *Other Sources of Flawed Analysis*

The plague of untrained or failing powers of observation is reflected in further confusions. We not only confuse cause and effect, we take the part to be the whole. We imitate the effect and assume we are generating the movement correctly; and we confuse the latest "thing" with the "real trick." Understanding how these confusions arise requires some history.

In the period from 1908 to the late teens in Europe three German researchers in the field of perception (all of whom wound up in America after WWII) began to draw distinctions between viewing a phenomenon as a mosaic of chance and interchangeable parts and as an integrated whole-form or Gestalt. Whereas in the former case each part had its own identity and each larger phenomenon was simply an aggregate or sum of smaller parts, in the latter case it was discovered that the whole of anything is in fact more than the sum of its parts. It is a synthesis, rather than mere aggregate, of not only quantities but of their attendant qualities determined in dynamic relationship to each other in that specific form. The best example is a chord of music. It is clearly more than the sum of its individual notes. One can play all the notes in sequence and not have a chord. Likewise, one can try to remember 10 numbers, but will do best and more naturally to group them into two sets of 3 plus four (or two and two). Then it becomes easy. Finally one can observe how two abstract figures have different qualities and give different feelings, even though the line length might be the same.

In the curved figure the line segments junction more smoothly, fluidly; in the angular figure the line are more definite, more identifiable, but the whole is jagged and tense. The same goes for movement. One style is easier to break down into its parts, the other more subtle and graceful. But gracefulness is closer to efficiency, for it makes body movement whole and continuous, seamless and economical. Human movement is not geometric and angular; it is ballistic and curved. It is complex and subtle because of this, and is too elusive for an eye not long schooled and astute in seeing, or at least for an eye without feet.

Where this takes us is from seeing to true observation. If we break movements apart from the whole and imitate individual motions, we will not know what technique feels like. If we push the leg up the hill, we will not only use power to make a cause rather than letting it rebound up hill as a result of the other leg extending, we will render the remaining total movement jerky and inefficient. It is a case where imitation does not equal understanding. Isolation of a single element does not lead us to the whole. We cannot simply copy what we see because that will not lead us to perceive and feel the movement the way it must most efficiently be. Athletes often do better just to watch whole-movement without isolating particulars, or at least work with related pairs of movements. And so rare is the young athlete who can articulate this deeper level of perception of movement that I recommend athletes do not attempt to teach each other.

Two examples of an extension of this mistake in observing. The assumption has been with us for some years that a longer enduring kick would produce more force and thus speed. The reasoning was that force multiplied by time would create greater total force. Biomechanics even stated so.[20] So hooked on the first and isolated insight we were oblivious to the second, which was that that principle applies only for the early, initial portion of an acceleration (a sprinter reaches max velocity 5 to 6 steps out, etc). After that the velocity is inversely proportional to the duration of the kick[21]

So we not only had skiers driving the leg and foot forward; we had them, erroneously, taking longer to kick. The result: slower speed at an increase in energy. We felt the energy and, again erroneously, assumed greater speed would result.

I have reviewed this topic in my chapter on traditional technique. Great force tends to derive from slower speeds, as the force velocity spectrum makes clear.

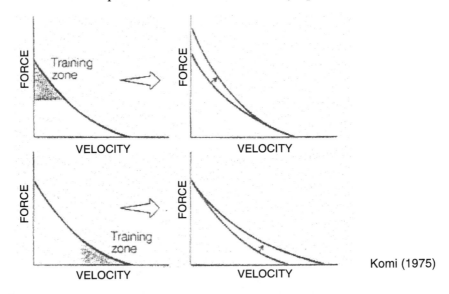

Komi (1975)

Americans need to spend some time reflecting upon this graph. We add the consideration that the Russians timed the kick movement at between .09 and .23 seconds, roughly the blink of an eye — too fast to feel. Feeling itself documents too much muscle tension, and tension, particularly in antagonist muscles, is a primary inhibitor of swift movement, both in terms of speed and of range of motion. I am reminded of Bob Nichols example of the great one-armed shotgunner, who had no left hand to control and "help" the shot and thus inhibit natural flow and follow-through.

Clearly we need not only to discriminate between seeing and observing, in which case the former represents impression and the latter insight. We also need to learn to discriminate between feeling as tension/ control and feeling as release/kinesthetic sense for movement.

I recall Eisner's critique of education as "shaping behavior."(Ch. 4) In analyzing technique the presumption was that the more elements of movement we could identify, the more things would be available to help the skier learn. Unfortunately this did not improve efficiency. In Eisner's words, it put "mind, invention, and emotion on the back burner," buried our skiers with an indiscriminate avalanche of detail, and left out the internal processes which could have provided the discriminating and coordinating agents. Had we added both electromyography and communication science to the athletes' sensations for refined movement, we could have saved time and improved results.

Once again, the educational process simply did not begin with true insight or respect for the body itself as a source. It needed to be shaped, reconstructed, to use the Civil War term, in terms convenient to us but imprecise and thus non-specific to the sport we try so diligently to understand. Our presumption to science in some critical areas has proven rather to have been intellectual conceit in which severe limitations in thought process were simply never recognized or admitted. In our hurry to help and to know, we rushed in. So feverish was our activity, however, our prey slipped away in the shadows before we caught sight of what it was. The best of weapons is no substitute for stealth in the approach.

## *Pitfalls of Our Culture*

Hurry and convenience also troubled our athlete testing protocols. Familiar problems appear: confusion of method with reality, number, because they are objective, with the truth about what is taking place with the athlete. Impatience lends overconfidence a hand in the name of greater productivity. But mechanistic notions from industry do not help, for the correct running of the machines of analysis does not equate with a correct interpretation of the humans to which they are applied. (Humans, Marcuse warned, must be subjects, not objects; but machines are now subjects and humans the objects.) Testing protocols for measuring maximum oxygen uptake and anaerobic threshold/Conconi point (*controversies surrounding these phenomena are beyond the scope of this inquiry. I take their educational value for what it is.) usually have the work load on a treadmill increase evenly every 60 seconds. Heartrate is documented as it climbs in relatively even response until a point at which it deflects clearly to the right.

Lactate measurements show something of a mirror curve, except that generally the heartrate deflects a little later. A three minute interval between increases in load brings the two deflection points close to vertically above each other. Conconi ultimately downplayed the differences in the shorter and longer testing protocols, but his own illustration showed the lactate line deflecting *prior* to the heartrate.

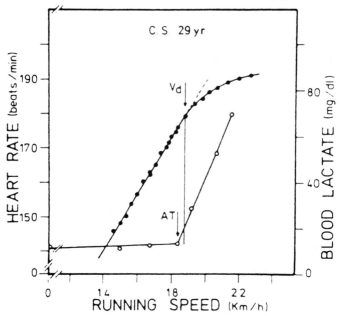

Running speed-heart rate relationship and blood lactate levels at various speeds.[22]

Conconi also noted the slightly slower running speed at that threshold (up to .4km/hr or 6.4m/min). In a 10 km time trial, that apparently small deficit would put the runner 166 meters behind — or a little less than half the track. That is then a very significant difference in ascertaining training intensity and speed at anaerobic threshold. In subsequent testing Conconi himself used the 1000m (3 minute) gradations of load for walkers, cross-country skiers and rowers.[23]

For endurance sport the three minute protocol is thus the most reliable. Whether the Finns came to the same conclusion independently or not, they use the same three minutes. So did the YMCA, in fact, many years ago.[24]

A comparison of the 60 and 3 minute protocols on the same American skier showed a difference in designated anaerobic threshold of 5 beats per minute (bpm), higher for the shorter interval between load increases. Using that figure for three months, he then came back down the five beats shown by both the three minute protocol and lactate curve. His fatigue levels were remaining too high with the higher threshold. Threshold heartrates skewed too high have been noted by others as well.

# The Confusion of Work with Performance

A final example of confusion is the notion than human beings can adapt along a linear path to ever increasing loads. In other words, the greater the load sustained in training, the greater the load to which the body will adapt. The harder the work, the faster the resulting speed, and regardless of whether the work is aerobic or anaerobic.

We are pretty well past this presumption now, except in many secondary schools. What is distressing is how long it hung on even in American scientific circles. Aside from some superficial evidence of limitless physiological adaptability, the ideal of hard work leading to greater and greater productivity and sounder moral fiber is the operant force here. And it comes from both industry and the complementary morality according to which the flesh must be subdued and beaten into proper shape. We still love the metaphor of the rugged athlete as a "machine," even though it leads us regularly astray. It is also part and parcel of the picture we have of heroes, Teddy among them.

Even as late as 1980 in Edmund Burke's standard text on sports physiology the rationale ran as follows:

> Now you might ask how you can best improve your AT [author's designation for anaerobic threshold]. We have not systematically compared various training programs as yet, so a conclusive answer is not available. However, we have produced increments in AT with an approach based on theoretically sound principles of specificity of training. Essentially this means that you must overload the specific physiological function in order to develop a training effect.[25]

He assumes any physiological function and prescribes training bouts indiscriminately above anaerobic threshold, according to the theory than the body will adapt to overloading of any kind.

Linear adaptability was clearly a widespread assumption in medical and exercise physiology circles. In 1982 the US Ski Team consulting physiologist wrote in the coaches newsletter that it was quite simple: if you want to race fast, you have to train as much as possible at race speed. At the time, he, like Londeree above, had never seen or tested a real year-round training schedule, either theoretically or, more reliably, up through the feet.

The point here is not to place blame but to describe a symptom of our scientific community, as well as our lay inclination to admire authority and blindly imitate heroes. Middle-class vertical mobility prizes the acquisition of authority, on any subject, as a mask of success, misunderstanding the connection between knowledge and power. And success is achieved through competition. In scientific fields no less than in others the temptation to go it alone with one's field and method, and to discount other related fields, leads to an ongoing limitation of our total understanding. In sports it leads to a sequence of experts, one traded in for the next, rather than the simultaneous collaboration which other nations thrive upon and which would bring our athletes predictably closer to the performance levels to which we aspire. Vertical position, hierarchies on the professional status and power rung takes implicit precedence over more patient, humble, and just attention to the total complicated nature of sports performance. Again and again the authority of power is confused with the authority of knowledge.

The numerical objectivity of the investigative protocol by itself does not produce an objective view of the athlete's complex interior. The first information on a topic is not the total needed and may even amount to a distortion if applied in isolation. Knowledge of the physical characteristics of a musical instrument does not explain the skill or physical dynamics which produce real music.

That confusion, which has been a root cause of the failure of sports science in cross-country skiing, is one to which we have been all too thoroughly cultured, as Richard Hofstader described it earlier in his essay on American education: "The American mind seems extremely vulnerable to the belief that any alleged knowledge which can be expressed in figures is in fact as final as the figures in which it is expressed."[24]

We are reminded yet again of the Zen saying that runs, "The finger pointing at the moon is not the moon." Norman Maclean put it less delicately in *Young Men and Fire*, "To woodsmen, if you don't know the ground, you are probably wrong about nearly everything else."[27]

My object throughout this book has been to re-examine the ground.

# *Epilogue*

As this book was going to press, news came of the hopeful results of America's male cross-country skiers in the Salt Lake City 2002 Winter Olympics. These results are all the more to be admired for having been achieved in a sports cultural context which has not favored the sort of development necessary for such success. Each of those skiers had to step out of mainstream American institutions and sports programs and essentially go it alone in order to achieve what they did. Two are much older skiers who have doggedly persisted, two younger skiers opted not to go to college in order to go to altitude and train as they knew was possible, and supported financially, only there in Park City, Utah. Another, John Bauer, put himself in the knowledgeable hands of longtime Russian coach Nikolai Anikin for four years in order to resuscitate and release his great potential.

Their stories need to remain in the forefront of our reflections if others in greater numbers are to follow. Congratulation, admiration and enthusiasm will not be enough. Respect for such gigantic efforts requires that we take the time to understand more fully the complex issues at the heart of America's sports culture. We are only just beginning to do so, and it is my hope that this book will help make the changes possible in both attitudes and institutions which will lead to a broader flourishing of our young athletes.

# Appendix 1

## Speed Development Program

Note 1.  The key to the success of this 7 week program lies in maintained clear distinctions between the various speeds/paces.

Note 2.  Between each repetition there is 2–3 minutes rest, a little more in FAP/sprint sessions. Between sets 5–8 minutes rest.

Note 3.  Rest includes light jogging, stretching, light plyometrics, paired resistance.

Note 4.  Number of reps = 450+hrs/yr. For fewer hrs/yr subtract 1-3 reps.

Definitions:   Swing (loose, tall, full striding) 60-80%

ANT (anaerobic threshold) 80-90%

FAP (sprint speed) 90-100%

**Week 1**
Wed    swing: 10x100m, 10x100m
Thurs  FAP: [3x30][2x30, 1x40][1x20, 30, 40]
Sat     ANT: 8x100
                    total: 3088m

**Week 2**
Wed    swing: 10x200, 6x100
Thurs  FAP: [4x30][1x20, 2x40][4x20]
Sat     ANT: 3x200, 6x100
                    total: 4100m

**Week 3**
Wed    swing: 6x300, 6x200
Thurs  FAP: [5x30][1x30, 2x40][1x20, 2x30]
Sat     ANT: 3x300, 5x100
                    total: 4450m

**Week 4**

Wed    swing: 10x250, 8x100
Thurs FAP: [3x20][3x40][1x20, 30, 40] (decrease wk.)
Sat     ANT: 8x100, 8x100
               total: 4920m

**Week 5**

Wed    swing: 6x300, 8x150, 8x100
Thurs FAP: [5x20][2x40, 1x50][1x30, 2x40]
Sat     ANT: 4x250, 4x200
               total: 5120m

**Week 6**

Wed    swing: 8x250, 8x150, 8x100
Thurs FAP: [5x20][2x40, 1x50][1x30, 2x40]
Sat     ANT: 3x300, 5x200
               total: 5440m

**Week 7**

Wed    swing: 10x200, 8x150, 10x100
Thurs FAP: [3x40][1x30, 2x50][1x40, 30, 20]
Sat     ANT: 2x500, 5x200
               total: 6340

# Appendix 2

## Acceleration Training for Distance Runners
## by Joe Rubio

**Strides**

mile pace over 100-200 meters
volume 2-3% of weekly mileage,
or 1% per session
recover between each with walk back to start
or 300 meter jog (full recovery!)

*Option*    fartlek of 15-30 seconds on, 15-30 off
after 15-20 minute warmup.

**Accelerations**    Over 100 meters, start at mile pace, steadily increase speed to
400 meter pace (very fast but never tight).
1% of weekly mileage
hard work on the anaerobic system

Beginning athletes should stick to strides for their first season.
There is danger in all-out efforts every rep, which can lead to injury.

# Appendix 3

# *Examples of Enhanced Plyometric Exercise*

*for muscle "stiffness"/springiness critical to maintenance of speed*

### Exercise 1.

1   2   3   4   5

1. the relaxed cord
2. getting underneath
3. standing relaxed, balanced, tubing stretched
4. drop! Natural shallow knee flexion and instantly …
5. rebound to toes! Even get a little air! … return to 3.

Two loops of half-inch surgical tubing 56" long are attached shoulder width to a beam (or at floor level). The ends of a 1" x 30-36" bar/dowel cushioned with pipe insulation is inserted into the loops and held with hands outside of the looped tubing. Begin with 3 x 10 reps and after several weeks go to 3 x 15 or more. The loops can be a little longer or shorter according to the height of the individual athlete.

**Exercise 2. Korchenny's Over-the-Beam Plyometric**

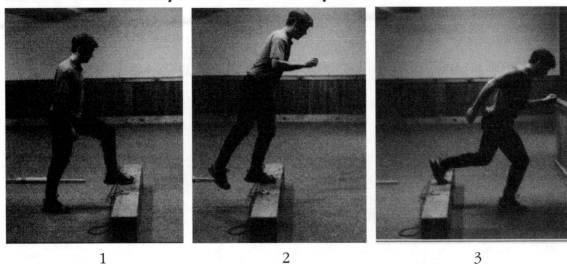

        1                            2                            3

1. Left foot on beam ...
2. spring up and over the beam without touching the right foot until it lands ...
3. on the other side. Return to position 1, again without touching the beam with the right foot.

Do as many as 15-20 crossings, then change feet. Difficulty is added by stepping further away on either side of the beam. Contact with the floor on either side should be as short as possible, with rapid rebound, as in all plyometrics. Avoid going deep into the knees.

# Exercise 3. Over-the-Beam Plyometric with surgical tubing enhancement

          1                               2                             3

1. Get comfortable and balanced before stepping up …
2. extend fully upward, then …
3. touch the floor and rebound back to position 1.

This exercise is more difficult, allows for fewer repetitions initially and requires patient, deliberate movements. The goals are springiness off the floor on either side of the beam and straightening the leg on top.

# Notes

## Introduction

[1]We have difficulty thinking of ourselves as such creatures of history, for that suggests we are less free than we would like. But former Surgeon General C.Everett Koop has made the same point about current medical education and its enduring dependence on the *Flexner Report* of 1910. So the equation might more accurately read: We are only free if we understand history. Only then can we improve on it.

[2]Alfie Kohn, *No Contest: The Case Against Competition* (Boston: Houghton Mifflin, 1992), p. 37.

[3]Mathew Arnold, "Culture and Anarchy," in *Prose of the Victorian Period,* ed. William Buehler (Boston: Houghton Mifflin, 1958), p. 465.

[4]Arnold, p. 465.

[5]Greene, Janet, *Putting Food By* (New York: Bantam Books, 1975), preface.

[6]Bob Nichols, *The Shotgunner* (New York: G.P. Putnam's & Sons, 1949), p. 116.

[7]Norman Maclean, *Young Men and Fire* (Chicago: University of Chicago Press, 1993) p. 104.

## Chapter One: A Letter to Parents

[1]Shane Murphy, ed., *Sport Psychology Interventions* (Champaigne, Ill.: Human Kinetics Press, 1995), p.47.

[2]Alice Miller, *The Drama of the Gifted Child* (New York: Basic Books, 1981), p.7.

[3]Ernst Herberger, et. al,. *Rowing* (Toronto: Sports Book Publisher, 1990), p. 192.

[4]Herberger, p.193.

[5]F. Klimt and Meyer, "Lauftempo durch Herzschlagfrequenzvorgabe," *Oster-reichisches Journal fur Sportmedizin*, 17:1, 1987, p. 31. The authors provide evidence for the shock effect of a 1000 meter run at a heartrate of 180 bpm on 10 and 11 year olds. Even after 10 minutes of rest both cardiovascular and metabolic (lactate) values remained elevated.

[6]V.N. Manshosov, *Training: Cross-Country Skiing* (Moscow, 1986), p. 48.

[7]Manshosov, p.58.

[8]Atko Viru, *Adaptation in Sport Training* (Boca Raton, Fla.: CRC Press, 1995), p. 283-286.

[9]*The Olympic Book of Sports Medicine* (London: Blackwell Scientific Publications, 1988), p. 65.

[10]Viru, p. 11.

[11]Viru, p.13.

[12]Miller, p. vi.

[13]Letter from Heikki Rusko, Finnish physiologist, to Richard Taylor, July 30, 1987

## Chapter Two: Coaches and Coaching

[1]Rudyard Kipling, *Captains Courageous* (Mattituk, NY: Amereon, 1896), p.71.

[2]Richard Rapaport, "To Build a Winning Team. An Interview with Head Coach Bill Walsh," *Harvard Business Review,* Jan.-Feb. 1993, p.113.

[3]Rapaport, p. 113.

[4]Bruce Olgivie and Thomas Tutko, "Sport: If You Want to Build Character, Try Something Else," *Psychology Today,* Oct. 5, 1971, p. 60-63.

[5]Olgivie and Tutko, "Sport:Ö"

[6]Alice Miller, *The Drama of the Gifted Child* (New York: Basic Books, 1981), p. 6.

[7]Miller, p.85.

[8]Miller, p.85.

[9]Carl Rogers, *On Becoming a Real Person* (Boston: Houghton Mifflin, 1961), p. 392.

[10]Rogers, p.392.

[11]J. D. Mac Dougall, "The Anaerobic Threshold: Its Significance for the Endurance Athlete," *Canadian Journal of Applied Sports Sciences,* no.2, 1977, pp. 137-139.

[12]MacDougall, p. 139.

[13]MacDougall, p. 139.

[14]Ben Londeree, "Anaerobic Threshold Training," in Edmund Burke, *Toward an Understanding of Human Performance* (Ithaca: Movement Publications, 1977), p. 42.

[15]Owen Anderson, "Planning Your Training for 1993: Should You 'Crash' Your Way to Better Performances?" *Running Research,* 9.1, 1993, pp.1-7.

[16]Arthur Weltman, et al., "Endurance training amplifies the pulsatile increase of growth hormone: effects of training intensity," *Journal of Applied Physiology,* 72.6, 1992, pp. 2186-2196.

[17]Anderson, p.7.

[18]Weltman, p. 2194.

[19]Ronald Blythe, *Akenfield,* (New York: Pantheon Books, 1969), p. 135f.

[20]Gordon Lawrence, *People Types and Tiger Stripes, A Practical Guide to Learning Styles,* 2nd ed. (Gainesville: Center For Application of Psychological Type, 1982), p. 2ff.

[21]Additional basic sources for the Meyers-Briggs Personality Type Indicator:

Isabel Briggs Meyers, *Introduction to Type* (Palo Alto: Consulting Psychologists Press, 1962).

Isabel Briggs Meyers and Peter Meyers, *Gifts Differing* (Palo Alto: Consulting Psychologists Press, 1980).

Otto Kroeger and Janet Thuesen, *Type Talk* (New York: Delacourt Press, 1988).

Richard Taylor, "Personality and Performance," *The Professional Skier,* Winter 2, 1988, p. 20-22.

Richard Bandler and John Grinder, *Frogs Into Princes* (Moab: Real People Press, 1979).

[22]Bandler, p. 61.

[23]Bandler, p. 16.

[24]Bandler, p. 30.

[25]Bandler, p. iiif.

[26]Bandler, p. 98.

[28]Bandler, p. 83.

[29]Bandler, p. 183.

[30]Bandler, p. 17.

[31]Bandler, p. 23.

[32]Bandler, p. 23.

[33]Bandler, p. 46.

[34]Bandler, p. 54f.

[35]Blythe, *Akenfield,* p. 308.

[36]Walt Whitman, *Song of Myself,* no. 47.

## Chapter Three: Affirming the Flesh: How Can We Be Tough? How Tough Can We Be?

[1]Bill Walsh, in "To Build a Winning Team: An Interview with Head Coach Bill Walsh," by Richard Rapaport in *Harvard Business Review,* Jan.-Feb.    1993, p.120.

[2]Jan Huizinga, *Homo Ludens, a Study of the Play Element in Culture* (Boston: Beacon Press, 1950), p.196.

[3] Rollo May, *Man's Search for Himself,* (New York: Dell Publishing, 1953), p.107.

[4]Kenneth Murphy, "Sowing the Whirlwind," *The Boston Globe,* Aug. 22, 1993, p. B16.

[5]Bill Moyers, quoted by D. C. Denison in "The Interview: Bill Moyers," *The Boston Globe Magazine,* April 14, 1993, p.8f.

Notes                                                                    303

[6]Jamake Highwater, *Dance Rituals of Experience,* (Pennington, NJ: Princeton Book Co. 3rd ed., 1992), p.26.

[7]Highwater, p. 27.

[8]Highwater, p. 27.

[9]Huizinga, p. 205.

[10]Norman Cousins, *Anatomy of an Illness* (New York: Bantam Books, 1979), p.65.

**Suggested Reading:**

Johann Huizinga, *Homo Ludens,* (Boston: Beacon Press, 1950).

Jay Coakley, *Sport and Society: Issues and Controversies* (St. Louis: Mosby, 1978).

Rainer Martens, *Joy and Sadness in Childrens' Sport* (Champaign, Ill.:Human Kinetics Press, 1978)

Leo Hendry, *Sport, School, and Leisure, Three Dimensions of Adolescence,* (London: Lepus Books, 1978).

Kathryn Groverned, *Fitness in American Culture,* (Amherst: Univ. of Mass. Press, 1989)

N. Norman Shneidman, *The Soviet Road to Olympus: Theory and Practice of Soviet Physical Culture and Sport* (Toronto: Ontario Institute for Studies in Education, 1978). This book is interesting not only because it states broad fundamental principles of sports—physiological development but also because it articulates the political, and, above all, social and cultural integration of sport into Soviet life.

**Chapter Four: Charge the Hill!**

[1]Wallace Stegner, *Where the Bluebird Sings to the Lemonade Springs* (New York: Penguin Books, 1992), p. 138.

[2]Rollo May, *Man's Search For Himself.* (New York: Dell Publishing, 1953), p. 107.

[3]Jean Baxter, "Framed for Reconstruction: Eastman Johnson's *The Old Stagecoach,* 1871," p. 3. Unpublished paper.

[4]Cf. Bill Moyers notion, in "The Interview: Bill Moyers," by D.C. Denison, *The Boston Globe Magazine,* April 4, 1993, p.8f. "Well, to us in the West, the body is a machine: If something goes wrong, you find the part that awry and replace it. That's a useful metaphor, but their [the Orientals'] metaphor is that the body is a garden, a living organism in which everything is interconnected. The physician then becomes a gardener, not a mechanic."

[5]Donald J.Mrozek, "Sport in American Life, From National Health to Personal Fulfillment, 1890-1940," in *Fitness in American Culture,* ed.Kathryn Grover (Amherst: University of Massachusetts Press, 1986), p.18. The very use of the word "corporate" — "having the characteristics of the body" — is perhaps the best example of how the body is preferred as metaphor while being ignored as fact.

[6]Mrozek, p. 18f.

[7]Mrozek, p. 19.

[8]Thomas J.Schlereth, *Victorian America: Transformations in Everday Life, 1876-1915* (New York: Harper Collins, 1991), p. 218f.

[9]Mrozek, p. 19.

[10]Larry Owens, "Pure and Sound Government: Laboratories, Playing Fields, and Gymnasia in the Nineteenth-Century Search for Order;" in *Isis,* Vol. 76, No. 282, 1985, p. 187.

[11]Mrozek, p. 27.

[12]Mrozek, p. 19.

[13]Mrozek, p. 19.

[14]Mrozek, p. 19.

[15]Kenneth Murphy, "Sowing the Whirlwind," *The Boston Globe,* Aug. 22,1993, p. B16.

[16]Schlereth, p. xiii.

[17]Frank Menke, *Encyclopedia of Sports,* (New York: Barnes & Co., 1944), p.xi. Cf. Schlereth: "Baseball eclipsed boxing as the nation's leading spectator sport by 1915." p. 224.

[18]This corresponds with Dudley Sargent's presence at Harvard, the founding of the American Association of Physical Education in 1895, and the advent of numerous sports governing bodies, as Menke notes in his history.

[19]John Brisben Walker, "XVII. Athletics and Health. The Department of Physical Culture," in *The Cosmopolitan Magazine,* Sept. 1904, p. 594.

[20]Schlereth, p. 217f.

[21]Claes J.Enebuske, *Progressive Gymnastic Day's Orders* (New York: Silver, Burdett & Co.,1890). Walker seems to be referring to this very book, for he practically quotes Enebuske's description of the unhealthy cramping effects of the student's body at his desk and the prescription of a "Two-Minute Exercise" to aereate to brain.

[22]Enebuske, p. vi.

[23]Enebuske, p. ix.

[24]Francesco Conconi, in tests conducted prior to the 1980 Olympics; reported in *Journal of Applied Physiology* (1982), 52:869-873; further in *European Journal of Applied Physiology* (1985)53:299-303; and in *Ultrasport,* Aug.1985, p. 70.

[25]Cf. Ulf Bergh, in *Physiology of Cross-Country Ski Racing* (Champaign: Human Kinetics Press, 1982. Originally published in Swedish, 1974), p. 59: "Running 'hard' can result in paying the price for excess tempo: high lactic acid buildup." Cf. also V.N. Manshasoff, *Training — Cross-Country Skiing* (Moscow, 1986), p. 58: If training levels remain at optimum-plus, then beginning improvement will soon be followed by a plateau and then progressive lowering of performance.

[26]Jeffrey L. Cruikshank, *A Delicate Experiment. The Harvard Business School 1908-1945* (Boston: Harvard Business School Press, 1987). Testing began at Harvard Business School in 1927 in Elton Mayo's Harvard Fatigue Laboratory. Mayo's goal was "a competent investigation of the physiological changes induced in the human organism by the conditions of its daily work." p. 165.

[27]Walker, p. 594.

[28]Walker, p. 593.

[29]Theodore Roosevelt, *An Autobiography* (New York: The MacMillan Co., 1913), p. 32f.

[30]Schlereth, p. 218f.

[31]Roosevelt, p. 31.

[32]Mark Sullivan, *Our Times, The United State 1900-1925. III: Pre-War America* (New York: Charles Schribner's Sons, 1930), p. 69.

[33]Sullivan, p. 71.

[34]Sullivan, p. 71f.

[35]Quoted in Sullivan, p. 99.

[36]Sullivan, p. 140.

[37]Edward Cotton, *The Ideals of Theodore Roosevelt* (New York: Random House, 1923), p. xiv f.

[38]Cf. Schlereth on the Victorian compulsion to quantify. p. 304.

[39]Richard Hofstadter, *Anti-Intellectualism in American Life* (New York: Random House), p. 329.

[40]Hofstadter, p. 331.

[41]Hofstadter, p. 331f.

[42]Hofstadter, p. 323.

[43]Hofstadter, p. 324. Cf. variety of types in *The Old Stagecoach.*

[44]Hofstadter, p. 324.

[45]Hofstadter, p .328.

[46]Hofstadter, p .326.

[47]As Hofstadter notes, p .326f.

[48]Hofstadter, p. 327

[49]Hofstadter, p. 329, 332.

[50]Hofstadter, p. 333.

[51]Hofstadter, p. 334.

[52]Hofstadter, p. 334.

[53]Hofstadter, p .335.

[54]Hofstadter, p. 336.

[55]Schlereth, p. xi.

[56]Schlereth, p. xiv.

[57]Hofstadter, p. 338.

[58]J.L.McBrien, 1916. *America First,* pamphlet (Cincinati, 1916), preface.

[59]Hofstadter, p. 338.

[60]Hofstadter, p. 339.

[61]Jane Green,"A Vision of Parity Brutally Extinguished," in *The Boston Globe,* July 5, 1992, p. 29.

[62]Hofstadter, p. 340.

[63]Hofstadter, p. 347.

[64]S. Hofstadter, p. 349.

[65]Mrozek, p. 23.

[66]Elliot Eisner, in his forward to Rudolf Arnheim's *Thoughts on Art Education* (New York: Oxford University Press, 1989), p. 3.

[67]Theodore Roosevelt, *An Autobiography*, p 31.

[68]William James, *Varieties of Religious Experience* (1902), 19th edition (New York: Modern Library, 1994), p. 105.

[69]Paraphrases Mrozek, p. 27.

[70]Mrozek, p. 28f.

[71]George Creel, "A Close-Up of Douglas Fairbanks," reprinted from *Everybody's Magazine* as an afterward in Douglas Fairbanks, *Laugh and Live* (New York: A.L. Burt, 1917), p. 177.

[72]Jane Jacobs, *The Death and Life of Great American Cities* (New York: Modern Library, 1993), p. 111.

[73]Jacobs, p. 111.

[74]Mrozek, p. 19f.

[75]Mrozek, p. 20.

[76]Jamake Highwater, *Dance: Rituals of Experience* (Pennington, NJ: Princeton Book Co., 3rd ed., 1992), p. 27.

[77]Highwater, p. 108.

[78]Highwater, p. 27.

[79]Highwater, p. 100.

[80]Highwater, p. 100f.

[81]Cruikshank, p. 165. Cf. footnote 26.

[82]*Tip Top Weekly,* New York, Nov.2, 1901.

[83]Harold M. Sherman, *Down the Ice* (Chicago: Goldsmith, 1932)

[84]Mrozek, p. 25ff.

[85]Fairbanks, p. 29.

[86]Fairbanks, p. 172.

[87]Fairbanks, p. 98.

[88]Mrozek, p. 26.

[89]Mrozek, p. 25.

[90]Cf. Mrozek, p. 26.

[91]Mrozek, p. 21.

[92]It is interesting that Theodore Roosevelt had had the same experience as Charles Atlas, had built himself up, and no longer had sand kicked in his face. Atlas thus profited from having Teddy, as well as his specific mentor, Bernarr McFadden, as models. S. Mrozek, p.32.

[93]Fairbanks, p. 103f.

[94]Mrozek, p.22.

[95]Mrozek, p.22.

[96]*Theodore Roosevelt, An Autobiography,* p.31.

[97]Mrozek, p.23.

[98]Mrozek, p.27.

[99]Mrozek, p.29.

[100]Mrozek, p.30.

[101]Mrozek, p.32.

[102]Mrozek, p.38.

[103]C. Everett Koop, *Koop* (New York: Harper Paperbacks, 1992), p. 52.

[104]Mrozek, p. 38.

[105]Arthur Lydiard, "Going Lydiard's Way," in *New Views of Speed Training* (Mountain Valley, CA: World Publications, 1971), p.24.

[106]Michael Blowen, *The Boston Globe*, May 21, 1994, p.29.

[107]Johan Huizinga, *Homo Ludens* (Boston: Beacon Press, 1950), p. 205.

[108]Mrozek, p. 42.

[109]Mrozek, p.42.

[110]Mrozek, p. 42.

[111]Mrozek, p. 43.

[112]Rollo May, *Man's Search for Himself* (New York: Dell Publishing, 1953), p. 105.

[113]*Harvard Business Review,* Jan.-Feb. 1993, p. 111ff.

[114]Theodore Roosevelt, *An Autobiography,* p. vi..

## Chapter Five: Putting Miles By

[1]Anikin, Nikola and Anikina, Antonia, *The Soviet Method of Training Cross-Country Skiers,* pamphlet, p. 4.

[2]Sweeney, H., "The importance of the creatine kinase reaction: the concept of metabolic capacitance," *Med. Sci. Sports Exerc.,* 26:1 Jan. 1994, p.35.

[3]Conconi, F., et.al., "Determination of the anaerobic threshold by a noninvasive field test in runners," *J. Appl. Physio: Respirat. Environ Exercise Physiol.,* 52:869-873.

[4]Baumann, W., *Protocol of the FIS Cross-Country Trainers' Seminar* 1982, Davos, Switzerland, p. 12.

[5]Daniels, Jack, *A System Approach to Running,* pamphlet, p. 2.

[6]Manshosov, V.N., *Training Principles: Cross-Country Skiing* (Moscow, 1986), p. 52.

[7]Franz, Birgit, "Zur Belastungsgestaltung im Nachwuchsbereich," *Information/ Dokumentation Sport* (Leipzig: Institut für Angewandte Trainingswissenschaft, 1995), p. 36.

[8]Shneidman, N. Norman, *The Soviet Road to Olympus* (Toronto: Ontario Institute for Studies in Education, 1978), p. 117.

[9]Cf. Anikin, p. 9.

[10] Cf. Ek, A., *Skidakning vs. rullskidakning,* pamphlet. Ek describes the manner in which the slower roller skis most precisely match the friction resistance of snow.

[11]The free flexing of the foot (plantar flexion) is of critical significance to propulsion. Thinking to imitate speed skaters early on, skiers turned to more rigid boot-binding systems, only to discover that speed skaters had invented a new "slap-skate" to gain that very plantar flexion the skiers had worked to hard to eliminate. S. Schenau, et. al., "A new skate allowing plantar flexion improves performance," *Med. Sci. Sports Exerc.,* 28:4 April 1996, p. 531ff.

[12]Suslov, F., "Does a Runner Need Strength?" *AFQ,* April 1991, p. 49.

[13]*The Olympic Book of Sports Medicine,* eds. Dirix, A., Knutgen, H.G., and Tittle, K., (Oxford: Blackwell Scientific Publications, 1988), p. 45f.

[14]*The Olympic Book of Sports Medicine,* p. 46.

[15]Koch, Christopher, "Endurance," *Bicycle Guide,* March 1990, p. 47ff.

[16]*The Olympic Book of Sports Medicine,* p. 46.

[17]Manshosov describes Soviet research showing 15–18 years of age (our secondary school period) as being the period of most accelerated cardiovascular development. p. 48.

[18]Bergh, Ulf, *Physiology of Cross-Country Skiing* (Champaign, Ill.: Human Kinetics Publishers, 1982), p. 34ff. Originally published in Sweden in 1974.

[19]*The Olympic Book of Sports Medicine,* p.184f.

[20]*Med. Sci. Sports Exerc.,* supplement to 24:5, May 1992, p. 55.

[21]Hoff, J., Hellerud, J., Wisloff, U., "Maximal strength training improves work economy in trained female cross-country skiers," *Med. Sci. Sports Exerc.,* 31:6 1999, p. 870ff.

[22]Bosco, C., Rusko, H., Hirvonen, J. "The effect of extra-load conditioning on muscle performance in athletes," *Med. Sci. Sports Exerc.,* 18:4 Aug. 1986, p. 418.

[23]Cf. Anikin and Anikina, p. 4.

[24]Cf. Suslov, "There is a strong connection between an athlete's anaerobic threshold and his muscles' oxidative capacities." p. 51.

[25]Bergh, p. 59.

[26]Manshosov, p. 58.

[27]Ivers, T., *The Fit Racehorse* (Cincinnati: Esprit Racing Team Ltd., 1983), p. 62. Quoted in my article in *JPSCI,* June, 1985, p. 14.

[28]Halle, Siri, "Man ma trives for a go fort!" in *Inside Sport,* Nr. 3-4, Vol. 2 (Osteras, Norge: Stiftelsen Norsk Skigymnas, 1991), p. 15.

## Chapter Six: Linking Base Training to Racing

[1]Novosad, J. and Waser, J., *Ski Sport* (Moscow, 1975), Ch. I, p. 1.

[2]*The Olympic Book of Sports Medicine,* p.184.

[3]Sharkey, Brian, *Training for Cross-Country Skiing,* Champaign, Ill. Human Kinetics Press (1984), p. 54.

[4]J.Helgerud, et.al., "Changes in Soccer Performance from Enhanced Aerobic Endurance." Abstract #947 in *Med. Sci. Sports Exerc.,* Vol. 32, #5, May 2000, Supplement, p. s208.

[5]Komi, P.V., and Häkkinen, "Strength and Power" in *The Olympic Book of Sports Medicine,* eds. Dirix, A., Knutgen, H.G. and Kittle, K. (Oxford: Blackwell Scientific Publications, 1988), p. 182.

[6]Novosad, J./Waser, J., *Ski Sport* (Moscow, 1975), Chapter II, p. 7.

[7]Herberger, Dr. Ernst, et.al., *Rowing* (Toronto: Sport Books Publisher, 1983). Originally published in East Germany as *Rudern* (Berlin, 1977), p. 178-194.

[8]Bompa, Tudor, *From Childhood to Champion Athlete* (Toronto: Veritas Publishing, 1995), p.146ff.

[9]Tesch, P., "Aspects of muscle properties and use in competitive alpine skiing," *Med. Sci. Sports Exerc.,* Vol. 27, No.3, 1995, p.313.

[10]Karlsson, J., "Profiles of Cross-Country and Alpine Skiers," *Clin. Sports Med.,* Vol. 3, 1984, pp. 245-271.

[11]Bergh, Ulf, *Physiology of Cross-Country Skiing* (Champaign, Ill.: Human Kinetics Publishers,1984), p. 67.

[12]Bellizzi, M., King, K., Cushmann, S., Weyand, P., "Does the application of ground forces set the energy cost of cross-country skiing?" *J. Appl. Physiol.* 85(5), 1998, p. 1742.

[13]Weyand, P., Sternlight, D., Bellizzi, M., Wright, S., "Faster running speeds are achieved with greater ground forces, not more rapid leg movements," *J.Appl. Physiol.* 89, 2000, p. 1995.

[14]Chelly, S. and Denis, C., "Leg power and hopping stiffness: relationship with sprint performances," *Med. Sci. Sports Exerc.* Vol. 33, No. 2, 2001, p. 328.

[15]Chelly and Denis, p. 330.

[16]Chelly and Denis, p. 331.

[17]Chelly and Denis, p. 331.

[18]Chelly and Denis, p.331.

[19]Arampatzis, A., Bruggemann, G., Klapsing, G., "Leg stiffness and mechanical processes during jumping on a sprung surface," *Med. Sci. Sports Exerc.* Vol. 33, No. 6, June 2001, p. 927f.

[20]Arampatzis, et.al., p. 929.

[21]Franz, Birgit, "Aktuelle Auffassungen zur Belastungsgestaltung in den Ausdauersportarten," in *Information/Dokumentation* Sport, Institut fur Angewandte Trainingswissenschaft, Leipzig 1995, p.35.

[22]Hiserman, Jim, "Develop a Fall Conditioning Program for Sprinters," *American Athletics,* Fall 1992, p.40 ff.

## Notes                                                        311

[23]Rubio, Joe, "Acceleration Training for Distance Runners," *American Track and Field*, Fall/Winter 2000.

[24]Korchenny, Dr. Remi, *Speed Improvement,* video tape, Ather Sport.

[25]Suslov, F., "Does A Runner Need Strength," *SFQ,* April 1991, p. 51.

[26]Keith, S., and Jacobs, I., "Adaptations to Training at Individual Anaerobic Threshold (IAT)," *Med. Sci. Sports Exerc.,* Vol.23, No.4, April 1991, p.533.

[27]Kuznezow, W.W., "Strength Training," US Ski Team pamphlet, p. 1. Also Counsilman, J.,"The Importance of Speed in Exercise," in Burke, Edmund, *Toward an Understanding of Human Performance* (New York: Mouvement Publications, 1977), p. 53.

Kuznezow: "It is the white [fast twitch] fibers which are synchronized during the development of power; a transformation of the red fiber will occur through special [endurance] training." p.1.

Counsilman: "The important thing to remember is that it's undesirable to enlarge or hypertrophy the red [slow twitch] fibers (through slower movements) for athletic events, whether for endurance or speed. Enlargement does not improve their endurance; it can actually impair it." p. 53.

[28]Numela, A., Hirvonen, J., Rusko, H., et.al., "Anaerobic Energy Production and Running Speed During the 400 Meter Sprint," *Med. Sci. Sports Exerc.,* Vol.23, No.4, April 1991, p. 36.

[29]*Trainingslehre* (East Germany), reviewed in *Athletic Performance Review,* Vol.2, No.3, 1987,p. 10f.

[30]*The Olympic Book of Sports Medicine,* eds. Dirix, A., Knutgen, H.G. and Kittle, K., (Oxford: Blackwell Scientific Publications, 1988), p.99.

[31]Marcinik, E.J., Potts, J., et.al., "Effects of Strength Training on Lactate Threshold and Endurance Performance," *Med. Sci. Sports Exerc.,* Vol. 23, No.6, June 1991, p.742.

[32]Crane, L., Davis, B., Kreider, M., et. al., "Comparison of Pulmonary Functions Between Endurance Athletes and Sprint Athletes," *Med. Sci. Sports Exerc.,* Vol. 23, No.4, April 1991, p. 24.

[33]Manshosov, V.N., *Training Principles: Cross-Country Skiing* (Moscow, 1986), p. 32.

[34]Artur Barrios, World Record Holder in 10,000m, quoted in Mark Will-Weber, "Running's Ups and Downs," *Coaching Challenge,* Fall 1991, p.9.

[35]Medbo and Burgers, "Effect of training on the anaerobic capacity," *Med.Sci.Sports Exerc.,* Vol.22, No. 4, Aug.1990, p.507.

[36]Houmard, et.al., "The effects of taper on performance in distance runners," *Med. Sci. Sports Exerc.,* Vol.26, No.5, May 1994, pp.624-631.

[37]Arthur Lydiard, the great New Zealand coach, summed up his critique of American track training as follows: "There are many athletes in the US who train like hell. And when the season starts, they continue to train very hard. We didn't train to train. When we started to race, we trained very lightly. The two key words are fresh and sharp. You have to be fresh and you have to be sharp if you want to race well." "Going Lydiard's Way," in *New Views of Speed Training,* (Mountain View, CA 1971), p. 22. Such light training I describe as "tickling your chemistry," as opposed to challenging your whole system.

[38]Paul Garvey, "Planning for Peak Performance," *The American Athlete,* Vol.4,No.3, Fall 1992, p.12.

## Chapter Seven: Racing: Farewell to "Charge the Hill!"

[1]Skinner, B.F., "On Having a Poem," Saturday Review, July 16, 1972, p.35.

[2]Watts, Alan, "Beat Zen, Square Zen and Zen," in *This Is It* (New York: Collier Books, 1958), p. 97.

[3]Simon, Jeff, "No Pain, Your Gain," *American Athletics,* Fall 1993, pp.54-56.

[4]Simon, p. 54.

[5]Simon, p. 56.

[6]Simon, p. 56.

[7]Novosad, J. and Waser, J., *Ski Sport* (Moscow, 1975), Ch. IV, p. 3.

[8]Novosad and Waser, Ch. IV, p. 49.

## Chapter Eight: Technique

[1]Highwater, Jamake, *Dance: Rituals of Experience,* 3rd Edition (Pennington, NJ, 1992), p. 27.

[2]Highwater, p. 112.

[3]Manshosov, V.N., *Training: Cross-Country Skiing* (Moscow, 1986), p. 53.

[4]Novosad, J., and Waser, J., *Ski Sport* (Moscow, 1975), Chapter I, p. 13.

[5]Novosad, Waser, Chapter II, p. 4ff.

[6]*The Olympic Book of Sports Medicine,* Dirix, A., Knutgen, H.G. and Tittle, K., eds. (Oxford: Blackwell Scientific Publications, 1988), p. 182.

[7]Novosad, Waser, Chapter II, p. 30f.

[8]Hay, James, *The Biomechanics of Sports Techniques* (Englewood Cliffs, NJ: Prentice-Hall, 1985), p. 77.

[9]Mann, R., Hermann, J., Kinematic analysis of Olympic sprint performance. *Inter-*

*national Journal of Sport Biomechanics,* Vol. 1, No. 2, May 1985, p. 151f.

[10]Mann, Herman, p. 153.

[11]Bobbet, M., Huijing, P., Van Ingen Schenau, G., The influences of jumping technique on the biomechanics of jumping. *Med. Sci. Sports. Exerc.,* Vol. 19, No. 4, Aug. 1987, p. 332.

[12]*The Olympic Book of Sports Medicine,* p. 182.

[13]*The Olympic Book of Sports Medicine,* p. 221.

[14]Carlsen, Johannes, *Skiing Technique and Motion Theory,* Swedish Ski Union Education Committee, Nov. 1975.

[15]Maier, S., Reiter, T., Skilanglauf Heute (1980). The authors trace the evolution of the prescriptive lift-off angle from 45 to 53 degrees, but their understanding remains limited by the vector model of analysis. Their book was translated as: *Cross-Country Skiing: Racing Techniques and Training Tips* (New York: Barron's Educational Series, 1980).

[16]Novosad, Waser, Chapter III, p. 7f.

[17]Novosad, Waser, Chapter III, p. 8.

[18]Novosad, Waser, Chapter III, 8.

[19]Cf. Taylor, R., "Technique is one movement," in *Nordic Skiing* 1981. "Cross-country skiing is one movement comprised of a continuous rhythmical curve of forces. Speed and endurance are factors of simple, natural momentum generated by muscle propulsion, elasticity, and body weight itself."

[20]Nichols, Bob, *The Shotgunner* (New York: G.P.Putnam's & Sons, 1949), p. 125.

[21]Nichols, p. 125.

[22]Nichols, p. 124.

[23]Nichols, p. 127.

[24]Jordan, Michael, *I Can't Accept Not Trying* (San Fransisco:Harpers, 1994), p. 30.

[25]Highwater, p. 33.

[26]Highwater, p. 33.

[27]Highwater, p.27.


## Chapter Nine: Skating

[1]Jordan, Michael, *I Can't Accept Not Trying* (San Francisco: Harper, 1994), p.30.

[2]Ehrig, Andreas, et. al., *"Untersuchungen zum Klappschlittschuh,"* in *Entwicklungstendenzen der Trainings- und Wettkampfsysteme in den Ausdauersportarten mit Folgerungen fur den Olympiazyklus 1996-2000* (Institut fur Angewandte Trainingswissenschaft, Leipzig 1996), p.108.

[3]Nelson, McNitt-Gray, Smith, *Biomechanical Analysis of the Skating Technique in Cross-Country Skiing,* Penn State University 1986, p.40.

[4]Penn State Study, p. 47.

[5]Penn State Study, p. 38.

[6]Bilodeau, B., Rundell, K., Roy, B. and Boulay, M., "Kinematics of cross-country ski racing," *Med. Sci. Sports Exerc.,* Vol. 28, No.1, 1996, p. 137. The authors refer to Humphreys, S.E, G.M. Street,and G.A. Smith, "Kinematics analysis of female Olympic cross-country skiers," *Med. Sci. Sports Exerc.,* 25: S170, 1993.

[7]Penn State Study, p. 45.

[8]Penn State Study, p. 46.

## Chapter 10: A Critique of Recent American Ski Science

[1]Peterson, Skogsberg, Zackrisson, *Muskelaktivitet under Olika Trainingsformer for Langakning på Skidor,* Diss. Stockholm, 1977.

[2]Frederick, E.C., "Synthesis, Experimentation, and the Biomechanics of Economical Movement," *Med. Sci. Sports Exerc.,* Vol.17. No. 1, Feb.1985, p.45.

[3] Frederick, p. 46.

[4]Skaard, Haldor, "Cross-Country Technique — Ideal, Norm or Adaptation?" *Protocol of the FIS Trainers' Seminar,* Davos, 1982, p.4.

[5]Skaard, p. 5.

[6]Baumann, W., "On Technical Training in Cross-Country Skiing Under Special Consideration of the Roller Ski," *Protocol of the FIS Cross-Country Trainers' Seminar,* Davos, 1982, p. 8.

[7]Cavanaugh, Peter, "Biomechanics: A Bridge Builder Among the Sports Sciences," *Med. Sci. Sports Exerc.* Vol. 22, No. 5, Oct. 1990, p. 548.

[8]Cavanaugh, p. 548.

[9]Cavanaugh, p. 549.

[10]Eisner, Eliot, "Forward" to Rudolph Arnheim, *Thoughts on Art Education* (Los Angeles: Getty Center for Education in the Arts 1989), p. 3.

[11]Taylor, Richard, "The Top Half," *The Professional Skier,* Winter 1986, p. 19ff.

[12]Taylor, Richard, "Plantar Flexion: Case Studies in Interpretive Method," *The Professional Skier,* Winter 1987, p. 42ff.

[13]Nichols, Bob, "The Gunner's Eyes," in *The Shotgunner* (New York: C.F. Putnam's Sons, 1949), p. 116.

[14]Nichols, p. 117.

## Notes

[15]Nichols, p. 118.

[16]Nichols, p. 117.

[17]Nelson, R., McNitt-Gray, J., Smith, G. *Biomechanical Analysis of the Skating Technique in Cross-Country Skiing,* Biomechanics Laboratory, Penn State University, 1986, p.48.

[18]Hofstadter, Richard. *Anti-Intellectualism in American Life* (New York: Vintage Books, 1962),p. 339.

[19]*The Olympic Book of Sports Medicine,* eds. Dirix, A., Knutgen, H.G. and Tittle, K. (Oxford: Blackwell Scientific Publications, 1998) p. 22.

[20]Hay, James. *The Biomechanics of Sports Techniques* (Englewood, NJ 1973), p. 71.

[21]Mann, R., Hermann, J., "Kinematic Analysis of Olympic Sprint Performance: Men's 200 Meters," *International Journal of Sports Biomechanics,* Vol.1, No. 2, May 1985, p. 151f.

[22]Conconi, F., Ferrari, M., Zigio, P., Droghette, P., Codeca, L., "Determination of anaerobic threshold by a noninvasive field test in runners," *J. Appl. Physiol.: Respirat. Environ. Exercise Physiol.* 52(4): 869-873, 1982, p. 871.

[23]Droghetti, C., et al., and Conconi, F., "Noninvasive determination of anaerobic threshold in canoeing, cross-country skiing, cycling, roller and ice skating, rowing, and walking," *Eur. J. Appl. Physiol.* (1985) 53, p. 300.

[24]*Y's Way to Physical Fitness* (3rd Edition), eds. Golding, Myers and Sinning (Champaign, Ill.: Human Kinetics Press, 1989), p. 92.

[25]Londeree, Ben, "Anaerobic Threshold Training," in Burke, Edmund, *Toward an Understanding of Human Performance* (New York: Mouvement Publications, 1977), p. 42.

[26]Hofstadter, p. 339.

[27]MacLean, Norman. *Young Men and Fire* (Chicago: Univ. of Chicago Press, 1993), p. 164.

## About Richard Taylor

Captain of the Dartmouth Ski Team in 1959, Richard Taylor went on to win the National 30 km championship the following year. He continued his training while in the Army with the US Biathlon Team in 1961-62, placing 14th in the World Biathlon Championships in Umea, Sweden and 6th in a World Cup Biathlon in Kuopio, Finland. He went on to captain the US Olympic Cross-Country Ski Team at the 1964 Olympics in Innsbruck, Austria. While at Dartmouth he studied English and German and continued his studies of German as a Fulbright Fellow at the University of Kiel in Germany. Taylor completed Ph.D. studies in German at Yale (without dissertation) in 1968. After teaching German for six years at the college level, he turned his attention to skiing and coaching.

As a cross-country skiing coach, Taylor was named one of eight Regional Coaches for the US Ski Team in 1975 and was an Assistant Coach at the 1980 Olympics in Lake Placid, NY. Named one of five Associate US Ski Team Coaches in the same year, his assignments included World Cup tours and the World Junior Championships. In 1984 he was Head Coach for the US team to the World Junior Championships in Trondheim, Norway. During this period he was also a staff member for US Ski Team Coaches Certification Clinics in 1979, 1980, and 1983.

In 1984 Taylor was named International Development Coach, a position he held until 1986, when he was named National Team Coach East. Among other activities, he was the US Cross-Country Ski Coach to the World University Winter Games in Italy in 1985, Czechoslovakia in 1987 and in Bulgaria in 1989.

Taylor has written articles widely on cross-country skiing in journals and magazines including *Nordic Skiing, Nordic World, Journal of the US Ski Coaches Association,*

*Cross-Country Skiing,* the *Rocky Mountain Ski Annual,* and *Psychology in Sport* (a book edited by Richard Suinn). He has lectured at numerous seminars, including the New England BIll Koch League meeting (1989), the Bates College Ski Coaches' Seminar (1991), the North American Cross-Country Ski Area Association Convention (1993), the New England Cross-Country Ski Coaches' Conference (1993), and the NENSA Coaches' Workshop (1998).

Since 1987 Taylor has been Director of Nordic Skiing at Gould Academy in Bethel, Maine, where he also teaches English, German, and Latin.

### To order additional copies:

For individual copies, send $30 plus $5 postage and handling.

6 or more books are $26.50 each. Please add $3 per book for postage and handling.

Maine residents add 5% sales tax.

For greater discounts on larger quantities, please write to the publisher below or e-mail the author at taylorr@gouldacademy.org.

Please send check or money order to:

> Mechanic Street Press
> P.O. Box 16
> Bethel, ME 04217